The Indian War of INDEPENDENCE 1857

The Indian War of INDEPENDENCE 1857

VEER SAVARKAR

ABHISHEK PUBLICATIONS
CHANDIGARH/NEW DELHI

ISBN : 978-81-8247-835-0
Copyright : Authors
First Edition : 2022
Price : 1200/-

Published by :
ABHISHEK PUBLICATIONS
SCO 57-59, Sector 17-C, Chandigarh -17
Delhi Office:
7/10, Ansari Road, Darya Ganj, New Delhi-2
Phone : 0172-5003768, 2707562
e-mail : abhpub@ yahoo.com
www.abhishekpublications.com

Printed at : Balaji Offset Naveen Shahdara Delhi-32

The Original Publisher's Preface

This book on the history of 1857 was originally written in an Indian vernacular. But owing to the unique nature of the book which, for the first time ever since the great War was fought, proves from the English writers themselves that the rising of the Indian people in 1857 was in no way an insignificant chapter in, or a tale unworthy of, a great people's history, pressing requests were made from many quarters to translate the work into the English language, so that, by translations into the other vernaculars the whole of the Indian nation might be enabled to read the history of the ever memorable War of 1857. Realising the reasonableness and importance of these requests and with the kind permission of the author, the publishers undertook the translation of the original into the English language. With the patriotic co-operation of many of their countrymen, they are able to-day to place this work in the hands of Indian readers.

The work of translating an Oriental work into a western tongue has ever been a task of immense difficulty, even when the translator has all the facilities which leisure and training could afford. But when the translation had to be done by divers hands and within a very short time, it was clearly foreseen by the publishers that the translation would be defective and unidiomatic. But the main point before the publishers was not to teach the Indian people how to make an elegant translation nor to show them how to write correct English—points to which they were supremely indifferent—but to let them know how their nation fought for its Independence and how their ancestors died 'for the ashes of their fathers and the temples of their Gods.' So, the publishers decided to run the risk of publishing the book as soon as it could expain the facts it had to tell, though none could be more conscious of the faults of the language than they themselves. Fifty years have passed and yet those who died for the honour of their soil and race are looked upon as madmen and villains by the world abroad ; while their own kith and kin for whom they shed their blood, are ahsamed even to own them! To allow this state of public opinion, born of stupid ignorance, and purposely and systematically kept up by a band of interested hirelings, to continue any longer, would have been a national sin. So, the publishers have not waited till the language of this translation could be rendered elegant, which would be more shameful — to let hideous calumny hover over and smother down the spirit of martyrdom, or to let some mistake creep into a book admittedly translated into a foreign tongue! The first, at the best, was a crime, and the second at the worst a venial literary offence. Therefore, the publishers owe no apology to, nor would one be asked for, by the Indian readers for whose special benefit, the work is published.

But, to those sympathetic foreign readers who might be inclined to read this book, we owe an apology for the faults of the language and crave their indulgence for the same.

London
May 10, 1909

The Publishers

The Story of This History

"An honest tale speeds best
By being plainly told."
—*Shakespeare*

Apart from the splendid merits of the subject matter dealt with in the warlit pages of this history of 'The Indian War of Independence of 1857,' the story of the thrilling vicissitudes through which this book had to pass does by itself entitle it to be placed on the classical shelf in any world library.

The Object and the Name of the Book

Veer Savarkarji, the famous author of this book, did himself explain in an article in the '*Talwar*', an organ of the Abhi Nava Bharat Revolutionary Society, which was started by him and published in Paris, that his object in writing this history was, subject to historical accuracy, to inspire his people with a burning desire to rise again and wage a second and a successful war to liberate their motherland. He also expected that the history should serve to place before the revolutionists an outline of a programme of organisation and action to enable them to prepare the nation for a future war of liberation. It would never have been possible to preach such a revolutionary gospel publicly throughout India or carry conviction so efectively as an illuminating illustration of what had actually happened in the nearest past would do. So he invoked the warriors of 1857 to deliver his message through their own mighty words and mightier deeds.

The ideal of absolute political Independence, and the conviction that the ultimate and inevitable means to realize that ideal could be no other than an *armed national revolt* against the foreign domination—were concepts which in those days—lay even beyond the horizon of the then political thought and action in India. The very mention of them was brushed aside as chimerical by the then extremists, was denounced as criminal by the loyal moderates and was even anathematised as immoral by the half-witted moralists! But these self-same concepts formed the two fundamental tenets of the A. N. B. (Abhi Nava Bharat) Revolutionary organisation. 'Reforms and a peaceful solution' formed the alpha and omega of the ambition of the then Indian National Congress itself. Independence, Revolution—let alone a War for Independence—were as a rule words almost unknown, unheard and inconceivably incomprehensible even to the highly patriotic Indian world. It was to familiarize this Indian patriotic world with at least these words in daily thought, and by their constant repetition, like that of a *Mantram* to hypnotize the youthful political mind into a sub-conscious attraction for the noble concepts, which the words connoted that Savarkar, who as a Historian would have called this book a history of the 'National Rising' or of the Revolutionary War of 1857, did, of a set design, name it the history of 'The Indian War of Independence of 1857.'

Veer Savarkar always emphasized the necessity in the Indian condition of carrying politics and patriotism to the camp, to the military forces in India, for rendering any armed revolt practical. The history of the Revolutionary War of 1857 proved beyond cavil or criticism that only some fifty years previously our ancestors had aimed to achieve absolute political independence, could bring about the active and armed participation in the National struggle of the military forces and could wage an inexorable war for the liberation or our motherland. He consequently felt that this history if told viewing it through such a, revolutionary perspective was most likely to animate the rising generation of India with the faith that there was no reason why it should not be practicable and even more faithful to try again as, at any rate, there was no other way to salvation. How far this expectation of the author was realized will be seen as this story proceeds.

Originally written in Marathi

This book was written originally in Marathi, in 1908, when Veer Savarkar was about twenty-four years of age. Some select chapters used to be reproduced in English, in speeches which Veer Savarkarji used to deliver at the open weekly meetings of the Free India Society in London. Perhaps through this channel or otherwise the detectives got some scent of the subject-matter of this book which their reports dubbed as revolutionary, explosive and highly treasonous. Soon a chapter or two of the Marathi manuscript were found missing, which, it was disclosed later on, were stolen by the detective agents, and found their way to the Scotland Yard, the headquarters of the British Intelligence Department in London. Nevertheless, the Marathi manuscript was sent to India by the revolutionists so secretly and cleverly that, foiling the strict vigilance of the customs authorities of the Indian Ports, it reached safely its destination. But the leading press-concerns in Maharashtra dared not run the risk of printing the volume. At last, the owner of a printing firm who was himself a member of the Abhi Nava Bharat Secret Society undertook to publish it. In the meanwhile, the Indian police too got some vague information that the volume was being published in Marathi. They, thereupon carried a number of simultaneous surprise raids on some prominent printing houses in Maharashtra. But fortunately, the owner of the Press, where the book was being actually printed got a hint through a sympathetic Police Officer and succeeded in smuggling out the Marathi manuscript to a safer place just before the search party arrived. The manuscript was later on sent back to Paris instead of to London, and fell into the hands of its author.

Finding thus that it was impossible to get it printed in India, it was decided to get the Marathi book printed in Germany where some Sanskrit literature used to be published in the Nagari script, But after a lot of waste of money and time, the scheme had to be given up as hopeless, owing to the uncouth and ugly Nagari type cast in Germany, and to the fact that the German compositors were absolutely ignorant of the Marathi language.

The History translated into English

The A. N. B. Revolutionary Party resolved thereupon to publish, at least, the English translation of this History of the Indian War of Independence of 1857 with a view to enabling the English speaking public, both in India and outside, to know its contents. A few highly intellectual Maratha youths in London, members of the A.N.B. distinguished graduates of Indian Universities studying Law, and candidates for the I. C. S. Examination volunteered to translate the voluminous work into English. After the translation was complete under the supervision of Sriyut V. V. S. Aiyer, efforts were made to get it printed in England. But the British detectives, too, were not idle, and made it impossible for any British printer to undertake the publication of it for fear of being prosecuted forthwith. The English manuscript was then sent to Paris; but the French Government at that time was so thoroughly under the thumb of England, with whom France had to ally herself in order to face combinedly the impending danger of a German invasion that the French detectives were working hand in hand with the British police to suppress the A. N. B. revolutionary activities in France; and under their threat, even a French printer could not be found ready to run the risk of printing this history. At last by a successful ruse, the revolutionists persuaded a printing firm in Holland to print the book. The British Intelligence Department continued to grope in the dark as the revolutionists publicly gave it out that the English translation was being printed in France. Before the British detectives could get any inkling, the volume was printed in Holland and the whole edition of the English translation was smuggled into France and kept secretly ready for the distribution.

In the meanwhile, before the book was sent to Holland for getting it printed, the British and the Indian Governments got so nervous, and dreaded so much the effects of Savarkar's writings that they proscribed the book which they admitted was not yet printed! This was so high-handed a step on their part that the English papers themselves resented this action of proscribing a book before its publication—a case almost unprecedented in a land which boasted of its Freedom of the Press. Veer Savarkar also did not spare the Governments and poured vials of ridicule on the proscribing order in a spirited letter which he wrote to 'The London Times'. He challenged in it, 'It is admitted by the authorities that they were not sure whether the manuscript had gone to print. If that is so, how does the Government know that the book is going to be so dangerously seditious as to get it proscribed before its publication, or even before it was printed? The Government either possess a copy of the manuscript or do not. If they have a copy then why did they not prosecute me for sedition as that would have been the only course legitimately left to them? On the contrary, if they have no copy of the manuscript how could they be so cocksure of the seditious nature of a book of which they do not know anything beyond some vague, partial and unauthenticated reports? The 'London Times' not only published the letter, but added a note of its own that the very fact that the Government should have felt it necessary to have recourse to such presumably, high-handed and extraordinary executive steps proved that there must be 'Something very rotten in the State of Denmark.'

After getting the English translation printed in Holland the revolutionists smuggled into India hundreds of its copies by ingenious devices. Many of them were wrapped in artistic covers specially printed with such innocuous and bogus names as 'Pick-wick Papers,' 'Scot's Works,' , 'Don Quixote' etc. Several copies got smuggled in boxes with false bottoms. It will be interesting to note that one such box, containing a number of copies under a false bottom, was taken into India by a youthful member of the Abhi Nava Bharat named Shikandar Hayat Khan who later on was known to fame Sir shikandar Hayat Khan, the chief minister of the Punjab. Even the vigilance of the Argus-eyed monster of the Bombay Customs House failed to spot these devices and thousands of copies did thus reach their destinations in India, addressed to many prominent leaders, members of Abhi Nava Bharat, leading libraries, colleges and especially to secret sympathisers who had access to several military camps throughout India. All these copies of this first edition of this history were sent free even the postal charges being defrayed by the A. N. B. Revolutionary Society. It was then openly published in France, was freely circulated and widely read by leading English historians, politician and revolutionary circles especially in Ireland, France, Russia, America, Egypt and Germany.

The 'Gadar' in America and the Second English Edition

In the year 1910, the British and the Indian Governments launched a violent campaign of persecutions and prosecution with a view to crushing the Abhi Nava Bharat Secret Society. Several Indian revolutionaries were hanged; several transported for life; hundreds sentenced to terms extending from ten to fourteen years of rigorous imprisonment. The heroic story of Veer Savarkar's arrest, escape, re-arrest, persecutions, prosecutions an consequent transportation to the Andamans for two life.sentences amounting to at least fifty years' imprisonment, is well-known to be recited here.

No sooner did the Abhi Nava Bharat organisation recover from this stunning blow then Madam Cama, the well-known brave Parsi lady, Lala Hardayal, Chattopadhyaya and other leaders of the A. N. B. Revolutionary Party decided to bring out the second English edition of this book. Lala Hardayalji organised the American branch of the A. N. B. and started his well-known newspaper *'The Gadar'*—(Rebellion) in America. Not only was the second English edition of this 'Indian War of Independence of 1857' published this time for regular sale to replenish the party funds; but translations of this History were published regularly in Urdu, Hindi and Punjabi languages secretly through the 'Gadar'. It aroused the Sepoys in the Army, as the 'Gadar' reached several camps in India and especially the large number of the Sikh agriculturists settled in America. Soon after that, the First World War broke out. How the Indian revolutionists in India and out-side joined hands with the Germans against England, how large amounts of arms and ammunitions were smuggled into India, how the *Komagatamaru* succeeded in landing revolutionary forces in India, how the Emden bombarded Indian ports, how mutinies broke out in Indian regiments stationed at Hong Kong, Singapore and Burma under the leadership of Gadar party and how this attempt by the Indian revolutionaries to invade India to liberate her was at last frustrated owing to the defeat of the Germans, is now a matter of history. Nevertheless, this revolutionary campaign proved to be a veritable rehearsal of the recent Military .Invasion attempted on. a mightier scale by Netaji Subhas Chandra Bose with the I. N. A. Throughout this later revolutionary movement, it became evident from the trials of hundreds of leaders and followers that this history of the first Indian War of Independence of 1857 proved to be a perennial source of inspiration, and even provided a detailed sketch of the programme of action. The demand for its copies was so great that they used to be sold and resold, in cases, for such fabulous prices as 300 Rupees each. Thousands of the arrested revolutionaries were found in possession of them, and possession of a copy of this book was taken to be a proof by itself of the complicity of the possessor in the revolutionory activities.

The Original Marathi Book is Dead !—Long live the Book!'

After the arrest of Veer Savarkar the manuscript of the original Marathi book was handed over to madam Cama in Paris. She kept it in her safe in the Bank of France with a view to placing it beyond the reach of the Agents of the British Intelligence Department. But the invasion of France by the Germans threw the Government of France itself into a hopless disorder. Madam Cama too, passed away. Consequently, when a searching enquiry was made regarding the whereabouts of the book, no trace of the manu'script could be found. The great Marathi *tome* was lost—no hope of its recovery was left. Marathi literature had thus suffered an irreparable loss.[1]

The Third Known English Edition of the History

As we are noting down only those editions of which we have definite knowledge, leaving out of count those of which rumour alone informs us, the next English edition we must take cognizance of, is that which, after the re-emergence of the revolutionary party on an all India basis, was printed and published in two parts, of course secretly, under Veer Bhagatsing's lead. It was sold widely at high prices and the proceeds went to swell the party funds. The few copies, almost religiously preserved even at the risk of prosecution and persecution, which can be rarely found even

1. The original Marathi book is not dead; the original Marathi manuscript changed hands after hands and was carried away to U.S.A. by Dr. Cutino of Goa, himself a member of the A. N. Bharat, and who was then in Europe, and now settled in U.S.A. He kept the manuscript with him till he came to know that the ban on it was lifted by the Government of Bombay in 1946. He then sent the manuscript with one of his friends back to India, who handed it over to Dr. B. S. Moonje; and the book at last reached the hands of shri Savarkar After India became independent.
Arrangements are now being made to publish the marathi original in this series.

today, belong, in the main, to this edition. The conspiracy cases which followed the arrest of Veer Bhagatsing and his leading comrades revealed the fact that copies of this book were found in searches in the possession of almost all the accused and that this History animated them to face martyrdom and guided them to chalk out the revolutionary programme—to organise an armed revolt to liberate our motherland!

The Indian National Army organised by Netaji Subhash Chandra Bose and the Fifth English Edition

The well-ascertained fifth edition came to light in the days when the last and the most determined effort was made to organize an army on the largest scale, yet recorded, to invade India to free her from the British bondage, by Rash Bihari Bose, the President of the Hindu Maha Sabha branch in Japan, and which army was later on commanded by Netaji Subhas Chandra Bose. Unimpeachable evidence recorded by patriots and warriors who took an actual part in the invasion shows that this 'History' was read and re-read in their camps and was looked upon as a veritable text-book for the soldiers and officers in the army. A stray copy of a Tamil edition was also ransacked. Its tattered pages were glued and the volume was rebound and circulated in the army. But it is not known when or by whom the Tamil translation was made and published.

The Sixth English Edition to Challenge the Ban on the Book

While throughout the last thirty or forty years the revolutionists were thus bringing out secretly, edition after edition of this history, an open public agitation was also going on in India demanding the raising of the Governmental ban not only on this history but on several other books written by Veer Sawarkar. Public meetings and protests made by literary societies went unheeded by the British Government in England as well as in India. Even when the so-called

National ministries formed by the Congressites came to power some ten years ago, they too did not raise the ban on Savarkarite literature as perhaps, it not only did not countenance but positively denounced the vagaries of the half-witted and even immoral doctrine of absolute non-violence to which the Congressites swore only verbal allegiance. But when the recent World War II was over and the present Congressite ministries came into power, the public demand for the raising of this ban grew so unruly that some enthusiastic patriots threatened to challenge and break the ban. They raised funds and secretly printed a new English edition in Bombay with a view to selling it openly and publicly courting arrests. They even informed the Congressite ministers of their intention.

The Ban Raised at Last after some Forty Years of Proscription

When matters came to this pass and as the Government too was inclined to reconsider the question, the ban on Savarkarite literature as a whole, which continued to be proscribed for some forty years in the past, was raised by the Congressite ministry at long last, upon which sane act they deserve to be congratulated.

The Book became the Bible of the Indian Revolutionists

It will be evident from the story as recited above that the book continued to be regarded as a veritable Bible by the Indian Revolutionists ever since the armed struggle for Indian Independence initiated by the Abhi Nava Bharat bands down to recent times when full-fledged armies marched to the battlefields under Netaji Subhas Chandra Bose. Directly and indirectly the book has influenced, animated and guided at least two generations in India in their struggles to free the Motherland. That is why the Nation itself made it a point of honour to keep the book alive as a national asset in defiance of the violent efforts of the foreign government to suppress and kill it. Its survival despite of it all is almost miraculous.

Miraculous too is the survival of its illustrious author who, in spite of untold sufferings and sacrifices, trials, tribulations and transportations, has been spared by Providence to witness the triumphant march of the Revolutionary principles and programmes which he as a Seer preached and as a Warrior fought to carry out.

The Book Pays our National Debt to the Memory of the Warriors of 1857

We cannot do better than to quote Shrijut Subbarao, the gifted editor of the Gosthi to illustrate the above truth:

'The British Raj in India has treated Savarkar's book as most dangerous for their existence here. So it has been banned. But it has been read by millions of our countrymen including my humble self. In trying to elevate the events of 1857, which interested Historians and Administrators had not hesitated to call for decades as an 'Indian Mutiny', to its right pose of 'Indian War of Independence'...All be it a foiled attempt at that! It is not a work of a Patriotic Alchemist turning base mutineering into noble revolutionaty-action. Even in these days what would the Mahatmic school have called the efforts of Subhas Bose's Azad-Hind-Fouj if Savarkar's alchemy had not intervened? True. Both the 1857 and 1943 Wars 'have ended in failure for our country. But the motive behind—was it mere Mutineering or War for Independence? If Savarkar had not intervened between 1857 and 1943, I am sure that the recent efforts of the Indian National Army would have been again dubbed as an Ignoble Mutiny effectively crushed by the valiant British-cum-Congress arms and armlessness. But thanks to Savarkar's book Indian sense of a 'Mutiny' has been itself revolutionised. Not even Lord Wavell, I suppose, can now call Bose's efforts as a Mutiny. The chief credit for the change of values must go to Savarkar-and to him alone. But the greatest value of Savarkar's book lies in its gift to the Nation of that Torch or Freedom in whose light an humble I and a thousand other Indians have our dear daughters named after Laxmibai, the Rani of Jhansi. Even Netaji Bose in a fateful hour had to form an army corps named after Rani of Jhansi. But for Savarkar's discovery of that valiant heroine, Rani of Jhansi should have been a long-forgotten Mutineer of the nineteenth century.

—Free Hindusthan, Special, 28th May, 1946

This history has literally resurrected from continuing to be entombed in oblivion the spirits of the bravest of the leaders, warriors and martyrs who fell fighting in 1857, and taught us to pay our admiring and loyal tribute to Nana Sahib, Bala Rao Kumgr Singh, Mangal Pande, Ahmad Shah, The Queen of Jhansi, Senapati Tatia Tope and hosts of our warriors. The names could never have been on the lips of millions today but for the researches of Veer Savarkar guided by a gifted intuition and on a par with such excavations as at Mohenjodaro.

It cannot but be a source of satisfaction to Veer Savarkarji that the expectations he cherished about this History, when he wrote it in his youth, should have been realised before his eyes. But we are afraid that his satisfaction in this case must be only partial. For he never could conceive that the 'Rising of 1857 was an event complete by itself. He looked upon the war of 1857 as but a campaign in the war of Independence in its entirety. He did not, therefore, mean the book to serve as merely the annals of the past but also as a source of inspiration and guidance to the Future. Consequently he must be expecting this History to continue to discharge its mission yet further till the end in view is accomplished. This end is clearly marked out by Veer Savarkar himself as the following passage will show.

The special tribunal, which tried him in 1910 for waging

war against the King (of course of England!) and sentenced him to transportation for life and forfeiture of his property, quotes in its judgement as an overwhelming proof of his 'guilt' the following statement issued by Savarkar in 1908 from London :

'The war begun on the 10th of May 1857 is not over on the 10th of May 1908, nor can it ever cease till a 10th of May to come sees the destiny accomplished and our Motherland stands free!'

Bombay
10th Jan. 1947

G. M. Joshi

CONTENTS

PART IV — TEMPORARY PACIFICATION

The Indian War of Indepedence

Author's Introduction

Fifty years having passed by, the circumstances having changed, and the prominent actors on both sides being no more, the account of the War of 1857 has crossed the limits of current politics and can be relegated to the realms of history.

When, therefore, taking the searching attitude of an historian, I began to scan that instructive and magnificent spectacle I found to my great surprise the brillance of a War of Independence shining in 'the mutiny of 1857'. The spirits of the dead seemed hallowed by martyrdom, and out of the heap of ashes appeared forth sparks of a fiery inspiration. I thought that my countrymen will be most agreeably disappointed, even as I was, at this deep-buried spectacle in one of the most neglected corners of our history, if I could but show this to them by the light of research. So, I tried to do the same and am able to-day to present to my Indian readers this startling but faithful picture of the great events of 1857.

The nation that has no consciousness of its past has no future. Equally true it is that a nation must develop its capacity not only of claiming a past but also of knowing how to use it for the furtherance or its future. The nation ought to be the master and not the slave of its own history. For, it is absolutely unwise to try to do certain things now irrespective of special considerations, simply because they had been once acted in the past. The feeling of hatred against the Mahomedans was just and necessary in the times of Shivaji—but, such a feeling would be unjust and foolish if nursed now.

simply because it was the dominant feeling of the Hindus then.

As almost all authorities on which this work is based are English authors, for whom it must have been impossible to paint the account of the other side as elaborately and as faithfully as they have done their own, it is perfectly possible that many a scene, other than what this book contains, might have been left unstated, and many a scene described in this book might be found to have been wrongly described. But if some patriotic historian would go to northern India and try to collect the traditions from the very mouths of those who witnessed and perhaps took a leading part in the War, the opportunity of knowing the exact account of this can still be caught, though unfortunately it will be impossible to do so before very long. When, within a decade or two, the whole generation of those who took part in that war shall have passed away never to return, not only would it be impossible to have the pleasure of seeing the actors themselves, but the history of their actions will have to be left permanently incomplete. Will any patriotic historian undertake to prevent this while it is not yet too late?

Even the slightest references and the most minute details in this book can be as much substantiated by authoritative works as the important events and the main currents of the history.

Before laying down this pen, the only desire I want to express is that such a patriotic and yet faithful, a more detailed and yet coherent history of 1857 may come forward in the nearest future from an Indian pen, so that this my humble writing may soon be forgotten!

THE AUTHOR

PART I

The Volcano

CHAPTER-I

Swadharma and Swaraj

IT is a simple truism patent even to the uneducated that the most tiny house cannot be built without a foundation strong enough to support its weight. When writers who profess to write the history of the Revolution that was encted in India in 1857 ignore this commonsense principle and do not try to discuss the real causes that led to it and impudently maintain that the vast edifice of the Revolution was built on a blade of straw, they must either be fools or, what is more probable, knaves. Anyway, it is certain that they are unfit for the holy work of the historian.

In all great religious and political revolutions, it is almost impossible to connect together links apparently inconsistent, without thoroughly understanding the principles which are at their root. On seeing a great work of machinery composed of innumerable screws and wheels doing work of tremendous magnitude if we do not understand how the power is produced, we may feel bewildering astonishment, but never the inner pleasure due to knowledge. When writers describe such stirring events as the French Revolution or the religious revolution of Holland, the very splendour and magnitude of the crises they paint, often, dazzle and confuse their mind's eye and they rarely gather sufficient coolness and courage to go deep into the underlying principles. But without an exposition of the hidden causes and the mysterious forces that worked beneath, the essence of a revolution can never be made plain. And therefore it is that history attaches more importance to the exposition of principles than to mere narrative.

While searching after principles, historians often commit another mistake. For every act, there are various causes, direct and indirect, general and particular, accidental and necessary. In their proper classification lies the true skill of the historian. In this process of classification many historians get mixed up and make the accidental into a necessary cause. These make themselves as ridiculous as the judge in the story who, in a cause of arson, put all the responsibility on the match instead of on the man who struck it. The real importance of any event can never be understood by this confusion of causes. Not merely that, but mankind begins positively to curse the memory of men who are represented as having started, with a light heart and private selfish motives, a Revolution in the course of which countless lives are lost and immense expanses of country devastated. And therefore, in writing the history of any event in general, and of revolutionary movements in particular, a writer cannot give a true idea of them by means of simple description, or even by tracing them backwards to accidental causes. An upright and impartial historian must try to discover the foundations on which the revolutionary structure was erected. He must try to discover and discuss fundamental causes.

Mazzini, in a critical article on Carlyle's French Revolution, has said that every revolution must have had a fundamental principle. Revolution is a complete rearrangement in the life of historic man. A revolutionary movement cannot be based on a flimsy and momentary grievance. It is always due to some all-moving principle for which hundreds and thousands of men fight, before which thrones totter, crowns are destroyed and created, existing ideals are shattered and new ideals break forth, and for the sake of which vast masses of people think lightly of shedding sacred human blood. The moving spirits of revolutions are deemed holy or unholy in proportion as the principle underlying them is beneficial or wicked. As in private life, so also in history, the deeds of an individual or a nation are judged by the character of the motive. If we forget this test, we cannot appreciate the vast difference between the empire-building wars of Alexander the Great and Italy's fight for liberty under Garibaldi. Just as to decide about the merits of these two different events one has to consider the prime motive of the chief actors in those wars, so also to write a full history of a revolution means necessarily the tracing of all the events of that revolution back to their source,— the motive, the innermost desire of those who brought it about. This is the telescope which will show clearly the lights and shadows obscured by the blurred presentation of partial and prejudiced historians. When a beginning is made in this manner, order appears in the apparent chaos of inconsistent facts, crooked lines become straight, and straight lines appear crooked, light appears where darkness is, and darkness spreads oves light, what appeared ugly becomes fair and what looked beautiful is seen to be deformed. And expectedly, or unexpectedly, but in a clear form, the Revolution comes into the light of real history.

The history of the tremendous Revolution that was enacted in India in the year 1857 has never been written in this scientific spirit by any author, Indian or foreign. And hence there are current, throughout the world, most extraordinary, misleading, and unjust ideas about that Revolutionary War. English authors have committed, in this respect, all the faults noted above. Some of them have not made any attempt beyond merely describing the events, but most of them have written the history in a wicked and partial spirit. Their prejudiced eye could not or would not see the root principle of that Revolution. Is it possible, can any sane man maintain, that that all-embracing Revolution could have taken place without a principle to move it? Could that vast tidal wave from Peshawar to Calcutta have risen in flood without a fixed intent of drowning something by means of its force? Could it be possible that the sieges of Delhi, the massacres of Cawnpore, the banner of the Empire, heroes dying for it, could it ever be possible that such noble and inspiring deeds have happened without a noble and inspring end? Even a small village market does not take place without an end, a motive; how, then, can we believe that that great market opened and closed without any purpose—the great market whose shops were on every battlefield from Peshawar to Calcutta, where kingdoms and empires were being exchanged, and where the only current coin was blood? No, no. The market was neither opened nor closed without a purpose. English historians have always ignored this point, not because it is difficult to ascertain it, but because it is against their interests to admit the truth.

Even more deceptive than this indifference, and one which changes or distorts the whole spirit of the Revolution of 1857 is the other device of English historians copied by their Indian sycophants, —the device, namely, of describing the rumour as to the greased cartridges as the moving cause of the Revolution. An Indian writer[1] drawing inspiration from English history and English money says, “Foolish people went mad simply at the rumour that cartridges were greased with cows’ and pigs’ fat. Did anyone inquire as to whether the report was true? One man said and another believed; because the second became disaffected, a third joined him, and so like a procession of blind men, a company of inconsiderate fools arose, and rebellion broke out." We propose to discuss later on whether people blindly believed the rumour about cartridges. But it will be plain to anyone who has read even the English historians closely and thought about the matter, that a great attempt has been made to father all the

1. वि.कों. ओक 'शिपायांचें बंड'.

responsibility of the Revolution on this rumour. It is not surprising that to one, who thinks that a mighty rising like that of '57 can be produced by such trifles, it was only 'a company of inconsiderate fools.' If the Revolution had been due only to the cartridges, why did Nana Sahib, the Emperor of Delhi, the, Queen of Jhansi, and Khan Bahadur Khan of Rohilkhand join it? These were not surely going to serve in the English army, nor were they compelled to break the cartridges with their teeth! If the rising were due wholly or chiefly to the cartridges, it would have stopped suddenly as soon as the English Governor-General issued a proclamation that they should not be used any more! He gave them permission to make cartridges with their own hand. But instead of doing so, or ending the whole by leaving the Company's service altogether, the sepoys rose to fight in battle. Not only the sepoys but thousands of peaceful citizens and Rajas and Maharajas also rose, who had no direct or indirect connection with the army. It is therefore clear that it was not these accidental things that roused the spirit of the sepoy and the civilian, king and pauper, Hindu and Mahommedan.

Equally misleading is the theory that the rising was due to the annexation of Oudh. How many were fighting, taking their lives in their hands, that had no interest whatsoever in the Oudh dynasty! Then, what was their motive in fighting? Nabob of Oudh himself was imprisoned in the fort of Calcutta; and according to the English historians, his subjects were very much disaffected under his regime. Then, why did Talukdars, soldiers, and almost every one of his subjects unsheath their swords for him? A 'Hindu' of Bengal wrote an essay in England at that time about the Revolution. In it the' Hindu' says, "You have idea how many simple and kind-hearted people who had never seen the Nabob, nor were ever again likely to see, wept in their huts when the sorrows of the Nabob were being related before them. And you do not also know how many soldiers were daily taking an oath, after the tears had flown, to avenge this insult on Wajid Ali Shah, as if a calamity had fallen on themselves in person." Why did the Sepoys feel this sympathy with the Nabob and why did eyes which had never seen the Nabob glisten with tears? It is plain, therefore, that the Revolution did not break out simply account of the annexation of Oudh.

The fear of greased cartridges and the annexation of Oudh were only temporary and accidental causes. To turn these to real causes would never help us in understanding the real spirit of the Revolution. If we were to take them as the real moving causes, it would mean that, without these, the Revolution would not have taken place—that without the rumour of greased cartridges and without the annexation of Oudh, the Revolution would not have been there. It would be impossible to find a theory more foolish and more deceptive. If there had been no fear of the cartridges, the principle underlying that fear would have cropped up in some other form and produced a Revolution just the same. Even if Oudh had not been annexed, the principle of annexation would have manifested itself in the destruction of some other kingdom. The real causes of the French Revolution were not simply the high prices of grain, the Bastille, the King's leaving Paris, or the feasts. These might explain some incidents of the Revolution but not the Revolution as a whole. The kidnapping of Sita was only the incidental cause of the fight between Rama and Ravana. The real causes were deeper and more inward.

What, then, were the real causes and motives of this Revolution? What were they that they could make thosands of heroes unsheath their swords and flash them on the battlefield? What were they that had the power to brighten up pale and rusty crowns and raise from the dust abased flags? What were they that for them men by the thousands willingly poured their blood year after year? What were they that Moulvies preached them, learned Brahmins blessed them, that for their success prayers went up to Heaven from the mosques of Delhi and the temples of Benares ?

These great principles were Swadharma and Swaraj. In the thundering roar of 'Din, Din,' which rose to protect religion, when there were evident signs of a cunning, dangerous, and destructive attack on religion dearer than life, and in the terrific blows dealt at the chain of slavery with the holy desire of acquiring Swaraj, when it was evident that chains of political slavery had been put round them and their God-given liberty wrested away by subtle tricks—in these two, lies the root-principle of the Revolutionary War. In what other history is the principle of love of one's religion and love of one's country manifested more nobly than in ours? However much foreign and partial historians might have tried to paint our glorious land in dark colours, so long as the name of Chitore has not been erased from the pages of our history, so long as the names of Pratapaditya and Guru Govind Singh are there, so long the principles or Swadharma and Swaraj will be embedded in the bone and marrow of all the sons of Hindusthan! They might be darkened for a time by the mist of slavery — even the sun has its clouds — but very soon the strong light of these self-same principles pierces through the mist and chases it away. Never before were there such a number of causes for the universal spreading of these traditional and noble principles as there were in 1857. These particular reasons revived most wonderfully the slightly unconscious feelings of Hindusthan, and the people began to prepare for the fight for Swadharma and Swaraj. In his Proclamation of the establishment of Swaraj, the Emperor of Delhi says, 'Oh, you sons of Hindusthan, if we make up our mind we can destroy the enemy in no time! We will destroy the enemy and will release from dread our religion and our country, dearer to us than life itself!'[2] What is holier in this world than such a

2. Leckey's *Fictions Exposed* and Urdu works.

Revolutionary War, a war for the noble principles propounded in this sentence, 'release from dread our religion and our country, dearer to us than life itself'? The seed of the Revolution of 1857 is in this holy and inspiring idea, clear and explicit, propounded from the throne of Delhi, *the protection of religion and country*. In the Proclamation issued at Bareilly, he says "Hindus and Mahomedans of India! Arise! Brethren, arise! Of all the gifts of God, the most gracious is that of Swaraj. Will the oppressive Demon who has robbed us of it by deceit be able to keep it away from us for ever? Can such an act against the will of God stand for ever? No, no. The English have committed so many atrocities that the cup of their sins is already full. To add to it, they have got now the wicked desire to destroy our holy religion! Are you going to remain idle even now? God does not wish that you should remain so; for he has inspired in the hearts of Hindus and Mahomedans the desire to turn the English out of our country. And by the grace of God, and your valour, they will soon be so completely defeated that in this our Hindusthan there will not remain even the least trace of them! In this our army, the differences of small and great shall be forgotten, and equality shall be the rule; for, all who draw the sword in this holy war for the defence of religion are equally glorious. They are brethren, there is no rank among them. Therefore, I again say to all my Hindi brethren, 'Arise and jump into the battlefield for this divinely ordained and supreme duty!'" The man who, after seeing such magnificent utterences by the Revolutionary leaders, does not understand its principles is, as we said, either a foot or a knave. What stronger evidence is needed to prove that Indian warriors drew their swords at the time for Swadharma and Swaraj, feeling it the duty of every man to fight for the rights given to man by God? These Proclamations issued at different times and places during the war make it unnecessary to dilate more on its principles. These Proclamations were not issued by nonentities; but they were orders issued from adorable and powerful thrones. They were burning expressions of the agitated feelings of the time. In these the real heart of the Nation had spoken out, when at the time of war, there was no occasion to conceal real sentiments through pressure or fear. This tremendous, heroic shout, 'Swadharma and Swaraj,' proclaims to the world the character of the Revolution in which 'all who draw the sword are equally glorious.'

But were these two principles understood as different and exclusive of each other? At least, orientals have never had the idea that Swadharma and Swaraj have no connection with each other. The Eastern mind has maintained a full and traditional belief, as is also said by Mazzini, that there is no vast barrier between Heaven and earth but that the two are ends of one and the same thing. Our idea of Swadharma, too, is not contradictory to that of Swaraj. The two are connected as means and end. Swaraj without Swadharma is despicable and Swadharma without Swaraj is powerless. The sword of material power, Swaraj, should always be ready drawn for our object, our safety in the other world, Swadharma. This trend or the Eastern mind will be often found in its history. The reason why, in the East, all revolutions take a religious form, nay more, the reason why Eastern history knows of no revolutions unconnected with religion, lies in the all-embracing meaning that the word 'Dharma' has. That this dual principle of Swadharma and Swaraj, always seen in the history of India, appeared also in the Revolution of 1857, should be a matter of no surprise. We have already referred to the first Proclamation of the Emperor of Delhi. Afterwards when Delhi was besieged by the English and the war was at its height, the Emperor issued another Proclamation addressing all Indians thus: "Why has God given us wealth, land, power? They are not for individual pleasure, but they are given for the holy object of defence of our religion." But where are now the means to attain this holy end? As said in the Proclamation given above, where is the gift of Swaraj, the greatest of all the gifts of God?

Where is wealth? Where is land? Where is power? In the plague of slavery, all this divine independence is all but dead. In the above Proclamation, in order to show how the plague of slavery was destroying India, full descriptions are given as to how the Kingdoms of Nagpur, Ayodhya, and Jhansi were trampled down into dust. And it awakens the people to the fact that they are guilty of the sin of destroying religion jn the house of God, having lost these means of defending religion. The command of God is, Obtain Swaraj, for that is the chief key to the protection of Dharma. He who does not attempt to acquire Swaraj, he who sits silent in slavery, he is an atheist and hater .of Religion. Therefore, rise for Swadharma and acquire Swaraj !

'Rise for Swadharma and acquire Swaraj !' What divine events in the history of India are due to the realisation of this principle! The poet-saint Ramdas gave the same dictum to the Mahrattas 250 years ago. 'Die for your Dharma, kill the enemies of your Dharma while you are dying; in this way fight and kill, and take back your kingdom !'[3]

This alone is the principle in the Revolutionary War of 1857. This is its mental science. The true and only telescope which will show it in its true and clear form, is the above verse of Ramdas.

Seeing at it through this telescope, what a spectacle comes into view! The war fought for Swadharma and Swaraj does not lose its lustre by defeat. The splendour of Guru Govind Singh's life is none the less, because his efforts did not immediately succeed at the time. Nor do we think the less of the rising of 1848 in Italy, because the Revolution failed completely at that time.

---

3. धर्मासाठी मरावें। मरोनि अवध्यांस मारावें।
मारितां मारितां ध्यावें। राज्य आपुलें॥

Justin McCarthy says: "The fact was that throughout the greater part of the northern and north-western provinces of the Indian peninsula, there was a rebellion of the native races against the English power. It was not alone the Sepoy who rose in revolt -it was not by any means a merely military mutiny. It was a combination of military grievance, national hatred, and religious fanaticism against the English occupation of India. The native princes and the native soldiers were in it. The Mahomedan and the Hindu forgot their old religious antipathies to join against the Christian. Hatred and panic were the stimulants of that great rebellious movement. The quarrel about the greased cartridges was but the chance spark flung in among all the combustible material. If that spark had not lighted it, some other would have done the work ... ... The Meerut Sepoys found, in a moment, a leader, a flag, and a cause, and *the mutiny was transformed into a revolutionary war*. When they reached the Jumna, glittering in the morning light, they had all unconsciously seized one of the great critical moments of history and converted a military mutiny into *a national and religious war*!"[4]

Charles Ball writes: " At length, the torrent overflowed the banks, and saturated the moral soil of India. It was then expected that those waves would overwhelm and destroy the entire European element and that, when the torrent of rebellion should again confine itself within bounds, patriotic India, freed from its alien rulers, would bow only to the independent sceptre of a native prince. The movement, now, assumed a more important aspect. It became *the rebellion of a whole people* incited to outrage by resentment for imaginary wrongs and sustained in their delusions by hatred and fanaticism."[5]

White writes in his *Complete History of the Great Sepoy War*: " I should be wanting in faithfulness as an historian if I

---

4. *History of Our Own Times*, Vol. III.
5. *Indian Mutiny*, Vol. I, page 644.

failed to record with admiration the courage displayed by the Oudhians. The great fault of the Oudh Talukdars from a moral point of view was their having made a common cause with the murderous mutineers. But for this, they might have been regarded as noble patriots, fighting in a good cause, *pro rege et pro patria* for the King and the Motherland"—for Swaraj and Swadesh!

* * *

CHAPTER-II

The Chain of Causes

IF it is true that the question whether India, bounded by the Himalayas on the north and the Ocean on the south, should be completely independent or not, was being solved on the battle-fields of the war of 1857, then the chain of causes begins from that day in 1757 when the question was first raised. On the 23rd of June in 1757, the question whether India should belong to the Indians or to the English was openly discussed, for the first time, on the field of Plassey. On that very day and on that very field, where it was first discussed, were sown the seeds of the Revolution. If Plassey had not been there, the War of 1857 also would not have taken place. Though a century had rolled by, the memory of that day was fresh in the heart of Hindusthan. In proof of this, witness the terrible scene on the 23rd day of June 1857, in Northern India. In the vast country from the Panjab up to Calcutta, wherever there was an open field, thousands of Revolutionaries were fighting the English simultaneously in different places, from morning till evening, after openly challenging them saying: 'To-day we are going to avenge Plassey !'

When, on the battlefield of Plassey, India had sworn to fight a war of freedom, England was, as it were, anxious to hasten the day of its fulfilment as much as possible. For,

Englishmen did not rest with sowing the seeds of the Revolutionary War at Plassey, but they made enormous efforts to encourage the growth of the plant all over India. Warren Hastings tended the plant in Benares, Rohilkhand, and Bengal. Wellesley did the same in the fertile fields of Mysore, Assai, Poona, Satara, and Northern India. This was not done without strong efforts, for the ground had to be ploughed not with ordinary ploughs but with swords and guns! What would ordinary ploughs avail against Shanwar Palace, the heights of Sahyadri, the fort of Agra, and the throne of Delhi? When these rocky portions had been broken and crushed, the smaller pieces left out by mistake were also next broken. The smaller princes fell under the strokes of English perfidy, oppression, and tyranny.

The English did not even feed well or pat on the back the brutes by whose strength they effected all these conquests. For a hundred years, they had been oppressing and maltreating the sepoys in their army. When the soldiers of the Mahrattas or the Nizam won important victories, they used to get Jahagirs and rewards. But the Company gave nothing but 'sweet words' of praise. The sepoys, whose swords won India for the English, were so barbarously treated that General Arthur Wellesley would drive the wounded sepoys to the mouth of guns instead of sending them to the hospital!

While the English had thus been sowing the seeds of discontent and hatred in almost all parts of Hindusthan, the time soon came when it appeared that their efforts would soon be crowned with success. The danger to the independence of India was first perceived by Nana Farnavis of Poona and Hyder Sahib of Mysore. From that day onwards the presence of this danger began to be seen, faintly at least, by the princes of India, and its effect was markedly seen in the 'mutiny' at Vellore. This rising at Vellore was a rehearsal of the great rising of 1857. Just as in a theatre, before the actual performance, several rehearsals have to be gone through, so in history, before the actual and final attainment of freedom, in order to harmonise the whole performance, several rehearsals in the shape of risings are necessary. In Italy, the rehearsals started as early as 1821, and only in 1861 was the play successful. The Rising at Vellore in 1806 was such a rehearsal on a small scale. In this rising, the sepoys had been won over by the princes and people. At markets, preachers disguised as Fakirs were preaching. To indicate the time or rising, *chapatees* even had been distributed. Hindus and Mahomedans together had risen in the name of religion and liberty. But this being the first rehearsal, they fell even as they were rising. Never mind! Before the final performance, how many rehearsals have to be gone through! Only the actors should boldly stick to their task, and never cease their rehearsals. And for producing this drama, both England and India were working day and night without rest. And those that were making ready to take part in the play were not common, poor, or ignorant folk. The Gadi or Tanjore, the Masnad of Mysore, the Raigarh of Sahyadri, the Dewan-i-Khas of Delhi were among the select actors. And to crown all, Lord Dalhousie landed on the shores of Hindusthan in 1846. There is not now much time left for commencing the task which was sworn to on the battlefield of Plassey.

From the above chain of causes, it will be clearly seen that, before Dalhousie landed in India, the seeds of discontent had gone deep, very deep, all over Hindusthan. Rajas and Maharajas, deprived of their kingdoms by the English, were burning in their hearts. The fact that the centenary of Plassey was approaching inspired a strange feeling of hope among the people; and in the very armies of the English, the sepoys were secretly chafing with rage and hatred. Even if India had had at this time a Viceroy who would strive to allay this secret discontent, it is very doubtful how far his efforts would have been successful. The question now was not whether the Company's rule should be good or bad; but the only question that used to be asked all over the country was whether the rule should exist at all. The one other force that was necessary for making an attempt to solve definitely this question was supplied when Dalhousie became viceroy; for he gave up the policy of coating poison pills with sugar before administering them to the victim, and began a system of open and direct oppression which did not fail to burn its way into the hearts of the masses.

Lord Dalhousie is described by English historians, as one of the founders of the English Empire. This fact alone is sufficient to form an estimate of his capacity and character. In a country where unjust wars of conquest and oppression of foreign nationalities and races are universally popular, it is no wonder that those who have committed the greatest injustice and oppression are the most honoured. Thus, he who is most unjust is deemed the most capable, and one has no better way of proving himself a great man in such a country than by committing a climax of injustice. In such an Empire, where there is such an emulation of injustice and oppression, Lord Dalhousie was given the significant title of a 'founder'; it is impossible to find a more suitable word to describe his character. With the result of a hundred years of wicked English policy behind him, obstinate by nature, possessed of boundless self-confidence, his flesh and blood permeated by the glory and pride of an unjust Empire, this bold, if not clever, man landed on the shores of our land saying openly, 'I will level the land of Hindusthan.'

As soon as Dalhousie landed, he saw at once that so long as Ranjit Singh's lions lived in the Panjab, it was impossible to achieve the object, dear to his heart, of levelling Hindustan. He, therefore, determined to throw somehow or other the lion of the Panjab in the cage of Slavery. But the Panjab lion had no ordinary claws. Seeing his cave threatened, he rushed out of the lair at Chillianwalla and, with a terrible stroke of his paw, mauled the enemy and made him bleed. But, alas! While the lion was standing at the mouth of the cave at Chillianwala, a traitor broke open the back-wall at Guzerat and the lion was surprised and captured. Soon the cave of the lion became his cage! Ranjit's Queen Chand Kuvar, died rotting in London! And the lion's cub Dhulip Singh, ate the beggar's bread at the hands of the Feringhi enemy!

After the annexation of the Panjab, Lord Dalhousie wrote in his despatch, the proud sentence that the extent of the British Empire was now continuous from the Himalayas to Cape Comorin. But now that the British frontiers had been pushed to the Himalayas on the north and to the seas on the south, it was inevitable that he should have an ambition to create an eastern and a western frontier suitable to these northern and southern ones. Then why delay? Send a 'peace' mission to Burma and the work is done. This peace mission so tightly embraced the peace of Burma that its ribs were broken and it expired! This very loving task was soon over and Burma was also annexed. Now, at last the whole of Hindusthan—from the Himalayas to Rameshwar and from the Sindhu to Iravady became red—but, oh! Dalhousie, do you not fear that it will soon be redder still?

Do we realise what is meant by the annexation of the Panjab and Burma? We cannot form an idea of it from mere names. The Panjab alone is a territory of 50,000 sq. miles and a population of four millions! It is the land watered by the five sacred rivers of the Vedas, on the banks of which the Rishis in ancient times had recited sacred mantras! To conquer such a region Alexander came from Greece, to defend such a region King Porus fought. After taking such a country, the ambition even of Ravana would have been satisfied; but the land-hunger of Dalhousie, was not satisfied even after swallowing not only the Panjab but also the extensive dominion of Burma. Though the frontiers of India were extended, there still remained the graves of ancient kingdoms within. Dalhousie therefore began to root these out and level everything. Not only did they occupy too much valuable space, but there was the fear that from these graves might one day rise the future avengers of India's wrongs.

In the grave at Satara was buried a magnificent Hindu Empire. And it is no wonder that Dalhousie, who was a believer in the Resurrection of Jesus was afraid that out of Satara might rise a future Hindu Emperor who would confound the foreigner and establish Swaraj. In April 1848, Appa Sahib, the Maharaja of Satara, died. At this news, Dalhousie decided to annex that State. And what was the reason? The King had no direct heirs! Even the cottage of the village labourer who has no direct heir is not confiscated but is given to his adopted son or to his near relatives. And Satara was not a peasant's cottage but an 'ally' of the English Government. In the year 1839, Pratap Singh Chhatrapati had been charged with having engaged in a conspiracy with the object of overthrowing the British Government, was dethroned, and in his place Chhatrapati Appa Sahib was appointed by the English Sirkar to succeed him. Mr. Arnold,[1] in his book *Dalhousie's Administration*, says 'It is not pleasant to dwell, on the circumstances of the dethronement —so discreditable they were'. After such shamelessly discreditable dethronement, the English established on the Gadi of Satara the brother, on account of the failure of legitimate sons. By this, the English practically acknowledged the right of the other relations—as is the invariable law laid

1. The first article in the treaty entered into by the Sirkar with the Chhatrapati, when he was placed on the throne of Satara, runs as follows:- "The valiant English Government on its part agrees to give the country or territory specified to the Government or State of His Highness the Maharaja Chhatrapati (the Raja of Satara); His Highness the Maharaja Chhatrapati and His Highness's sons and heirs and successors are perpetually, that is from generation to generation, to reign in sovereignty over the said territory.'

down by the Hindu Shastras—to succeed to the throne. The only truth about this whole affair is that Dalhousie, with the habitual treachery of his nation, overrode this open aknowledgement knowingly and deliberately, because it was profitable to do so.

No one could under any pretext say that the English, in any of the various treaties concluded with the various Rajas, had refused to acknowledge the right of adopted children to succeed to their adoptive parents' thrones. In 1825, the Company, while acknowledging the right of the adopted child of the Raja of Kota to succeed, openly declared: "*The Prince of Kota must be considered to possess the right, in common with all other Hindus, of adopting a son and successor in conformity with the rules of of the Shastras.*'[2]

Again, in 1837, when the Raja of Oorcha adopted a successor, the English acknowledged him and promised :-

"Hindu sovereigns have a right to adopt, to the exclusion of collateral heirs, and the British Government is bound to acknowledge the adoption, provided it is regular and not in violation of the Hindu law."[3] It may be safely asserted that nowhere else but in English politics could be found the audacity of denying the very existence of those promises which were given most definitely and which are contained in their own documents. Not only by these declarations but on innumerable other occasions, the English have acknowledged the right of the native princes to adopt in accordance with the Hindu Shastras. Suffice it to say that, within the short period of two years (1846-47), the English Government had consented to the succession to the Gadi of innumerable adopted sons, and acknowledged their rights.

Indeed, to try to seek, in the language of promises and

2. The Parliamentary Papers, 15th February, 1850, page 153.

3. Parliamentary Papers, 15th February 1850, Page 141.

treaties, the root cause of annexing these states, is to work in a wrong direction altogether. The real truth of the matter is that Dalhousie had come to reduce all India to a dead level and the grave of the Hindu Empire at Satara was trying to raise its head. Obviously, therefore, though Pratap Singh and Appa Sahib had both adopted in accordance with the Hindu Shastras, ths English annexed the Raj under the pretex of failure of legitimate heirs. The Gadi of Satara ! The same Gadi on which Shivaji was crowned by the hand of Gaga Bhatt! The same Gadi to which Baji Rao I, dedicated all his triumph, before which he bowed low! O Maharashtra! behold that same Gadi, on which Shivaji sat, and to which homage was paid by Santaji, Dhanaji, Niraji, and Baji has been broken to pieces by Dalhousie! Go on, if you will, with your petitions and deputations. What if Dalhousie does not listen to these? In England at least, you think, the Directors will listen to you? Dalhousie is apparently a mere man; but, who knows, perhaps the Directors in England might be more than men. None in Maharashtra had seen these sami-Gods. It was, therefore, thought proper that Rango Bapuji, an excellent and loyal man should go to England to lay the grievances of Satara before the 'Home' authorities. Success or no success, the game was at least they thought, worth trying. But how long would they wait, hoping against hope, for the success of their mission? For how long would Rango Bapuji go on wearing away the very pavement of Leadenhall Street? Yes, Rango Bapuji will go on clinging to his impossible hope till he is mocked at and insulted, till every penny is spent in feeing English barristers with crores of Rupees so that he has not money left even for his passage, and until he receives the insolent reply that they refuse to give back Satara !

While Rango Bapuji was busy packing for London, Dalhousie's attention was being absorbed by a new affair; for, an occasion had risen by which he could weed out the miserable shrunken shrub of the *Raj* of Nagpur. Raghoji Bhonsle. the rightful owner of the Nagpur Gadi, died suddenly at the age of 47. The Raja of Berar was an ally of the English Government,[4] and this very friendship of the English was the cause of his destruction! Those who knew that the English hated them were spared but all those who foolishly believed that the English were their friends were mercilessly and treacherously involved in ruin. The kingdom of the Berars was not the Englishman's *jahgir*, nor was it a feudatory state dependent for existence on his sweet will and pleasure. It was an independent state on an equality with Feringhi Sirkar. J. Sylvian has defied the British Government to show on what grounds and by what show of justice, either eastern or western, they could have the right of annexing such a *Raj*, merely because the king died childless. Obviously it was a game of legerdemain or sleight-of-hand; one removes and the other, his accomplice, conceals it quietly! While the one cuts off the head, the other, his accomplice, goes on asking loudly by what law he dared commit the deed—as if murderers and highway robbers need the law to back them up. In 1853, then, Dalhousie at last laid his murderous knife at the throat of 'his friend', showing as a reason that the Raja had not adopted a successor. Raja Raghoji had every hope of a child but died suddenly. Even if he died without a child, the right of adopting passed at his death to his legal wife. If the English had not acknowledged at any time previously the heirs adopted by the queens of deceased Rajas, we should have had nothing to say. But it remains a fact that the English had acknowledged the adoption by Daulatrao Scindia's widow in 1926, the adoption by Junkoji Scindia's widow in 1836, the adoption by the widow of the Raja of Dhar in 1834 and the adoption by the queeen of Kishangarh in 1841. Not one, not two, but many such adoptions have the English acknowledged. But we should

---

4. The treaty of 1826 begins as follows: Treaty of perpetual friendship between the Honourable East India Company and His. Highhness the Maharaja Raghoji Bhonsle, his heirs and successors.

not forget the fact that, on those occasions, it was to their advantage to acknowledge these heirs. In this case, on the other hand, it was not to their advantage to acknowledge the adoption by the widow of Raghoji. The real point at issue, then was one of advantage to the English Government, and everything was determined on that issuse. While the Raj of Nagpur was annexed because no adoption took place, the Satara kingdom faced a similar fate because the adopted heir should not have a right to succeed to the throne! Impossible for logic to step in here.

By annexing Nagpur, Dalhousie robbed an extensive tract of 76,832 sq. miles, with a population of 46,50,000 people and an enormous annual income. While the poor Ranees were weeping themselves hoarse, a loud knock came on the palace gate. The door was opened and in rushed the English troops. Horses were let loose from the stables, elephants—after forcibly pulling down the Ranees riding on them—were taken to the bazaars for sale, and silver and gold ornaments were removed from the palace and were sold by public auction in every street. The necklace that adorned a queen was lying in the dust of the bazaars. Elephants were sold for 100 Rupees! After this you will hardly be surprised to learn that horses, fed on richer food than Dalhousie had for his own dinners, were sold for 20 Rupees and that a pair of horses, on which the Raja himself used to ride, was sold for 5 Rupees! Elephants with the *howdas* on them and horses with their caparisons were sold, but the Ranees still remained with their jewels. Why not sell the jewels? So, the jewels also went the way of other things, and no Ranee had a single jewel left on her person. But even here the 'friendship' of the English could not stop. So, they began to dig the floor of the palace! And, Heavens, in the very bedroom of the Ranees the Feringhi's pickaxe began its desecrating work! Reader, start not yet, nor tremble, for the pickaxe has only started the work; and will do further deeds, nay, is doing it. For, see you not it has broken the bedstead of the Queen, and is digging the very flooring underneath the bed? And shall we say it? All the while the Maharanee Annapoorna Bai was on her death bed, and was even then dying! While the Dowager Queen of the great family of the Bhonsles of Nagpur was on her death-bed, groaning with agony and for the insult to the throne and the family, in the neighbouring room, in that bed of the Queen, the Feringhi's pickaxe was doing its work! What a terrible accompaniment to the groans in the next room! And why all this? Because Raghoji died before adopting a successor![5]

Ranee Annapoorna Bai died, groaning for the insufferable insults flung at her ancient dynasty. But the hope of Ranee Banka to get justice from England was not yet dead! This vain hope was at last destroyed, but not until she had tried the immensely expensive remedy of feeing English barristers with lakhs of Rupees. And what did Ranee Banka do then? She spent the rest of her life in 'loyalty' to the Feringhi ! While the Lightning was working destruction at Jhansi, Banka, seeing that her sons were ready to unsheath their swords for Swaraj, threatened them that, if they did unsheath their swords, she would herself inform the Feringhis of their designs and advise the Feringhis to behead them![6]

* * *

CHAPTER III

Nana Sahib and Lakshmi Bai

BLOW YOUR TRUMPETS loudly now, O Heralds of History, for soon there are to arrive on the scene two great heroes! These are two bright pearls in the necklace of Mother India. Now when dark night has overspread the

---

5. *Dalhousie's Administration*, pp. 165-168.
6. Banka, thy name shall go down to History as Banka the treacherous.

horizon of the whole country these two alone are shining as luminous stars. They are fiery *Akalis* ready to avenge their country's unjust wrongs with the last drop of their blood. They are two martyrs sacrificing their lives for Country, Religion, and Freedom. They are two witnesses sword in hand, to prove that the blood of Hindustan that gave birth to Shivaji is not yet dead. They are two noble souls that could entertain in their hearts the grand and holy ambition of Swaraj. They are two crusaders in the Holy War, glorious even in their defeat. Therefore, O readers, stand up in all awe and reverence for the noble figures of Nana Sahib Peshwa and the Queen of Jhansi are coming on the stage of History!

We do not know which to describe more-the splendour of the mountain tops of Matheran in the holy Maharashtra, or the green, velvet-soft, grassy meadows adorning the feet of those hills. In the lap of the graceful plateau below, almost overhung by the sky-reaching peaks of the Matheran, there nestled a tiny little village called Venu, heightening the beauty of the already beautiful region. Among the old and respectable families of Venu, the family of Madhavrao Narayan Bhatt was the most prominent. Madhavrao and his noble wife Gangabai, though living in circumstances of domestic poverty, were happy in the enjoyment of mutual love. In the small house of this good family, all faces beamed with joy and happiness in 1824, for the good Gangabai had given birth to a son. That son of Madhavrao and Gangabai was no other than the Peshwa Nana Sahib, at the very sound of whose name the Feringhi shudders with fear,—that same Nana who has made his name immortal in history as a hero who fought for liberty and for his country.

About the same time, the last Bajirao had abdicated his throne and was leading a life of retirement on the banks of Ganges, many Maratha families had followed him and, hearing that Bajirao was generous enough to support them in good state on his pension, many new families also emigrated thither. Among the latter was the family of Madhavrao, who went to Brahmavarta in 1827 to seek the generosity of Bajirao. There, the little son of Madhavrao captivated the heart of Bajirao, and little Nana Sahib became a great favourite of the whole Durbar. His spirit even in childhood, his serious mien, and his intelligence made a deep impression upon Bajirao, who eventually resolved to adopt him. On the 7th of June, 1827, Bajirao formally placed him on his lap and adopted him. At this time Nana was only two-and-a-half years old. In this manner, the child, born in the village of Venu became, by a stroke of luck, the heir presumptive to the throne of the Peshwas !

It was no doubt a great good fortune to be made heir to the seat of the Peshwas of the Mahratta Empire. But, O brilliant Prince, do you realise the great responsibility accompanying this good fortune? The throne of the Peshwas is not an ordinary thing! It was on this that the great Baji sat and ruled an Empire. It was for this that the battle of Paniput was fought. On this have been poured the sacred waters of the Sindhu for the anointing of generations of Peshwas; on this the treaty of Wargaon had been made and, most important of all, on this is to come, or why, already has come, the contaminating touch of slavery. Do you realise all this? To be a heir to a throne is to undertake, to guarantee the protection and dignity of that throne. Then will you or will you not guard the dignity of the Peshwa throne? Either the Gadi should be adorned with the crown of victory, or it should be burnt in a brilliant pyre of glory, like the proud women of Chitore! There is no third way of saving the glory of the Peshwa's throne! O brilliant Prince! Think of this terrible responsibility, and then sit on the *Gadi* of the Peshwas! Since your father gave reason for the taunt that the Peshwa's Gadi surrendered, the whole of Maharashtra has become black with shame, and all desire that if the *Gadi* is to end after all, it should end even as it began—that if it is to die, it should die fighting! Sit proudly on that *Gadi*, O young Nana, so that History may say with pride that the *Gadi*, whose first Peshwa was Balaji Vishvanath, had for its last occupant Nana Sahib!

At about the same time in sacred Varanasi, there lived in the retinue of Chimnaji Appa Peshwa, Moropant Tambe and his wife Bhagirathi Bai. Little did the couple know at the time that their name would become immortal in History! This couple had the good fortune of giving birth to a daughter who was to be a veritable flashing sword in the hands of Hindusthan. This couple hardly understood its good fortune. Do the thorny branches know that, in the spring, a rose, delighting all with its fragrance, would spring forth from out of them! But though the branches knew it not, still, as soon as the spring time of Hindusthan came, the flower did come forth! It was in 1835 that Bhagirathi gave birth to the heroine, Ranee Lakshmi Bai. This brave woman's name in youth was Manu Bai.

When Manu was hardly three or four years old, the whole family left Benares and went to the court of Bajirao at Brahmavarta. There she was so much liked by all the people that they called her 'Chhabeli'! Prince Nana Sahib and the sweet Chhabeli ! When two such children braced each other in childish affection, what a sight must it have been to the people of Brahmavarta ! What eyes would not glisten with joy to see Prince Nana Sahib and the Chhabeli playing together in the armoury and learning their lessons in sword-play—lessons which they were destined to use in later life for the defence of their country and their religion? How limited, indeed, is the vision of man! When Nana Sahib and Lakshmi Bai were learning sword-play together, the spectators did not see the future glory of these brilliant children and now who do see their glory have no longer the good fortune to see those children's games of the past! Still, if, to remove the short-sightedness of these eyes of flesh, we put on the spectacles of imagination, then we can easily see those games of the past. While Nana Sahib and Rao Sahib (his cousin) were learning their lessons under their tutor, this Chhabeli too would closely watch them, and thus she learned to read, though stumbling often. Nana Sahib would be sitting in *howdah* on an elephant and the sweet child would affectionately call up to him, 'Won't you take me too?'[1] Sometimes Nana would lift her up, and both would learn to ride the magnificent animal. Sometimes Nana would be on a horse and wait for Lakshmi to come and join him; just then she would come up galloping with a sword at her side, with her hair slightly dishevelled by the wind, and her fair complexion becoming ruddier by her efforts to curb the spirited horse. And both would start away at a smart pace. At this time, Nana was eighteen years old and Lakshmi Bai was seven; what a pleasant memory to us that the heroine should have started her training for the holy war at the age of seven? These two jewels were extremely fond of each other from their earliest childhood. In Brahmavarta at that time, were being brought up three of the most important characters of the Revolutionary War of 1857, Nana Sahib, Queen Lakshmi Bai, and Tatya Tope. It is said, that on every festival of Yamadvitiya, these two, Nana Sahib and Lakshmi Bai—historical brother and sister—used to perform the ceremony of *Bhaubij*. We can well picture to ourselves the sweet attractive spirited Chhabeli, with a golden dish and with lamps in her hand, performing the ceremony. Such occasions when a Lakshmi Bai is waving the sacred lamp round the face of a Nana Sahib, such occasions make history more romantic than romance!

In the early life of Nana Sahib and Manu Bai, we have the key to their future greatness. Their flesh and blood, even in early childhood, had been permeated by the love of Swaraj and a noble sense of self-respect and pride of ancestry. In

1. Parasnis's Life of the Queen of Jhansi.

1842, the Chhabeli was given in marriage to Maharaja Gangadhar Rao Baba Sahib of Jhansi, and thus became Maharani Lakshmi Bai. of Jhansi. She was extremely popular at the Court of that place and gained the affection and devoted loyalty of all her subjects, as the later part of this history will show.

In 1851, the Peshwa Bajirao II died. Let not a single tear be shed for his death! For after losing his own kingdom in 1818, this blot in the escutcheon of the Peshwas spent his time in helping to ruin the kingdoms of other kings! He saved considerably on the pension of eight lakhs of Rupees allowed to him by the Company's Government, and invested it in the notes of the Company. Later, when the English went to war with Afghanistan, he helped them with a loan of fifty lakhs out of his savings. Soon after, the English went to war with the Sikh nation of the Panjab. And all were in hopes, and the English in fears, that the Mahratta at Brahmavarta would make common cause with the Sikh *misalas* against the English power. When almost the whole of India was fighting against Aurangzeb, Shri Guru Govind Singh, after a defeat in the Panjab, had come into the Maharashtra, it is said, to enter into an active alliance with the Mahrattas. Now it seemed that the Mahrattas would go into Northern India on a similar mission, and perform the unfulfilled promises of the alliance. But Baji, spoiled the sport at the eleventh hour. This Baji —this Peshwa of Shivaji and his descendants— spent money out of his own pocket and sent one thousand infantry and one thouand cavalry to the assistance of the English! This Bajirao had not troops to protect his own Shanwar Wada, but he could spare troops enough to help the enemy to desecrate the house of Guru Govind Singh! O unfortunate nation! The Mahrattas should take the kingdom of the Sikhs and the Sikhs should take the kingdom of the Mahrattas—and all this for what? In order that the English might dance in joy over the corpses of both! We have rather to- thank the God of Death that such a traitor—this Baji—

died before 1857.

Before his death, Baji Rao made a will by which he bequeathed all the rights of succession and powers of the Peshwa to his adopted son Nana Sahib. But immediately on the news of Baji Rao's death, the English Government announced that Nana Sahib had no right whatsoever to the pension of eight lakhs. What must have Nana Sahib thought on hearing this decision of the English? The conflict of passions in his heart is portrayed to some "extent in the despatch written under his direction. It says: 'It is simply unjust that the high family of the Peshwa should be treated by the Company so lightly as this. When our throne and kingdom were handed over to the Company by Shrimant Bajirao, it was done so on the condition that the Company should pay eight lakhs of Rupees every year, as its price. If this pension ,is not to last for ever, how can the surrender of the kingdom, which was given as a consideration for this pension, last for ever in your hands? That one part alone should be bound by the contract, while the other intentionally fails to do its part is absurd, unjust, and inconsistent.'[2] Then follows a clear and well-reasoned 'passage refuting the theory that he being an adopted son, cannot get his father's rights, citing authorities from Hindu Shastras, from rules of politics and customary law. After that, the despatch of Nana Sahib continues: 'The Company puts forward another excuse to cease to pay the pension, namely that Bajirao II has saved a considerable sum which is quite sufficient to defray the expenses of his family. But the Company forgets that the pension was given as a condition of the treaty, and there is no single clause in the treaty directing the mode in which the pension should be spent. The pension is the price of the kingdom given, and Bajirao would heve been justified had he saved even the whole of the pension! We ask the Company whether they have got the least right to question the manner

2. Nana's Claims against the East India Company.

in which the pension is expended? Nay, can the Company ask even its own servants as to how they spend their pensions or what they save out of it? But it is strange that a question, which the Company dare not ask even of its own servants, is raised in the case of the heir to a royal dynasty, and is made the pretence to break a treaty.' With this argumentative and spirited despatch, Nana's faithful ambassador, Azimullah Khan, left for England.

Of the important characters in the Revolutionary War or 1857, the name of Azimullah Khan is one of the most memorable. Among the keen intellects and minds that first conceived the idea of the War of Independence, Azimullah must be given a prominent place. And among the many plans by which the various phases of the Revolution were developed, the plans of Azimullah deserve special notice.

Azimullah was very poor by birth. He rose gradually on the strength of his own merits, and at last became the trusted adviser of Nana Sahib. His early poverty was such that he served as a waiter in the household of an Englishman. Even while in such a low state, the fire of ambition was always burning in his heart. He took advantage of his profession as a *Baberchi* in order to learn foreign languages, and in a short time he had learned to speak English and French with fluency. After acquiring a knowledge of both these languages, Azimullah left the service of the Feringhis and began to study in a school at Cawnpore. By his extraodinary ability, he soon became a teacher at the self-same school. While still serving as a teacher in the Government school at Cawnpore, his reputation as an able scholar reached the ears of Nana Sahib, and he was introduced at the Brahmavarta Durbar. Once, at the Durbar, his wise counsels were appreciated and valued by Nana Sahib, who would take no important step without first conculting Azimullah. In 1854, he was made the chief representative of Nana Sahib and sent to England. His face was noble, his speech, sweet and silvery. Knowing very well the customs and manners of contemporary English life, he soon became very popular among Londoners. Attracted by his pleasant and silvery voice, his spirited mien and Oriental magnificence, several young English women fell in love with Azimullah. There used to be a crowd, in those days, in the. parks of London and on the beach at Brighton, to see this jewelled Indian 'Raja'. Some English women of respectable families were so much infatuated with him that, even after his return to India, they would send him letters couched in the most affectionate terms. When, later, Havelock's army captured Brahmavarta, he saw there the original letters written by some English ladies to their' Darling Azimullah !'

But though English women were captivated by Azimullah, still the East India Company would not leave their stern attitude. They put him off for some time with beguiling words, and at last gave the stereotyped answer, 'We entirely approve of the decision of the Governor-General that the adopted son of Bajirao has no claim whatever to his father's pension'. Thus, as regards the principal object of his mission he was disappointed, in a way. We say 'in a way'; because at this very moment, a new inspiration, a new hope, was rising in his heart. There was no necessity of any foreigner's consent to realise this hope, but it depended for its realisation on his own country and countrymen! How to get the consent of his own men? How to acquire the independence of his country by force when it could not be acquired by *Sama, Dama or Bheda* (conciliation, money, or division)? These thoughts breathed a new hope and a new life into Azimullah's heart.

At this self-same moment, right in the heart of London, a Brahman was sitting, brooding over the means for the attainment of that which he was unable to obtain by petition or by prayer and his heart, filled with vengeance born of despair, was planning dozens of schemes for the attainment of his object. This was Rango Bapuji of Satara. Azimullah, the representative of the Peshwa, used often to visit him, and they both used to hold secret consultations. Leaving these two—one, the representative of the Chhatrapati of Satara himself, and the other, the representative of the Prime Minister of the Chhatrapati—to the quiet and secret solution of the problem of saving the Hindu Empire, let us turn our attention to the activities of Nana Sahib.

Fortunate will be the day when a complete and systematic history of the life of Shrimant Nana Sahib Peshwa will be before the world. Meanwhile, until such a day arrives, it would not be out of place to recount in brief some of the details of his life about this period, as published by the English historians, bitter enemies of Nana Sahib as they are. We have already related incidentally the story of his youth. He had married a cousin of the chief of Sangli. While in the north, in 1857 the Revolution was being resolved upon, this relation of Nana Sahib was making strenuous efforts to achieve the same end in Maharahtra by working in the Patwardhan State. Nana had made Brahmavarta his home after the demise of his father. This city was in itself very beautiful, while the sacred Bhagirathi which flowed close to the city walls greatly added to its beauty. The palace of Nana commanded a most charming view; before him stretched the quiet waters of the Bhagirathi; the banks were cheerfully alive with throngs of men and women; and beautiful temples of famed architecture raised their cupolas all along the banks. The Palace of the Peshwa was a grand structure. Its political, administrative, and other offices, and the large shops and well-kept roads inside the gates, amply testified to the activities within the palace. The many extensive halls within this palace were decorated with rich carpets and gorgeous tapestries. Most valuable china selected with faultless taste, magnificent.candelabra studded with diamonds, beautifully carved mirrors, carved ivory of finest workmanship, gold art works richly set with diamonds, in short, all the luxury and taste and splendour of the Hindu palace were to be seen there.[3] The steeds and camels of Shrimant Nana Sahib were caparisoned in silver. Nana's fondness for horses was well known, and it is said that none could excel either him or Lakshmi Bai in horsemanship. His stables were a fine collection of splendid breeds. His special hobby was animals, and people even from far-off parts used to come to Brahmavarta, to see his deer and his gazelles brought from various parts of India, his camels, and his pointers. Yet, be it noted that, above all things, it was on his splendid collection of arms that Shrimant prided himself most. It included arms of all kinds and for all purposes, -swords of best-tempered steel, modern long-range rifles, and big guns of various sizes.

Immensely proud of his high birth and conscious of his noble ancestry, Nana had quietly made up his mind that he would -either live as became that noble parentage, or pass away from memory altogether. It is a significant fact, that in the main hall and in a prominent place were hung the portraits of those great and capable men who had adorned Mahratta history.[4] What did those faces speak to him? What did the portrait of Chhatrapati Shivaji say to him? What a tumult of feeling must have arisen in his mind when he saw Baji Rao I, the Bhau of Panipat, the youthful and regal Viswas, the wise Madhava, and statesman Nana Farnavis, in the portraits before him! The very consciousness that he was born in a family which could boast of such great names must have been constantly impelling him to what thoughts? Nana, there is no doubt, must have felt, and felt terribly, the woeful humiliation of petitioning to his enemies for a pension for that Empire, of which his ancestors were the Prime

3. See Thomson's *Cawnpore*. Peculiar importance attaches to this man and his book owing to the fact that he was one of the two men who survived massacre at Cawnpore.

4. Charles Ball's *Indian Mutiny*, Vol. I, page 304.

Ministers, nay, rulers. Thc stories of the noble deeds of the great Shivaji, whose memory he fondly cherished, must, without doubt, have set ablaze in his heart the flames of anger and vengeance. A Sanskrit proverb says, 'The honourable prefer death to dishonour,' and Nana was above all honourable. Generous as a prince, pride was his greatest wealth—as it always is of the brave. Hence he could not bear the idea of accepting any invitation from the European officers about him. For, was he not, as the Peshwa, entitled to the salute of guns, which the Company was not willing to fire in his honour? He was serious constitutionally and his habits were simple. He had not a trace of extravagant habits or vices.[5] An Englishman who had observed him closely on many occasions says, that, at the time he saw him, he was really about twenty-eight years of age, but he looked forty. He was inclined to *embonpoint*; his face was round; his eyes, restless like those of a tiger, were piercing and of great lustre; his complexion was like that of any Spaniard; his conversation was characterised by a touch of humour.'[6] In the Durbar, he was dressed in *kinkhabs*. Englishmen used to admire the jewellery he displayed about his person and his crowns studded with diamonds. His generous and sympathetic heart, had effectually won the love of his subjects. His kindness to his subjects would be quite natural, but it is significant that Shrimant was habitually generous even towards those very English people, who, turning ungrateful, had deprived him of his all. If any youthful English couple wanted change of air, the rich equipage of Maharaja Nana Sahib was ready at their service. Many a 'Sahib' tired of living in Cawnpore, used to pay a visit with his 'memsahib' to the town of Maharaja Nana Sahib, and presents of rich shawls and valuable pearls and diamonds were made to them

---

5. 'A quiet and unostentatious young man not at all addicted to any extravagant habits.' -Sir John Kaye.

6. Trevelyan's *Cawnpore*, pages 68-69.

7. Trevelyan's Cawnpore, pp. 68-69.

on the occasion of their leaving Brahmavarta.[7] It may be seen clearly from this that the poison of individual hatred never touched the noble soul of Nana. The elevated and heroic ideal, of generously treating those very enemies with social courtesy and obligation, whom, on the battlefield, you would remorselessly destory, has again and again been celebrated in the epics and histories of Hindusthan. The Rajput heroes used to treat their bitterest enemies with splendid generosity. Be it noted, therefore in this connection, that there was considerably cordiality between Nana and the English at this time.[8] As long as they could feast at the palace of the Shrimant, the English officers and their wives were heaping friendly praise upon him, but as soon as he lifted the sword of righteousness in the cause of Swaraj and Swadesh on the battefield of Cawnpore, what ignominy and what low abuse they heaped on him!

Shrimant was well educated, and had the refinement of culture. He took great interest in politics and political affairs. He used to watch and closely study the ever changing affairs or great nations, and for that purpose would closely follow the English press. He used to have the daily papers read to him every moring by Mr. Tod, an Englishman afterwards massacred at Cawnpore. He thus was able to observe, with his lynx-eye, all the political changes in England and in India. When heated discussions were taking place over the question of annexing Oudh, Nana was of opinion that that act would inevitably force on a war.[9]

As this description is compiled from the histories written by Nana's enemies, it is to be noted that those virtues which

---

8. 'Nothing could exeeed the cordiality which he constantly displayed in his intercourse with our countrymen. The persons in authority placed an implicit confidence in his friendliness and good faith, and the ensigns emphatically pronounced him a capital fellow. ,- Trevelyan's Cawnpore.

9, Charles Ball's *Indian Mutiny*, Vol. I, p. 304.

his enemies ascrib to him must have been a distinct feature in his character. For it cannot be expected that English historians, with their terrible hatred for Nana, could acknowledge willingly his eminent virtues except where absolutely necessary. The tardy acknowledgment of such virtues is the more significant, as after this slight confession of truth, these very historians have wreaked to the full their devilish vengeance on Nana for having leaped forth into the battlefield. The poisonous pen of English historians has taken a fiendish delight in calling him a '*badmash*' a 'highway robber', a 'fiend' and, 'Satan', and has been heaping upon him low, vulgar, and dishonest abuse. But even if all this abuse was deserved, still the single fact, that Nana fought for Swarajya and bled for Swadesh, is sufficient to establish his loving memory in the heart of us Indians. It was essentially necessary that the whole world should realise the fact that a grand and terrible vengeance is visited sooner or later on those who dare to commit the sin of depriving Hindusthan of Independence. Nana was the incarnation of vengeance of the land of Hind! Nana was the Narasimha Mantra of this land! Yes; this one fact will impress Nana's memory on the tablet of our hearts! Yet with this particular merit of Nana, when one further remembers the individual instances of his generosity, his pride of birth, and above all his noble and patriotic heart, one's head bows in loving adoration of that grand personality; and then rises before one's mind's eye the fair and noble form of Nana, with his huge strength, crown on his head, his bright, and alert eyes red with injured pride, the sword (worth three lakhs of Rupees) by his side keen and ready to leap forth from the scabbard, and his body all aflame with anger and keen desire to avenge the Swarajya and the Swadesh!

Ye, conflicting emotions, stop! What a terrible tumult is happening there! The insolent message, the last, has come to Nana from the English, that he has not a vestige of claim to the penson of Baji Rao; nay that he must even give up the proprietary rights to Brahmavarta; and this, the Company further claimed, was justice! Justice? Now the English need not take the trouble of giving a definite reply whether it was justice or injustice! Extensive preparations are in progress and there, on the field of Cawnpore, will be determined the issue of the question. It is there that the question, whether it is justice or injustice to injure the heart of a Mahratta, will be fully discussed. Decapitated, headless trunks, mutilated bodies, flowing streams of blood—these will determine the issue. Aye, and the vultures sitting on the well of Cawnpore will listen to this discussion and give a definite answer to the issue raised, Justice or Injustice?

While splendid preparations were being made for this extraordinary ceremony at Nana's palace, his Chhabeli sister was not sitting idle. Before her had come the same question—Justice or Injustice? When she adopted her darling Damodar as her son, soon after the sudden death of her husband in 1853, the English annexed Jhansi, refusing to recognise the rights of adoption. But Jhansi was not a state which could be annexed by mere word or letter. Not the Banka of Nagpur, but the dear sister Chhabeli of Nana—Ranee Lakshmi Bai was ruling there! As if she cared a whit for this 'annexation'! From her proud heart, seeing this low and heartless cunning of the English, pealed forth the thunders born of injured pride and a sense of honour, and through these the lightning of Jhansi declared, I Give up my Jhansi?-I will not! Let him try to take who dares!!' 'Meri Jhansi doongi nahin !!' [10]

* * *

10. Dalhousie's Administration, Vol. II.

S-2-3

CHAPTER IV

Ayodhya

We have no hesitation in saying that Lord Dalhousie is one of those Indian administrators who are accused of more sins of administration than they are really guilty of. Officers like Dalhousie are nothing more than mouthpieces of tyranny. They merely execute the commands of the 'Home' authorities. To refer all responsibility for tyrannous misdeeds committed in India to such mouthpieces would be as unjust as it is irrational. Dalhousie was purely a creature of the circumstances in which he was placed. The major portion of the responsibility, for good as well as for evil, therefore, rests on those who created the situation. As long as the general policy is dictated from 'Home' those whose duty is merely to execute it can act no more honestly than Dalhousie did. It would certainly be unjust to hold Dalhousie responsible for all those combined acts and deeds which had to flow directly from the situation created for him by his masters in England and his assistants in India. Dalhousie merely reaped that harvest of political robbery the seeds of which had been sedulously sown for a hundred years by his predecessors. The intrigues born of political avarice had been sown long before and Dalhousie's regime was the season in which they bore fruit. But for this heritage of iniquitous power behind him, how many kingdoms could Dalhousie have annexed? It was chiefly because generations of his predecessors had prepared the way for him by slowly undermining the foundations of the different kingdoms of India that Dalhousie was enabled, by the mere stroke of his pen, to annex so many of them.

It was in 1764 that the relations between the Company and the ruler of Oudh were first established. Since then, the servants of the Company had been steadily trying to usurp the fertile land of Ayodhya. Having first compelled the Nabob of Oudh to keep English regiments in his pay for 'protecting' him they obtained from him in return Rs. 16 lakhs (£ 160,000) per annum as the pay for these regiments. By such forced protection and voluntary compulsion, the treasury of the Nabob was rapidly emptied; and then the English suggested to the Nabob (it was a veiled command) that replacing of all the native army of the Nabob by English regiments would be a valuable step towards the effectual 'protection' of the Principality. A treasury which could not afford to pay even the pay of the 'subsidised troops' could certainly not pay the salaries of the 'additional' troops forced on the Nabob, and the English thoroughly knew this fact. Indeed, the additional demand *was* made *because* the English knew this fact. At last it was forced (most unwillingly!) upon the notice of the Company that, if the Nabob had an empty treasury, he had at least a tract of territory and, so, with the sole object ot looking after the welfare and well-being of the Nabob, the Company deprived him, at once and for ever, of a territory yielding a net revenue of about two crores of Rupees (£ 2,000,000) and forced him to accept the services of this extensive army of English soldiers. This territory was the land of Rohilkhand and the Doab.

After robbing all this land from the territory of Oudh the English signed an agreement that, as the Nabob had surrendered all and every right over this tract of land, the rest of the territory belonging to the Nabob should remain hereditarily in the family of the Nabob. Another article in the treaty provided that the Nabob should not oppress his subjects. After this treaty which was concluded in 1801, the Nabob was made to advance to the Company, whenever they wanted financial aid, crores of Rupees. The whole kingdom of Oudh was in the hands of the Company's army officers, the treasury became empty by forced loans and contributions, and it was impossible for the Nabob to administer his territory independently or to introduce internal reforms. But the philanthropic company kept on urging upon him, pointing to the articles in the treaty of 1801, to alter his administration so as to make his subjects happy and contented. How was it possible for the Nabob to do so ? The Company thwarted all his eftorts to reform the finances. Those old laws in the kingdom which ensured the happiness of the people were abolished by the Company and new ones were introduced. The subjects suffered so much in consequence of these new laws that even the Company had to acknowledge its mistake and did do so ten years after. Thus, while on the one hand the Company unlawfully interfered in the internal administration of the kingdom, on the other hand it insisted that the subjects of the Nabob should have no complaints. The first made him empty his treasure to satisfy their exorbitant demands; and when, to satisfy their further demands which they insisted on being satisfied at once, the Nabob taxed his subjects, down comes the Company on the Nabob's poor devoted head and charges him with maladministration, because, forsooth, the subjects complained against the new taxes. The Nabob's administration was thus paralysed, but, at the same time, if by any chance the people, with one voice, rose against the injustice and attempted to get a reform of the constitution, English bayonets and swords of the 'subsidised' troops were ever ready to smother the united voice of the nation. And still, the Company persisted in requiring that there should be no complaints in the kingdom! Thus, while on the one hand they renderded it more and more impossible either for the Nabob or the people to reform the administration in any way, on the other hand their strict and persistent demands for a better administration grew steadily louder and louder! 'As a matter of fact, the true and effectual way for the introduction of an administration which would render the people happy would have been to call the British Resident back and to give the Nabob a free hand in the administration of his dominion. Thus, the whole guilt of the unrest in his territory rests on the head of the Company.'[1] Such is the clear and unmistakable evidence of Lord Hastings. But in spite of this, the Company threatened that, if the Nabob did not render his administration conductive to the happiness of his subjects, the Company would consider it a violation of the treaty of 1801.

This treaty of 1801 was cancelled and the Nabob entered into a fresh agreement in 1837. This treaty impaired the authority of the Nabob considerably, but he signed the new agreement simply with the intention of rescuing himself from the cunning treaty of 1801. In the year 1847, Wajid Ali Shah succeeded to the throne of Oudh. This new Nabob determined from the first to destroy the poisonous white worm which was killing the life out of the state, and with that object began reforms in the army which was the life of the kingdom. This youthful prince introduced strict regulations as to the discipline of the Sepoys and even personally supervised their drill. All the regiments had to undergo the drill every morning before the Nabob, who used to dress in the uniform of the commander-in-chief of the troops. He issued strict orders that every regiment that was late in presenting itself on the parade ground should be liable to a fine of Rs. 2000 (£ 200) and he, at the same time, bound himself to pay the same amount as fine if he himself failed in 'his duty.[2]

The Company of course, could not bear to see the Nabob develop his strength. The British Resident, therefore, in a short time forced the Nabob to give up these military activities and at the same time suggested that, if he so desired to increase the strength of the army, the Company was quite willing to increase the 'subsidiary' force; the only condition they could impose being that the Nabob should, every year, pay a further additional sum towards its expenses and upkeep.

I.Charles Ball's Indian Mutiny, Vol. I. p. 152.
2. Native Narratives af the Mutiny by Metcalfe, pp. 32-33

The hot-blooded Nabob was quite indignant. But he was forced to give up his daring scheme of military reform and was reduced to complete inactivity. Yet, the benevolent East India Company went on arguing that the Nabob should render his administration happy to his subjects.

But now, the Nabob need not even think as to how to render his rule happy. For Lord Dalhousie has arrived in India with the express and benevolent object of taking upon himself (as representative of the E. I. Coy.) all the responsibility for the good administration of all the independent states of India. With his keen political insight, Lord Dalhousie soon realised that the treaty of 1837 was, as a matter of fact, a great blunder. For in the annulment of the old treaty was lost a very strong and a very hyper critical reason for the annexation of the independent principality of Oudh. The article in the treaty of 1801, demanding that the Nabob should rule for the happiness of his subjects, was an incontrovertible argument for annexing Oudh at the sweet will of the Company. How could this mistake of 1837 be repaired? Why, by simply denying the fact that the treaty was ever entered into. Without any indirect methods, the Nabob was informed that no such treaty as the one of 1837 was ever entered into. A short time after the treaty of 1837, the English, as it would appear, remembered the treaty perfectly well. Indeed in 1847, Lord Hartington had publicly and unmistakably acknowledged this treaty. Col. Sleeman in 1851 had further testified to the treaty. Nay, in that very year 1853, not only was mention made of this treaty, but it was actually appended to the list of the existing treaties in the Company's records for that year![3] So the English denied, aye, altogether, that there was ever any such tieaty; the very existence of a treaty which they had acknowledged just a minute before was denied by them even before the pen which had written the acknowledgement had been laid

3. Dalhousie's Administration, Vol. II, p. 367

down! And thus, Wajid Ali Shah was informed that the company would consider it necessary to take over the administration of his kingdom if he did not introduce the happy regime!

But it must not be forgotten that all these important issues had been decided on long before Dalhousie even reached the shores of Hindusthan. All his predecessors, moved by unholy designs, had prepared the way to swallow this province, and their endeavours, characterised by low cunning, had almost succeeded. To Dalhousie was reserved the last act of consummation, the last stroke of policy, and this absorbed all his attention. It would have been out of question to 'conquer' Oudh by sending an expedition into the territory as was done in the case of the Panjab or Brahmadesh (Burma) , for as yet not a single man in the Oudh territory was for the English. The charge that the Nabob did not carry out the friendly intention he professed was also out of question, for had not the Nabob helped the English on all occasions, when help was needed? And had not the Nabob freely supplied the English with money from his pocket? Had he not supplied the English even with provisions, when they were pressed hard in many of their compaigns ?

Nor could there be any excuse, as in the case of Nagpur, that the Nabob had no direct heir; the palace was full of the Nabob's legitimate children. Nor was their trouble about adoption as in the case of Jhansi, for the present king was the legitimate son of the late king and had, further, sat on the throne for years. In short the Nabob of Oudh had not committed any of the above, 'crimes' which cost other princes their kingdoms. But though the Nabob had thus avoided every other 'crime', still the demented fool had committed one unpardonable crime! What crime could cry louder than this, that the land of Oudh was very fertile, teeming with crops and rich in every way? Even the dry language of the Blue Book has broken forth into poetic eloquence when describing the beautiful and rich land of Oudh !

The Blue Book says: 'In this beautiful land, everywhere within twenty feet, and in some places even within ten feet, of the surface, there is plentiful supply of water. This splendid tract is most charming, nodding with whole forests of tall and towering bamboo trees, cooled by the shade of mango trees and green with rich and verdant crops. The deep shade of the tamarind, the fragrance of the orange trees, the rich hue of the fig trees, and the sweet all-pervading scent of the pollen of flowers lend an additional glory to a scene naturally beautiful !'

That no wise Englishman should hesitate to pull down a Nabab who was guilty of such an enormity as possessing such a beautiful tract of territory all for himself, Dalhousie realised but too well and so, in the year 1856, the fiat went forth that Oudh was to be annexed. And what was the reason alleged? Of course this, that the Nabob was not reforming his administration.

But, England, couldst thou justify thy rule over India for a day, if thou acknowledgest the plea of unrest and maladministration as sufficient? There is the vice of opium-eating in China, absolute rule in Afganisthan, why, under thy very nose Russia has reached a climax of lawlessness and tyranny ; yet couldst thou dare for that reason to drag the Chinese Emperor and the Amir and the Tsar from their thrones and annex their kingdoms? How couldst thou acquire the right of gagging the mouth of your neighbour and binding his hands and feet and taking possession of his house, because, forsooth, he kept his things not quite in proper order? Even the treaty of 1801 did not give the Company the right of annexing Oudh, under any circumstances. And was not that very absence of good administration, at which the Company pretended so much indignation, a thing brought about by their own agency? Arnold, the biographer of

Dalhousie and the historian of his regime, asserts that the Nabob of Oudh Was guilty of many a crime besides that! In the first place, he used to give presents of shawls to his servants of either sex; further that he had a fireworks display on the 11th of May; why, more- one morning he urged Shah Begum and Taj Begum to a dinner! What more horrible crime could he commit? All thanks to the English who bore patiently such gross acts on the part of the Nabob as taking medicinal drugs in the mornings, and desisted from dethroning him! But the patience of the English could endure no more! For, one day the Nabob was present when some stallions were let on the mares for breeding purposes.

It is a wonder that malicious as the English historians were, trying hard to noise far and wide the incapacity of the Nabob for good administration, by such silly, trifling accusations, they should have taken the trouble to come to Hindusthan to witness such occurrences as these. Even in their own country, throughout the various royal palaces, they could have gathered enough material of worse nature; and in that case, their time would certainly have been more profitably employed in annexing and confiscating the estates of their own princes and lords, in order to put an end to violations and outrages of a far more nefarious kind!

As soon as the British Resident received the order that the Nabob should be informed of the decision of Dalhousie—a lasting stain on his regime—the Resident went to the Nabob's palace and began to insist that the Nabob should sign a document stating that he was perfectly willing to give over his dominions to the Company. The Nabob read the document and flatly refused to sign. To make the Nabob sign this document, the Resident began attempts to bribe the Ranee and the Vizier and the threat was also given that a refusal by the Nabob to sign the document would result in even his pension being stopped. The Nabob was overwhelmed with grief at this and began even to weep.

But it was of no use. Seeing at the end of three days that the refusal was still persisted in, the British army, insolently setting aside the Nabob's authority, entered Lucknow and took forcible possession of the whole *Ryasat*, including his palace. The Zenanas were looted, the Begums were insulted, the Nabob was hurled from the throne, palaces were turned into stables for the soldiers of the English and thus began a happy beginning of the good administration of the so-far-badly-managed kingdom of Oudh.

Though the ruling prince of Oudh was a Mahomedan most of the big land-owners under him were Hindus. Jahgirs and Talukdari rights had continued from father to son in the families of these Zemindars for generations. Hundreds of villages were administered under the single authority of each of these proprietors. They possessed forts and had small armies under them to protect these Jahgirs. No wonder, then, that these Zemindars very soon incurred the displeasure of the Company. With a view to reduce all to the same level of poverty, the sordid roller of the Company's land revenue administration began to devastate the land. The Talukdars were deprived of their numerous villages wholesale, their lands were confiscated, their forts were demolished, and allover the land of Ayodhya one long wail of suffering rent the air! The Amir of yesterday became a Fakir to-day. The descendants of ancient and noble families were driven from village to village at the behest of a raw white youth of yesterday; insults were everwhere given; whole families were reduced to dust.[4]

---

4. Kaye says with reference to the Zemindar: The charges, against him were many and great, for he had diverse ordeals to pass through and he seldom survived them all. When the claims of a great Ta!ukdar could not be altogether ignored, it was declared that he was a rogue or a fool. .. They gave him a bad name and they straighatway went to ruin him. .. It was at once a cruel wrong and a grave error to sweep it away as though it were an encumbrance and an usurpation.

The English claimed that they were doing these things for the poor agriculturists and villagers. Tyrannous land owners oppressed the Ryot: hence, these protectors of the Ryot were introducing new methods to deliver the Ryot from the cruel grip of the landowner. How many Ryots and bow many villages were deceived by these false pretensions will soon be witnessed on the battle-fields of Ayodhya. Faithful villagers, attached to their masters, used to visit these homeless Zemindars and Talukdars, robbed and driven from door to door, and used to pay them faithful homage in the profuse flow of sincere tears. Thus, there was terrible suffering—right from the Nabob of Oudh to the villagers; not a place but witnessed wholesale looting, even burning misery, oppression, and tyranny, and did not hurl terrible curses and vowed vegeance; not a homestead but looked desolate, terribly desolate! Such was the beneficent administration that was substituted in Oudh for the misgovernment of the Nabob!

The world-wide difference between Swarajya and foreign rule was, thus, brought painfully to the notice of all Oudh. All their previous history stood before them vividly. They realised full well now that even death was preferable to living in slavery. How long to look on, while the Swadesh was reduced to dust and Swarajya was no more? They hated intensely these insults and this shameful condition.

At this very time, the roller of the lnam Commission was working in other provinces in order to destory the stamina of Zemindars and Vatandars in those provinces and reduce them to, the level of those classes in Oudh. Those lands and those Jahgirs which had been won by the Sanad of the Sword were being abolished wholesale, because they could not show documentary evidence of Sanads of paper. That the work of the Inam Commission was terrible may, to some extent, be realised from this single fact that nearly 35000 big Jahgirs and extensive Inams were inquired into by the Inam

Commissian and of these, within, the space of ten years, three-fifths were usurped! By this means, all over India, property of every kind was rendered insecure. Thrones of princes, Vatans of Sardars, lands of Zemindars, Talukas of Talukdars, houses of citizens, the lands dedicated to the temples, the fields of agriculturists—all these were, in this terrible conflagration, burned to ashes. Even life was rendered insecure. No one could be sure that the few morsels of food which he was allowed to-day would be spared to him to-morrow. The contrast between Swarajya and foreign government, independence and slavery, stood naked in all its horrible aspects before the people.

Thus did the English administer benevolently in this extraordinary way these vast dominions of our Indian princes which had been so far badly administered!

* * *

CHAPTER V

Adding Fuel To Fire

To ALLOW the existence of slavery under which such unjust acts of oppression (as have been mentioned in the last chapter) and hundreds of other unmentionable crimes (which have been left unmentioned, being, indeed, too numerous to mention) are committed and encouraged and to bow the head in submission to. the perpetrators thereof, is not this the very destruction or Religion? What religion is there which has not condemned dependence and slavery? The ultimate goal of true religion is likeness unto the nature of the Supreme Being that moves everything, of Him who made all beings capable of becoming all-perfect. There must not be imperfection in man if he is to be like the All-Perfect. But how can there be anything but imperfection in a country where there is slavery? God is the essence of justice, and slavery is absence of justice. God is the essence of freedom slavery is absence of freedom. Hence, where there is God there cannot be slavery, and where there is slavery there cannot be God or Godliness. Where there is no place for God, there can be no religion. In short, true religion cannot exist where slavery, the nursery of injustice, is rampant. Slavery is the straight road to Hell and true religion is a means of attaining Heaven. To walk in the path leading towards Heaven, the shackles of slavery must be broken. This was the practical philosophy which Sri Samartha Ramdas gave to Shivaji and Sri Pran Nath taught Chhatrasala, and this advice to win Swaraj for the sake of religion, by fighting and dying for it, began to echo in the hearts of the people trodden under slavery, in 1857, two hundred years after it was originally given.

Those, who had thrust this slavery — unnatural, born of injustice, —on Hindusthan, had already begun the destruction of religion not only in India but all over the world. For, what religion is there which has not condemned injustice? But not satisfied with the tacit insult of the religion of India, from the very day he set foot on the Indian soil upto the terrible battles of 1857, the Feringhi had been making steady and unceasing attempts to trample the Hindu religion and the Moslem faith. The head of the whole English nation was turned at the immeasurable success which had attended the attempt to Christianise (?) the indigenous ignorant races of Africa and America, and they had strong hopes that in India too, in a few days, the Crosss would be everywhere triumphant. That the English fully believed that Hindusthanis would be ashamed of their religion when they saw the light of western civilisation and give it up, that they would consider the Bible more sacred than the Vedas and the Koran, and that they would be gathered together in the fold of the Church, leaving their Temples and Musjids,—is fully and unmistakably seen from the literature of that time and from the writings and speeches of Englishmen of the first half of the last century. The chairman of the Directors of the East India Company, Mr. Mangles, said in the House of Commons, in 1857:—

'Providence has entrusted the extensive empire of Hinduthan to England in order that the banner of Christ should wave triumphant from one end of India to the other. Everyone must exert all his strength that there may be no dilatoriness on any account in continuing in the country the grand work of making all India Christian.'

Macaulay, in 1836—when schools in which English education was to be given were first opened in Bengal, had expressed a hope amounting almost to a conviction that, in thirty years there would be no idol-worshipper left in Bengal.[1]

The mind of the Feringhi was filled with such contempt and such hatred for the Hindu and Moslem faiths—the two principal religions of India—that very prominent writers, forgetting even ordinary conventionalities, constantly heaped shameful abuse on the two religions whenever they got a chance.

The constant insistence by the East Indian Company to make India Christian was due to a very obvious reason. Once the religions in India died, the national feeling of the people would also die; individuality would die and it is infinitely more easy to rule a nation whose individuality is dead than to rule one which has a clearly marked individuality. Thus, the question was one of diplomacy rather than of religion, and the reason why England did not lift the sword for the solution of the problem was also to be found in diplomacy. England had learnt many lessons from the history of Aurangzeb. Both the strength and weakness of the policy of that monarch

1. 'It is my firm belief that, if our plan of education is followed up, there would not be a single idolator in Bengal 30 years hence Macaulay's letter to his mother, Oct. 12, 1836.

had been carefully studied by the English. Learning the wisdom of Aurangzeb, that the destruction of the religion of a conquered race makes the problem of retaining it in perpetual slavery much easier, the English had avoided his folly of open persecution for religion. Hence the stolid and continuous efforts of the English to make India Christian by indirect means -only and not openly.

Rev. Kennedy wrote at the time, 'Whatever misfortunes come on us, as long as our Empire in India continues, so long let us not forget that our chief work is the propagation of Christianity in the land. Until Hindusthan, from Cape Comorin to the 'Himalayas, embraces the religion of Christ and until it condemns the Hindu and the Moslem religions our efforts must continue persistently. For this work, we must make all the efforts we can and use all the power and all the authority in our hands; *and continuous and unceasing efforts must be kept on until India becomes a mangnificient nation, the bulwark of Christianity in the East!* If, with such uninterrupted perseverance, we continue our efforts, then I do not doubt that, by the grace of God, we shall be successful in the end!'

No wonder, then, that every citizen of India—seeing that English authorities and missionaries were using such language openly—began to feel that, under the English Raj, everyone would eventually be forced to be Christian. With the disappearance or Swaraj, the Rajas and Maharajahs, who made rich gifts of Inams and Jahgirs to Temples and Musjids, were also disappearing. In this powerless state-instead of new Inams being granted, instead of fresh gifts of money being showered on Temples and Musjids as when there was Swaraj—even those Inams and the money remaining yet in their hands were being taken away forcibly from the temples and mosques. And there is no wonder that, seeing that there was no protection for their religions, the Hindus and the Moslems alike were pained and grieved. Nor is it to be wondered at that the blood of both the Hindus and the Mahomedans boiled with rage at being openly described in official and private documents as 'heathens' a peculiarly abusive epithet. And yet, there was every indication that the Feringhis, who cared more for increase of commerce than of the Christian religion and were the devotees more of Mammon than of Christ—the Prince of Poverty, would therefore desist from attacking the relgious prejudices of the people by open violence.

As if with the express purpose of proving the falsity of such an idea, the English in the insolence born of unbridled power very soon began an open and violent interference with the religions of Hindusthan. Even while efforts were being made to pass in Calcutta the law for the abolition of suttee, public opinion in India began to suspect deeper designs on the part of the Government. Even before this law for the abolition of suttee had passed through the Councils of Calcutta, the prisoners were prevented from observing their religions. A few days more saw the passing of the Widow Remarriage Act, in the face of the loud protests of the Hindus. No sooner had this law been passed than Lord Canning expressed his opinion that the law for the abolition of polygamy was to be brought into the Legislative Council, and he exerted himself to pass it as speedily as possible through the Council. The question we have to answer here is not whether the law which the Company was going to introduce was good or bad. 'What we want, in this place, to say is that neither the Hindus nor the Mahomedans could be certain as to where the attack on their religious customs would stop, seeing that the English, in the exercise of their authority for the passing of these laws, had begun the dangerous habit of interfering by force with the religious customs of the people. These laws may be good or bad nor may it be necessary to attach to them the slightest import-tance; but this much is clear that any changes in the social habits based upon religious texts can be brought about only by the authority of those religions and through their adherents. When a foreign administration professing an alien religion, after making promises never to interfere with the religious beliefs of the people endeavours to change by force the hereditary customs, the established religious belief of the people, on the strength of a majority composed of men professing the foreign religion in the council and on the strength of despotic authority, and that, when the public opinion clearly and unmistakably expressed, of the adherents of those religions was opposed to such a change, while, in the Council, the men who belonged to these religions had no authority at all-then, indeed, there was not the least difference between the tyranny of Aurangzeb and the tyranny of the Company's *Raj*. To-day law regarding only suttee has been passed; who could say that, when this injustice was swallowed by the people what other laws the Company would not pass? The English hated idolatry as much as they did suttee. To-day the law for the abolitIon of suttee was forced on the people against their will; who knows that, to-morrow, a law for the prevention of idol-worship would not be thrust on the people under the pretext of reform? One injustice begets another. To allow the continuance of this system of interfering with religion by means of laws made by aliens was to follow the lifting of the sword of Aurangzeb. And when the English had begun to take up the role of Aurangzeb, there was no other remedy than that India must produce a Shivaji or a Guru Govind. And such was the usual impression allover India.

And this idea the Christian missionaries began to strengthen themselves. In their street preachings at various places, they used to say openly that India would soon be Christianised. The Sirkar had already begun to pass one law after another to destroy the foundations of the Hindu and Mahomedan religions. Railways had already been built in such a way as to offend the caste prejudices of the Hiudus. The larger mission schools were being helped with huge grants from the Sirkar. Lord Canning himself distributed thousands of Rupees to every mission, and from this fact it is clear that the wish was strong in the heart of Lord Canning that all India should be Christian. Why, if the would-be converts are afraid that they would lose their property by conversion, a law shall at once be passed to prevent this!

Hardly had the missionaries exhausted their sermons and lectures, when news came that a law had been passed that all the rights and privileges of converts to the property of their unconverted relatives should remain intact even after conversion. Another fact also came to light, that huge salaries were to be paid to the bishops and even archbishops from the Indian treasury. The insistence of every Englishman, from the highest officer in the Government to the commonest missionary of the towns, had reached such a pitch that the white superior in Government offices began to insist on all the 'black' clerks under him to become Christian! While the officers were ready to lay the axe at the root of Indians' religions, at the expense of India's money, themselves living on the fat of India—the Government did not move at all in the matter. For, what was the Government but Lord Canning and his councillors? And, this Canning and this Council had surpassed all other officers in their holy zeal for coversion and were feeding the missionaries with lakhs of Rupees—those missionaries who defiled the people and heaped unrestrained abuse on their sacred religions. Under such circumstances the people were reasonably afraid that a greater danger was in store for their religion under the British *Raj*. The English missionaries tried to allay the terrible unrest by an attempt to christianise the sepoys, the chief strengh of the people of India, believing that the disaffection of the ordinary people would be no danger to them at all. That the low cunning of this trick was plainly understood by the people will be seen unmistakably from the proclamations of the 'Mutineers'. That the complaints and grievances mentioned in these proclamations are literally true can be collected even from the reluctant confessions of the English historians themselves. Except in the time of actual warfare, all days were days of leisure to the Sepoys. How were these days of leisure utilised by colonels and captains and other officers in the English army? Why, in constantly poisoning the ears of the Sepoys with talks on Christianity! Do you think even this preaching was conducted in simple and decorous language? Not at all. Abuse, unrestrained filthy abuse was heaped on the name of Ramchandra, the sacred name, the mere mention of which makes the heart of every Hindu fill with love and with devotion, and on the name of Mahomed, the very mention of whose name fills all Moslems with reverence and awe. The Koran and the Vedas were openly defiled and images were desecrated! If any Sepoy retaliated on these fiendish Feringhis and returned abuse for abuse, the poor Sepoy's *roti* and *ghee* would be taken away by the authority of the missionary colonels. Why, very soon things came to such a pass that living in the English barracks meant the sacrifice of one's religion. For, if any Sepoy accepted the Christian religion, he was praised loudly and treated honourably; and this Sepoy was promoted in the ranks and his salary increased, in the face of the superior merits of the other Sepoys! A soldier renegade giving up his religion became a Hawaldar and a Hawaldar, untrue to his religion, was promoted to be a Subhedar Major![2]

Seeing that the Sepoys in the army were poor, ignorant, and short-sighted; feeling that when the military was christianised the christianising of the people was only a question of time; considering the question every way, the English had come to the conclusion that the chief attack must be delivered on the Sepoy in the army. And in accordance with this opinion, from many directions, secret and open attacks on the Hindu and Moslem faiths had already begun

---

2. *Causes of the Mutiny* by a Bengali Hindu.

to be delivered. Not only that, but some commanders and colonels did not hesitate even to declare publicly through newspapers, that they had entered the army with the express purpose and object of destroying the religion of the Sepoy. The Commander of the Bengal infantry himself writes in the Government Report that he had been continuing uninterruptedly for 28 years the policy of christianising the military and that it was a part of military duty to save the souls of heathens from Satan! Who could dare to say that the fears of the Sepoy were unreasonable as to the impossibility of preserving their religion in the face of the attempts to undermine it, continued day and night by these *padre* heroes who stumped the country with port-folios of military orders on the one hand, and the Bible in the other? Everywhere there was a strong conviction that the Government had determined to destroy the religions of the country and make Christianity the paramount religion of the land.

An Englishman, to show how the hatred of the Feringhi was raging tumultuously in the hearts of both Hindus and Mahomedans, says - A Moulvie of my acquaintance, living outwardly on terms of intimacy with me, was on his death-bed. I was with him at the time and I asked him what was his last wish before he died. He looked very disconsolate and gloomy at this question. On being asked why he looked so gloomy, he said, 'Truly, I assure you that I repent exceedingly that I did not kill even two Feringhis in my life!' On another occasion a respectable and learned Hindu said boldly, 'We wish you to be gone and our native rule to be established, that we may continue in the ways of our fathers!'[3]

While this tumult of disaffection was raging everywhere Dalhousie himself made a further attack on the Hindu

3. Rev. Kennedy, M.A.

religion. Even English historians who consider it their duty to support all the actions of the Government find it impossible to support this enormity. When the civilised Christian hero, Dalhousie, came forward to trample under foot the noble custom of adoption, one of the tenderest, most noble, loving, and sacred commandments of the Hindu Dharma Shastras and endeared to the people of all ages allover India, all India from one end to the other was shocked. The magazine required only lighted match to explode with violence and this act of Dalhousie supplied it.

To add fuel to this raging fire, orders were issued to the Indian sepoys that they should use the new cartridges! Soon after the promulgation of the order for using new cartridges for the new rifles, factories were opened for the manufacture of these cartridges in various places. A certain kind of fat had to be used for the greasing of these cartridges so that they might be smooth and well-lubricated, and orders soon followed that the sepoys should bite off this greasy portion with their teeth instead of tearing it away with hands as formerly. Immediately afterwards schools were even opened that the sepoys might learn how to use these rifles and also how to bite the cartridges with their teeth, and the Government reports from various quarters stated that the sepoys were immensely pleased with the long range of these new rifles.

One day, a Brahmin Sepoy belonging to the village of Dum-Dum, very near Calcutta, was going to the military barracks with his *Lota* full of water. At that instant, a scavenger came and asked to drink from the *Lota*. The Brahmin replied that his Lota would be rendered unclean by his touch. The scavenger replied, 'Enough of caste pride now! Do you not know that soon you would bite with your teeth the flesh of the cow and the fat of the pig? The new cartridges are being expressly greased with these materials for this purpose!' When he heard this, the Brahmin ran wild with excitement towards the camp, as if the very devil was in him; and in a few minutes, the sepoys became excited—a crowd of mad men?—and horrible whisperings were in the air. Suspicions arose that the Feringhis had arranged a cunning plot to defile their religions by greasing the cartridges with cows' blood and pigs' fat. The Sirkar replied that, far from such a plot being devised by them, the very story that the cartridges were greased with cows' blood and pigs' fat was absolutely without fonndation.

Who was it then that spoke the lie? Was it the Sirkar or the sepoys ? If the cartridges were really greased with cows' blood and pigs' fat, was it the result of mere ignorance or of conscious purpose on the part of the Government? That the English did not know with what material the cartridges were greased cannot be held for a moment. For in 1853, when these cartridges were introduced for the first time and when 'native' sepoys from Cawnpore, Rangoon, Fort William and other places, not suspecting that unclean things had been used in their manufacture, had bitten off these cartridges with full confidence in their superiors, even then the English authorities knew with what the cartridges, were greased. In December 1853, Col. Tucker has mentioned this fact very clearly in the Government reports.[4] Why, even the Commander-in-Chief knew the fact and, in spite of this, the very things prohibited by the two religions were used and even factories for their manufacture were opened right in India! After ascertaining well this fact from the low caste Indians working in those factories, the sepoys of Barrackpore spread this news all over India. Even lightning travels not so quick! Within a fortnight, not a Hindu or a Mahomedan but was talking of cartridges and nothing but cartridges, wherever he was. And the stronger this public indignation grew, the stronger and more frequent grew the assertions on the part of the authorities, from the Governor-General

4. Kaye's Indian Mutiny, Vol. I, P.880.

down to the lowest white soldier that the story of the cartridges was a mere fabrication.

These statements of the Feringhi Government were not only absolutely false, but they were put forward deliberately with the knowledge that they were false. The fact that the very Commander- in-Chief was aware of it four years before, was now being openly denied by the Government. That in the factory at Dum-Dum cartridges were not greased with cows' and pigs' fat, that the ignorant and superstitious sepoys had started this wholly unfounded rumour—such were the assertions of the English historians until a very recent date. But now, there does not seem to be the slightest doubt that the Government was well aware of this fact. The contractor who had undertaken to supply the fat for the cartridges had in clear words, made a distinct agreement in his contract deed, drawn at that very time, to supply cows' fat. The agreemment was that the cartridges should be greased with the fat of the cow, the Sacred Mother, buying the same at the rate of two pence (two annas) per pound. And the sepoys should bite these cartridges with their teeth! When this cunning scheme was exposed, the Feringhi Government immediately issued orders that, thereafter, whatever fat was to be used for the cartridges should be only from sheep or goats, and cows' and pigs' fat should never be used. If these orders mean anything they mean that so far the cartridges were being greased with cows' and pigs' fat. It was necessary for them to issue this new regulation because they knew this fact. From the Government documents published by Forrest it is clear beyond any doubt that, in the fat used for the cartridges, cows' and pigs' fat was mixed, and that this fact was known to the highest English authorities in the land.[5] And when the sepoys refused to bite these cartridges, the Feringhi military authorities used to swear that this was altogether false. Not only that, but they were threatened with severe punishment if they refused to obey the military orders through their silly prejudices. But when, regardless of these threats, it appeared that the sepoys were going to dare everything for the protection of their Dharma, then the Sirkar quietly retreated back and yielded on one point, allowing the sepoys to use a certain paper instead of fat. But what guarantee was there that a Government which could stoop to the meanness of using pigs' and cows' fat would not use some other mean trick of the same nature to make the paper substituted for the lubricating mixure smooth? If once unconsciously they were defiled with cows' and pigs' meat thrust in their mouths, then the missionary colonels and *padre* commanders would say, 'Look here, you have now been christianised!.' If, on the one hand, the military superiors tried to soothe the indignation and anger of the sepoys by false denials and lowly retractations, on the other hand, they provoked them still more by distributing on the parades thousands of big pamphlets full of abuse of Rama and Mahomed to spite their religions. The beginning of the agitation against the cartridges was started early in January apd, before the month had ended, the Government had to yield on yet another point-a fresh regulation allowed the soldiers to use the fat they themselves prepared. Further, Birch, at the same time, by means of another Government memorandum, assured all the sepoys that not a single'

5. Says Kaye : 'There is no question that beef fat was used in the composition of this tallow. (Vol. I, p. 381) Says Lord Roberts: , The recent researches of Mr. Forrest in the records of the Government of India prove that the lubricating mixture used in preparing the cartridges was actually composed of the objectionable ingredients, cows' fat and lard and that incredible disregard of the soldiers' religious prejudices was displayed in the manufacature of these cartridges.'- *Forty Years in India*, p. 431.

objectionable cartridge had been sent into the army! The Prince of Lies could not have been more versatile! Twenty-two thousand and five-hundred cartridges from the Umballa depot alone and fourteen thousand from the Sialkot depot had been already sent in 1856! In the rifle classes in various places, even at that very moment, practice in the use of these cartridges was being given! In the Gurkha Regiments, the cartridges were being openly introduced! And military authorities used to threaten the sepoys that they would be physically forced to use the cartridges. Why in one or two places, when the sepoys were obstinate in their refusal to use these cartridges, whole regiments were punished severely.

So, the sepoys determined that, whether they had to use these cartridges or not, they would not rest quiet until they had destroyed this political slavery and this dependence which was at the root of all this trouble. What religion can a slave have? The first step towards Dharma is to be a free man of a free county.

Rise, then, O Hindusthan, rise! Even as Shri Ramdas exhorted 'Die for Dharma; while dying, kill all your enemies and win back Swarajya; while killing, kill well.' Murmuring such sentiments to himself, every sepoy in India began to sharpen his sword for the fight for Swadharma and Swarajya!

* * *

CHAPTER VI

Lit up the Sacrificial Fire

IT IS then inevitable that we must resist sword in hand and wage a relentless struggle to win back our political independence and to safeguard the honour of the ashes of our fathers and the temples of our gods. We must hence hasten first to propitiate the God of War, the Lord of Hosts, even as Indrajit did before he marched on to the battlefield as the 'Puranas' tell us, to 'Secure the unconquerable Chariot which he expected to appear forth out of the blazing Sarificial Fire. True it is that Indrajit was foiled in his attempt to secure it because unrighteous was his cause. But our cause is just, it is righteous! We need not fear frustration. Even though we know that to fight fot what we call Right does not unfailingly win through its inherent justificability or righteousness unless and until it is upheld by proportionate Might, even then to fight for our Right to the best of our might is in itself a heroic joy which fills the warrior with a divine intoxication.

Lit up the Sacrificial Fire then, for we must propitiate the Lord of Hosts, the God of War!

Dig the Sacrificial Fire-pit on the altar wider and wider,. deeper and deeper! Well and good. Lo! the Fire of National Indignation is already bursting forth into flames! As the first sacramental rite, the Sankalpa, the declamatory vow, has already been proclaimed a hundred years ago as early as the year. 1757 A.D. So, as the first sacrificial offering, throw the Field of Plassey into the flaming pit!

Where is the Kohinoor of the Panjab? Here has Dalhousie himself offered to help us and brought it, snatching it away from its rightful owner the Khalsa of Guru Govindsingh! What sacrificial offering can be more igniting the hungry Fire than thc Gem of 'the purest ray serene', this ancient historical emblem of Indian Sovereignty? Throw then, the Kohinoor of Punjab in.

The next immediate offering must be Burma. So let its King Theeba be exiled and into this crackling Fire pit, throw in the kingdom of Burma too.

How do you forget the Throne of Shivaji himself? What is the good of its keeping rotting at Satara! We must respect the right of precedence due to it! Help us, Oh obliging

Britania, by doing your worst with your ravenous claws and relegating the kings there to the graves—where they might yet rule freely—bring here the Maratha throne quick! That the Fire of National indignation may get more fed, fat and fierce, throw the throne of Satara in!

The Gadi of Nagpur by itself could be but a poor offering for such a wild, warlike God. Hence bring ye, with the Gadi all the empty palaces, elephants, horses and the very Ranees too, not only with their jewels, rudely robbed but with their shrieks and weepings and wailings and in this Sacrificial Blazing pit throw it all altogether!

Even though the flames are rising like huge columns leaping forth into the skies higher and higher yet they must be lit still more intensely and fiercely. So throw the lightning of Zansi in!

Ah ! Hear you not now the rambling so deep, so roaring in the bowels of this blazing fire pit, this 'Yagnya-Kund'? Surely some great explosive Revolutionary Birth is getting into line, form and figure! Feed up, Feed up the mighty sacrificial fire with anything and everything that is intensely combustible and at hand. So throw the Nabob of Oudh in! In with the Gadi of Tanjore! In with the Nabob of Arcot! Push in Raj Anguli, Sambalpur, all the Talukdars, Jahagirdars, Inamdars, Vatandars in fact all those who can affix a 'Dar' to their titles, depriving them of all their proprietary rights and possessions and making them all 'Nadars' throw in, throw in !

And now has come the time for Dum Dum! Hasten ye all, friends and foes, and bring all the new cartridges in millions from , the Dum Dum type factories spread throughout India, dip them in cow's blood, boil them in pig's fat and throw into this all absorbing, all consuming Jaw of Fire! There, from the white-heat point the wild fire has risen to War-heat!

Dancing on the blazing flames out of the Sacrificial fire pit, behold, arises at last the presiding Deity, terrible to look at ! Salutes innumerable to Thee, O War God, O Lord of Hosts! Under, whose fierce insolence, tyranny and injustice are ground and burnt to ashes, by the mighty hammer in whose hands the shackles of slavery get knocked down to pieces and Nations are set free and whose hundred and one red hot tongues are lolling out from hundred and one mouths athirst up lick up battlefulls of blood when loaded war clouds burst out on Nations fighting for life, for death,-that aspect of Thee, O Spirit of War, O Har—the terrible! We contemplate, we worship! Be propitious! Wilt thou, O Lord, sharpen the edge of our sword and bless it with Victory?

'If not, perchance, with victory-with Vengeance will I bless your sword! ! —vengeance, the force deterent, the Nemesis which tyranny dreads like death and which holds in the hollow of its hands the seeds of a Victory to come!!'

* * *

CHAPTER VII

Secret Organisation

WHILE the forces of the Revolution were thus maturing themselves all over India, as described in the last chapter, in Brahmavarta a Programme was being prepared as to how to organise properly all the materials for the war so as to bring the the War of Independence to a successful conclusion.

In the third chapter, we left Rango Bapuji and Azimullah Khan holding secret interviews with each other in some London rooms. Though history cannot record the exact conversation the Brahmin of Satara held with the Khan Sahib of Brahmavarta, still, it is as certain as anything can be that the map of the rising was being prepared by these two in London. After leaving London, Rango Bapujl went straight to Satara. but it was not possible for Azimullah Khan to go direct to Hindusthan. The extent of the dominions and the diplomacy of those against whome the war was to be waged were not now confined to Hindusthan alone. Hence, it was necessary to attack the British Empire in as many places as possible. It was also essential that it should be ascertained from what quarters in Europe direct help or moral sympathy could be expected in the coming War or Independence. With this object, Azimullah Khan made a tour in Europe before returning to India. He went to the capital of the Sultan of Turkey famed throughout the world as the Khalifa of all Moslems. Being informed that in the Russo-Turkish War then going on the English had been defeated in the important battle of Sebastopol, he stayed some time in Russia. Many English historians have a suspicion that Azimullah had gone there to ascertain whether Russia would pursue the war against England in Asia, and if possible, to enter into an offensive and defensive treaty. When the trumpet of National War had blown, all people openly declared that the Nana had completed a treaty with the Tsar of Russia and the Russian army was ready to fight against the Feringhis. If we bear this in mind, the above suspicion is strengthened. When Azimullah was in Russia, he had an interview with the well-known writer Russell, the military correspondent of the London *Times*. The poor man could not have even dreamt that, immediately after the Turko-Russian War, he would have to send from Hindusthan news of the wonderful activities of his guest. As soon as Azimullah heard the news of the defeat of the English, and that the Russians had beaten the attack of the united forces of the English and the French on the 18th of June, he obtained admittance into the English camp. His dress was Hindusthani and rich like that of a prince. As soon as Russell came out, Azimullah said to him,

'I want to see this famous city and those great Rustoms, the Russians, who have beaten the French and the English together.'[1] Undoubtedly, Azimullah was a past master in irony and satire. This curiosity on the part of Azimullah to see these brave Rustoms who defeated both the English and the French, Russell undertook to satisfy, by inviting him to his tent. On that day, till the shades of sunset closed round them completely, 'he was looking with marked interest at the fire of the Russian guns.' One cannon-ball of the Russian guns burst right at his feet, but he did not move. The gay Azimullah, before returning home in the evening, said to Russell, 'I have my serious doubts whether you could ever capture this 'Strong fortified position.' That night, Azim slept in Russell's tent, and he left next day, early in the morning. On the table was left this note:- ' Azimullah Khan presents his compliments to Russell, Esq., and begs to thank him most truly for his kind attentions.'

It is difficult to say where Azimullah went after leaving Russia. Yet, from the mention in the Proclamation of Cawnpore later on, it would appear as certain that he was trying to put through some diplomatic scheme in Egypt also.[2] So, Azimullah then 'completed his European tour and returned to Brahmavarta. As soon as Azim reached Brahamvarta,

---

1. The above account is published in Russell's *Diary*, a very well-known book. Russell was military correspondent of the London '*Times*' in the war of 1857. He was personally present in most of the affairs that he describes.

2. Lord Roberts has come across a genuine letter from Azimullah to the Sultan of Turkey about the oppression in Hindusthan. He says 'regarding this' There were numerous letters from his English fiancees .and two from a Frenchman. ..It seems probable that Les principales -*choses*' to which Lafont hopes to bring satisfactory answers were invitations to the disaffected and di.,loyal in Calcutta and, perhaps, the French settlers in Chandernagore to assist in the effort about to be made to throw off the British yoke. A portion of the correspondence was unopened and there were several

the whole political atmosphere of the palace was changed. *Jaripatka* which had waved triumphant and vitctorious all over India lay so long in dust in the palace; the glorious drum of the Peshwas at the beating of which thousands of Mahratta swords had advanced on the battlefields and performed such deeds of wondrous valour, that drum hitherto only sounded melancholy to the ear; and the royal signet of the Peshwas on the sealing of which had depended the fate of the Mogul Empire had so far been lying sealing its own widowhood in the palace. But now all these appeared to be thirlled with extraordinary life. The dust-soiled *Jaripatka* shone forth again; the old drums which had almost forgotten their martial music were practising again the forgotten military airs; and the regal seals seemed to be eager, extremely eager. The eyes of Shrimant Nana Sahib, 'excited like those of a tiger, brilliant and fierce,' since the arrival of Azimullah Khan, flashed more fierce from injured pride and shone more brilliant as he drank inspiration from the words of Shri Krishna, 'Therefore, get ready for battle.' Every corner of' Brahmavarta echoed with those eternal words, *Tasmat yuddhaya, yujyaswa*. For, in Swadesh, even in their own Hindusthan, the people have been reduced to be slaves and have foreign masters : the Swaraj is no more, they have lost their natural rights of liberty! All the attempts to win back the country and its independence by conciliation and by money, and by appeal, had: so far failed; hence, be ready for war. 'If you are killed, you will get to heaven; if you win, you will enjoy the earth; so, be, ready for war; you will not be committing any sin thereby' -it was such heavenly

letters in Azimullah's own handwriting. Two of these were to Omar Pasha of Constantinople and told of the Sepoy's discontent and the troubled state of India generally. '

—Forty Years in India p. 429.

inspiration that gave to Nana's eyes extraodinary brilliance![3] He studied the conditions of his country, saw the sufferings of his countrymen, noticed the destruction of his religion and, diagnosing all these chronic symptoms, he came to the conclusion that nothing but the sword could cure that terrible disease of slavery. Though it is not clear what was the ultimate ideal which he set before himself, still, it would appear that, in his opinion, the first thing to do was to drive the English out by unsheathing the sword and thus get independence; and then, to set up an Indian Government under the banner of the united authority of all the Indian princes. Before his eyes rose. clear the history of how Swadesh fell into slavery through the turmoil of internecine quarrels. Before him, on the one side was the portrait of Shivaji Maharaj, on the other of Baji Rao, his father. By seeing these two pictures side by side, he could well contrast the past glory and the present shame! And, hence, Nana's programme was first to fight a united fight, to make. India free and, by removing internecine warfare, to establish the rule of the United States of India which would, thus, take its rightful place in the council of the free nations of the earth.

He, also, felt that the meaning of 'Hindusthan' was thereafter the united nation of the adherents of Islam as well as. Hinduism. As long as the Mahomedans lived in India in the capacity of the alien rulers, so long, to be willing to live with them like brothers was to acknowledge national weakness. Hence, it was, up to then, necessary for the Hindus to consider the Mahomedans as foreigners. And moreover this rulers hip of the Mahomedans, Guru Govind in the Panjab, Rana Pratap' in Rajputana, Chhatrasal in Bundelkhand, and

---

3. ' Nana's object, then, was to lay the foundations of his future sovereignity at Cawnpore. The mighty power exercised by the Peshwas was to be restored; and to himself, the architect of his own fortunes, would belong the glory of replacing that vanished sceptre. There can be no doubt that some such thoughts influenced him'- Trevelyan : p. 133

the Mahrattas by even sitting upon the throne at Delhi, had destroyed; and after a struggle of centuries, Hindu sovereignty had defeated the rulership of the Mahomedans and had come to Its own all over India. It was no national shame to join hands with Mahomedans then, but it would, on the contrary, be an act of generosity. So, now, the antagionism between the Hindus and the Mahomedans might be consigned to the Past. Their present relation was one not of rulers and ruled, foreigner and native, but simply that of brothers. with the one difference between them of religion alone. For, they were both children of the soil of Hindusthan. Their names were different, but they were all children of the same Mother; India therefore being the common mother of these two, they were brothers by blood. Nana Sahib, Bahadur Shah of Delhi; Moulvi Ahmad Shah, Khan Bahadur Khan, and other leaders of 1857 felt this relationship to some extent and, so, gathered round the flag of Swadesh leaving aside their enmity, now so unreasonable and stupid. In short, the broad features of the policy of Nana Sahib and Azimullah were that the Hindus and the Mahomedans should unite and fight shoulder to shoulder for the independence of their country and that, when freedom was gained, the United States of India should be formed under the Indian rulers and princes.

How to achieve this ideal was the one all-absorbing thought of everyone in the palace of Brahmavarta. Two things were necessary for the success of this terrible war that was to be waged to win back freedom. The first thing was to create a passionate desire in Hindusthan for this ideal; the second was to make all the country rise simultaneously for the purpose of achieving it. To turn India's mind into the channels of freedom and to guide India's hand to strike for freedom, these two things it was necessary to accomplish; and this in such a manner that the Company's government should not suspect anything while the scheme was yet unripe. Not forgetting historical experience but guided by it, a secret organisation was resolved upon and, at once, started at Brahmavarta. To obtain all information about this secret society, either now or in the immediate future, is as difficult as it is to obtain the information about any other secret society. But upon the facts that occasionally come to light, one 'cannot but admire the skill of the organisers.[4]

A little before 1856, Nana began to send missionaries all over India to initiate people into this political ideal. In addition to sending missionaries to awaken the people, Nana also sent tried and able men to the different princes from Delhi to Mysore, to fill their minds with the glorious ideal of the United States of India and to induce them to join in the Revolution. These letters, which were sent into every Durbar secretly pointed out how the English were playing the game of reducing India to insignificance by annexing Swadeshi kingdoms under the pretext of 'no heir', how those states which were spared yet would soon be reduced to the same fate as the others and how, under the yoke of slavery, country and religion were both being trampled under foot; and they concluded by exhorting the princes to work for the Revolution which was to make them free. Direct evidence is available that messengers and letters from Nana were sent to the states of Kolhapur and Patwardhan, to the Kings in Oudh, the princes in Bundelkhand, and others. The English arrested one of such messengers at the Durbar of Mysore. The evidence given by this man is so important that we give it word for word below :— 'Two or three months before Oudh was annexed, Shrimant Nana Sahib had begun sending letters. First, no one would reply, for no one hoped for any success. After Oudh was annexed, however. Nana

4. Trevelyan says in reference to this: 'No society of rich and civilised Christians who ever undertook to preach the gospel of peace and goodwill can have employed a more perfect system of organisation than was adopted by these rascals whose mission it was to preach the gospel of sedition and slaughter.' -*Cawnpore*, p.39.

began a regular battery of letters, and then the opinions of Nana began to appeal to the Sirkars of Lucknow. Raja Man Singh, the leader of the Purbhayas, was also won over. Then the Sepoys began to organise amongst themselves and the Sirkars of Lucknow began to help them. No replies to letters were received till Oudh was annexed; but as soon as that was accomplished hundreds of people came forward boldly and replied confidentially to Nana. Next came the affair of the cartridges and. then, the disaffection was so great that letters were simply showered on, Nana.'[5] This very agent has given a long list of the letters sent by Nana to the various Durbars.

While agents of Nana were moving from one Durbar to another from Delhi to Mysore in order to draw them into the War of Independence, it was in the Dewan-i-Khas of Delhi. more than in any other Durbar, the seeds of Revolution began to take root. The English had not stopped at merely taking away the *Padshahi* of the *Padshah* of Delhi, but had recently decided even to take away the title of *Padshah* from the descendant of Babar. The Emperor, though reduced to such an extremity, and Zinat Mahal, the beloved, clever, and determined Begum of the Emperor, had already decided that this last opportunity of regaining the lost glory should not be allowed to go by, and, if dying was the only resource, then,

5. 'For months, for years indeed, they had been spreading the network of intrigues allover the country. From one native court to another, from one extremity to another of the great continent of India, the agents of Nana Sahib had passed with overtures and invitations discreetly, perhaps mysteriously worded to princes and chiefs of different races and religions, but most hopefully of all to the Mahrattas ...There is nothing in my mind more substantiated than the complicity of Nana Sahib in widespread intrigues before the outbreak of the Mutiny. The concurrent testimony of witnesses examined in parts of the country widely distinct from each other takes this story altogether out of the regions of the conjectural.' Kaye's *Indian Mutiny*, Vol. I, pp. 24-25.

they should die the death which would only befit an Emperor and an Empress. At this juncture, the English were engaged in a war with Persia. Seeing that a simultaneous rising in India would be a help, the Shah of Persia began to open diplomatic correspondence with the Emperor of Delhi. In the Declaration of the Emperor of Delhi, it had been made quite clear that a confidential agent had been sent to Persia from the Delhi Durbar. While this intrigue was going on at the Durbar of the Shah, right in the city of Delhi agitation was started to stir the public feeling to its very depths. For this work, even public Proclamations were sometimes posted up on the walls of the town. In the beginning of 1857, a Proclamation couched in the following terms appeared boldly: 'The army of Persia is going to free India from the hands of the Feringhis. So, Young and old, big and small, literate and illiterate, civil and military, all Hindusthanee brothers should leap forth into the field to free themselves from the Kaffirs.'[6] Though these Proclamations were ever and anon posted in public places, still the English could hardly trace the persons who posted these Proclamations; and Indian newspapers used to publish these Proclamations and to criticise them in mysterious language. The various *Shahzadas* and their retainers in the palaces of Delhi openly and secretly spread disaffection, and were engaged in weaving a network of conspiracies. In the grounds of Prince Nawab Bakht, for six years, Sergent Fleming's son had been practising riding. But when, in the beginning or April 1857, this English youth went to the residence of Vizier Mahbub Ali, the prince, excited beyond measure, said, 'Away, get away, get away from here. I boil with rage when I see the face of any Feringhi !' So saying, the Prince spat on him![7] Other people were working more secretly and quite differently from the

6. Kaye's *Indian Mutiny*, Vol. II, p. 30
7. *Military Narrative* (p. 374) : 'Jawan Bakht commenced abusing, declaring that the sight of the Kaffir Feringhi disturbed his serenity, spat in his face, and desired him to leave.'

manner of this abusive prince. Mrs. Aldwell says in her evidence, that she had personally heard Mahomedan mothers asking their children to pray that the English should be destroyed root and branch.[8] Mukund Lal, Private Secretary of the Emperor of Delhi, says: 'Sitting at the doors of the royal palace, Moguls and others within the palace used to discuss the Revolution openly. The Sepoys would rebel soon; the army of Delhi would rise against the English; and then, all people, along with the army, would throw off the Feringhi yoke and enjoy Swaraj — such definite opinions were current. All people were inspired with the hope that, when once the *Raj* was won, all power and all authority would remain in their own hands.' Thus, in every cellar, in every house in Delhi, thc disaffection only awaited for a spark which should explode everything up.

Like the capital cities of Delhi and Brahmavarta, Lucknow also, the capital of Oudh, the last victim that had fallen a prey to the greed of Dalhousie, began to catch fire from the flames of the War of the Revolution. The Nabob of Lucknow and his Vizier were now residing near Calcutta. To all appearances, thc Vizier of Lucknow looked as if he was wasting his time in luxury; as a matter of fact, however, Vizier Ali Nakkhi Khan was as much absorbed in his dangerous conspiracy near Calcutta as Nana Sahib himself was. One cannot help feeling wonder struck at the schemes—secret, extensive, and daring—which Al Nakkhi Khan was weaving to seduce the Sepoys in Bengal and to prepare them to join him at the right moment already fixed upon. Confidential agents were sent by him, in the garb of Fakir or Sanyasis, to preach 'sedition' to the Sepoys. He opened correspondence with the Indian officers in the army to make them understand fully what immense advantages Swaraj could confer as compared with the service of the Company. How the English had committed an unpardonable

8. Trial of the King of Delhi

crime in annexing Oudh, how the royal family of the Nabob had been treated with insult, and how the very Queen and Begums were expelled with violence from the palace—pictures of such heart-rending tyranny were drawn with such pathos that the brave Sepoys began to weep profusely. And then and there, Sepoys would take the water of the Ganges in their hands, or would swear by the Koran, that they would live only to achieve the destruction of the English rule. When *Subahdar* Majors, *Subahdars*, and *Jamadars* and the bigger officers were all sworn in, the whole regiment was naturally bound over. The Vizier of Oudh, by the use of such tactics, won over the- whole army in Bengal.[9] In Fort William itself, in Calcutta, the Revolutionary agents of Ali Nakkhi Khan moved silently.

After sending letters to the various Durbars from Brahmavarta, Nana exerted himself thoroughly to awaken all the latent power of the people. When Brahmavarta, Delhi, Lucknow, Satara, and such other big and prominent princes figured conspicuously in the Revolutionary Organisaton, how could this organisation suffer for want of money? To preach to all those who were a power among the people, thousands of Fakirs, Pundits, and Sanyasis were sent out in an incredibly short time. It is not true to say that all these Fakirs were true Fakirs; for, some of the Fakirs and Sadhus lived with the grandeur of Amirs. Elephants were given them for

9. Some of the letters of the Sepoys of Barrackpore fell into the hands of the English. Kaye adduces the following letters as evidence for the above. 'The second grenadier said that the whole regiment is ready to join the Nabob of Oudh.' 'Subahdars said that they would join the Nabob of Oudh.' Subahoar Madarkhan, Sirdar Khan, and Ram Shahi Lal said, 'That in treachery no one could come up to the level of the 'Beti-choot' Feringhis. Though the Nabob of Oudh gave up his kingdom, he could not even get a pension.' Many other letters, like this, the English came across afterwards.—Kaye's *Indian Mutiny*, Vol. I. p. 429. (These regiments consisted of the sepoys from Oudh, Agra, and were only stationed in Bengal.—Author's note).

travelling, Guards armed to the teeth travelled with them and every stage on their way was a regular camp. Provided with such paraphernalia, they could influence and impress the people better, and the Sirkar also had fewer reasons to suspect them. Influential and noble Moulvies were appointed to preach the political *Jehad*, and they were rewarded with thousands of Rupees. Through towns and villages, these Moulvies and pundits. these Fakirs and these Sanyasis began to travel, from one end of the country to the other, preaching secretly the war for political independence. Just this start was wanted, for this same trick was begun independently by other groups of the Revolutionary Organisation. After these paid missionaries came volunteers. Begging from door to door, they began to sow, in all direction, the principles of independence, patriotism, and love of Dharma—for the awakening of strength among the people. This work of preparing for revolutionary rising was done so cautiously and secretly that not much inkling of what was going on could reach even such cunning people as the English, until the explosion actually took place. When such a Fakir or a Sanyasi went to a village, a strange agitation and an unrest began in that village, and of this the English were sometimes cognisant. Whisperings went on in bazaars; 'sahibs' were refused water by the *Bhishtis*, *Ayahs* left English homes without permission; Baberchis purposely stood before the *Mem-Sahibs* half-dressed; and Indian messenger boys walked insolently and slovenly before their 'masters', when sent out.[10] These Fakirs and Pundits used to walk round and about the military cantonments more particularly. From Barrackpore to Meerut, Umballa and Peshawar, they started secret societies and, more than that, practically surrounded every military cantonment. The Hindu and Moslem Sepoys in the army being very devoted to their religious teachers, the Sirkar, though they might suspect them, could hardly proceed against them. For, they feared that the Sepoys would

10. Trevelyan's *Cawnpore*.

find in it another grievance against the Government. And, if the Sirkar did, by any chance, suspect them, these political Sanyasis sowed the seeds of the Revolutionary War in the very houses of the Sepoys in the neighbouring village. The authorities at Meerut were at last compelled to ask a Fakir, who was lodging near the Meerut military cantonment, to move away. As soon as this order came, like a simple, innocent man, this grand person left the camp on his elephant, only to go to a neighbouring village and establish himself securely in the houses of the Sepoys![11] That patriot Moulvie Ahmad Shah, whose sacred name has cast a halo round Hindusthan, whose glorious achievements we shall have to describe very soon, began similarly to tour through the country preaching the Revolutionary War. At last, when he began to preach in Lucknow itself, to thousands and tens of thousands in open meetings, that there was no other way of saving the country and the religion than by killing the English, he was arrested for sedition and sentenced to be hanged!

It was the custom to have a Mullah and a Pundit in every regiment for religious purposes. Taking advantage of this, the Revolutionaries entered the service as regimental Mullas and Pundits. At the falling of the night, they used to preach Revolution to the Sepoys secretly. Thus, these political Sanyasis toured from village to village for two years preaching Revolution, and at last succeeded in sowing the seeds of the terrible war to come.

While itinerant Sanyasis and itinerant preachers preached in the villages and the country, local preachers were being sent to the bigger towns. In all the important places of pilgrimage where thousands of people congregated, the ever-existing dumb dislike of the usurping Feringhi rule was intensified into active hatred by the Revolutionary preachers. The stir that was created at all the holy places on the banks

11. *The Meerut Narrative.*

of the Ganges, how the *Sankalpa* (resolution) of Revolutionary War was made along with the usual *Sankalpa* for the bath—these and other facts will soon be narrated in the history of the rising of those places. The hatred of the Feringhis in those *Kshetras* (holy places) was so strong, that open prayers were started by the priests in the temples of Benares, on behalf of their own rulers belonging to their own religion.[12]

In order to make clear to the common people, in simple and clear language, how Swadharma and Swatantrya — Religion and Independence-were being insulted, the all-comprehensive programme of the Revolutionary party had not left out of their consideration any of the festivals or the *Tamashas* in which people took interest and congregated in large numbers. The dolls in the doll-theatres began now to speak a strange language and to dance a dangerous dance; at police stations, under the shades of trees in *Dharmasalas*, and at public squares, *Powadas* and *Lawanis* (ballads and epic lays) were sung with the gusto of a new mysterious interpretation. The fame goes and there is a strong conviction everywhere that the song of Allah-Udal, one of the most popular songs in Northern India, does at once rouse in the hearers the martial craving for war. This heroic martial song, sung with spirit by minstrels, would cause the arms of the hearers tingle and itch for battle, and their blood would begin to boil on listening to the exploits of their ancestors; then, the subject would suddenly be changed and before their eyes would be forced the image of their present helplessness. And the hearers would be roused to rise against the Feringhi and act in the present the heroism they admired in the past. Itinerant groups of *Tamashgars*, so innocent in themselves that the Government was not even cognisant of their existence, were used for the Revolutionary War by these consummate Revolutionists. Starting from Calcutta, they

12. *Red Pamphlet.*

went on to the Panjab and, in the nights, exhibited their peculiarly dangerous *Tamasha* to their fellow countrymen.[13]

These *Tamashgars* could not preach Revolution to the women, and so it would appear that the leaders of the Revolution sent out quack doctors and their wives-female gipsies-amongst the people, to move them with a new life and revolutionary discontent. The trick of using gipsies for this purpose was excellent. These gipsies used to foretell the destruction of English, depict the evil machinations of the alien rule and prescribe revolution as the only remedy and spell that could and would get rid of this evil which had possessed their Motherland! The coming narrative will show what a terrible hatred of the English had grown amongst the women and how anxious they were to destroy this rule. Thus, the war was preached in temples and *Tirthas*, in *Kshetras, jatras*, and in festival, on the road and in the house, amongst the Sepoys and the citizens, in *Natakas* and in *Tamashas*, to men as well as to women.

Everywhere was this hatred of slavery and the desire for Swaraj manifested. 'My religion is dying, my country is dying: my people have been reduced to a condition worse than that of dogs! '—such were the fears that moved every heart; and an unconquerable desire arose in every heart, from prince to pauper to make that country live and that people rise to the height or men. And the passionate conviction went forth that streams of of blood were but a small price to achieve that independence; and that, therefore, 'Din! Din!' and 'Har! Har! Mahadev!' — the war cries of the Indians — must rend the air.

To instil into every heart the one great desire for independence, and rouse it to action, there could be no more effective weapon than poetry. When the mass of the people are possessed by an idea which struggles for adequate

---

13. Trevelyan's *Cawnpore, Short Narratives.*

expression, the poet, who realises the idea more intensely than the rest, gives it a beautiful expression, which at once touches their hearts and makes them love the idea still more. Hence the great part that national songs play in all revolutions. The national songs are an expression of the national soul under the sway of a strong ideal. They unite the hearts of the people with ease. When the soul of the land of Bharata was swayed by an intense passion for liberty, for the protection of Swadharma and the attainment of Swarajya, strange indeed would it have been if the heart of the nation did not burst into song. The principal court bard of the Emperor of Delhi had himself composed a national song which was to be sung by every throat in Hindusthan, and the Emperor of Delhi, in person, had ordered that this should be sung on all occasions of public ceremony. It described the heroic deeds of the past and painted a pathetic picture of the present fallen state. In that national song was echoed the cry of the nation that those persons, whose heads had been crowned but yesterday with imperially aggressive independence, should be reduced to the condition of slaves to-day, that their religion which yesterday was the state religion should to day be unprotected, and that heads crowned recently with glory should, alas, be trampled to-day under the foot of the foreigner.[14]

While the national song was educating people about their past glory and their present fall, a prophecy, that emblazoned the star of future hope and encouraged all, was heard, in the land. Prophecies are the leaps of the mind into the future. As soon as the heart of India began to long for Swaraj, the

---

14. A mandate had, of late, gone forth from the palace of Delhi enjoining the Mahomedans, at all their solemn gatherings, to recite a song of lamentation indited by the regal musician himself which described in touching strains the humiliation of their race and the degradation of their ancient faith, once triumphant from the northern snows to the southern straits but now trodden under the foot of the infidel and the alien. — Trevelyan's *Cawnpore*.

prophecies too began to point to Swaraj. From the northern snows to the extreme south, young and old circulated the prophecy that, thousands of year ago, a holy, ancient sage had foretold that the Feringhi *Raj* would end exactly a hundred years from the date of its creation! Indian newspapers gave wide publicity to this prophecy and interpreted it to mean that the Company's *Raj* would fall to pieces on the 23rd of June, 1857. This one prophecy led to the performance of such wonders in Hindusthan that it may safely be asserted that, but for this prophecy, several portions of this history would have to be written in a different way altogether. The year 1857 was the centenary of the battle of Plassey and the Company's rule would end in that year—this idea created a strange hope and an extraordinary inspiration which moved every part of Hindusthan since the beginning of 1857. After a considerable heated discussion between various English historians as to who foretold this, it has at last been decided beyond doubt that it was the stratagem of the Hindus, since it was according to their almanacs that the 100th year of Plassey fell in the year 1857. By this national prophecy, the impression of which is indelibly indited on some of the most important pages of this history, an extraordinary wave of agitation came over the hearts of the young and old, and everyone began to be ready to turn the prophecy into an actual fact.

The secret organisation of the revolution, which was first started in Brahmavarta, was now growing at a tremendous rate.[15] By this time, nuclei had been established in various places in Northern India and regular communication had been established between them. Rango Bapuji was trying hard to

15. Malleson says at the end of his voluminous history: ' Of this conspiracy, the Moulvi was undoubtedly a leader. It had its ramifications all over India--certainly at Agra where the Moulvie stayed sometime—and almost certainly at Delhi, at Meerut, at Patna, and at Calcutta where the ex-King of Oudh and a large following were residing. '-Vol. V .p. 292.

create nuclei of this organisation in the Deccan. The palace at Brahmavarta was the focus of the activities at Cawnpore; the same function was performed for Delhi by the Dewan-i-Khas of that premier city. The great and saintly Ahmad Shah had woven fine and cleverly the webs of *Jehad*—the War of Independence—through every corner of Lucknow and Agra. Kumar Singh, the hero of Jagdishpur had taken the leadership of his province and, in consultation with Nana, had been busy gathering materials for war. The seeds of the *Jehad* had taken such root in Patna that the whole city was a regular haunt of the Revolutionary party. Moulvies, Pundits, Zemindars, farmers, merchants, vakils, student, of all castes and creeds, were ready to give up their lives for the sake of Swadesh and Swadharma. A very prominent leader of this secret organisation was a book-seller! Near Calcutta, the Nabob of Oudh and his Vizier, Ali Nakkhi Khan, had seduced all the Sepoys and were ready for the occasion. The Mahomedan population of Hyderabad began to call secret meetings. The coils of the Revolution began to wind themselves. round the Durbar of Kolhapur. The states of Patwardhan, and the father-in-law of Nana, at Sangli, were ready to fight—with, their followers—under the banner of the united nation, in the coming war. Why, right in Madras, in the beginning of the year 1857 the following proclamation began to appear from the walls of the city: "Countrymen and faithful adherents of your religion, rise, rise ye, one and all, to drive out the Feringhi Kaffirs! They have trampled under foot the very elements of justice, they have robbed us of Swaraj; determined are they to reduce to dust our conntry. There is only one remedy, now, to free India from the insufferable tyranny of the Kaffir Feringhis. and that remedy is to wage a bloody war. This is a *Jehad* for Independence! This is a religious war for justice! Those who fall in such battles will be their country's *Shahids*. Opened wide are the doors of Heaven for the *Shahids*. But Hell is burning fierce to engulf those wretches, those cowardly traitors, who turn away from this national duty! Countrymen, of these, which would ye have? Choose now, even now!"

To link together the innumerable groups of various provinces which were working separately, men were employed to travel about secretly and letters were rarely used. If letters were used at all, they were written in a mysterious language, any mention of names being avoided. But when, after some time, the English persisted in opening any and every letter that appeared suspicious to them, the leaders, in order that their schemes should not come out and not even a trace should be known to others, began to carry on their correspondence in a kind of cipher; a sort of code was formed composed of dots and numbers, and this was used by them on all occasions![16]

While everywhere activity of this kind was going on, the blunder as to the cartridges, born of the criminal desire to spite the religious feelings of the Sepoys, was committed by the English. This filled the cup of their iniquity! Every soldier vied with every other to fire the first shot, at the proper time, in the war to be waged for the object that was foremost in the minds of all their fellow-countrymen. We have already described how Nana and Ali Nakkhi Khan had acquired perfect control over the Sepoys of every regiment, and how thousands of Fakirs were sent into the regiments to seduce the Sepoys to patriotism. But after the mean and cunning trick was played by the English in respect of the cartridges, every Sepoy began, on his own account, to urge every other Sepoy to take the oath of fighting for their common country. In these two months, thousands of letters were sent from Barrackpore, in the name of the Nabob of Oudh, to the regiments stationed in the Panjab, in Maharashtra, and at Meerut, Umballa and other places. When immense bags full of letters were carried in the post, the English had their suspicions roused, and they—especially Sir John

16. Inne's *Sepoy Revolt*. p. 55

Lawrence—began to open these letters. All this time an extraordinary self-confidence had bean created in the Sepoys. The English asked the Sepoys wounded in the battle of Kali Nadi and ordered to be blown from cannon mouths how they dared to rise against them; and the Sepoys replied, 'If Sepoys are united, the whites would be like a drop in the ocean.' A letter of one of these opened by the English says, 'Brothers, we ourselves are thrusting the foreigners' sword into our body. If we rise, success is assured. From Calcutta to Peshawar, there will be an uncontested maidan.' The Sepoys used to call together meetings secretly in the night. All resolutions were passed in the general meetings, and all decisions passed in the inner circles were obeyed strictly and by all. When they used to come to the secret societies, they used to conceal their identity by covering their faces completely, leaving only their eyes uncovered, and then speak about the thousand and one oppressions commited in the country by the English.[17] If anyone of the members was suspected of telling the name of the conspirators to the enemy, he was immediately put to death. In order that common deliberation should take place between the various regiments, it was arranged that on festive occasions one regiment should invite another to a feast and, on this pretext, united gatherings were carried on successfully. Meetings of selected Sepoys were held in the houses of the *Subahdars*. Though all political and religious wrongs were -explained and commented on to the lowest Sepoy in the army, though every Sepoy knew about, and was anxious for a fight with

---

17. 'These incendiary fires were soon followed by nocturnal meetings. Men met each other with muffled faces and discussed in excited language the intolerable outrages the British Government had committed upon them.' Kaye's *Indian Mutiny*, Vol. I, p. 365. 'On the parade ground, about 1300 men were assembled. They had their heads covered so that only small part of the face was exposed. They said they were determined to die for their religion.'—*Narrative of the Indian Mutiny*, p. 5.

the English, still the knowledge of how to rise, when to rise, and who were the leaders of the various groups was not imparted to all. The work of deciding all these things was left to the officers, and everyone was made to swear either by the water of the Ganges, or by the leaf of Tulsi, or by the Koran, that each one would do what the regiment should undertake to do. When one regiment was thus bound together, the chief committee of that regiment began negotiations with the chief committee of another regiment; each swore faithfulness to the other and they worked together. The mutual oath of the regiments, like the mutual oaths of the Sepoys were determined and decisive. Every regiment was a unit in the higher organisation. The English afterwards gathered a good deal of material to determine what this organisation was, and Mr. Wilson gives the following information about the society, in the Government report: 'From the available evidence I am quite convinced that the 31st of May, 1857, had been decided on as the date for simultaneous rising. Every regiment had a committee of three members; and this committee used to do everything connected with the Mutiny. The Sepoys had no idea what decisions were arrived at. The Mutual agreements between the various regiments simply amounted to agreeing to do what the other regiments would do. The committee had to decide on all important schemes, to do all the correspondence, and several other things. All came to the one important decision that the Sepoys should rise on the 31st. As it was a Sunday, they would be able to find a large number of European officers in church. All European officers, along with these, were to be murdered. Then all the treasuries, that would be full with the proceeds of the Rabbi crops, were to be looted. Jails were to be broken open and prisoners released. For in the North-Western provinces, from the prisoners alone an army of nearly 25,000 people could be formed.' As soon as the rising took place, the powder-magazines and armouries were to be taken possession of. All forts and strategic positions were to be taken, wherever possible. Such was the secret structure of the Revolutionary Organisation, and it had bound together the whole army.

To supply the sinews of war to the secret organisation, the *Sahukars* of Lucknow, the palaces of Nana and Vizir Ali Nakkhi Khan, the Mahal of Delhi, and other heads of the Revolutionary party were sufficient. While the Sepoys were concerting their secret schemes, some secrets, now by a trifling mistake, now through a traitor, leaked out. Then, the English Government issued orders that the whole regiment about which the suspicion of disaffection arose should be at once dismissed. That was most excellent. Why? The Government thus actually gave to the country so many volunteer Sanyasis to spread the fire of Revolution all round. The various Durbars of Hindusthan, the ordinary people, and the military—these three divisions of the people were linked together by the indefatigable efforts of the able Revolutionary leaders. There still remains the class of civil officers. An outline of the particular part which this class played in the structure of the Revolution must be given. The coming pages will clearly show that most of the more prominent Indian civilians in Northern India had taken a leading part in the 'mutiny'. From the *Patel* and *Kulkarni* of the village to the native judge of the high cort, Hindu and Mussalman officers of all ranks, pleaders and clerks, had joined the Revolutionary Organisation secretly. The fact that the Government had not the least idea of the extensive organisation is easily explained; for these native officers alone are the eyes with which the Government was to see anything. But, on the other hand, it had been decided that, until the critical moment, these Government officers should not show even the least opposion to the Sirkar. Not only that, but very often it happened that, when it was necessary to arrest a Revolutionary leader, these Indian officers, who were the accomplices of this man, used to treat him as cruelly as an English officer would do, and used to sentence him to heavy punishment. When the Meerut

Sepoys were tried, it was the native judges that passed heavy sentences on them; but it came to light that these very judges were scheming for a Revolution. Anonymous proclamations were posted at every square of the city of Lucknow, written in very strong language, to agitate the masses. These proclamations were couched in fiery and violent language. We give the following as the specimen. 'Hindus and Mahomedans, rise unitedly and decide, once for all, the fate of the country; for, if this opportunity is allowed to slip by, not a single way will be left open to the people even to preserve their lives. This is the last chance. Now or never!' Tbough the, English authorities knew well that proclamations were issued every day, they could do no more than tear them of; and still, every time they were destroyed, new ones were put up. The police used to declare that it was impossible for them to find out as to who put up these posters and when they were put up. The English came to know the reason soon after. The police themselves were the prominent members of the Revolutionary party.[18]

Not alone in the revolutions of Russia, but in the Revolution in India, too, the police were found to be in sympathy with the people. The programme, then, of the civil officers was to join secretly in the Revolutionary organisation of their countrymen without giving up Government service and, when the right time came, to work on under Swarajya, performing those very functions which they were all doing under the English Government.

Now that the wheels of the secret machinary of the Revolution were set in motion, it was necessary to arrange that all the various motions should be synchronised. With this purpose, in Bengal, a messenger of the Revolutionaries went to the cantonments, taking a red lotus in his hand. He would give the red lotus into the hands of the chief Indian officer in the first regiment. The chief would pass it on to

18. *Red Pamphlet*: Part II.

the nearest Sepoy. The Sepoy would pass it to the one next to him, and so the red lotus would pass from Sepoy to Sepoy through the hand of all the thousand Sepoys, and then the last Sepoy would return it back to the Revolutionary messenger. That was enough! Without a whisper or a word, the messenger would pass on like an arrow, and as soon as the next regiment was in sight, he would give, the red lotus in the hands of its chief officer. In this way, the organisation, so full of poetry, became impressed with one opinion, with revolution, with blood. The red lotus was the final seal of the organisation. What a tumult of thoughts must be raging in the mind of every Sepoy when he touched the red flower! That courage which it would have been impossible for the eloquence of orators to inspire was imparted in those warlike fellows by the dump lotus flower and by the mute eloquence of its red, red colour![19]

A lotus flower! The symbol, the poet-appointed symbol, of purity, victory, light! And its colour red, vivid red! The very touch of the lotus flower makes every heart bloom. When the Sepoys, hundreds upon hundreds, were passing on rapidly from hand to hand this lotus flower, the eloquence of it must have been full of wild suggestions and wilder aspirations. "The red lotus, really made all the people one; for, in Bengal, both the Sepoys' and agriculturists were found giving expression to this one sentiment, 'All is going to be red!', with a movement of the eyes which betrayed an extraordinary, mysterious pregnancy of meaning".[20] 'All will

19. 'A man appeared with a lotus flower and handed it to the chief of the regiment. He handed it on to another—every man took it and passed it on and, when it came to the last, he suddenly disappeared to the next station. There was not, it appears, a detachment, not a station in Bengal, through which the lotus flower was not circulated. The circulation of this simple symbol of conspiracy was just after the annexation of Oudh'.—*Narrative of the Mutiny*: p. 4 (The book also gives the picture of the flower).
20. Trevelyan's *Cawnpore*

be red'—with what?

This red lotus and this suggestive sentiment had made all 'one-voiced' as far as individuals were concerned. But, it was also necessary to make all the principal nuclei one-voiced through mutual visits. So Nana came out from the palace of Brahmavarta to link together into one chain the various links—the nuclei of the organisation. With him started his brother, Bala Sahib, and his amiable and witty councillor, Azimullah. And why did they start? 'For a pilgrimage!' Indeed! A Brahmin and a Moslem are starting together, arm in arm, to visit the holy, religious, places,—an event without a precedent!

This was in the March of 1857. Most essential was it now, indeed, to visit at least once the places of pilgrimage and the first that they visited was Delhi. Only the Dewan-i-Khas or, perhaps, the atmosphere of Delhi could speak about the accents with which the consultations were carried on! At this very time, a judge of Agra, one Mr. Morel, came to see Nana. The latter gave him such a hearty welcome that he did not have the least suspicion about the different kind of welcome which Nana was busy preparing for the English and which he was going to offer within a month or two. After supervising all arrangements at Delhi, Nana went to Umballa. On the 18th of April, he reached Lucknow, the important centre among the various nuclei. On that very day the people of Lucknow had followed the *buggy* of Sir Henry Lawrence, Chief Commissioner Sahib, and pelted him with a shower of mud .and stones. And now Shrimant Nana had come there! This infused the whole city of Lucknow with an almost uncontrollable joy and excitement. Nana started in a huge procession through the chief streets of Lucknow, and a strong confidence was instilled in the Revolutionary party on seeing their would-be commander. Nana voluntarily went to Sir Henry Lawrence and told him that he had come to see Lucknow out of simple curiosity. Sir Henry issued orders to all the officers to show due respect to Nana. Poor Sir Lawrence! He did not know what this simple curiosity meant. After visiting Lucknow, Nana went to Kalpi. The diplomacy of Nana was actively going on, this time with Kumar Singh of Jagdishpur who was in intimate correspondence with him about this time.[21]

Thus, after personally visiting the leaders of the principal nuclei at Delhi, Umballa, Lucknow, Kalpi etc., and drawing up a clear programme and a definitely outlined map of the future campaign. Nana returned to Brahmavarta about the end of April. [22]

While, by visiting the principal leaders, Shrimant Nana was touring to determine the date and bring about the necessary unity of purpose, strange bands of secret messengers of Revolution were going about at express speed throughout the length and breadth of India, to prepare the people for the great day. These messengers were not a new thing at all. Whenever the work of Revolution was started, these agents-*Chapatees*-have as a rule done the work of carrying the errand far and wide in the land. For in the Mutiny of Vellore, too, *Chapatees* were used to perform the same function. These angels with unseen wings were flying through every secret corner of the country, setting the mind

21. *Red Pamphlet.*

22. Nana must have gone during this tour to many other cities, but, as English historians have not expressly mentioned them, they cannot be given. The following quotation is rather important: 'After-wards, the worthy couple (Nana and Azim), on the pretence of a pilgrimage to the hills, visited the military stations all along the main trunk road and went so far as Umballa. It has been suggested that their object in going to Simla was to temper with the Gurkha regiments, stationed on the hills. But finding, on their arrival at Umballa a portion of the regiment were in cantonments. they were unable to effect their purpose with these men and desisted from their proposed journey, on the plea of the cold weather.'-Russell's *Diary*.

of the whole country on fire by the very vagueness of the message. Whence they came and whither they went no one could say. To those alone who were expecting them these straflge symbols carried the exact message and spoke with limited significance; as for those whom they took unawares, illimitable was the conversation that they carried on ! Some silly Government officers tried to get hold of these *Chapatees*, cut them to small crumbs, powdered them, and powdered once more, and tried if they could give some message; but, like witches the *Chapatees* had no tongue when they were asked to speak. The *Chapatees* spoke only to those it meant to speak to. It was made from wheat or millet flour. Nothing was written on it; yet it inspired the men who knew it with a strange Revolutionary energy at its very touch. The *Chowkidar* of every village had it. He ate a bit of it first himself and gave the rest, as *Prasad*, to those who asked. The same number of *Chapatees* were made afresh and sent to the inhabitants of the neighbouring vIllages. The *Chowkidar* of the latter place would send it to yet another village and, so, this fiery red cross of India travelled from village to village, kindling with flames every village it touched. Speed on, Angel of Revolution, speed on! Go thou forth to preach the Gospel to all the dear children of India, that the country is ready for a holy war, to make everyone of them free, Dash on, Messenger, to all the ten directions, not stopping even at midnight, piercing the air with the age-inspiring cry, 'The Mother goes forth to the war! March on ! March on !! Save her!!!' The gates of the cities are closed; still wait not thou till they open—but fly over through the air. The mountain defiles are deep; broken are the steep ascents; the rivers are wide, the forests are dangerous; still dread thou not, but speed like an arrow with this terrible national message. On thy speed depends the life or the death of the Desh and the Dharma. Hence cover as many miles as thou possibly canst and race with the wind! When the enemies destroy one shape of thee, go thou miraculous Angel, assuming hundreds of forms at this critical period of our national existence! In every shape and form of thy speed create for thyself a thousand tongues. Invite all-wife and husband, mother and child, sister and brother—to come with their relatives to accomplish the predestined task! Invite the spears of the Mahrattas, the swords of the Rajputs, the *Kirpan* of the Sikhs, the Crescent of the Islamites—invite one and all to make the ceremony a success. Call the Goddesses of War at Cawnpore! Call the Goddess of the forts in Jhansi! Call the Goddesses of Jagdishpur. To bless the work of national Revolution, bring with thee all thy relations, drums and trumpets, flags and banners, clarionets and war-songs, thunderings and war-cries. The martial spirit of the nation is awaiting the signal. Tell them all, The auspicious hour is soon to strike; so, be ready!'

Ready! Friends, be ready! And, O unfortunate Tyranny sleeping unconsciously and proud on the green, green hills, be thou ready too! The world might believe that a hill appearing green from a distance is really green. Nor does it fully know yet what a mistake it is to trample under foot the crown of such a hill. Trample, aye, trample! Now shines forth the year 1857, and in a moment it will be clear that the description of Kalidas applies literally to India. 'In those whose wealth is their penance and patience, forget not there is a concealed fire, which, if it bursts forth, can consume the whole world!' O world! Our India has certainly patience as its prominent feature; but do not, on that account, take undue advantage of it for within her heart, whose treasure is all-forbearing calmness, resides concealed the terrible fire of vengeance too. Hast thou ever beheld the third eye of Shankar? That is calmness itself while it is closed; but from it can issue the flames which can reduce the whole universe to ashes! Hast thou ever beheld a volcano! Apparently it is clothed with soft green vegetation; but let it once open its jaws, and then all sides will begin to pour forth boiling lava. Like unto that this living volcano of Hindusthan, fierce as the third eye of Shankar, has begun to boil. Terrible streams of lava in its interior are bubbling up tumultuously. Dangerous mixtures of explosive chemicals are being formed, and the spark of the love of liberty has fallen on it. Let Tyranny take heed when it is not yet too late! Neglet it in the least, and a thunderous explosion would teach insolent Tyranny what a volcanic vengeance really means!

END OF PART I

PART II

The Eruption

CHAPTER I

Shahid Mangal Pandey

OF all the surprising incidents connected with the Revolution of 1857, the most striking was the secrecy with which the vast movement was organised. The clever English administrators had so little information about the source of the movement. Even after the tremendous revolutionary upheaval all over Hindusthan, that, even a year after open mutiny had broken out, most or them still persisted innocently in the belief that it was due to the greased cartridges! The English historians are now beginning to understand that the cartridges were only an incident and they themselves now admit that it was the holy passion of love of their country and religion that inspired the heroes of the war of 1857.[1]

---

1. Malleson says: ' In this lesser sense, then, and in this only, did the cartridges produce the mutiny. They were instruments used by the conspirators, and those conspirators were successful in their use of the instruments only because, in the manner I have endeavoured to point out, the mind of the Sepoys and of certain sections of the population. had been prepared to believe every act testifying bad faith on the part of their foreign masters,'

Medley says: 'But, in fact, the greased cartridges was merely the match that exploded the mine which had, owing to a variety of causes, been for a long time preparing.'

' Mr. Disraeli dismissed the greasing of the cartridges with the: remark that nobody believed that to have been the real cause of the out-break.'—Charles Ball's *Indian Mutiny*, Vol. I. page 629.

One author goes further and says: That the fear about the cartridges was mere pretext with many is shown beyond all question. They have not hesitated to use freely when fighting against us, the cartridges which, they declared, would, if used, have destroyed their caste.'

We cannot sufficiently admire the skill of the leaders like Nana Sahib, Moulvie Ahmad Shah, and Vizir Ali Nakkhi Khan, who perfected that organisation with such secrecy under the very nose of the English officials in Hindusthan. It is difficult to find a parallel to the capacity for secret organisation displayed by these men, who successfully taught the necessity of mutual help and united action to the Hindus and Mahomedans, and infused the revolutionary spirit among all classes of the people-sepoys, police, zemindars, civil officials, peasants, merchants and bankers; and who harmonised all these conflicting elements into an army fired with the sacred purpose of freeing the motherland; and all this, without letting the English have any adequate suspicion of this vast upheaval. Just as this secret organisation was becoming ripe, the Government began to force the greased cartridges on the soldiers in Bengal. It appeared probable that the first experiment would be made on the 19th regiment. It was the month of February. Of all the regiments stationed in Bengal, the 34th was most anxious to start the Revolution. This regiment being stationed at Barrackpore, Vizir Ali Nakkhi Khan who stayed near Calcutta had bound the whole regiment by oaths in favour of the Revolution. Some companies of this regiment had been sent to the men of the 19th, and these had brought over the whole of that regiment to the national cause. The English had no notion of this and decided to force the cartridges first on the 19th regiment as an experiment. But the regiment openly refused to accept them and made plain their determination even to draw their swords, if necessary. Seeing this, the English, in pursuance of their policy, began to put down the 'natives'. But the English officers soon saw that they were not the 'natives' of past days. The clashing of swords soon convinced them of that. But they had quietly to pocket this insult, because, in the whole province, they had no white troops with which to overawe the Sepoys. To remove this difficulty, an English regiment was ordered from Burma to Calcutta in the beginning of March. The order went forth that the 19th regiment was to be disarmed and disbanded. It was decided to execute this order at Barrackpore!

But the Barrackpore regiment was not going to see quietly the spectacle of its countrymen being dishonoured. The sword of Mangal Panday positively refused to rest in its scabbard. The 34th regiment wanted to leave the Company's service quite as much as the 19th. Hence all patriots thought it was best that the Company itself disbanded the 19th. The wiser leaders counselled patience for one month until all were consulted. And letters had already been sent from Barrackpore to various regiments to fix the signal day. But Mangal Pandey's sword would not wait!

Mangal Pandey was a Brahmin by birth. He took up the duties of a Kshatriya and was a valiant young soldier. Into the heart of this young and brilliant Brahmin who loved his religion more than his life, and who was pure in his private life and undaunted in battle, the idea of the freedom of his country had entered and electrified his blood. How could his sword be patient? The swords of martyrs never are. The crown of martyrdom shines only on the head of those, who, regardless of success or failure, bathe their cherished ideals with their hot blood. But from this apparently useless waste of blood does the sacred image of victory spring forth. The idea that his brethren were going to be insulted before him fired Mangal Panday's heart, and he began to insist that his own regiment should rise on that very day. When he heard that the leaders of the Organisation would not consent to his plan, the young man's spirit became uncontrolable, and he at once snatched and loaded his gun, and jumped on the parade-ground, shouting, 'Rise! ye brethren, rise! why do you hold back, brethren? Come and rise! I bind you by the oath of your religion! Come, let us rise and attack the treacherous enemies for the sake of our freedom.' With such words, he called upon his fellow-soldiers to follow him. When Sergeant-major Hugson saw this, he ordered the Sepoys to arrest Mangal Panday. But the traitor-Sepoys whom the English had been used to count upon upto now were nowhere to be found. Not only did no Sepoy move to arrest Panday at the orders of the officer, but a bullet from Panday killed the officer, and his corpse rolled on the ground! Just at this time, Lieutenant Baugh came upon the scene. While his horse was prancing forth on the parade, another bullet from Panday struck the horse and brought both the horse and the rider to the ground. While Panday was loading his gun again, the officer got up and aimed his pistol at Panday ; but the latter, undismayed drew out his sword. Baugh fired but missed his mark ; he then drew his sword ; but before he could use it Panday struck him down rolling again. While another white man was charging Panday, a Sepoy smashed his head with the barrel of his gun; and a shout arose from among all the Sepoys. 'Do not touch Mangal panday!' Immediately, Colonel Wheeler came and ordered Mangal Panday's arrest. Another shout arose, 'We would not even touch the hair of this sacred Brahmin.' The colonel, on seeing the blood of Englishmen flowing and the Sepoys in such a mood, speedily retreated to the bungalow of the general. On the parade Mangal Panday continued waving his hands full of blood in the air, shouting tremendously all the time, 'Rise! Brethren, rise!' When General Hearsey heard this, he took some European soldiers and rode hastily towards Panday. Seeing that he would soon fall into the hands of Feringhis and preferring death to falling into the hands of the enemy, Mangal Panday turned the gun towards his own breast, and immediately his sacred body lay wounded on the parade ground. The wounded young soldier was taken to the hospital .and the English officers returned to their tents, amazed at the bravery of this Sepoy. This was on the 29 of March 1857.

Mangal Panday was, then, tried before a court-martial.

During the inquiry, attempts were made to compel him to reveal the names of other conspirators. But the valiant youth bluntly refused to do so. He also said that he had no personal malice against the officers whom he shot. If there had been any personal malice, Mangal Panday's name would have been in the list of assassins and not of martyrs. But Mangal Panday's brave deed was done through devotion to a high and noble Principle. His sword came out of its scabbard to defend his country and religion, 'thinking alike of victory and defeat,' as the Bagavat Gita enjoins. He came out with the firm resolution to die rather than face the insult to his country and religion. In this his bold attempt, his bravery as well as his patriotism are worthy of the highest praise. He was condemned to be hanged. The 8th of April was the day fixed for the execution. Whatever might be the inspiring splendour in the actual blood of martyrs, the very names of martyrs inspire us with noble sentiments! What, then, must be the power of the martyr over those who believed in him when he was before them in flesh and blood, ready to undergo martyrdom? It is no wonder that a divine love for him inspired all those who saw Mangal Panday. Not even a low-class man could be found in the whole of Barrackpore to act as executioner. At last four hangmen had to be brought from Calcutta to do the dirty work! Mangal Panday was carried to the scaffold on the morning of the 8th, surrounded by soldiers. He walked with a steady step through the ranks and ascended the scaffold. While he repeated once more that he will never give out the names of any of the conspirators, the noose dropped and the glorious soul of Mangal Panday left the body and went to Heaven!

This was the first skirmish of the Revolutionary War, and so died the first martyr. We always ought to remember with pride in our heart the name Mangal Panday, whose blood was the source of the river of martyrdom! The seed of freedom that had been sown for the three years and more, was first watered with hot blood from the body of Mangal

Panday! When the time comes to get its crop, let us not forget who first boldly came forward to nourish it!

Mangal Panday is gone, but his spirit has spread all over Hindusthan; and the principle for which he fought has become immortal! He gave not only his blood but his sacred name also to the Revolution! It has become a nickname for all those who fought for religion and country in the war of 1857 whom friends and foes alike called by the appellation of 'Panday.[2] Let every mother teach her son the story of this hero with pride.

* * *

CHAPTER II

Meerut

THE seed of revolutionary martyrdom soaked in the blood of Mangal Panday was not long in taking root. The Subhadar of the 34th regiment was charged with holding secret revolutionary meetings at night and beheaded. And when documents were found proving that the 19th and 34th regiments had secretly planned to raise a revolution, they were both disarmed, disbanded. This was a 'punishment' in the eyes of the Government, but the Sepoys of these regiments looked upon it as a great honour. The European regiments were kept ready on that day, and the English officers were confident that the Sepoys would repent of their disobedience after being disbanded. But thousands of Sepoys willingly laid down their arms like some unholy object, and

2. The name has become a recognised distinction for the rebellious Sepoys throughout India.'—Charles Ball.
'This name was the origin of the Sepoys generally being *Pandays*'- Lord Roberts's *Forty-one years in India.*

broke with pleasure the chains of slavery. They tore away their boots and uniforms and proceeded to take a bath in the neighbouring river, as if to wash away the sins of slavery. It was the custom for the Sepoys to buy military caps out of their own money, so the Company allowed them to take them back a their private property. But were they going to don the emblem of slavery again after the purificatory bath in the river? No, no. No one would commit such an impiety! The days are gone when India would don other people's caps! Throw away these slavish caps! Thousands of caps began to fly in the air! But through the obstinacy of the force of gravitation, they fell again on India's soil! The Goddess has been polluted again! Run, Sepoys, run even before the English officer, tear those other badges of slavery, and trample these into dust. Thousands of Sepoys began to trample upon the polluted caps; and, seeing the Sepoys dance upon caps, which was an insult to their authority, the English officers were petrified with astonishment and rage.[1]

Mangal Panday's blood not only sowed the seeds of freedom in the regiments stationed in Bengal, but electrified also Umballa on the other side of India. Umballa was the chief head-quarters of the English army, and the English Commander-in-Chief Anson stayed there. The Sepoys at Umballa struck upon a new plan, that of burning the house of every officer that went against them! Every night the houses of tyrants and traitors used to receive the unwelcome visit of fire. The work was done so swiftly and secretly that it seemed as if the God of Fire himself had become a member of the Secret Society. There were so many fires and thousands of Rupees were offered to discover the culprit, but no revolutionaries played the part of a traitor! At last, the Commander-in-Chief Anson wrote to the Governor-General in despair, 'It is really strange that the incendiaries should never be detected. Everyone is on the alert here, but

1. *Red Pamphlet*, part I, page 34.

still there is no clue to trace the offenders.' Towards the end of April, he writes further: 'We have not been able to detect any of the incendiaries at Umballa. This appears, to me extraordinary; but it shows how close are the combinations among the miscreants who have recourse to this mode of revenging what they conceive to be their wrongs, and how great is the dread of retaliation to anyone who would dare to become an informer!' The English Empire is based on Indian treachery So, in Umballa, when not a single man turned traitor, the Commander-in-Chief of the English became helpless and began to thirst secretly for revenge, at the same time wondering at the: secret conspiracy of the Sepoys!

The fires had now begun in various places in Hindusthan. It is but natural that there should be sparks blown up here and there before the vast final conflagration broke out. Since the visit of Nana Shib, Lucknow was in commotion. There also the houses of foreigners and traitors began to take fire! The plan fixed upon was that on the 31st of May the whole of Hindusthan should burst out in a universal conflagration, so that the English should have no room to escape and thus die in the country they wanted to keep enslaved! Though the Lucknow branch of the Secret Society had consented to this plan, the valiant Sepoys could not restrain themselves. Besides, the exciting speeches every night in the meetings of the Society and the sight of burning houses inflamed them still more. On the 3rd of May, four such uncontrollable Sepoys rushed into the tent of Lieutenant Mecham, and said, 'Personally, we have no quarrel with you, but you are a Feringhi and must die!'[2] The lieutenant, frightened out of his wits at the sight of the fierce-looking Sepoys, implored them for mercy and said, 'If you like you can kill me in a second. But what will you get by killing a poor individual like me? Some other man will come and take my place. The

2. Charles Ball's *Indian Mutiny*, Vol. I, page 52.

fault is not mine but of the system of Government. Then why don't you spare my life?' At these words, the Sepoys cooled down and remembered that their real aim was to annihilate the whole system at once, and returned. But this news reached the officers, and Sir Henry Lawrence disarmed the regiment by means of a trick.

But at Meerut, things were taking a more lively turn. Some Englishmen formed the novel idea of testing if the Sepoys really objected to the cartridges. And they decided to force them on a company of cavelry on the 6th of May. It seems only five of the ninety Sepoys there touched the Cartridges! Once more the same cartridges were given them to be used. Again they all refused to touch them, and went away to their camps. When this news reached the General, he tried them before a court-martial and sentenced all the eighty-five Sepoys to rigorous imprisonment ranging from eight to ten years!

This heart-rending scene occurred on the 9th of May. These eighty-five Sepoys were made to stand under the guard of European infantry and artillery. All the Indian Sepoys were also ordered to stand by to witness the scene. Then the eighty-five patriots were ordered to take off their uniforms. Their uniforms were torn away, their arms were snatched off, and all the eighty-five were handcuffed. Those hands which so long held only swords to pierce into the hearts of the enemy, such martial hands were now loaded with handcuffs! This sight inflamed the hearts of all the Sepoys present; but, seeing the artillery on the other side, they did not draw their swords then and there. Then the eighty-five Sepoys were told that they were sentenced to rigorous imprisonment for ten years, and these religious martyrs were hurried away to their prisons, bending under the heavy prisoners' chains! What sign their compatriots made to these religious martyrs at the time, the future will soon unfold. This sign must have encouraged them! We will destory the foreign slavery, under which to refuse cartridges mixed with the blood of cows and pigs is an offence punishable with ten years' hard labour! We will soon break not only the chains tightening round your legs but also the chains of slavery riveted for one hundred years round the feet of our dear Motherland! This must have been the meaning of the sign that they made.

This was in the morning. The Sepoys could not possibly control themselves any longer. They returned to their barracks, smarting inwardly under the insult and shame of seeing their brethren being imprisoned by foreigners for what was nothing more than an act of self-respect in defence of their religion. When they strolled out in the bazaars, the womenfolk of the town said to them scornfully, 'Your brothers are in prison, and you are lounging about here killing flies! Fie upon your life!'[3] How could they, already chafing under injury, hear women taunting them so in the open street, and still remain doing nothing? All Over the lines that night there was a number of secret meetings of the Sepoys. Were they to wait now till the 31st of May? Were they to sit like dummies, while their compatriots were rotting in prisons? Were they going to wait till others rose, when even the women and children of the town were calling them traitors in the streets? The 31st was yet very far off, and were they to remain till then under the banner of the Feringhis? No, no. To-morrow is Sunday, and before the sun of to-morrow sets, the chains of these patriots must be smashed, the chains of the motherland must be smashed, and the banner of Independence must wave forth! Immediately messengers were sent to Delhi, 'We will be there on the 11th or the 12th, keep everything ready.'[4]

Sunday dawned on the 10th of May. The English had so little information about the secret preparations of 1857, that they had no idea about the meetings of the Sepoys at Meerut,

3. J.C. Wilson
4. *Red Pamphlet.*

much less of their communications with other Sepoys. They began their day with the usual peaceful pursuits. Horse-carriages, cold appliances, fragrant flowers, airing, music and singing, all was going on in full swing. The servants in a few Englishmen's houses suddenly left their services, but this did not cause more than a moment's surprise. But here in the Sepoys' camp the point was being debated, whether there should be a general massacre or not. The 20th regiment said that, when the English were in church, they should rise with the shout of 'Har, Har, Mahadev!' and massacre all the English, civil and military, men and women, on the way to Delhi. This plan was agreed upon at last. At that time, the church bells began to toll in the air. The Englishmen with their wives were strolling towards the church. Meanwhile in the town of Meerut, thousands of people, even from the villages, were gathering together with old and broken weapons! The citizens of Meerut also prepared themselves for the country's cause. Still the English had not any serious information about this! At five o'clock, the bells were tolling for prayer-only it was the last prayer of the Englishmen before they were despatched to give an account of their sins! There, in the Sepoy lines, however, the air resounded to the fierce shout 'Maro Feringhi ko!' —' Kill the foreigner!'

At first hundreds of horsemen galloped towards the prisons to free their compatriots. The jailors, also, being members of the revolutionary party, left the prison and joined their brethren, when they heard the cry, 'Maro Feringhi ko!' In a moment, the walls of the prisons were razed to the ground! A patriotic blacksmith came forth and smashed the chains of all the prisoners. What a wonderful sight when the liberated prisoners embraced heartily their brethren ; their deliverers! With a loud war-cry, the heroes rode their horses and marched towards the church along with their brethren, leaving the hated prison behind. In the meantime a company of infantry already started the Revolution. Colonel Finnis of the 11th regiment had approached towards them on horseback and begun to threaten them haughtily in the usual manner. But the Sepoys rushed at him like death. A Sepoy of the 20th regiment emptied his pistol at him, and both the horse and the rider fell dead on the ground. Infantry and artillery, Hindu and Muslim, were thirsting for the blood of the Englishmen! This news spread to the bazaars of Meerut and Meerut was ablaze; and everywhere the Englishman was killed, wherever he was found. The people of the bazaars took swords, lances, sticks, knives, anything in fact that came to hand and were running about in the lanes. All the buildings that were in any way connected with English domination—bungalows, offices, public buildings, hotels—all were burning in a blaze. The very sky of Meerut wore a threatening aspect; there rose clouds of smoke, terrible flames of fire, and confused shouts from a thousand throats; and, above all of them could be heard the terrible cry, 'Maro Feringhi ko!' As soon as the Revolution began, according to the plan previously agreed upon, the telegraph wires to Delhi were cut and the railway line was strictly guarded. The night being dark, the English who survived were utterly confused. Some hid themselves in stables; some passed the night under trees; some on the third floor of their houses; some in a ditch; some disguised themselves as peasants, while others fell at the feet of their butlers. When darkness was falling, the Sepoys were already marching to Delhi, and it was the townsmen of Meerut that were accomplishing the work of revenge for the wrongs and oppressions of a century. The hatred towards the English was so violent that stone houses where they resided, which could not be burnt were pounded down! The bungalow of Commissioner Greathed was set fire to. He was still hiding inside. The rumour went about that the people of Meerut had risen in arms and surrounded his bungalow. Then the Commissioner fell at the feet of his butler and implored him for his and his family's life. The butler gave the mob a ruse and led them away, and the Commissioner fled away from the crumbling bungalow. The mob dragged Mrs. Chambers out of her bungalow and killed her with knives. Captain Craigie clothed his wife and children in horse clothes to disguise their colour, and hid them all night in an old demolished temple. Dr. Christie and Veternary surgeon Phillips were battered to death. Captain Taylor, Captain MacDonald, and Lieutenant Henderson were hotly pursued and killed. Many women and children died in the burning houses. As more and more English blood was spilled, the terrible cry of the Revolutionaries and their spirit became more and more violent. Passers-by began to kick about English corpses! If in the middle somebody showed pity in striking down the English, thousands of men used to run there crying, , 'Maro Feringhi ko!' They would point to the mark of the handcuffs round the wrist of any lately manacled Sepoy present in the company and would shout, 'We must revenge this!' Then swords flashed out without any thought of mercy.

Meerut was about the last place where the Revolution should have started in the natural course of events. There were only two Sepoy regiments of infantry and one of cavalry, while there was a complete riflemen battalion and a regiment of dragoons of Europeans there. Besides, the whole of the artillery was in the hands of the Europeans. Under these circumstances the Sepoys had no chance of success. Therefore was it that, immediately after the rising, the Sepoys went away towards Delhi, leaving the work of revenge to the townsmen of Meerut. It was. very easy to have stopped the Sepoys on the way and to have crushed them. But even English historians are ashamed of the cowardice, mismanagement, and want of foresight among the civil and military officers there. Colonel Smyth of the Indian cavalry ran away to save his life when he heard that his regiment had risen against the English. When the chief officer of the artillery was getting his guns ready and parading them, the Sepoys were already on the way to Delhi. Even then, the English army, instead of following them, remained inactive all night, as if cowed down. To tell the truth, when Meerut rose, the English were absolutely dumb founded. They could not form any idea of this unprecedented and sudden rising till the next day! On the other hand, the Sepoys had a clear programme before them. It was this to rise immediately, to release the prisoners, and massacre the English. Either the English were frightened at the sudden rising, or the citizens of Meerut, plundering and burning on all sides, made it impossible for the English to see where the real rising was. When they would be busy taking their bearings, the Sepoys were to have marched towards Delhi. This march towards Delhi was a very cleverly organised plan. There is not the least doubt that the leaders of the Secret Society showed unexampled skill in taking hold of Delhi at the first heat, thus making the Rising openly national in a moment, and destorying the prestige of the English. And the plan was as quickly executed as it was cleverly arranged. Before the English got news of the rising, the telegraph wires between Meerut and Delhi were cut, the road was guarded, the patriotic heroes were liberated from prison, the blood of English despots was flowing on the ground, and two thousand Sepoys, with their drawn swords wet with English blood, raised the significant cry of, 'To Delhi, to Delhi!'

* * *

CHAPTER III

Delhi

NANA SAHIB Peshwa had been to Delhi towards the end or April and all were anxiously awaiting Sunday, the 31st of May, agreed upon as the day of rising. If the whole of Hindusthan had risen simultaneously on the 31st of May, history would not have had to wait longer than 1857 to record the destruction of the English empire and the victorious Independence of India. But the premature rising of Meerut benefited the English much more than the Revolutionaries.[1] It is true that the spirited and patriotic women of the Meerut bazaars, who taunted the soldiers and goaded them on to release their comrades, have added one most honourable episode to our history. But the Meerut Sepoys, by their rising, unconsciously put their brethren in unforeseen confusion by warning the enemy beforehand![2] All the Sepoys at Delhi were Indian. They too had become restless since the heroic martyrdom of Mangal Panday. But the Emperor Bahadur, Shah and the Empress Zinat Mahal had tactfully restrained them. Just at this moment, a message from the Meerut branch of the Society was delivered to the Delhi branch, 'We are coming to-morrow; make the necessary preparations!' Hardly had this unexpected and strange message been delivered at Delhi when two thousand Sepoys were already on the march from Meerut, shouting, 'Delhi! Delhi!' Night herself was then sleepless. How could she sleep amidst the terrible noise produced by thousands of horses stamping and

---

1. 'It is certain, however, that if this sudden rising in all parts of India had found the English unprepared but few of our people would have escaped the swift destruction. It would then have been the hard task of the British nation to reconquer India or else to suffer our Eastern empire to pass into an ignominious tradition.' Malleson, Vol. V. 'The calamitous revolt at Meerut was, however, of signal service to us in one respect in as much as it was a premature outbreak which disarranged the preconcerted plan of simultaneous mutiny of Sepoys all over the country, settled to take place on Sunday the 31st of May, 1857.'— White's *History* page 17.

2. From this combined and simultaneous massacre on the 31st of May, 1857, we were, humanly speaking, saved by the frail ones of the bazaar. The mine had been prepared and the train had been laid, and it was not intended to light the show match for another three weaks. The spark which fell from the female lips ignited it at once and the night of the l0th of May saw the commencement of the tragedy never before witnessed since India passed under British sway.'—J. C. Wilson's *Official narrative.*

neighing, the clanging of swords and bayonets, and the fierce shouts and secret whisperings of the marching revolutionaries? When day dawned, the Sepoys were astonished to find that the Meerut artillery had not been following them. The Sepoys forgot all the fatigues of the night and, without losing a minute, marched on with vigour. Delhi is about thirty-two miles from Meerut. At about eight in the morning, the first part of the army was in sight of the sacred Jamna. Seeing the holy Jumna which seemed by its cool breezes, consciously to encourage the heroes, bent on the holy work of Freedom, thousands of soldiers saluted her, shouting, 'Jai Jumnaji!' Horses began to gallop on the bridge of boats leading to Delhi. But did the river Jumna understand their sacred mission? It was necessary to let her know this and get her blessings before marching on. Then catch hold of that Englishman there walking along the bridge, and let his blood be poured into the dark Jumna! This blood will tell her the reason why these Sepoys are galloping so hurriedly towards Delhi!

After crossing the bridge of boats, the Sepoys were already at the walls of Delhi. When the rumour reached the English officers, they collected the Sepoys on the parade-ground and began to treat them to lectures on loyalty. Colonel Ripley, with the 54th regiment started to oppose the Meerut Sepoys. The Sepoys of the 54th regiment told their Colonel when starting, Show us the Sepoys of Meerut and we will then see.' The colonel said '*Shabash*' (Well done)! and the regiment marched towards the Revolutionaries. As they advanced they saw the Meerut cavalry galloping towards the fort. Just behind the cavalry, there were also coming on, the infantry dressed in red garments and thirsty for English blood. As soon as the two armies saw each other, they saluted; and the army of Delhi met that of Meerut on friendly terms! When the Meerut army raised the cries of 'Let the English rule be destroyed!' and 'Long live the Emperor!', the Delhi army replied by shouting, 'Kill the Feringhis!' In a moment, Colenel Repley, who, in confusion, began to shout, 'What is this!', 'What is this!', was riddled with bullets and fell down, dead. All the English officers of the army of Delhi were similarly killed. After having thus sealed their patriotism with English blood, the horsemen of the Meerut cavalry descended and heartily embraced their comrades from Delhi! Just then the historic Kashmir gate of Delhi opened, and this army of the heroes of liberty entered the town of Delhi with the cries of 'Din! Din!'

The second part of the Meerut army was also trying to enter Delhi by the Calcutta gate. The gate was first barred, but at the terrible knock of the Sepoys, it began to open slowly, and soon the watchman at gate joined the Sepoys with cries of 'Din! Din!! The Sepoys who entered by the Calcutta gate turned towards the bungalows of the English at Daryaganj, and the buidings there were all ablaze before long. Those Englishmen who escaped the fire succumbed to the sword. The English hospital was near by and it was found that it had given shelter to the English bottles! It is natural that the Sepoys were enraged at the temerity of this hospital, after it had seen the example of the bungalows of Daryaganj being razed to the ground for sheltering Englishmen! So they broke all bottles and after punishing the hospital, they began the hunt for English blood in all the houses of Delhi! But what is an army without a banner and what are mere cloth banners for an army like this? So, wherever an English head was found, it was struck at the ends of lances, and with such terror-striking flags did the army push forward at a rapid pace!

In the Royal palace of Delhi, Sepoys and townsmen were crowding together, shouting, 'Victory to the Emperor.' Commissioner Fraser was entering the gates of the palace, wounded. A man called Nuzul Beg standing near him pierced him in the cheek. At the sign, all the Revolutionaries ran up the stairs, trampling Fraser down all the way up. The Sepoys did not stop there, trampling him, but went upstairs to the room in which Jennings and his family were living. An attempt was made by someone from inside to bolt the door, but a furious knock of the Sepoys burst it open. Jennings, his daughter, and a guest fell to the sword in an instant. Where is that Captain Douglas, who was running already dying with terror, all through the streets of Delhi? Kill him, too! And this Collector hiding in the corner? Give him also leave of life! Well, now there is not a trace of Feringhi authority left in the palace of Delhi! Now, Sepoys, you can surely rest a while! Let the cavalry pitch their quarters in the palace, and let the Sepoys who had marched all night take a little rest in the palace in the Dewan-i-Khas.

In this way the palace of Delhi came into the hands of the army of the people, and the Emperor, the Empress, and the leaders of the Sepoys held a conference as to future plans. It was now evidently foolish to wait till the 31st May as previously arranged; so after a little hesitation, the Emperor decided openly to take the side of the Revolutionaries. As this was going on, a large part of the artillery of Meerut, who had also risen, arrived at Delhi. They entered the palace and gave a salute of twenty-one guns in honour of the Emperor and of freedom. The little hesitation that remained in the mind of the Emperor, even after the pleadings and arguments of the Revolutionary Sepoys, now completely disappeared after this thunder of cannon; and the hundred Imperial yearnings in his heart awoke with a flash. The leaders of the Sepoys, with their swords dipped in English blood, stood before the dignified and magnificent person of the Emperor, and said, 'Khavind! the English are defeated at Meerut, Delhi is in your hands, and all the Sepoys and people, from Peshawar up to Calcutta, are awaiting your orders. The whole of Hindusthan had arisen to break the chains of English slavery, and to aquire their God-given independence. At this time, take up the flag of Liberty in your own hands, so that all the warriors of India may assemble to fight under it! Hindusthan has begun to flight to get back Swaraj and if you accept her leadership, in a moment, we will either drown all these Feringhi demons in the oceans to give them as food to the vultures!'[3] The Emperor grew spirited after hearing this unanimous and exciting eloquence on the part of the leaders, both Hindu and Mahomedan. The memories of Shah Jahan and Akbar rose before his mind's eye, and a divine inspiration inflamed into his heart, that, rather than continue in slavery, it would be preferable even to die, in the attempt of liberating one's country. The Emperor said to the Sepoys, 'I have no treasury and you will get no pay!' The Sepoys replied, 'We will loot the English treasuries all over India and lay them at your feet!'[4] When the Emperor, at last, declared that he would accept the leadership of the Revolution, there was a thundering roar of applause in the vast multitude assembled in the palace!

While all this was going on in the palace, in the city outside there was terrible confusion. Hundreds of the citizens of Delhi took up any arms they could get hold of, and joined the Revolutionaries and were roaming about to kill any stray Englishmen in the streets. About twelve o'clock the bank of Delhi was besieged. The family of Beresford, the manager of the bank, was killed, and the whole bank was demolished. The mob then turned to the printing office of the 'Delhi Gazette.' The compositors were busy setting into type the news from Meerut. Suddenly, there was a roar of 'Din! Din!!' outside, and in a moment, all the Christians in the building were despatched. The types were thrown away, the machinery was smashed, and everything that was made impure by the touch of the Englishmen was destroyed. The great wave of Revolution then rushed on ! But see the yonder church.! Is it fair that it should hold its head high in the march of this Revolutionary War? From this very church

3. Charles Ball's Indian Mutiny, Vol. I, page 74.
4. Metcalfe

have prayers gone forth to Heaven to perpetuate English dominion in India! Has this church preached once at least to its congregation that their dominion in India is a sin and a crime against liberty? On the contrary, this partisan church has sheltered under her wings these tyrants, to protect them and to look after their material more than their spiritual welfare. We have already got the reward for allowing this den of cruelty to be established in our midst, in the shape of cartridges mixed with cows' and pigs' blood! Run to that church! Why are you looking on? Smash that cross, take away those pictures from the walls, pound down that pew, and shout 'Din!' Every day the bells ring in the church. We shall, also, peal them on our way back. Peal on, bells, peal on ! You are pealing so much to-day and still no Englishman comes to the church! How do you like the touch of these brown hands? Fall down on the ground! Our comrades are ready to trample you down! When all the bells fell down with a crash, the mob smiled to each other in a ghastly way and said to one another, '*Kya tamasha hai*!' what fun !'

But there, on the other side, there was even a more ghastly scene taking place. There was a big arsenal of the English army near the palace. In this arsenal there was a vast quantity of ammunition useful for war. At least 900,000 cartridges, 8 to 10 thousand rifles, guns, and siege-trains were there. The Revolutionaries decided to capture this arsenal. But this work was not at all so easy. If the Englishmen in the arsenal were so inclined, they could kill a large number of the attacking force; they had only to light a match. It was thus wery dangerous to attempt to capture the arsenal. Still, without it, the life of the Revolution was not safe for a moment; so thousands of Sepoys made ready to carry out the task. They sent a message in the name of the Emperor to the officers of the arsenal, asking them to surrender. But such paper messages never conquer kingdoms! Lieutenant Willoughby did not even condescend to reply to the note. At this insult, thousands of infuriated

Sepoys began to mount the wall of the arsenal. Within the walls were nine Englishmen and some Indians. When they saw the flag of the Emperor of Delhi flying on the Fort, the Indians speedily joined their comrades, and the nine Englishmen began to fight with the courage which despair gives. It was evident that the handful of Englishmen could not hold out long before the terrible onslaught of the Sepoys. They had already determined to blow up the arsenal in case all hope of saving it for England was gone; because they were not certain of their lives being spared even if they were willingly to hand over the arsenal. On the other hand, the Sepoys also, in spite of a certainty of losing a large number if the arsenal was blown up, fiercely continued the assault. To their aid came also hundreds of the citizens of Delhi. Suddenly the terrible boom and crash, as if of a thousand cannon, which both sides had been expecting every moment, rent the air, and volumes of flame and smoke went up to the skies! The nine English heroes, instead of handing over the arsenal to the enemy, set fire to it themselves and gave up their own lives. With that one crash, twenty-five Sepoys and about three hundred men in the neighbouring streets were literally blown to pieces!

But it was not in vain that the Revolutionaries, at last, got hold of the arsenal at the cost of so many men who fell victims in the blowing up of the arsenal. The Sepoys got a good store of arms, each getting four guns. As long as the vast arsenal was in English hands, the Indian Sepoys in the chief cantonment were under the English officers. True, they had refused to attack their brethren; but they did not also rise against the English. At about four o'clock in the evening, the thundering crash was heard which shook the whole of Delhi. The Sepoys in the cantonment suddenly came together and fell on the Englishmen, crying 'Maro Feringhi ko!' They killed Gordon Smith and Revely, and wherever an Englishman was found, he was killed. The national vengeance awakened after a century, crushed down men, women, children, houses, stones, bricks, watches, tables, chairs, blood, flesh, bones—anything that had any relation with the English! In the end, at the strict orders of the Emperor, many Englishmen were saved from massacre and made prisoners in the palace. But such was the popular fury against the Feringhi despots that, after a struggle of four or five days, the Emperor was compelled to hand over the fifty English prisoners to the mob! On the 16th of May, the fifty Englishmen were taken to a public *maidan.* Thousands of citizens, assembled to witness the scene, burst forth in imprecations against English rule and the faithlessness of the English. When the order was given, the Sepoys killed the fifty in a second. If any Englishman attempted to ward off a Sepoy's sword and implored for mercy. loud cries of 'Revenge for handcuffs!', 'Revenge for slavery!', 'Revenge for the arsenal!', would rise up, and the bent English head was soon severed from the body! The massacre of the English began on the 11th and ended on the 16th. In the meanwhile hundreds of Englishmen ran away from Delhi to avoid death. Some blackened their faces and disguised themselves as 'the despised' Indians; some died of heat, while running away, in the woods and forests; some learnt by heart the songs of Kabir and attempted to escape through the villages in the guise of Sanyasis; but were killed by the villagers when the disguise was seen through. Some were cut by the villagers as , 'Feringhis' when they sat down under the trees in fatigue after walking long, long distances; and a few with the assistance and hospitality of kindly villagers at last safely reached the English camp at Meerut. The hatred against English rule was so great that, at the news of the massacre of Delhi, hundreds of villages determined never to allow an Englishman to set foot within their limits. But in none of those villages, not even in Delhi itself was a single English woman outraged.[5] The fact is proved by the enquiries of the English themselves and is universally admitted by the English historians. And still what lies were not circulated in England by the English missionaries at that time? We have no hesitation in saying that nobody has ever dared to make false statements more mean, despicable, or wicked, than the false descriptions given, at the time, by English missionaries 'from personal experience,' about the events at the time of the massacre! What can one think of the love of truth of a nation which allows its citizens to say falsely that English women were made to walk about naked in the streets of Delhi, that they were outraged openly, that their breasts were cut, the small girls were outraged, and so on? And these were priests, too! The Revolution of 1857 did not take place because the Indians wanted white women; It was brought abour, rather, to remove all traces of white women from India!

In this manner, the storm raised by the violent ravings of the women of the Meerut bazaars, dug up, by the roots, in one stroke, the poisonous tree of slavery which had been standing in the country for a hundred years! The chief cause for this extraordinary success of the Revolutionaries in five days was the ardent desire among all classes of the people to get rid of English slavery. From the women of Meerut to the Emperor of Delhi, there was a strong desire in every heart to achieve Swaraj and protect religion. This desire had already been put into shape by the secret societies. Therefore was it that in five days the banner of Swaraj could be won on the historic capital of Hindusthan, Delhi. On the 16th of May, there was not even a trace left, in Delhi, of English domination. Such was the hatred against the English

5. 'However much of cruelty and bloodshed there was, the tales which gained currency of dishonour to ladies were, so far as my observation and enquiries went, devoid of any satisfactory proof.'- Hon. Sir Wm. Muir, K.C.S.I. Head of the Intelligence Dept.

that anyone who uttered a word of English was mercilessly thrashed! The rags of the English flag were being trodden down upon the streets; and the flag of Swaraj, from which the stains of slavery had been washed away by hot blood, was flying at the head of the Revolution! The wave of liberty rose so strong that in five days there was not even one traitor in the whole of Delhi. Men and women, rich and poor, young and old, Sepoys and citizens, Moulvies and Pandits, Hindus and Mahomedans—all attacked the foreign slavery with their swords drawn under the banner of their country. It was on account of this extraordinary patriotism and love of freedom, and a confirmed hatred of the English, that the words of the women of Meerut could raise the throne at Delhi once more from the dust!

These five days will be ever memorable in the history of Hindusthan for yet another reason. Because these five days proclaimed by beat of drum the end for the time being at any rate of the continuos fight between the Hindus and Mahomedans dating from the invasion of Mahamud of Ghazni. It was proclaimed first that the Hindus and the Mahomedans are not rivals, not conquerors and the conquered, but brethren! Bharatmata (Mother India) who was, in times past, freed from Mahomedan yoke by Shivaji, Pratap Singh, Chattrasal, Pratapaditya, Guru Govind Singh, and Mahadaji Scindia—that Bharatamata gave the sacred mandate that day, 'Henceforward you are equal and brothers; I am equally the mother of you both!' The five days during which Hindus and Mahomedans proclaimed that India was their country and that they were all brethren, the days when Hindus and Mahomedans unanimously raised the flag of national freedom at Delhi. Be those grand days ever memorable in the history of Hindusthan!

* * *

CHAPTER IV

The Interlude and the Punjab

THE news of the liberation of Delhi travelled with lightning rapidity, and by its suddenness absolutely staggered for a moment Indians as well as the foreigners. Englishmen could not even grasp for a time the meaning of what had come to their ears. Lord Canning was fast asleep there in Calcutta, in the certainty that peace was reigning all over India, and Commander-in-Chief Anson was preparing to go to the cool heights of Simla. When first Canning got a scrappy telegram to the effect that Delhi was free, he could hardly believe his eyes. The Indians were in a consternation quite as much as the Englishmen, because this unthought-of rising at Delhi spoiled all the preconcerted plans of the Secret Revolutionary Organisation. And the Englishmen were not, now, likely to repeat the tactical mistakes which they committed while confused at the sudden rising in Delhi. They got an opportunity to retrieve their mistakes, being forewarned of the future great danger by this sudden shock. The throne of Delhi could now be wrested from the Emperor in a couple of days by a sudden onslaught. Whereas, if the rising had taken place simultaneously in all places on the 31st, as arranged previously, the complete success of the Revolution would have been assured in the course of a single day. Though that plan failed on account of the sudden rising at Meerut, the taking of Delhi at once openly gave the Revolution a national character, and the sudden news had brought about an extraordinary awakening in the whole of Hindusthan. Now, the question was whether to take advantage of this awakening and rise at once, or wait till 31st as arranged before. What were the plans adopted by the Centres? Would not a rising without consultation of the rest produce confusion similar to that of the rising at Meetut? Such were the questions which the Revolutionary leaders in other places put to themselves and wasted their time with.

There is no other life-killing poison to a revolution than indecision. The sooner and the more sudden the spreading of a revolution the greater are its chances of success. If delay is made after the first start and breathing time is given, the enemy gets time to guard himself; those who rise prematurely lose confidence, when they see no one joining them; and a clever enemy, profiting by the past, puts obstacles in the way of those who want to rise later. Therefore, to give the enemy time between the first rising and the spreading of a revolution is always harmful to the Revolution. But that is exactly what happened. This sudden rising in opposition to their previous plans confused the Revolutionary leaders in various places and they could, for the time being, neither hold back nor rise.

The inevitable idleness of the Revolutionary party was of the hightest advantage to the English. They never had occasion to hear such terrible news since first they set foot on the soil of Hindusthan. The swords of the very Sepoys who so long maintained and extended their power were now turned against them. English Sovereignty fled from this spectacle at Meerut to Delhi, only to find the old Emperor, who strangled her with the left hand and wrested her crown away with the right! This English Sovereignty full of gory wounds, spat upon even by the women at Meerut, with hair dripped in English blood, with necklaces of bones, with all her ornaments including the crown snatched away by the people—this English Sovereignty now tried to enter Calcutta with a terrible moan! The English dominion in India has not the slightest natural strength! In this month of May, there was only one white regiment right from Barrackpore to Agra. a distance of 750 miles. Under such circumstances, if the whole of this region had risen according to the plan of the Revolutionary party, not one but even ten Englands put together could not have been able to hold Hindusthan! This white regiment was stationed at Danapur. There was a considerable number of white troops in the Punjab on the frontier, but it was necessary to maintain them there. Under these circumstances, the first effort of Lord Canning was to bring as many white troops together as possible. Just at the time, fortunately for the English, the war with Persia had come to an end and orders were sent to that army to return at once to India. At the end of the war with Persia, the English had picked up a quarrel with China and had ordered troops thither; but when this storm arose in India, Canning determined to stop the army on its way to China. Besides these two, the English regiments which were to have gone to Rangoon were detained at Calcutta, and orders were issued to the Governor of Madras to hold in readiness the 43rd infantry and the Madras fusiliers.

While this white army was marching towards Calcutta from all directions, Canning made one more attempt to pacify the Sepoys. He issued a proclamation and ordered it to be posted in every town and village. It was worded in the usual manner and contained the usual stuff. It said, 'We had no intention to interfere with your religious and caste affairs. We have not the least intenion of insulting your religion. If you like it, you can make cartridges with your own hands. It is a sin on your part who have eaten the salt of the Company to rise against it.' But who was now going to pay attention to such empty proclamations? Where the question at issue was whether the English ought to have, at all, the right of issuing proclamations in India or not, to issue a new proclamation was not to pacify but to exasperate the people. Hindusthan had no time to read these proclamations, for all eyes were turned to the magnificent Proclamation that went forth from Delhi! It was a strange sight, two proclamations at once, one of freedom at Delhi, the other of slavery at Calcutta. Hindusthan at that time welcomed the Proclamation of Delhi. And, therefore, Canning laid aside his pen and ordered the Commander-in-Chief to direct his guns immediately towards Delhi.

Commander-in-Chief Anson was at Simla when he got

the telegram announcing that Delhi had become free. When he was thinking what he was to do, he got Canning's order to take Delhi at once. The ignorance of the English about the plans and the strength of the Revolution was so extraordinary, that they perfectly believed that they could take Delhi in a week and could quell the rising before a month was over. Sir John Lawrence, Chief Officer in the Punjab, also sent urgent messages to Anson to capture Delhi. But Anson knew better than either Canning or Lawrence what it meant to take Delhi and he determined to wait until sufficient preparations were made. Hardly had Anson left the heights of Simla and arrived at the army headquarters at Umballa, when there was a tremendous uproar at Simla ! A rumour was abroad that the Gurkha Naziri battalion had also risen, and at that the English at Simla lost all courage. In that year, the heat was un sufferable to the English even at Simla! It appeared that the English would now have to pay a very heavy price for the royal pleasures, which they had so long enjoyed in cool bungalows and beautiful pleasure-gardens. There was a general uproar that the Gurkha regiment was coming, and women and children ran wherever they could get away. In this race, the men, naturally, even with loads on their backs, left the women and children far behind! This exhibition of English courage was open for two days, but it was closed afterwards as no Gurkhas were to be seen. About this time, similar scenes were being enacted, also at Calcutta. Often the rumour would get about that the regiment at Barrackpore was in arms against the English; and Englishmen, women, and children would be seen running towards the fort. Some booked passages to England, some prepared all their luggage in readiness to run away to the fort, and some would hide in corners in their offices and leave their work aside! Such was the panic created by Meerut and by Delhi—and yet Cawnpore was still to come.

As soon as Anson arried at Umballa, he began to prepare the siege-trains to besiege Delhi. There was never such a danger to the English in India before; but, now that it appeared, their real weakness came forth into prominence. Their state was absolutely deplorable. It became impossible for Anson to expedite matters. The English officers ordered about Indian soldiers just as they liked, but they could not do the same to their own soldiers! How could the English soldier give up in a day his haughtiness and his luxurious habits? And it was now out of question to get an Indian to help in everything. Carriages, labourers, provisions, even stretchers and ambulances for the wounded could not be got! Adjutants, quarter-masters, commissaries, medical chiefs-none could get his department ready and everyone was in a fix. What a shadowy thing is English power in India, without the help of the Indians themselves! When once the Indians were roused, the English found it extremely difficult even to march from Umballa to Delhi, because 'natives of all classes held aloof, waiting and watching the issue of events. From the capitalists to the coolies, all shrank alike from rendering assistance to those whose power might be swept away in a day.[1] If the Indians had always kept aloof like this, then, indeed, as the above writer says, English power might have been swept away in a day. But such a brilliant day had not yet arisen in 1857 ! The year, 1857, was the dawn after a long night's sleep. Those who saw the vision of the brilliant day to come woke up and left their beds, but others, who thought it was still night, clung to their covers of slavery and went again to sleep. Amongst these sleepy heads, the honour of Rip Van Winkle was very keenly contested between the states of Patiala, Nabha, and Jhind. These states had it in their hand either to establish the Revolution firmly or kill it. These states lay between Umballa and Delhi and without their support the English rear was quite defenceless. Even if these states had remained passive like the others, the Revolution had a great chance of success. But when Patiala, Nabha, and, Jhind began to deal blows at the Revolution even more cruel than

1. Kaye's *Indian Mutiny*, Vol. II.

those of the English, the chain between Delhi and the Punjab was suddenly snapped. These states despised the invitation sent to them by the Emperor of Delhi, killed the Sowars that brought the message, showered money on the English from their own treasuries, mustered their armies, and protected the regions through which the English armies were to pass, and attacked Delhi along with the English; and when the Punjab Revolutionaries left their hearths and homes to defend the national flag at Delhi, these Sikh states, these disciples of Guru Govind Singh, cruelly tortured and murdered them!

When the English were sure of the help of Patiala, Nabha, and Jhind, they mustered up courage. The Raja of Patiala sent his brother with sepoys and artillery and ordered him to guard the Thaneswar Road, and the Raja of Jhind took up the strong position of Panipat. When these two most important stations were thus guarded, the roads from Delhi to Umballa and uninterrupted communication with the Punjab were perfectly secure; and the Commander-in-Chief left Umballa on the 25th of May and marched towards Delhi. But Anson had become quite disheartened since the news of the freedom of Delhi. He had now, besides, to be roasted in the terrible heat of plains, of which he had great terror having passed his time hitherto amid the cool shades of Simla. Emaciated by these mental and bodily worries, the Commander-in-Chief succumbed to cholera on the 27th of May, just as he arrived at Kamal. On the same day, Sir Henry Barnard took charge of his office.

In this manner, the English army, after burying the old Commander-in-Chief, was marching under the new one towards Delhi. At that time, the English were so hopeful of victory that they were openly boasting that they would fight in the morning and drink the blood of the enemy in the evening at Delhi! While this army was marching, from Umballa, the world saw the secreted poison in the black hearts of these white Sepoys !

The army at Meerut was composed of 'heathens!' It is, of course, an example or the savage nature of Indian country and religion that they massacred' harmless' Englishmen at Meerut and Delhi, relying on the 'rumours' about cartridges! But let not what is concealed be laid open before the world! Otherwise God will despise truth more than false rumours and civilisation more than barbarity! Ah, it will require pools of blood to wash these blasphemies away!

On the way from Umballa to Delhi, in thousands of villages. all those that could be easily caught were immediately put before a court-martial in rows after rows, and were condemned to be hanged and killed in a brutal and barbarous manner! At Meerut, the Indians no doubt killed the alien English but it was not done savagely enough. They simply cut off their heads with a blow of the sword. But the English, be it said to their credit, corrected this mistake. Hundreds of Indians were condemned to be hanged before a court-martial in a short time, and they were most brutally and inhumanly tortured, while scaffolds were being. erected for them. The hair on their heads were pulled bunches by bunches, their bodies were pierced by bayonets, and then they were made to do that, to avoid which they would think nothing. of death or torture—cows' flesh was forced by spears and bayonets in the mouths of the poor and harmless Hindu villagers![2]

Ah! but it still remains to be told to my 'barbarous' readers what this court martial was and is. Hundreds of innocent villagers were herded together, and then they were given 'justice'. When there was a revolution in the Netherlands, Alva had established a similar court. The inquiry before this court was so thorough that sometimes the judge would go to sleep. When the time of sentence came, he would be awakened, and with a grave look at all the prisoners before him, he would say, 'Let these be hanged!' This historical

2. *History of the Siege of Delhi.*

death-chamber of the Netherlands was doubtless reformed and improved upon by the English! For their judges never went to sleep. Not only so, but, before their appointment, they had to take an oath that they would give the death sentence, without thinking of guilt or innocence![3] The place, where, after such a holy oath, English officers sit down in order to condemn all 'natives' guilty or innocent, to be hanged. is known in the English language as a court-martial!

Wreaking all along the line of his march such a demoniacal vengeance on thousands of innocent men for the handful of Englisbmen killed at Delhi and Meerut, Commander Barnard sought to join the white troops at Meerut before marching right up to Delhi. It has already been noted that the English had considerable force at Meerut. This force was coming down from Meerut to join the army from Umballa. But the national army of Delhi came forth to fight with the Meerut army before the junction could be effected. On the 30th of May, the opposing armies met on the banks of the river Hindan. The right of the Indian army was safe on account of powerful guns, and the English could do nothing against it. While the fight was raging on this side, the left of the Indian army could not stand before the English onslaught. There was confusion in their ranks, and they retreated to Delhi, after leaving five guns in the field. But before the English could take possession of the guns one brave Sepoy of the 11th regiment, rather than leave his place, chose death instead. Others might do their duty or not, but he was determined to do something for his country before

---

3. 'Officers as they went to sit on the court-martial swore that they would hang their prisoners, guilty or innocent and, if any dared to lift up his voice against such indiscriminate vengeance, he was instantly silenced by the clamours of his angry comrades. Prisoners condemned to death after s hasty trial were mocked at and tortured by ignorant privates before their execution, while educated officers looked on and approved.' — Holfes's *History of the Sepoy War*, Page 124.

he lost his life. With this noble inspiration, this Sepoy of the 11th regiment seeing that the guns would otherwise fall into the hands of the English, purposely fired into the arsenal, when the English crowded round the captured guns. There was a tremendous explosion and Captain Andrews and his followers were burnt down, and several Englishmen were injured. After placing so many heal of the enemy before his Motherland, he then placed before her his own martyr's head! Just as the English historians are always singing the praises of Captain Willoughby who blew up the arsenal at Delhi, we shall also sing the praises of this brave Sepoy, the martyr for the cause of his Motherland. But, alas, even his name is not known to history! About this hero, Kaye says: 'It taught us that, among the mutineers, there were brave and desperate men who were ready to court instant death for the sake of the national cause!'[4]

As the English were, thus, completely successful in this first battle, they expected Delhi to fall in a day or two, and used to enquire every time, by post, for news of the fall! But how different were matters in reality! Though, when this unprecedented and sudden revolution first burst out into flames, Delhi had not yet the tact and boldness to lead and guide it, yet every heart in Delhi was full with the intense desire not to rest until the mother country was free, so long as God gave them life. So, the Sepoys despised by the populace all night on the 30th on account of the defeat they had sustained, came out to fight again on the 31st. When the guns of the Revolutionaries started their havoc, the English also replied with their artillery. Since the guns of the Revolutionaries were directed on this day with good aim and the Sepoys fought with stubborn courage, the loss of life on the English side was considerable. The hot sun of May, also, became unbearable to the English. The English tried the tactics of the previous day, but that would not succeed. The

4. Kaye's *History of the Indian Mutiny*, Vol. II, page 138

English prepared for a general assault towards the evening. But the Revolutionaries rained a perfect shower of cannon balls on the advancing English and, before the broken ranks of the English could reform to advance, they retired from the field in good order. Never mind, Sepoys, in one day you have shown great improvement. Even if you are so defeated again tomorrow, even then, the English are done for. For now they have not enough strength left even for petty skirmishes. On the first day of June, an army was seen marching towards the rear of the already straitened English camp. The English were utterly confounded when they found this army to be composed of brown soldiers! They Were preparing with despair in their hearts, to defend themselves, when they soon discovered that this army was not the army of the Revolutionaries, but only the Gurkhas under Major Reid coming to help them. The English army from Umballa was helped by the Sikhs, the army from Meerut was helped by the Gurkhas! Under these circumstances, what were the poor Revolutionaries of Delhi to do ? The two English armies, effected a junction on the 7th of June. At the same time, the siegetrain prepared with the help of the Raja of Nabha also arrived safely. The Sepoys of the 5th regiment were entreating the Gurkhas to revolt and capture the siege train as soon as it arrived at Umballa. But the Gurkhas flatly refused to serve their country and their religion, and the siege-train arrived at Delhi And the united army of the English arrived scatheless right up to Alipur, near Delhi.

Hearing that the English army had arrived at Alipur, the Revolutionaries again came out of Delhi and met the English army near Bundel-ki-Sarai. At this moment, the English army was in a most efficient condition, with all the necessary complement of artillery and other engines of war, good commanders, fresh and numerous soldiers, and an advantageous position. The Revolutionaries had nothing but the goodness of their cause to support them. Their leader was a prince who had never seen a battlefield in his life.

Their number was swelled by more camp followers than regular soldiers. And besides, they had become disheartened at seeing their countrymen, the Sikhs and the Gurkhas, helping the enemy. The English on the other hand assured themselves that the battle would only be a great *Tamasha* (a show). But the glorious ideal of Swaraj had filled the hearts of the Sepoys with a new inspiration and a new courage which discount all odds. Such, was the valour they showed that the English were soon convinced that it was not a *Tamasha*, but a real, grim, life-and-death struggle. The Delhi artillery was so powerful that the English artillery could do nothing against it. While the artillerymen and officers of the English were falling, the Delhi artillery became more and. more fierce. At this, the English ordered their infantry to rush, the artillery of the Revolutionaries. The English soldiers came right up to the artillery and the field arsenal, and still the Revolutionaries would not budge an inch! In the fight for Swa-dharma and Swaraj, these Sepoys behaved like true heroes and did not leave their posts till English bayonets pierced them through! But these brave heroes had not, at that time, a proper leader, or one who would, at least stand by them to the end, if not lead and encourage them. For, while they were dying for their country and religion, pierced by English bayonets but still sticking to their posts, their Commander-in-Chief had run away towards Delhi at the first roar of cannon! Just then, the English cavalry charged the left, and Hope Grant with his horse artillery charged the rear of this unfortunate army. The field was lost and this army, harassed by compatriots and foreigners alike, after fighting all day, was routed, and retreated to Delhi. General Barnard in order to follow up the victory ordered the English army to push forward, and it arrived at the wall of Delhi towards evening. The result of this day's fight was that the Revolutionaries lost the control of the territory surrounding Delhi, and the English got an advantageous position to attack the fort itself. It is necessary to record here that English historians applaud the Gurkha regiment under Seymour for conspicuous bravery in this battle.

In English eyes, the names of these Gurkhas have become favoured and honoured, for this extraordinary eagerness and unparalleled bravery in cutting the throats of their mother's sons!

The English won the battle of Bundel-ki-Sarai with the help of the Gurkhas, but the battle destroyed all the fancies of their imagination; for, it killed the vain hope of the English soldiers that they would spend the night in Delhi and spill the arch-enemy's blood. The unpleasant truth, that there were not only disorderly camp followers in the Revolutionary army, but that here, on the walls of Delhi, swords flashing with the fire of righteousness were now unsheathed for the protection of Swa-dharma and Swaraj, was forced upon the notice of the English by this stubborn battle! In this battle, the English lost four officers and forty-seven men, besides one hundred and thirty wounded. But the thing which spread more sorrow and despair in the English army than all these losses, was the death, in the thick of the battle, of Adjutant-General Colonel Chester. It will be seen later on, how English historians surpass English novelists when they give the losses of the Revolutionaries. But even in this din of the first battle, it is necessary to say that, as regards the number of cannon which the English captured on that day, one gives thirteen, and the other says they were exactly twenty-six! We should also note that both these were military officers present in the fight!

In this manner, on the evening of the 8th June, the English army encamped outside the walls of Delhi. The work of bringing the armies from Umballa and Meerut safely to Delhi depended solely on the movements in the Punjab It is, therefore, here necessary to see what were the effects of the Meerut rising in this important province, what the Swadeshi men did there, and how far the plots of the English against them were successful. When the Sikh Empire was broken, and the Punjab fell finally into the hands of the English, Lord Dalhousie pursued an administrative policy in that province which was calculated to destory the two virtues of love of freedom and martial spirit among the Sikhs. When the administration of this newly-acquired province came in to the hands of the two officers Sir Henry Lawrence and Sir John Lawrence, they completely disarmed the people, enlisted most of the Sikh Sepoys in the English army, brought the larger portion of the European army in Northern India into the Punjab, and directed everything in such a manner that the mass of the people should attend only to agriculture as the chief means of their subsistence and do nothing else. When people become mere peasants, they lose their martial qualities; they become hungry for 'peace' and do not easily give their consent to revolutionary projects which might interfere with their agriculture. This deep and profound statesmanship of the English proved successful in the Punjab and, within ten years of the destruction of the Sikh empire in the Punjab, the majority of the Sikhs began to take to the plough and left their swords altogether, and those that still retained the sword put it into the hands of the English in order to put down their own countrymen! In these circumstances, the chief officer in the Punjab, Sir John Lawrence, was sure that there would be no trouble there. Like other English officers he had no adequate idea about the impending danger till the beginning of May, and he too had intended to leave Lahore for summer and go to the cool air of the Murree Hills. Just then, the news of Meerut and Delhi electrified the Punjab. The clever Chief Commissioner grasped the grave import of the news and stayed where he was, in order to fight those who were preparing to overthrow the English empire.

At this time, the greater part of the Punjab army was at Mian Mir. As the camp of Mian Mir was very near Lahore, the Lahore fort was allowed to be garrisoned purely by

Sepoys. In the camp at Mian Mir, though the Sepoys outnumbered the English soldiers by four to one, the English officers had no suspicion about them until the news from Meerut arrived, and when the news did arrive they found it difficult to ascertain whether they were or were not secretly in communication with the Meerut Sepoys. At this time, the chief officer of the army of Lahore was one Robert Montgomery. This Robert Montgomery and Sir John Lawrence were both trained in the school of Dalhousie. They were gifted with rare coolness and courage and could preserve their presence of mind in the midst of the most unexpected difficulties. It was necessary to find out how far the spirit of national freedom had awakened among the Punjab Sepoys. A Brahmin detective was employed to ascertain the state of mind of the Sepoys. This Brahmin did the work of treachery exceedingly well and reported to Montgomery, 'Sahib, they are steeped in revolt—they are so far steeped in revolt' —and so saying he put his hand to his neck. This account of the Brahmin removed the veil from the eyes of Lawrence and Montgomery. They saw cleary that the Revolution was well organised not only in northern India, but that the fire was smouldering also in the Punjab, only waiting for the right moment to burst into flames. Thanking the premature rising at Meerut for having enabled him to discover this terrible secret, Montgomery immediately ordered the Sepoys to be disarmed. On the 13th of May, in the morning, a general parade was called out at Mian Mir. To keep the Sepoys confident in their sense of security, a grand ball was given to the English residents. Before the Revolutionaries guessed the secret of this apparent hunting after pleasure, in these conditions, they were suddenly surrounded by English cavalry and artillery. It was impossible for the Sepoys to see through this deceit and, when the usual parade movements were going on, the artillery were ordered to be in readiness to fire, and the confused Indian regiments were peremptorily ordered to give up their arms! The thousand Sepoys indignant with rage but overawed by the strong force of artillery, threw down their arms and, without a word, walked away to their lines.[5]

While this ceremony of disarming the soldiers, who, by their valour, had saved the lives of Englishmen in Afghanistan was going on, a battalion of the English force was sent to the fort of Lahore. This battalion, with the help of the English artillery in the fort, disarmed the Sepoys there and turned them out of the fort and occupied it. If there had been the slightest delay or slackness in this manoeuvre, within a fortnight, the whole of the Punjab would have been burning with Revolution; for, the different regiments of Peshawar, Amritsar, Pilhur, and Jullunder were anxiously waiting for the moment when the Sepoys of Mian Mir would attack the Lahore fort. When the news spread that English had disarmed the Mian Mir Sepoys and taken the Lahore fort, English, prestige gained a great deal of ground in the Punjab.

But a position of even greater importance than the Lahore fort was the Govindgurh of Amritsar. This latter, being a holy place of Sikhs and there being a probability of the Sikhs being aroused if anything happened there, the Sepoys had their eye on it. The rumour arose that the Sepoys, disarmed at Mian Mir, were going towards Amritsar to take Govindgurh. The English perceived the danger and requested the Jat and Sikh peasants to protect Amritsar! This request was acceded to by these loyal traitors, and the fort of Amritsar, like that of Lahore, fell into English hands. Before the 15th of May, the two towns of Lahore and Amritsar were kept, at least for the time being, from joining the Revolution.

---

5. 'Had the Punjab gone, we must have been ruined. Long before reinforcements could have reached the upper provinces, the bones of all Englishmen would have been bleaching in the sun. England could never have recovered the calamity and retrieved her power in the East.

-*Life of Lord Lawrence*. Vol. II, page 335.

After completing all these measures for the security of the Punjab, Sir J. Lawrence began to extend his labours to places outside his own province. When the news from Delhi reached him, he said it was not a rebellion but a national revolution. Still he nursed the fond hope that if Delhi could be taken within a short time there would be no rising anywhere else. With this idea, he sent letter after letter to Genera! Anson to take Delhi before June. Not only this, but he began to send contingents from the Punjab to make up the complement of the army of Ambala, while taking upon himself the responsibility of keeping the Punjab at peace. The first instalment of this assistance was the Guide Corps Regiment under Daly. John Lawrence had great confidence in Daly's bravery; and therefore selected him to lead the Guide Corps and march towards Delhi. Daly marched towards Delhi by forced marches and joined the English army at Bundel-ki-Sarai the day after the battle. In the siege of Delhi were now two traitor regiments-the Gurkhas under Bead and the Punjabees under Daly. The English were exceedingly fond of these two regiments. And who can say that this love was undeserved? The regiments deserved it fully, considering thec measure of their treachery!

While Daly's regiment was marching towards Delhi, John Lawrence took a minute survery of the political situation of the Punjab. In that territory, Hindus, Mahomedans, and Sikhs were often at daggers drawn. The Punjabees had not yet the common national awakening of the Hindus and Mahomedans as the people of Northern India had. As a matter of fact, it was barely ten years since they had lost their freedom. But the very Sikhs, who in 1849 fought furiously with the English, were now in 1857, embracing them. The key to this extraordinary historical mystery is to be found in the fact that the Revolution of 1857 came so soon after the loss of their independence. Those brave, illustrious, spirited followers of the Khalsa, who so hated Mahomedan slavery that they fought continuously for one hundred years and made the Punjab free, would certainly not have tolerated the slavery under the English if they had realised the nature of English rule. But before the ignorant Sepoys realised the fact that English rule was nothing short of slavery, before they had time enough to understand it fully, the Revolution of 1857 broke out. The English domination came into India at a time when a revolution was taking place in Indian politics. Various small groups of accumulated waters, divided for centuries, were trying to break the dams that separated each from the rest and unite into a vast river. The vast river is the United Nationality of India. The great united and compact nations of the world of to-day passed before their unity, or even for the sake of their unity, through an intermediate stage of disorganisation, internal strife, and disorder. If we look at the strife in Italy, in Germany, or even in England under the Romans and the Saxons and the Normans, if we see the mortal enmity between different races, provinces, and religions, and the inhuman persecutions in the course of mutual vengeance, we shall realise that the strife in India was a very small matter. But who can deny that the above countries have now united their several people into strong and powerful nations to-day, because they had been melted in the furnace of internal strife and fire of foreign despotism?

By a similar process of historical evolution, Bharatabhumi was in the course of creating a great nation out of the heterogeneous elements that inhabited it. The steam roller of English slavery was strong enough to crush out all the differences among the people of Northern India and make them unite to throw it off; but in the Punjab, ten years were not enough to make them realise the nature and effect of that slavery, in those days. And therefore, the Sikhs and the Jats could not conceive the idea and help in the realisation of a United Indian Nation.[6]

The men who represented the English Government in the Punjab understood this weak link in the chain of the Revolution and turned it to their advantage, They began the policy of increasing the ha tred of the Sikhs and the Jats for the Mahomedans. They were reminded of an ancient prophecy which was current among the Sikhs, that the Khalsa would one day march on Delhi the spot where the Mogul Emperor formerly killed their Guru—and raze it to the ground. Now the time had come for the prophecy to be fulfilled! But if, according to this prophecy, only the Khalsa Sahib were to march on Delhi and conquer, what would be the gain to the English? Instead of Bahadur Shah, a Ranjit Singh might rule at Delhi. It is natural that those whose interests lay in ousting both Bahadur and Ranjit from the throne of India should think it advisable to change this one-sided prophecy a little! In this revised and enlarged edition of the prophecy it was so written that Delhi would be razed only when the Khalsa and the Company would join hands! What a prophecy! But the pity is that it turned out true! The English took every unscrupulous advantage of the situation. To fan still further the hatred of the Sikhs for Delhi, a false proclamation was posted that the first order of the Emperor was to massacre all the Sikhs! Poor old Emperor! What an irony! At that very moment, he was everyday going about the streets of Delhi and saying that this war was only against the Feringhi and no damage should evermore be done even to the hair of any Indian.[7]

Though the Revolutionary party tried their utmost, the

---

6. Sir Jobn Lawrence in a letter wrote :- 'Had the Sikhs joined against us, nothing, humanly speaking, could have saved us. No man could have hoped, much less foreseen, that these people would have with-stood the temptation to avenge their loss of national independence.'- October 21st, 1857.
7. Metcalfe.

Sikhs turned to the side of the English. But in the Punjab, many regiments were composed of the non-Punjabee Hindusthanee people and all of them had prepared their minds to fight against the English, and were waiting for the appointed signal. It was not only Sepoys that vowed for freedom, but some patriotic sections of people outside the camp also were sowing the seeds of revolution everywhere. The English soon discovered that even after the disarming of the Mian Mir Sepoys the solid ground on which they were so confidently relying was being undermined. Though the forts of Lahore and Amritsar were secure, the arsenal at Ferozepore was undefended. On the 13th of May, a parade was ordered to ascertain if the Sepoys there showed any signs of mutinying by endeavouring to take the undefended arsenal. But the Sepoys behaved so coolly at parade as not to give the slightest room for suspicion of the passions that were tearing their hearts. Therefore, their disarming was not thought of; but only the two regiments were stationed apart from each other. One of the regiments was made to march through bazaar in the town. How little the English knew what was being exchanged at that bazaar ! The spirit of independence was strengthened among the Sepoys there, if that were possible, by the pleadings of the shopkeepers and the customers and before the regiment came out of the bazaar, they laid aside their doubts and hesitations and made a firm resolve. In the moment, there was raised a war-cry and the English could only blow up the arsenal as they thought it was difficult to save it. The Sepoys then, hurried towards the walls of Delhi, from where the National Flag was calling out to all Indians to rally round it! At the same moment, the town of Ferozepore also rose and burnt to the ground the bungalows, tents, hotels, and churches of the English. And the people began to roam about hunting for Englishmen. But the latter had been warned by telegrams from Meerut and were, already, hiding in the barracks. The English army which came to pursue the Sepoys, killed everyone they came across, and, after following them for some distance, returned, boasting of their indiscriminate massacres and inhuman cruelties.

The English were as much afraid of the Afghan tribes beyond the border as of the armies of the Indian Revolutionary party. When the secret propagation of the Revolution of 1857 was still in progress, the Secret Society of Lucknow had asked the help of the Amir of Kabul. From a letter which fell into the hands of Mr. Forsyth in August 1855, it is abundantly clear that Mussulmans of Lucknow were intriguing with Amir Dost Mahomed. It saids .Ayodhya is now annexed, and when Hyderabad is also swallowed up even the name of Mahomedan rule will not be heard of! Some remedy must be found to prevent this in time. If the people of Lucknow rise for the sake of Swaraj, Sire, to what extent can we rely upon your help?' To this question of Lucknow, the diplomatic Amir replied enigmatically, 'We will see to it.' But the Amir of Kabul having recently concluded a treaty with England, the English were afraid of the Mahomedan tribes on the frontier near Peshawar rather than of the Amir himself. Some Mullahs were sent to preach among these tribes and exhort them not to rise against the English. The English officers at that time near Peshawar were all bold, diplomatic, and clever in war. The danger on the side of Peshawar was avoided, though with very great difficulty, by the promptness of men like Nicholson, Edwardes and Chamberlain who were heartily supported by such an able officer as John Lawrence. They found out at very first stroke how to enlist these Mahomedan tribes on their own side. Their greed for money was exploited and they were bribed to enlist in the English army. After buying these mountaineers with money, Sir John formed a moving army to put down the unrest smouldering everywhere in the Punjab. In this army were English soldiers and experienced and tested Sepoys in whose disloyalty to the country the English could put implicit faith. Hardly was this corps formed when it found important work to do; for, the news of the disarming at Mian Mir had created a tremendous agitation in the Indian Sepoys stationed at Peshawar.

The bold English officers at Peshawar decided to strike the first blow and they prepared to disarm the Sepoys. But the English commander and other officers felt very much grieved at the impending insult to the Sepoys of their regiments. These English officers, on account of the marvellous secrecy of 1857, would not believe that their Sepoys had secretly joined the Revolution. However, Cotton and Nicholson surrounded them with European troops on the 21st of May and gave the order to disarm. Seeing that it was impossible to escape from this sudden situation, all the Sepoys laid down their arms. And their officers also, unable to look on calmly at that insult, threw down their arms and decorations and joined the Sepoys in hurling curses on the Company!

When the troops at Peshawar were disarmed, the English found an opportunity to turn their attention to the 55th regiment stationed at Hotimardan. The Government of the Punjab was perfectly certain that this regiment was also revolutionary; but the chief officer of the Sepoys there, Colonel Spottiswoode, did not share the Government's suspicions. He was continually insisting that his Sepoys would never rise against the English; still the Government persisted in its order to disarm them. Colonel Spottiswoode felt very much chagrined; and when, on the 24th of May, the Sepoy leaders came to him and asked him if the rumour that the English army was marching against them from Peshawar was true, he gave an evasive reply and the Sepoys went back dissatisfied. The English were really marching from Peshawar to destroy this regiment, as they did at Peshawar. Rather than see the wicked and disgusting affair, Colonel Spottiswoode retired to his room and committed suicide! At this news, the 55th regiment attacked the treasury, took up their arms and flags,. looted the treasure, broke the chains of the slavery to the foreigners, and marched on towards Delhi! But Delhi was not near. The whole of the Punjab, full of English soldiers, had to be crossed and, besides, an English army was pursuing them. Under these circumstances, success was so difficult that they questioned within themselves as to whether it would not be wiser for them to lay down their arms like their comrades at Peshawar and surrender to the English. But the heroes decided that it was better to have the noose of death round their necks than the chains of slavery round their feet, and they made it known by shouts to the English army following them, 'We will die fighting!' And, in truth, did the heroes of this 55th regiment lay down their lives on the battlefield fighting for the freedom of their country! The story of this 55th regiment is simply heart-rending. The pursuit had been so hot that Nicholson was often on horse-back for 24 hours without dismounting. Hundreds of them died in the fight and others escaped beyond the frontier, fighting as they went. But who would give shelter to the Hindus there? The Mussulman hordes began to receive them in a terrible manner. Isolated Sepoys were forced to become Mahomedans there. Thus these unfortunate Sepoys fighting in defence of their religion turned towards Kashmir for shelter, thinking that Gulab Singh, the Maharaja of Kashmir, would be able to protect them: When hundreds of these Hindu Sepoys were walking through the stony regions, without food, without clothes without a fire to warm them, towards Kashmir, weeping that there should be no one on earth who would protect their sacred religion, the English organised massacres of these Sepoys at various places, and they were killed like wild beasts! But, still, some of the Sepoys escaped towards Kashmir, in the fond hope of finding a protector of Hinduism. Protector of Hindus! Alas! Sepoys, you will soon be undeceived. When the Rajput-born Gulab Sing of Kashmir heard that these helpless Sepoys who were ready to jump into the jaws of Death to save the honour of their Hindu religion were coming towards him, he prohibited them from entering his country! Nay more, after giving orders that any of these Hindus found in his territory should be instantly killed, he very proudly let the English Durbar know of his valiant deeds! Now, Sepoys, either you change your religion and surrender to slavery or embrace death! Of these, martyrs, you have done well in choosing death! The English were so cruelly slaughtering them wherever they found them that the permanent scaffolds on the maidans began to rot by the flow of constant streams of Hindu blood! Still the English were not satisfied, Scaffolds-permanent scaffolds-were tired of performing executions, and then, the mouths of guns were opened. And of 55th regiment which had not spilt a single drop of English blood, every one of the men who had not been hanged was blown from the mouth of the gun! A thousand Hindus were, thus, slaughtered in no time. But, even at this last moment, (says Kaye a little ashamed at this terrible bloodshed), 'Brave and sullen they went their doom, asking only to die like soldiers at the cannon's mouth, not as dogs in the noose of the gibbet.'

As regards the massacre of these brave people, in a manner which would bring shame upon even savages, English historians generally say that, though this was undoubtedly cruel, 'the severity of the hour would be the humanity of all time!' The cruelty was desired in the interests of humanity! English historians, remember this your own sentence, 'The severity of the hour would be the humanity of all time!' As you now know the meaning of this sentence, you will also remember it exactly on a future occasion. It is well that you perpetrate this cruelty for the sake of humanity, but do not forget that the Hindu Nana is there at Cawnpore!

One more thing must be told here. Those English historians who vie with each other in dramatic descriptions of the massacres committed by the Revolutionaries, attempt at the same time to suppress purposely and consciously the inexcusable, unprecedented, and inhuman atrocities committed by their own countrymen. Before the massacre of this unfortunate but patriotic regiment, Heaven alone knows what brutal tortures they were subjected to by the demoniacal English! For English historians have clean wiped off from history this incident and left no trace of it at all. Kaye himself says, 'Though I have plenty of letters with me describing the terrible and cruel tortures committed by our officers, I do not write a word about it, so that this subject should be no longer before the world !' Here is a historian, indeed! What proof have we that the ruffians, who stuffed cow's flesh in the mouths of harmless inoffensive peasants on the road to Delhi, did not also cram the throats of these brave Hindu Sepoys of the 55th regiment in the same manner before blowing them from guns!

While these inhuman atrocities were going on in the direction of Peshawar, here in Jullunder, the smouldering fire of the Revolution was bursting into flame. John Lawrence had started the policy of disarming Sepoys wholesale, in the Punjab; and Jullunder and Pilhur would have been so treated long ago but for the admirable self-restraint and organising power of the Pilhur Sepoys. The Sepoys in the Jullunder Doab, like their comrades allover the Punjab, had made preparations for a rising. It was clearly given out by a patriotic Hawaldar, taken prisoner in the assault on Delhi, and the Government reports have recorded the same, that all over the Jullunder Doab, it had been decided to rise simultaneously. The plan was that when the Jullunder army should send a corps to Hoshiarpur, the 31st infantry should rise and march to Pilhur; on their arrival, the 3rd regiment at Pilhur was to rise and all together were to march to Delhi. Similar plans had also been made in other places; but, before the time of putting them into execution, the secret leaked out and the English were forewarned. The Pilhur regiment, however, observed great secrecy till the last moment. When the siegetrain was being taken to Delhi, they could easily have broken it up, but not to spoil the general plan, this regiment kept outward peace till the right moment. At last, on the 9th of June, the signal agreed upon was made at Jullunder—the bungalow of the colonel of the Queen's Regiment was set on fire. At this signal, the Jullunder Sepoy rose in revolt at midnight. As a matter of fact, the English had European soldiers and artillery there, but the rising of the Sepoys was so unanimous and sudden that, at their terrible war-cries, the English lost their nerve, English men, women and children began to run away to p]aces of safety. But the Jullunder Sepoys had no time to waste in massacres. Since the English guns were aimed at the flag of freedom in Delhi, every heart was drawn towards that place. When Adjutant Bagshawe began to interfere unnecessarily, one horseman galloped towards him and shot him dead. The English military officers of the place had, to the end, confidence in the Sepoys and informed the higher authorities that they need not be disarmed; and they really did trust the Sepoys. For this. the Sepoys not only refrained from massacring them wholesale but spared the life of those also that had not yet left the place. Thus, the Jullunder army kept its plan well and the officers who trusted them were spared their life. In this, the Sepoys showed great magnanimity.[8]

8. The English have circulated a myth and have called it the Black Hole of Calcutta and the whole world is execrating the memory of Siraj-ud-daulah for this wild invention of an English forger's brain. Here is a blood-curdling story of a real black hole which the perpetrator himself has confessed to. 'In the Punjab, near Ajnala, in a small island, many a Sepoy who had simply fled away from a regiment, which was 'Working under the reasonable fear of being disarmed and shot by the Government for suspicion, was hiding himself. Cooper with a loyal body of troops took them prisoner. 'The entire number, amounting to two hundred and eighty-two, were then conveyed by Cooper to Ajnala. Then came the question what was to be done with them. There was no means of transporting them to a place where thay could be tried formally. On the other hand, if they were summarily executed, other regiments and

And yet, although the Government and their officers had treated them kindly and they were thankful to them for their trust, they did not allow these private relations to come in the way of the national cause, and they gave up their body and soul to the cause, when the war-bugle for country and freedom sounded.

Before beginning the revolt at midnight, they had despatched a horseman to inform their Pilhur comrades. As soon as this messenger of freedom from Jullunder arrived, the Pilhur regiment also rose. Now it only remained for the Jullunder men to marchs to Pilhur! It was not an easy task, for it was necessary to avoid. the English artillery and cavalry; but such was the tumult and confusion among the English and so clear was the map drawn by the Revolutionaries that, at last, all the Jullunder Sepoys arrived at Pilhur in perfect order. Seeing thousands of their comrades. coming to meet them, the Sepoys of Pilhur marched in a body to receive them. The comrades heartily embraced each other, and the vast army under the leadership

---

intending rebels might take warning by their fate, and thus, further bloodshed might be prevented. For these reasons, Cooper, fully conscious as he was of the enormous responsibility which be was undertaking, resolved to put them all to death. Next morning, accordingly, he brought them out in tens and made some Sikhs shoot them. In this way, two hundred and sixteen perished. But there still remained sixty-six others who had been confined in one of the bastions of the Tahsil. Expecting resistance, Cooper ordered the door to be opened. But not a sound issued from the room; forty-five of them were dead bodies lying on the floor. For, unknown to Cooper, the windows had been closely shut and the wretched prisoners had found in the bastion a second Black-Hole. The remaining twenty-one were shot, like their comrades. J-8-57. For this splendid assumption of responsibility, Cooper was assailed by the hysterical cries of ignorant humanitarians. But Robert Montgomery unanswerably vindicated his. character by proving that he had saved the Lahore division.'-Holmes's *History of the Indian Mutiny*, page 363.

of Swadeshi Jamadars and Subahdars marched towards Delhi. On the way was a river and beyond the river was the city of Ludhiana awaiting to kiss the dust ot these heroes' feet. The very morning, the English officers of Ludhiana had received a telegram announcing the rising at Jullunder. But it was too late. The officers had no hope of keeping the Sepoys there under control. For, before the Government telegram arrived, the Sepoys had got the information that their- comrades had already left Jullunder! The English officers at Ludhiana resolved to bar the way of the army coming from Pilhur on the river Sutlej which flows between the two towns. The bridge of boats on the river was destroyed and the English, the Sikhs, and the auxiliary troops of the Raja of Nabha were protecting the bank of the river. When the Revolutionaries got this information they began to cross the river at night, four miles up the river. Some of their number had just crossed the river in boats, some were still crossing, while some were yet on the other bank. In this state, the English and the Sikhs began their artillery-fire on them. It was about ten at night and the Revolutionaries could not find the whereabouts of the Eaglish army. Besides, their guns had not yet crossed the river. In this difficult situation, the English and the Sikhs, with their artillery, fell upon them. But, when the shock of the first attack was passed. the Sepoys, without moving an inch, kept up a steady fire on the enemy. The ranks of the Sepoys, though disordered for a moment on account of the sudden attack of the enemy defended their position for about two hours. Just then, a Sepoy's bullet went right into the chest of the English commander, Williams, and he fell dead on the field. Now, the moon had arisen to dispel the midnight darkness and to throw her cool rays on the heads of the devotees of freedom. In this moonlight, the Revolutionaries saw the whole strategy of the English, and they left their position and attacked. the English boldly. Not being able to hold out before this attack, the English army as well as the loyal Sikhs took to their heels!

Proud of victory that they had just won against the combined forces of the English and the Sikhs, the Sepoys entered the town of Ludhiana about midday. In the city, there was a certain Moulvie who always used to preach to the people to break away from English slavery and establish Swaraj. On account of the Moulvie's lectures, this town had become a powerful centre of the Revolutionary party in the Punjab. When the sign came that the time had come to deal the last blows at the chains of slavery the whole town rose. The Government stores were looted and burnt. Churches, the houses of Englishmen, the presses of English newspapers, all were burnt. There was rivalry among the citizens to, accompany the Sepoys and show them the stations of Englishmen and especially the houses of 'native dogs' who used to wag their tails under the protection of the Englishmen! Prisons were broken. Whatever belonged to the Government and whatever was English was burnt down. That which could not be burnt down was razed to the ground. In this manner, Ludhiana also began to, glow with the Revolutionary fire.

But it was desirable for the Revolutionaries to go to Delhi. It would have been a great strategic and moral advantage if the Sepoys could have held Ludhiana fort, as it was the key to the Punjab; and if Ludhiana had also been a centre of the Revolution, like Delhi, it would have been a terrible shock to the English power. This was, no doubt, known to the Sepoys. But it was impossible for them to remain in Ludhiana under the circumstances. They were all mere Sepoys without a leader. They had no ammunition. If, at such a juncture, there had been at Ludhiana a Nana Sahib, or a Khan Bahadur Khan, or a Moulvie Ahmad Shah, they would never have left Ludhiana. Now, they could do nothing but march towards Delhi. And so they proceeded towards Delhi, crying that they would now decide, at the wall of Delhi itself, the question of slavery or Swaraj. The English were so much demoralised then that, though the Sepoys used to march in procession by day, yet no one dared to suggest pursuit!

But the enforced idleness of the Revolutionary party at other places for three weeks after the Meerut rising, was completely taken advantage of by the English in the Punjab. Because there were large forces of European troops in the Punjab, it became easy either to disarm the Sepoys, or compel them to revolt under odds of time and place, and then destory them. Seeing that the Sikh princes and people were joining them instead of the Revolutionaries, the English expelled all the Hindusthanees in the Punjab from the frontier up to the Sutlej and crushed the seeds of the Revolution in that part of the country. At this time, not only the Sepoys, but thousands of peaceful and well-to-do non-Punjabee Hindusthanees in towns and villages, were deported at the mere will of the authorities. And when the Punjab was, thus, completely in hand, the movement of European troops towards Delhi began on a large scale. There were two chief reasons why the Punjab remained in English hands. One was that the Sikhs sided with the English. If they had even been indifferent, the English could not have retained the Punjab for a single day. The Revolutionaries, naturally, spared no pains to bring over the Sikhs to their side. As soon as Delhi was free, a devoted servant of the Emperor sent him a long, detailed, and very interesting account of the state of feeling in the Punjab. In it, the faithful servant Taju Din says, 'The Sikh Sardars in the Punjab are all idle and cowardly, and unlikely to join the Revolutionaries. They have become the playthings of the Feringhis. I saw them personally in private, had conversation with them, and spoke to them. most earnestly. I asked them, 'Why do you join the Feringhis and become traitors to Swaraj? Won't you be better off under Swaraj ? Therefore, at least for your own gain, you ought to join the Emperor of Delhi!' To this they replied, 'See, we are all waiting for the opportunity. As soon as we get the order of the. Emperor, we will kill these Kaffirs in a day.' .... But I believe they are thoroughly untrustworthy.' So when horsemen came, with the order from the Emperor to the Sikh kings, they were assassinated! This was the first and most important reason why the English found it so easy to keep their hold on the Punjab; yet we cannot say that it was impossible to drive the English away from the Punjab, in spite of the opposition of the Sikhs. If advantage had been taken of the laxity of the English till the month of May, and if there had been a simultaneous rising according to the original plan, then, the Sikhs too would have been terrorised to join the Revolutionaries, or, at leest, there would have been a division among them; and, whatever else might have happened, the English could not possibly have taken hold of thousands of Sepoys separately and put them down. It cannot be maintained that in the Punjab there was no desire for Swaraj. The Brahmins of Thaneswar and the Moulvies of Ludhiana, the shop-keepers of Ferozepore and the Mussalmans of Peshawar, were wandering about, preaching everywhere a holy war for the sake of Swadharma and Swaraj. The writer of the above-mentioned letter says, 'If a Sirdar from the Emperor together with an army can be sent thither, the Punjab will be free in the moment. The Sepoys at different places will rise and rally round your banner. The English will have to leave in haste. And I am certain that all Hindus and Mahomedans will bow to your glorious throne. Besides, it is desirable that the rising should be made in this month of June, for English soldiers find it hard to fight in the sun. They die quickly even before fighting begins. As soon as you see this letter, you should send a Sirdar with an army into the Punjab.' etc, etc. Though popular sympathy in the Punjab was with Delhi, the Revolutionaries could not take advantage of it. The reason is that the wave of Revolution was inevitably checked for three weeks after the freedom of Delhi. If according to the pre-arranged plan, there had been universal and simultaneous risings, the English could not have moved anywhere; solitary and helpless regiments could not have been disarmed in the Punjab; the wave of

Revolution would have daily gained in volume, and undecided and hesitating people like the Sikhs would have been carried away with it; and, seeing a glorious and successful beginning, those who sympathised but dared not throw in their lot with the Revolution would have become emboldened and,—India would have been free.

In short, on account of the treachery of the Sikhs and the premature rising at Meerut, the roots of the Revolution in the Punjab were all weeded out. And the Punjab being the back-bone of Delhi, the news was very discouraging to the Delhi patriots.

We have given, above, the movements of the Revolutionaries and of the English in the Delhi and the Punjab during the three weeks. The English had been making all possible preparations during these three weeks, and large contingents of European troops were constantly being sent from Calcutta to Allahabad. In Bombay and Madras, in Rajputana and Sind, a minute inquiry was made as to the sympathisers of the Revolutionary movement, and great efforts were being made to crush it in time, as was done in the Punjab. And, thanking God for this previous warning of the Revolution, they began to be confident that they had extinguished the flames in various places. While these preparations were going on during these weeks on the side of the English, on the side of the Revolutionaries all possible outward quiet was maintained in general except for some small risings that took place here and there. This was the state of affairs on both sides, on the 30th of May. We must now turn to the succeeding events-how this was immediately altered, how the growing confidence of the English was dashed to the ground, how the flames of the Revolution burst again with redoubled vigour in spite of the great losses it had sustained during these three weeks. Revolutions are not regulated by fixed laws. They are not accurately working machines like clocks or watches. They have their own way of marching. They can only be regulated by a general principle; but they brush away minor rules by their very shock. Revolution has oply one watchword-'Dash on!' All sorts of new and unthought of circumstances might arise during its progress, but one must not stop; one must overcome them and press forward.

Tell us now, O Muse of History, how Nana Sahib, the Moulvie of Lucknow, the Ranee of Jhansi and other grand heroes clung to this principle with such extraordinary persistence! And fail not to tell, also, O History, how all Indians could not cling to it as these heroes did! Come and sing the songs of glory and of praise with us in the first part, and, also, come and weep with us later on !

* * *

CHAPTER V

Aligarh And Nasirabad

JUST as the tremendous shock was shaking the whole of North-Western India, towards Umballa and the Punjab, so also in the South, another part of the country was trembling through another of its waves. In the town of Aligarh, below Delhi, there was the regiment called the '9th Native Infantry.' Some detachments of this regiment were stationed at Minpur, Itawa, and Boland. The Government had such confidence in this regiment, that they thought that it would never revolt even though all the Sepoys in India should rise against them. Though the officials heard rumours that, in the bazaars of Boland, secret revolutionary societies were rife, they believed that the 9th regiment was sure to stand aloof from them, and remained idle in this sense of false security.

About the month of May, the places about Boland selected , from amongst them a revered, faithful, and freedom loving Brahmin, and deputed him immediately to Boland town. The Brahmin walked away with quick steps, his heart overwhelmed with conflicting emotions of hope of success and fear of failure of the errand on which he went, towards the military station of Boland, which on the one hand was relied upon by the English for loyalty, and, on the other, was looked upon with hopeful eyes by the Mother country. Will my compatriots listen to my pleadings for the freedom of the Mother-country and for the protection of religion? Or will they cling again to the dread and dark narcotic of slavery, and draw their swords against me for having disturbed their sleep, when I wanted to wake them and show them the brilliant vision?' With such feelings surging in his heart, but with his face beaming with a quiet light of peace, this Brahmin entered the station with his extraordinary message. He was well received and his message was welcomed. As to the plan of rising, the Brahmin said that they should all rise suddenly amidst the noisy jollity of a great marriage procession, massacre the English, and proceed to Delhi. Of course, there was nobody there against the principle of overthrowing English dominion, but a discussion began as to the fitness of this mode of realising the principle at Boland. Just then the Brahmin was arrested on the information of three Sepoys of the regiment. He was immediately sent from Boland to Aligarh, the chief station of the regiment, and sentenced to be hanged in the presence of all the Sepoys. While this was happening at Aligarh, the three loyal Sepoys were being disgraced and spat upon at Boland. The whole camp of Boland heaped curses on them and went, without the permission of their officers, to Aligarh where the Revolutionary messenger had been taken. On the evening of the 20th May, the Brahmin was to be hanged. The whole regiment was made to attend at the execution. What was to be done now? If they were to wait till the 31st of May, the Brahmin would be hanged. As they whispered to each other, 'He is going!', and looked up, they beheld that the Brahmin's body was hanging on the scaffold, delivering a terrible oration of REVENGE! What an oration! Instead of strings of words, streaks of blood were flowing incessantly! The dead Brahmin could never in his life have delivered such an oration as he was delivering from the scaffold without uttering a single word! For, in an instant, a sepoy broke forth from the ranks and, pointing his sword towards the body of the Brahmin, he exclaimed, 'Friends! This martyr bathes in blood !' This shaft from the mouth of that brave Sepoy, entered the heart of the thousands of Sepoys quicker, even, than it takes for a spark to explode a powder-magazine! They, at once, drew out their swords; and these thousands of Sepoys, mad with rage, began to dance with delirium, thundering, Death to the Feringhi rule!'

It is no wonder that the English officers were at their wit's end after this scene. Not only did the, 'most loyal' 9th regiment rise, but it spoke out that, if the English wanted to save their lives, they should leave Aligarh at once! Taking advantage of this generosity, the officers at Aligarh with their wives and children, and all the other Englishmen and women there, including Lady Outram, left Aligarh quietly. Before midnight not a trace of English rule remained at Aligarh !

The news of the freedom of Aligarh arrived at Minpur on the evening of the 2nd May. It has been said above that a detachment of the 9th infantry was stationed here. Anybody can imagine from the account of their brethern's doings at Aligarh, what the thoughts of the Sepoys of this detachment would have been. The officers at Minpur got information that a certain Raje Nath Singh, who had fought against the English at Meerut, had gone to a place called Jivanti. They, therefore, sent some Sepoys to arrest him. But these Sepoys of the 9th regiment, instead of arresting him, took him safely out of Jivanti and reported to the officers that no one of that name stayed there. A Sepoy called Ram Din Singh was sent by the officers under guard to Aligarh, for disobedience. When he was halfway, the Sepoys on guard released him, broke his chains and quietly returned to Minpur! This regiment, fired with patriotism, was only waiting for the signal to rise. But in order that the enemy might not cripple them before the simultaneous rising, they apparently kept such good behaviour that the 9th regiment was regarded as the 'most loyal!' regiment in the whole of India! But since the above-mentioned tour of the Brahmin, not only the Sepoys but the whole mass of the people of the Aligarh district also, were in a rage. The Minpur detachment of the 9th regiment had been sent to the Aligarh district to quell the growing discontent, and, when it returned to Aligarh, the butchers, and even loafers in the bazaars, asked them questions like, 'When are you going to kill the Feringhis?', 'When are you going to rise for freedom?' How would Sepoys have liked to postpone a work for which even butchers and loafers were impatient? Just then came the news of Aligarh. Seeing that their comrades had risen, they thought it disgraceful to wait any longer, and so they rose that same day. They, also, spared the life of all Englishmen who fell into their hands, took plenty of arms and ammunition from the arsenal, loaded it on camels, and started on the 23rd to Delhi.

At the same time, a similar movement was going on amongst the garrison of Itawa. The chief magistrate and collector at Itawa, Allen O. Hume, as soon as he heard the news from Meerut formed a select corps to guard the roads round about Itawa, with the help of the assistant magistrate Daniell. On the 19th this corps met a handful of Sepoys coming from Meerut. The few Sepoys surrendered and were ordered to lay down their arms. The Meerut Sepoys pretended to obey the order, disarmed the enemy of his suspicion, and then suddenly took up their arms and massacred their captors! Before this news got about, the Sepoys entered a Hindu temple near by, and hid themselves there with all their arms. When the collector of Itawa, Mr.

A. O. Hume, heard this, he and Daniell took some Indian soldiers and marched to attack the temple. At first Mr. Hume was confident that the handful of Sepoys must have been killed by the populace even before his little corps attacked them! But when they came near the temple, they discovered that the townsmen, instead of killing them, were singing their praises and giving them provisions. Though the villagers thus belied his expectations, Daniell thought that at least his Sepoys and police would stand by him. With immense confidence, he gave the order to attack the temple and himself rushed forward. But who followed him? Only a single Sepoy was inclined to obey his order! But this white commandant and his black slave were both despatched in an instant by bullets from the Sepoys in the temple, and Mr. Hume, who was proudly coming up, left the Sepoys in peace at the temple and took to his heels!

On this day, the 19th of May, a rumour was afloat that the army at Itawa was going to rise. But the headquarters were at Aligarh, and as the order to rise had not yet come, the Sepoys at Itawa remained quiet. And it would have remained so till the 31st of May, but for the fact that in the meantime the self-sacrifice of the Brahmin martyr set the Revolutionary flames going. When on the 22nd, the news came that Aligarh had risen, Itawa rose also. On the 23rd of May, the whole army rose, shouting, 'Har! Har! Mahadev!', sword in one hand and a lighted torch in the other. The Sepoys then attacked the English camp. They looted the treasury, broke prisons, and told the English that, unless they left the place instantly, they would be indiscriminately massacred. In this terrible plight, the English took their wives and children with them and ran wherever they found a way! Mr. Hume himself, profiting by the magnanimity of the Sepoys, disguised himself as an Indian woman and ran away,[1] When Hume ran away, it was proclaimed by beat of drum

1. *Red Pamphlet,* part II, page 70.

that Itawa was independent, and all the Sepoys went away to join the chief division of the regiment marching towards Delhi.

Thus the regiment rose like one man. In places so far apart as Aligarh, Boland, Minpur, and Itawa, the programme was perfectly carried out—looting the treasury, announcing freedom, sparing the life of the English when at the mercy of the sword, and after securing a good supply of provisions and ammunition, marching to Delhi. The regiment which the English thought would be the last to rise, thus rose sword in hand long before the others. The English, thereafter, could not feel themselves secure of anything!

There is a small town called Nasirabad about twelve miles from Ajmer. In this town there was a company of English soldiers and the 30th native infantry, besides the artillery. There were, also, the 1st Bombay Lancers and the 15th regiment which had been lately brought from Meerut. In the last regiment, the hatred of the English and the desire for driving them out were strongest. And it would have been a wonder, if the thousand political preachers from Meerut would have let go this opportunity of explaining personally to the Nasirabad Sepoys the resolutions of the Secret Society at Meerut. Excepting some men of the Bombay Lancers, the whole Sepoy army was unanimous, and resolved only to wait a suitable opportunity. This came on the 28th of May, for on that day, the discipline in the artillery was very lax. Thus, at the appointed signal, the 15th regiment from Meerut took possession of the artillery. To take it back the English officers together with the Bombay Lancers marched upon them. But, in a very short time, the Lancers retired with wisdom, and the English officers fell dead on the ground. Newbury was not only killed but his body was blown to pieces! Colonel Penny and Captain Spottiswoode also fell in this skirmish. Then,leaving all hope of the city, the English ran away to Biau. The Revolutionaries took the treasury, and their unanimously elected commander gave presents to the Sepoys in the name of the Emperor of Delhi. The houses of the Englishmen were burnt. Then that army composed of thousands of Sepoys marched towards Delhi brandishing their arms to the tune of enthusiastic military airs!

* * *

CHAPTER VI

Rohilkhand

BAREILLY was the capital of the province of Rohilkhand. The English had wrested the kingdom away from the Rohilla Pathans who had been ruling the province. There was a population there of brave, strong, and spirited Mussulmans, biding their time to take revenge for this insult. Rohilkhand and its capital must also be counted among the places where the Revolutionary propaganda against English rule was spreading fast about the year 1857. In Bareilly, at this time, were stationed the 8th Irregular Cavalry, and 18th and 68th regiments of infantry, and a battery of Indian artillery. Over this force, the chief officer was Brigadier Sibbald. About the month of April, some Sepoys had expressed their doubt about the cartridges, but the Government did not pay any serious attention to them, and forced the Sepoys singly to accept them. Once or twice again there was some tumult and growing disaffection among the Sepoys, but the Government could not see its danger.

The news of the Meerut rising reached Bareilly on the 14th of May. Thereupon, the Englishmen sent all their families towards Naini Tal and ordered the cavalary to be in readiness. The cavalry was also Indian, but it had the special and complete confidence of the English. All the Sepoys, including the cavalry, were called on parade on the 15th of

May, and the chief English officer preached to them loyalty and good behaviour. He said that the new cartridges were thenceforth to be stopped, and that the Sepoys should use the old cartridges to which they had no objection. Nay more, he said he would himself trample into the dust any new cartridges which he saw on the field and thus tried to remove the Sepoy's fear about the cartridges. As a matter of fact, to dilate upon cartridges now was superfluous. The Commander-in-Chief had issued an order that throughout Hindusthan, the new cartridges were, thenceforth, to be stopped. When the Government thus drew back immediately after the Meerut rising, and stopped, of their own accord, the use of the cartridges upon which they insisted so much before the month of May, the people and the Sepoys saw in the new order nothing but a sign of fear and weakness. The error of the theory that the Sepoys revolted solely on account of the cartridges, was now to be clearly proved at Bareilly. The Brigadier told the Sepoys that he would himself smash these cartridges, and tried to reassure them; but the days were gone when such words could pacify them. What was the use of giving orders about cartridges? Where the question at issue was whether the English should any longer have the power of giving any orders whatsoever in the land, to give further orders was to inflame the quarrel. To lecture now about good or bad cartridges was an unpardonable digression!

For the people of Rohilkhand had now received an urgent and pressing invitation from the Swadeshi throne of Delhi to hold aloft the flag of Indian freedom. Was this invitation one that could be lightly treated?

'From the commander of the army at Delhi to the commander of the army at Bareilly, hearty embraces. Brothers, there is a fight with the English proceeding at Delhi. By the grace of God, even the first defeat that they have received at our hands has demoralised them more than ten defeats would have done them at other times. Innumerable

Swadeshi heroes are coming to Delhi. At such a time, if you are dining there, come here to wash your hands. The Padishah of Shahs and the Home Splendour, our Emperor of Delhi, will give you a great welcome and fitly reward your services. Our ears are anxious for the sound of your cannon and our eyes are thirsting to see you. Come! Come at once! For, Brethren, how will the rose-tree flower without spring? How will a child live without milk?'

Was this an invitation to be rejected? While the invitation was on its way, Khan Bahadur Khan, the descendant of Hafiz Rahmat, the last independent Rohilla chief, was weaving the nets of the secret society. Khan Bahadur Khan used to get two pensions from the English, one as the descendant of Hafiz Rahmat, and the other as a judicial officer under the English. He was known throughout the province as a great favourite of the English. The Government also had great confidence in him. And he was the life and centre of all the secret societies of Bareilly! But though this invitation asked the people of Bareilly to come at once, they decided to wait till the 31st of May, in accordance with the plans originally arranged. All the Sepoys were doing their duties without, in the least, disobeying the English officers. A few days before, a hundred of the revolted Meerut Sepoys came and lived secretly in the 'lines' themselves, and stirred up the revolutionary spirit by the narrative of the events at Meerut, and then left. Still, the Sepoys kept the peace outwardly. The Subahdars of the regiments even went so far as to request the Europeans to bring their families! But before this request was fulfilled, a rumour arose on the 29th of May that the Sepoys had taken oath, at the time of the morning bath in the river, that they would massacre the English at two o'clock! Immediately the English got ready the loyal cavalry regiment. They, also, came together and formed without murmur. But the whole day passed and the Sepoys- never rose. The English retired at night, saying that though the rumour was false, it at least incidentally proved that the cavalry could be relied upon. Just then, sure and certain information came that the cavalry had sworn, long before, never to lift their swords against their comrades or help the English! The English now could not make up their minds what to believe. Not only the 29th, but also the 30th passed away without any incident. And, on the latter day, the conduct of the Sepoys was so good if anything, it was more loyal than ever-that the civil and military authorities made up their minds that the danger was surely past and that there was no longer any reason for fear!

The 31st of May dawned. Early in the morning, the house of Captain Brownlow was set on fire. But the English had not much reason to be particularly fearful of anything serious. The day was Sunday. The Sunday military parade passed off smoothly as well as the reports of native officers. The English officers even observed that the Sepoys were more than usually quiet that day. The English prayed in their churches. There was not the least sign of trouble anywhere.

The clock struck eleven. A gun was fired among the Sepoy lines. Hardly had the echo died out, when a noise of clanging rifles and shrill shouting rent the sky! The rising at Bareilly was so carefully planned, that it was arranged beforehand who was to kill which Englishman. As soon as it was eleven, the 68th regiment attacked the Englishmen near their lines. Small detachments quickly went to the various bungalows, and the rest attended to the straggling Englishmen, to go to their houses and burn them. On hearing this noise and tumult, the terror-stricken Englishmen ran towards the cavalry lines. All the civil and military officers had decided to come together there for refuge. As soon as they arrived there, they ordered the cavalry regiment to march on the Revolutionaries. But the Indian head of that regiment was also a Revolutionary. Mahomed Shafi galloped towards the Revolutionaries and ordered the horsemen to follow him. They followed him, shouting, 'Die for religion, come, the green flag is calling you!' Still the English tried to collect together a few that remained, and attempted to come near the parade ground, but finding it impossible to stand before the terrible onslaught of the Revolutionaries, they all turned their backs and began flying towards Naini Tal. Brigadier Sibbald was killed in the first affray. Captain Kirby, Lieutenant Fraser, Sergeant Walton, Colonel Troup, Captain Robertson—all the Englishmen that fell into the hands of the Revolutionaries were killed. Only thirty-two officers escaped the massacre and safely reached Naini Tal. In this way, the English power at Bareilly was made to end in six hours.

When the English flag was hauled down and the flag of freedom began to fly at Bareilly, the Subahdar of the Sepoy artillery, Bakht Khan, accepted the commandership of all the Sepoy troops. We will hereafter have occasion to refer to him at the time of the siege of Delhi. He delivered an enthusiastic oration to all the Sepoys as to their conduct after acquiring freedom and their duties in sustaining the newly established Swaraj.[1] And now, this Swadeshi brigadier went through the town in the carriage of the English brigadier. Behind him followed the new officers seated in the carriages of their English predecessors. Khan Bahadur Khan was accepted by acclamation as the ruler of Rohilkhand in the capacity of Subahdar of the Emperor. After all the houses of the English at Bareilly had been burnt down and looted, Khan Bahadur Khan ordered the imprisoned Englishmen to be brought before him. He had acted as judge under the English administration and knew English justice thoroughly. So, he appointed a court for the trial of the English criminals. Among them were the Doctor, the son-in-law of the Lieutenant-Governor of the North-Western provinces, the principal of the Government college at Bareilly, and the District Judge oC Bareilly. Only the day before, loyal Khan

1. Charles Ball's *Indian Mutiny*, Vol. I.

Bahadur Khan had been sitting beside them as a friend. Today, one was on the throne and the others in the prisoners' dock! The jury took their oaths as usual, and took their seats on the bench. The prisoners were charged with various crimes involving treason and were all sentenced to be hanged, and the six Englishmen were forthwith executed. As the Commissioner of Rohilkhand had escaped with his life, Khan Bahadur Khan issued a proclamation that the Feringhi commissioner had absconded. and a reward of one thousand rupees was offered to anyone who would bring him, dead or alive. After having thus firmly cemented his authority with English blood, Khan Bahadur Khan sent word to Delhi that Rohilkhand had become free. The Revolution began that morning at eleven, and before sunset, the messenger announcing Rohilkhand's freedom set out for Delhi!

The announcement that the whole of Rohilkhand had become free was not a vain boast. While the artillery at Bareilly was shaking the English power to pieces, English blood had already begun to flow at Shahjahanpur. This latter town is about forty-seven miles from Bareilly, and was the headquarters of the 28th infantry. The news of Meerut reached Shahjahanpur on the 15th of May. But since the Sepoys gave no indication whatever of their plans to the authorities, the 31st of May dawned there like other days, in peace and happiness. It being Sunday, the English were in church; but before their prayer was half-finished, the Sepoys ran towards the church! When the chaplain came out to see what the matter was, his hand was cut off and the massacre began. The city magistrate Ricketts fell while running. Labadoor was killed in the church itself. Only one batch of the Sepoys had come to the church while the other had been sent to the English cantonment. The latter had already started killing and burning. The assistant magistrate ran into the verandah for life, but was killed. Doctor Bowling began to address a few words to the Sepoys. The Sepoys, also, were listening to his words, but unfortunately, he called them, in the course of his speech, 'seditious.' In reply to this 'charge,' a bullet came whizzing and he dropped dead. The Revolutionaries who had gone to the church had only swords and sticks with them; so, now, they returned to the lines to take their rifles. In the meanwhile, some Englishmen, together with the women and children, with the help of some Sikh Sepoys and the native cooks and servants, ran to the house of a neighbouring Raja for safety. But the Raja explained to them his helplessness and asked them to 'move on.' The fugitives then went away towards Mahmadi. Thus, before the evening of the 31st of May, Shahjahanpur also became free.

To the north-west of Bareilly, at a distance of about forty-eight miles, is the district town of Moradabad. Here was stationed the 29th infantry regiment and half a batallion of native artillery. A fine opportunity came to test their loyalty, after the news from Meerut had gone there. The English authorities got information on 18th of May that some of the Meerut Sepoys had camped near Moradabad. The 29th regiment was ordered to make a night attack on them. In obedience to that order, the Sepoys attacked the Meerut Revolutionaries while they were asleep in the woods, but, however, in some ways or other, in spite of the determined attack under these conditions, all but one of them succeeded in escaping. The night was so dark! The English officers also thought that the darkness helped the Meerut Sepoys to escape though attacked under such odds. It has now transpired, however, that the attack was a mere sham; nay more, some of the Meerut sepoys, said to have escaped in the forest, actually slept that night, in the Sepoy lines at Moradabad! However for the time being the English had entire confidence in the 29th regiment on account of the loyal night-attack which it made. And nothing in its conduct was calculated to dispel it till the end of May.

On the morning of the 31st, however, all the Sepoys

began to form on the parade-ground. The English were about to ask the reason of their assembling thus without permission, when the Sepoys spoke authoritatively in the following manner :— 'The rule of the Company is at an end! Therefore, you should leave this country immediately and go away, or else you will be massacred! If you cannot go at once we will allow you two-hours to prepare for departure. But you must vacate Moradabad as soon as the two hours are over.' The Moradabad police also announced that thenceforth they would not obey the orders of the English, and the citizens supported them! When these three simultaneous notices were given, the English people at Moradabad—the judge, the collector, the magistrate, the surgeon and others—with their families, ran away from Moradabad without the least attempt at remonstrance. Any Englishmen who were found in Moradabad after the time limit had expired were killed. Commissioner Powell and others became Mahomedans and thus saved their lives. The Sepoys took possession of the treasury and all government property, and before sunset the green flag began to fly on Moradabad.[2]

There is also another district town, called Budaun, between Bareilly and Shahjahanpur. Mr. Edwardes was then collector and magistrate of the district. Since the English government came into Rohilkhand, the old Zemindars were being frightfully oppressed with heavy taxes and otherwise. Therefore, the big Zemindar and their tenants were very much disaffected. In fact, the land-tax in Budaun was so oppressive, that Edwardes himself knew that Budaun was perfectly ready, and only waiting for a chance to drive out the English; and for this reason he asked military help from Bareilly. But the situation in Bareilly, as has already been described, was not such that help could be sent to Budaun. However, a message from Bareilly came that troops under-

2. Charles Ball's *Indian Mutiny.*

European officers would be despatched on the 1st of June. At. this news Edwardes felt happy and on the 1st June sat with his eyes towards the road from Bareilly. He soon saw a government man coming galloping on towards Budaun. In the hope that he would be the forerunner of the succour which he expected, Edwardes hastily interrogated him. But in reply, instead of an assurance of help from Bareilly, he got the message that, at Bareilly itself, the English power was at an end! There were Sepoys kept at Budaun to guard the treasury, and Edwardes asked their head, 'Bareilly has become independent; what about Budaun?' The head replied that the Sepoys under him were loyal and that there was no cause for anxiety. But in the evening, the town of Budaun rose in revolt!

The Sepoys at the treasury, the police, and the leading citizens announced, by beat of drum that the English rule was at an end. Thus, the whole district went willingly into the hands of Khan Bahadur Khan. The Sepoys took the treasure and marched towards Delhi and all the English officers at Budaun began to run about in the forests at night. Under privations of food and clothing for weeks, hiding everywhere, sometimes in the stable of some villager, sometimes in deserted houses, English, collectors, and magistrates, and English women, were running about to save their lives. Some of them were killed, some died and some lived under the protection of kindly 'natives!'

In this manner, the whole province of Rohilkhand rose in a day! In Bareilly, in Shahjahanpur, in Moradabad, in Budaun, and other district towns, the military, the police, and the citizens issued Proclamations and deported the British Power in the space of a few hours! The English power was smashed and the Swadeshi government was put in its stead; British flags were torn down, and green flags began to fly in the court-house and police stations and offices. India assumed the role of ruler and England was put in the prisoner's dock!

This extraordinary transformation took place in a whole province in a few hours! What wonder that not a drop of Swadeshi blood was shed in freeing the whole of Rohilkhand? Instead of saying 'Rohilkhand is dependent,' all said 'Rohilkhand is free,' and the thing was done! On one day, unanimously, everywhere and at once, the police, the Sepoys, and citizens rose and drove away the few English officers in the district towns. No more pains than this were required to make the province free! A strong organisation of secret societies, and the swift and clever execution of the plan proposed, these were the two things which enabled Rohilkhand to free itself from the English and accept the rule of Khan Bahadur Khan.

All the Sepoys went away to Delhi to fight under the leadership of Bakht Khan, the head of the Bareilly above-mentioned. Then, Khan Bahadur Khan formed a new force to keep order in the province and the capital. Almost all citizens were formed into a militia. The civil departments were also organised and almost all the previous holders of offices were confirmed in their posts. And the chief posts, occupied previously by Europeans, were now given to Indians. The government land-tax was assessed in the name of the Emperor of Delhi. Courts of justice were opened as before and the former officers were retained. In short, there was no break in any department or its work on account of Revolution, except that, instead of Englishmen, the Chief officers were Indians. Khan Bahadur Khan personally wrote an account of the doings in his province to the Emperor, and the following Proclamation was posted throughout Rohilkhand. 'Residents of Hindusthan! The long-looked-for festival of Swaraj has arrived! Are you going to accept or refuse it? Are you going to take advantage of this great opportunity or are you going to let it go out of your hands? Hindu and Mahomedan Brethren! Be it known to all of you that, if these English are permitted to remain in India, they will butcher all and put an end to your religion! The residents of Hindusthan have so long been deceived by Englishmen, and have cut their necks with their own swords. So, now we must repair this sin of treachery to our country! The Englishmen will try, now also their old work of deception; they will try to incite the Hindus to rise against Mussalmans, and the Mahomedans to rise against the Hindus. But, Hindu Brethren! do not fall into their nets. It is hardly necessary to tell our clever Hindu brethren that the English never keep their promises. They are adepts in the art of trickery and deceitful imposture! They have all along been trying to root out all other religions on earth but their own! Have they not pushed aside the rights of adopted childern ? Have they not swallowed up the countries and kingdoms of our Kings? Who took away the kingdom of Nagpur? Who took away the kingdom of Lucknow? Who has trampled under foot both Hindus and Mahomedans? Mussulmans, if you revere the Koran, and Hindus, if you revere the cow-mother, forget now your minor differences and unite together in this sacred war! Jump into the battlefield fighting under one banner, and wash away the name of the English from India in streams of blood! If the Hindus will join hands with the Mahomedans in this war if they will, also, take the field for the freedom of our country, then, as a reward for their patriotism, the killing of cows will be put a stop to. In this holy war, he who fights himself, and he who helps another to fight, by means of money, will attain earthly and spiritual freedom! But, if anyone will oppose this Swadeshi war, then, he will strike at his own head and be guilty of the sin of suicide!'

Leaving Rohilkhand for the present to make its preparations for defending the Swaraji which it has got back, we shall go to Benares and Allahabad to see what is taking place there.

* * *

CHAPTER VII

Benares and Allahabad

ABOUT four hundred and sixty miles from Calcutta lies the the ancient city of Benares, on the banks of the sacred Ganges, shining in all her historical glory. Benares is surely the queen of all the cities that have been built by the side of the cool, clear and holy waters of the Bhagirathi. The rows of houses mounting higher and higher from the banks of the Ganges, the domes of tall temples with golden steeples glittering in the sun, the thick rows of trees gracefully raising their heads to the sky, the grand harmony of the innumerable bells sounded in the temples, and above all, the sacred temple of Vishweshvara, all these give a unique splendour to the city of Benares. The pleasure-seekers go there for amusement, the devoted for prayer, the Sanyasis for contemplation, and holy for salvation. All these achieve their various purposes in the holy city. For people who are satiated with pleasures of the world, holy Benares is a place of retirement, and for those unfortunates whose hopes and desires of happiness in this world are shattered by the jealousy and spite of cruel and wicked men, Benares and the sprays of the cool Ganges are a heaven of rest.

Thanks to the English, there was no want of such unfortunate men in 1857 coming to end their days of toil in that heaven of refuge and peace. Several Hindu and Mahomedan nobles, helpless since the palaces of Delhi and Poona and Nagpur etc. were closed to them, and the plundered royal families of Sikh and Mahratta princes, were telling their tale of woe in Benares in every temple and every Musjid. In this holy city, it is no surprise that the degradation of Swadharma and the destruction of Swaraj were being hotly discussed among both Hindus-and Mohomedans. The military station of the province was Sikroli, which was a short distance from Allahabad. There was the 37th infantry, the Ludhiana Sikh regiment, and a cavalry regiment; the artillery was purposely kept in the hands of Englishmen. Among the Sepoys, the desire to rise for Swadharma and Swaraj had been secretly fomented by various means. As the year 1857 approached, signs were evident that there was a tremendous agitation among the populace of Benares. The chief commissioner of the city, Tucker, Judge Gubbins, Magistrate Lind, and other civil officers, as well as captain Olpherts, Colonel Gorden, and other military officers had from the first taken great precautions for the safety of the English at Benares. For, in that city, the popular agitation often outstepped the limits of serecy and sometimes became almost uncontrollable. Purbhayyas openly shouted prayers in the temples, 'God, release us from the rule of the Feringhis.'[1] Secret societies were formed to ascretain the strength of the movement in other places. When the month of May came, there was quite a number of Mahomedan preachers in the Sepoy camp, proclamations were affixed to the city walls and public squares asking the people to rise,[2] and at last, things went so far, that Hindu priests began holding public prayer-meetings in the temples to pray for the destruction of the English and the victory for Swaraj. About the same time, the prices of grains went up enormously, and when English officers went about explaining how, according to the laws of political economy, the grain merchants would, in the end, be the losers if prices rose any more, people said boldly to their very faces, 'It is you who have made everything dear in our country; and now you come to lecture to us!' The English were so much terror-struck at this ugly manifestation of popular fury, even before the rising, that Captain Olpherts and Captain Watson themselves insisted that the English should vacate the place! At last Gubbins said, pathetically, 'I will go on my knees to you not to leave Benares!', and the plan of evacuation was temporarily postponed! And,

1. Report of the Joint-Magistrate, Mr. Taylor
2. *Red Pamphlet.*

indeed, why should it not be so ? for have not the Sikh nobles established a volunteer corps, now, to protect the English? And has not the descendant of Chet Singh whom Warren Hastings trampled down, also joined the English? When there is so much 'loyalty' yet, there is no reason why the English should leave Benares!

But, while the English of Benares, relying on the strength of this loyalty, had given up the idea of leaving Benares, terrible news began to come from the direction of Azimgarh. Azimgarh is situated about sixty miles from Benares, and the 17th native regiment was posted there. In this regiment, a tremendous agitation commenced since the 31st of May, and the magistrate, Mr. Horne had been delivering sweet speeches to pacify the Sepoys! But the days were gone when such empty lectures would have pacified soldiers. The 31st of May dawned, and the Barracks at Benares were set fire to, the sign for the other Sepoys in the province to rise. So, the rising must take place in the first week of June. To-day is the 3rd of June and good day. For, don't you see that the treasure of Gorakhpore, together with the treasure of Azimgarh altogether seven lakhs of Rupees is being sent to Benares? What better opportunity can you desire or expect?

The twilight of the 3rd of June was slowly changing to the darkness of the night at Azimgarh. All the English officers of Sepoy regiments were dining together at the club, and the women and children were playing and frolicking near by. Immediately, the party heard a tremendous noise. The English had by the first week of June learnt by heart the meaning of these sudden crashes. Even the sudden hush in the midst of their jollity looked like a mutual whisper of 'The Sepoys have risen!' Just then followed a thundering noise of drums and clarionets! Not a moment passed before the white people, with the picture of the Meerut events before their mind's eye, started running for dear life. Officers, women and children despaired of life. But the Azimgarh Sepoys, seeing this unfortunate people suffering a worse agony of death, relinquished all thoughts of revenge. They took charge of them in order to protect them from being harmed by stray Sepoys, and ordered them to leave Azimgarh at once. But what about some of the over enthusiastic Sepoys who had sworn to shed English blood on that day?[3] Well then, Lieutenant Hutchin- son and Quarter-Sergeant Lewis, at least your bodies must fall a prey to our bullets! Enough, let the rest run away alive. If they cannot run, we have no objection to their leaving in carriages! But the officers and their wives complained, 'Who will give us carriages now?' But the Sepoys replied gallantly, 'Do not be anxious; we will give you carriages.' With such extraordinary magnanimity, the Sepoys brought carriages, took away the handcuffs of the English, put them in carriages, and even gave a few Sepoys as guard; and thus, the whole caravan, including all the flags and other signs of English rule, started forth for Benares! On the other side, the treasure of seven lakhs, the English store of ammunition, the prison bearing the stamp of British rule, offices, roads, barracks—all fell into the hands of the Sepoys. And who was foremost in all this work? It was the police, the police whom the English trusted for information about a possible rising in order to save their lives! The police were as well undermined and as harmless on the surface as the Sepoys. When the appointed time came, they began by hoisting the flag of Swaraj on the English houses and prisons. Some Englishmen who did not find room in the carriages going to Benares ran away in the night to Ghazipur. When the sun rose the next day, it gazed in admiration at the marvellous transformation that had taken place during its short absence, and shone delightfully on the revolutionary flag flying at Azimgarh. The Sepoys, in the flush of victory, drew up a great military procession; and to the strains of martial music and banners unfurled marched away to Fyzabad.

---

3. *Narrative*, p. 58

Although the news of the freedom of Azimgarh reached Benares, there were hopes amongst the English that Benares at least would be safe. Sine the news of the Meerut rising, John Lawrence in the Punjab and Lord Canning in Calcutta had been straining every nerve to send English troops to the cheif centres of the Revolution. Since the northern army was busy in the siege of Delhi, there was perfect helplessness in the parts south of Delhi, and English officers sent pathetic requests to Calcutta, saying, 'For God's sake, send us Europeans!' We have already described how, by this time, Lord Canning had, called European troops from Bombay, Madras, and Rangoon, and, had retained in India the army destined for the now abandoned, invasion of China. Out of these troops, General Neill, with the Madras fusiliers had, about this time, arrived at Benares. The first succour of European troops, and that too under a bold, able, and cruel general like Neill, restored the confidence of the English, at Benares. Just then, the English army at Danapur also came to Benares. As there was extraordinary unrest in Benares, and there was clear evidence that the Sepoys were also concerned in the Revolutionary propaganda, the English thought that they should make an attempt to crush the Revolution in its embryo. From the first, the English were confident that this could easily be done by the combined strength of General Neill's troops, the Sikh nobles and soldiers, and the artillery. The news of Azimgarh' reached Benares on the 4th of June and it was decided after considerable discussion that the Sepoys should be disarmed before they rose. Accordingly, a general parade was ordered that afternoon.

Hearing this order, the Sepoys guessed the rest. They also got the secret information that the English held the artillery in readiness. When on the parade maidan the English officers gave them the order to lay down their arms, it was clear to them that they would be first disarmed, and then blown, from the mouth of guns. Therefore, instead of laying down, their arms, they attacked the neighbouring arsenal and fell on the English officers with fierce cries. Just then, there arrived on the scene the Sikh regiment intended to overawe them. The Sikhs were at the time possessed of such a spirit of loyalty to England, that they fell at the feet of the English and prayed to be given a chance of fighting the Sepoys, at least for a short time! A Hindu Sepoy attacked their commander Guise and he dropped down dead in an instant. Hardly had Brigadier Dodgson arrived to take his place, when a Sikh Sepoy, at the inspiration of the moment, shot him! But the other Sikhs, unable to forgive this great crime, hacked him to pieces! The Sikhs, were waiting for the reward of this loyal deed, when the English artillery opened fire on them all! Seeing the confusion going on between the Hindu and the Sikh Sepoys, the English authorities must have suspected that the Sikh regiment also had deserted them. On account of this misunderstanding, they opened fire on all indiscriminately. Now the unfortunate Sikhs had no other way left but to join the Revolutionaries! All the Indians, together, attacked the artillery thrice. This was about the only prominent occasion in the history of 1857 when Hindus, Mahomedans, and Sikhs, unitedly fell upon the English! But at that very moment, the Sikhs were making extraordinary efforts to expiate this sin! While the battle between the English and Sepoys was raging near the barracks, there was a fear that the townsmen would also rise.

In this fear, English officers, women, and children were running about in the streets. Then the Sikh Sirdar, Surat Singh, rushed forward to protect them. The treasury at Benares, besides, containing lakhs of Rupees, also contained the most valuable ornaments, wrested by the English from the late Sikh Queen. And this treasury was guarded by the Sikhs! It was here impossible that the Sikhs would not entertain the idea of taking hold of the treasury and taking back the ornaments belonging to their Queen who had been deported by the English. But their leader, the loyal Surat Singh, came forward and arranged that his co-religionists should not touch any of them! And, soon, lhe treasure was transferred to the guard of English soldiers. At lhis time, a Pundit, called Gokul Chand, had also joined the side .of the English. Even the Raja of Benares placed his all-his influence, his wealth, and his power—his everything at the feet of his lord—not Kashi Vishweshwara, but-the English! The Sepoys alone did not surrender in spite of the hot fire but retired fighting out of the field and spread all over the province.

No doubt, the English, following John Lawrence's plan in the Punjab, crushed the Benares rising in embryo; but the news that Benares had risen spread with lightning rapidity all over Northern India, and the different Revolutionary centres, which were waiting with their eyes directed towards Benares, began a series of risings. Javanpur rose on the 5th of June. When the news arrived at Javanpur that the Sepoys from Benares were coming there in all haste, the English officers began to deliver lectures on loyalty to the Sikh Sepoys stationed there. But these lectures had hardly ended when the tramp of Benares Sepoys was heard rapidly approaching! The few Sikh Sepoys at Javanpur who belonged to the Sikh regiment at Benares at once joined the Revolutionaries, and the whole was ablaze in the flames of the Revolution. Seeing this, the joint magistrate, Cuppage, again stood up to lecture, but, from the audience, came a whizzing bullet instead of applause, and the magistrate sahib fell down dead! Commanding officer Lieutenant Mara also fell shot by a bullet. After this, the Revolutionaries attacked the treasury and ordered all the English to clear out of Javanpur. Now, the Benares cavalry too entered the town. They had taken terrible oaths to kill every Englishman they met. Seeing an old deputy collector running, the Sowars ran after him. Some Javanpur men tried to mediate, Give the poor man his life, he has treated us very .kindly.' But the

Sepoys replied, I Can't help it; he is an English-man and must die!'[4]

Even in times of such excessive hatred, the Revolutionaries gave permission to Englishmen who surrendered, to lay down their arms and run away quietly. Making use of this permission, most of the Englishmen vacated Javanpur and departed in a short time. They hired boats on the banks of the Ganges to go to Benares. But, when in the middle of the stream, the boatmen looted them and left them on the sands! There, at Javanpur, the whole town came out, looted and burnt English houses, and mixed into dust all the signs of their power. The Sepoys took as much treasure as they could carry and marched towards Ayodhya. Then, the -old women of the town and paupers who had never had a rupee in their lives, were placed in charge of the remaining treasure. They helped themselves with it plentifully, and showered blessings heartily on Swaraj and the Revolution!

In this way rose Azimgarh on the 3rd of June, Benares on the 4th, and Javanpur on the 5th. The whole province of Benares was in flames. If the chief town of a province falls to the enemy, the Revolution, as a rule, loses strength in that province. For the whole province to depend on the capital in times of Revolution is regarded as a most dangerous fault in Revolutionary tactics. Mazzini says, 'Wherever our flag flies, that is our capital.' The capital must follow the Revolution and not vice versa. However accurately the map of a Revolution might have been drawn in the beginning, it is impossible that events will happen in a settled order during its course ; therefore, though it fails in the capital, the province must never give it up. Undoubtedly, Benares gave a very good illustration of this principle. For though the capital of the province, the city of Benares, fell into the grip of the English, in the province itself, the cyclone of the

4. Charles Ball's *Indian Mutiny*, Vol. I, page 245.

Revolution arose at once and enshrouded the whole atmosphere. Zemindars, peasants, Sepoys,—all began to consider English rule as unholy as cow's flesh! Even small villages, if they heard that an Englishman was within their boundaries, would beat and drive him out![5] Especially the people were so disgusted not only with Englishmen but with everything they had done, that they could not bear to see anything connected with the English before their eyes! They drove away Zemindars appointed by the English—good or bad—and put the old hereditary Zemindars instead. In one week disappeared, completely, English methods of taxation, their prisons, and their courts of 'justice'! The telegraph lines were cut off; the railway lines were dug up; behind every hillock and every bush were hidden villagers thirsting for English blood and money; and most of all, in village boundaries, warders were parading so that the English should get not only no provisions but not even any information! In these circumstances, the misery of the English knew no bounds! And still, the city of Benares had been frustrated in its attempt at freedom, and the Sepoys who rose had marched to Oudh! When the attempt of the 4th of June at Benares failed and wholesale arrests followed, an important fact came to light.[6] Only from such incidental events it is possible to understand how the machinery of the Secret Organisation had been worked. Three of the most active

5. 'At every successive stage of this military revolt, the fact of a deep-seated and widespread feeling of hatred and an unappeasable revengefulness for an assumed wrong is more plainly developed. The desire for plunder was only a secondary influence in producing the calamities to which the European residents of various places were exposed.'—Charles Ball's *Indian Mutiny*, Vol. I, page 245.

6. 'No sooner had it been known in the districts that there had been an insurrection at Benares, than the whole country rose like one man. Communications were cut off with the neighbouring stations and it appeared as if the Ryots and the Zemindars were about to attempt the execution of the project which the Sepoys failed to accomplish in Benares.—*Red Pamphlet* page 91.

agitators and a millionaire banker were arrested at Benares. When their houses were searched, some very violent letters written in cipher and received from the chief centre of the Revolutionary organistation, fell into the hands of the Government. The most important of these letters came from 'a head leader.' Their substance was as follows:- 'The Benares citizens should rise at once. Kill Gubbins, Lind, and other Englishmen. The money for this work will be given by the banker ....' When the house of this banker was searched, a store of 200 swords and rifles was discovered!

This is a short account of the rising of the province of Benares. Here the people never massacred Englishmen as at Meerut or Delhi. In the whole province not a single English woman was killed. Nay more, when national anger in the heart was demanding 'Revenge!', the people cordially bid farewell to the English there, themselves assisting sometimes to yoke the animals to their carriages. Look on this picture and on that which will now follow!

We do not say that the English should have sympathised with Benares in its attempts to attain Swaraj. But we do maintain that the English could never be justified in the atrocities that they committed in the Benares province, so totally incommensurable with the provocation they received either from the Sepoys or the people in that province. That English have never spared to hurl the most vile and lying abuses on the heads of the Revolutionaries, and hence, on all Indians, for their 'cruelties'. Now, when we shall have described below how a brave commander of the 'civilised' English army treated the people in the Benares province, and when it is said that all the facts that we shall give are from the accounts of the English themselves, it will be superfluous and unnecessary to add anything to it. Let the imperial world judge for itself.

After the Benares rising, General Neill organised detachments of the English and Sikhs to keep 'order' in the neighbouring villages. These bands used to enter villages occupied by defenceless peasants. Anybody whom they met was either cut down or hanged. The supply of those to be hanged was so great that one scaffold was soon found to be insufficient, even though worked day and night; therefore, long time of permanent scaffolds was erected. Though, on this long range, people were half killed and thrown away, still, there was a crowd of waiting candidates! The English officers gave up as hopeless the silly idea of cutting down trees and erecting scaffolds; so, thenceforth, the trees themselves were turned into scaffolds. But if only one man were to be hanged on each tree, what has God given so many branches to a tree for? So, 'natives', were left hanging on every branch, with their necks tightly roped to them. This 'military duty' and this Christian mission went on incessantly night and day. No wonder the brave English got tired of it. So the necessary seriousness in this religious and noble duty was mixed with a little humour for the sake of amusement. The rude manner of catching hold of peasants and hanging them on the trees was altered to suit the taste of art. They were first made to mount on elephants. Then the elephants were taken near a high branch, and after the necks were tied tightly to it, the elephants would be moved away.[7] Still, when the elephants were gone, the countless unshapely corpses used to hang on the branches and the English passers-by were bored with the unchanging monotony of the scene. Therefore, when 'natives' were hanged, instead of being hanged straight they were made into all sorts of figures. Some were killed in the shape of English figure '8' and some in the shape of '9'![8]

---

7. *Narrative*, page 69.

8. 'Volunteer hanging parties went out into the districts and amateur executioners were not wanting to the occasion. One gentleman boasted of the numbers he had finished off quite' in an artistic manner, with mango trees for gibbets and elephants as drops, the victims of this wild justice being strung up, as though for pastime, in 'the form of a figure of eight.' -Kaye and Malleson's *History of the Indian Mutiny*,. Vol. II, page 177.

But in spite of these various efforts in different directions, there were still hundreds of thousands of 'black' men living! Now, to hang all these would require an amount of rope that could not easily be had! The 'civilised' and 'Christian' nation of England was landed in this unthought-of difficulty. By the grace of their God Himself, they hit upon a new plan, and the first experiment was so successful that, thenceforth, hanging was abandoned for the new and scientific method. Village after village could thus be razed to the ground! After setting villages on fire, and keeping the guns in position to overawe them, how long will it take to burn thousands of natives? This setting fire to villages on all sides and burning the inhabitants, was so amusing to many Englishmen that they sent letters to England giving a humorous description of these scenes. The fires were so quickly and skilfully lighted that no villager had any chance of escape at all! Poor peasants, learned Brahmins, harmless Mussalmans, school children. Women with infants in their arms, young girls, old men, blind and lame, all were burnt in the mass of flames! Mothers with suckling babes also succumbed to these fires! Old men and women, and those unable to move away even a step from the fire, were burnt in their beds![9] And if a solitary man were to escape the fire, what then? One Englishman says in his letter, 'We set fire to a large village which was full of them. We surrounded them, and when they came rushing out of the flames, we shot them!'[10]

And was it only a solitary village that was thus treated? The English sent various detachments to the various parts of the province to burn villages. Out of the many batches, one officer, out of the many officers of a batch, says of one of his many outings, 'You will, however, be gratified to learn that twenty villages were razed to the ground!'

---

9. Charles Ball's *Indian Mutiny*, Vol. I, pp. 243-244.
10. Charles Ball's *Indian Mutiny*, Vol. I, pp. 243-244.

And all this account is only a summary of what has accidentally appeared in the works of English historians, who openly swear, 'it is better not to write anything about General Neill's revenge!'

Enough ! To add even a word more of our own to it, is to spoil this naked picture of the inhuman barbarity of the English!

And, therefore, your terror-struck eyes, look now towards the love-waves of the happy union of the Bhagirathi and the Kalindi rivers. The city of Allahabad, eternally laved by the calm, noble, and graceful waters at the union (Sangama), is situated about seventy miles from Benares. To the holy purity of the Prayaga-Kshetra, the vast fort built under the reign of Akbar gave an additional beauty. Allahabad is the key to all the important roads leading from Calcutta towards the Punjab and Delhi. Here, the fort of Allahabad has the imperial grace of a tall, strong, and great commander appointed to guard over the movements of these provinces. In the Revolution of 1857, he who held this fort held the key to the whole province. Such being the case, both sides made extraordinary efforts to acquire or retain the command of this most important fort. The plan of the Revolutionary' party was that the Sepoys as well as all the citizens of Allahabad should rise simultaneously. While the secret organisation was working up towards this goal, the Prayaga Brahmins had been of the greatest use in inspiring into the cities the ideals of Swaraj. These influential Hindu priests had been long sowing the seeds of the Revolutionary War, not only among the citizens of Allahabad, but also among the Hindu population in the whole province. With the traditional Hindu prayer at the time of the bath, was coupled the holy and religious prayers of the Revolution. Also, among the vast Mussalman population of the town, the Mullahs were very busy. Thousands of Mussalmans were only awaiting the signal with a firm determination to offer their blood on the battle-field in the cause of country and religion. The English, at the time, quite expected this. They seem to have been firmly convinced that all Mussalmans were their mortal enemies. The well known writer of the *Red Pamphlet* says, 'The Mahomedans, too, have shown that they cherish in their hearts the proselytising doctrines of their religion and that, as Christians, they will ever detest and take advantage of every opportunity of destroying Feringhis.' True as this is in general, it was more true still in this city. At Allahabad, the Moslems were more advanced than lhe Hindus. They were most prominent in the management of the machinery of the secret society. The efforts of Hindus and Mahomedans for the freedom of their country became, at last, so great that the very judges and Munsiffs of the Government joined the secret society![11]

Allahabad being the chief station of the province, the English should have taken extraordinrary precautions to guard the fort. But, on account of the ignorance till the beginning of May about the internal agitation in the whole country, the military preparations at Allahabad had been very bad. At Allahabad itself, the men who were spreading all around the fire of Revolution had kept such skilful secrecy that the Government did not think it necessary even to keep a single English soldier there! When the news from Meerut came, this important station had only the 6th Sepoy regiment and about two hundred men of a Sikh regiment from Ferozepur. Soon after, the Oudh cavalry was brought there, and the fort, together with the vast store of arms and ammunition. was kept entirely in the hands of the Sepoys. The English officers at the head of these Sepoys were strong in the belief that their Sepoys were very loyal. Especially the 6th regiment was undoubtedly the first in loyalty! One day, after hearing the news of Delhi, they sent word to their officers, 'Khavind', give us the order to go to Delhi and cut

---

11. Charles Ball's *Indian Mutiny*, Vol. I, page 268.

those mutineers to pieces. We are anxiously waiting.' This extraordinary symptom of loyalty was admired everywhere. From the Governor-General himself came the order to give public thanks to the 6th regiment, 'for this unparalleled faithfulness and loyalty.' Just then a citizen brought the information that the 6th regiment was secretly hand in glove with the Revolutionaries! Seeing this, the 6th regiment caught two revolutionary preachers and handed them over to the officers as a tangible proof of their loyalty. Now, why base suspicions? But, if the Government still suspects our loyalty, then the officers should come amongst us and see for themselves how pure our hearts are! The English officers came on the 6th of June into the lines and saw that their heart was indeed full to the brim with loyalty everywhere. Nay, some of the Sepoys actually ran up to the officers, embraced them heartily, and affectionately kissed them on both cheeks.[12]

And the same night, everyone of the Sepoys of the 6th regiment rushed out, sword in hand, shouting 'Maro Feringhi ko!' (Kill the Feringhis!).

While the Sepoys were moving heaven and earth in order that their plans might not be frustrated and they themselves might not be disarmed as at Benares, the English were removing their families into the fort for protection under the charge of the Sikhs and the cavalry. The news from Benares came to Allahabad on the 5th. On that day, there was so much agitation in the town that the English pointed some guns in the direction of the bridge towards the Benares side and closed the castle-gates. At. night, the English officers whom the Sepoys had only then affectionately kissed had assembled at the mess for dinner, when at a distance the terrible bugle began to blow! The sounds of the bugle, as it were, conveyed the information that the loyal 6th regiment had also risen!

12. *Narrative.*

That evening, the order had been given to the Sepoys to take the guns which were on the Benares bridge into the fort. But it seemed that the hitherto traditional loyal practice of obeying all the orders of the English was suddenly discontinued that evening; for, the Sepoys themselves issued an order that the guns shall be taken not to the fort but to the cantonment! The officers called the Oudh cavalry to punish the Sepoys for this extraordinary disobedience. The young and promising officers, Lieutenant Alexander and Lieutenant Harvard, got the cavalry in order and marched on the Sepoys. At this time the morning was just rising. When the cavalry was brought face to face with the insolent Sepoys, the English officers gave the order to attack and rushed boldly forward, hoping that thousands of horses would gallop behind them and trample down the handful of Sepoys. But, behold the cavalry refused to draw their swords against their own countrymen and did not move! At this, the Sepoys raised a tremendous shout of applause. Lieutenant Alexander was hit in the chest and fell down, his body was cut to pieces, and then all the Indian. Sepoys embraced each other and marched to the camp. Two horsemen had already galloped to the camp and given the news to their brethren in the camp. The scene that followed on the parade ground was unparalleled! Whenever an English officer gave a word of command, whiz came a bullet! Plunkett, Adjutant Steward, Quarter Master Hawes, Pringle, Munro, Birch, Lieutenant Innes, all fell down dead! The excited mass of humanity on, .the parade ground was now going about setting fire to the houses of Englishmen. When they heard that there were many Englishmen at the mess-house, an attack was made and every Englishman there was killed! It has been already said that the most important thing in Allahabad was the possession of the fort. In it were the Englishwomen and children and a vast store of ammunition, and it was entirely in the hands of the Sikhs. All the Sepoys; were now waiting for the firing of the gun, the settled sign that the Sikhs and the few Sepoys with them had also risen and driven. out the English.

But within the fort, the Sikhs showed their true treachery! They not only refused to take away the English flag from the fort but helped the English officcrs to disarm and drive out the few Sepoys that had found their way inside. The English express even now a sense of astonishment as to how the Sikhs stuck to them at that juncture. In half an hour, the extensive fort of Allahabad would have fallen into the hands of the Revolutionaries. That is to say, in half an hour, the backbone of English rule would have been smashed! But the Sikhs spent that half an hour in hacking their own countrymen and their mother country! Though the Sepoys in the fort rose again and, again Sikhs instead of joining them, disarmed them and drove them out at the orders of the English. And thus, the fort continued to be in English hands.

But Allahabad did not fortunately consist of these four-hundred Sikh traitors alone! As the time for the Sepoy rising; in the fort approached, the city of Allahabad rose also. The terrible shouts on the parade-ground were echoed from the town itself. At first, the houses of Englishmen were destroyed; then Sepoys and the people together broke the prison. No hearts could be more full of hatred against the English than those of the hundreds of prisoners there. So, as soon as they were released, they shouted hoarse cries and ran first to the quarters. where the English resided! The Revolutionaries had a special eye on railways and telegraphs! The railway officers, the lines, the telegraph poles and wires, engines, were all crushed to pieces! In spite of all the precautions taken by the English, some English-men fell into the hands of the Revolutionaries. They despatched them quickly! Then, the half Feringhis, who, relying on the protection of the English, used to treat the 'natives' with insolence, came in for their turn. Those who had been against the Revolution had their houses attacked. The lives of only those were saved who took oaths, 'We will fight against the English!' On the morning of the 17th, the Revolutionaries captured the treasury containing nearly thirty lakhs of Rupees. Then in the afternoon, a great Revolutionary flag was taken in procession and hoisted on the police station. And while the town and the fort were thus involved in the flames of Revolution, all the Sepoys and the citizens saluted it!

Almost at the same moment, the whole province of Allahabad rose like one man! Everywhere, things were altered so quickly that, after a short time, no one would have believed that the English had ever been ruling there! In every village the embroidered flag was hoisted and a stray Englishman was beaten away or killed and the roots of English rule were, as it were, uprooted! Oh, how superficial really are the roots of slavery in spite of the centuries of efforts made to drive them in! And, especially, an unnatural seed like that of slavery, how can it take root?

Most of the Talukdars in the Allahabad province were Mahomedans and their tenants were Hindus. Thus, the English had considered it impossible that these two would unite and that the whole mass of the people would rise against them. But, in this memorable first week of June, how many of such impossibilities were realised! Without even waiting to hear about the rising of the city of Allahabad, all the villages of the province rose simultaneously and declared their independence! Hindus and Mahomedans, because they fed on the same Mother's milk, rose together to strike blows at English rule! Not only the able-bodied Sepoys, but also old military pensioners enrolled themselves as national volunteers. Twisting their white moustaches, they would organise bands. Those who were too weak and old to do anything themselves would explain to younger men important points in military strategy and give advice on knotty points of tactics. Can we wonder that the noble ideals of

Swadharma and Swaraj which thrilled youth even in superannuated Sepoys had thoroughly permeated all classes of the population?[13] Shop-keepers, Marwaris, and Banias, even, took such an important part in that popular agitation that General Neill in his report makes a special reference to their hatred of the English! 'The majority of the chief merchants and others have shown the worst spirit towards us. Many of them have taken active part against us.' But, even after this, the English were boasting that the peasants would take their side. But Allahabad shattered this vain delusion to pieces! The peasants took a leading part in the Revolutionary War of 1857, as, perhaps, they never had done in, any political agitation before. Under the banner of their old Talukdars —not the new ones appointed by the English— the peasants threw their ploughs and ran with lightning speed to join the war for freedom. They had compared the English Company with their old kings; and they were firmly convinced that their own Swaraj was a thousand times better than the Feringhi Company's rule. Therefore, when the hour of consummation arrived, they began the work of revenge for the wrongs of decades. Everywhere, Swaraj was hailed with shouts of delight and even the children in the streets began to spit on slavery! It is true; even children spat, for children of twelve or fourteen would organise processions in the streets with the Revolutionary flag. The Engtish arrested such a procession and sentenced the little boys to death! Hearing this sentence, an English officer felt so ashamed that, with tears in his eyes, he came to the chief commandant and requested him to release the children. But it was of no use! And the children who committed the crime of raising

13. 'And with them went on not only the Sepoys who, a day cbefore, had licked our hands, but the superannuated pensioners of the 'Company's native army who though feeble for action, were earnest in -'their efforts to stimulate others to deeds of cowardice and cruelty.'- Xaye's *Indian Mutiny*, yol II, page 193.
See also *Red Pamphlet*.

the flag of independence were all publicly hanged! Will not the murder of these little angels fall back on the head of the assassins? The whole province shook with tremor; peasants and Talukdars, old and young, men and women, all arose with the cry, 'Har, Har,' to smite the chains of political slavery. 'For, not only in the districts, beyond the Ganges but in those lying between the two rivers, the rural population had risen and, soon, there was scarcely a man of eitter faith who was not arraigned against us.[14] And, for the success of these huge efforts of the whole populace and for the freedom of the Motherland, the Prayaga Brahmins and Mullahs began to send forth prayers unto Heaven!

It is difficult to find in Indian history another Revolution, so exciting, so quick, so terrible, and so universal! It was almost an unheard of thing in India that the powers of the people should awaken with a start and begin to shed pools of blood for the freedom of the country, even as thundering clouds shed rain. Besides, the sight of Hindus and Mahomedans fighting side by side for Hindusthan realizing their true interests and natural comradeship, was truly magnificent and inspiring. After having set up such a terrible whirlwind, shall we wonder that Hindusthan could not firmly keep it under control? The wonder is that Hindusthan could raise such a whirlwind at all. For, no nation has been able to control a Revolution suddenly. If we compare the Rising with the French Revolution, we will find that the inevitable incidents of any Revolution—like anarchy, confusion, outrage, selfishness, and looting, were not fewer there than in India. This was a vast experiment made by India. So we need not be surprised if, in the province of Allahabad where the experiment was so successful, there were, also, some mistakes and confusion. The hereditary feuds of Zemindars, the excessive poverty—the corollary of long slavery, and the enmity of centuries between Hindus and Mahomedans

14. Kaye's *Indian Mutiny*, Vol. II, page 195.

and the natural occasional misunderstandings during the efforts to extinguish it, all these made it impossible that there should not be anarchy for some time, when the first shock of the Rising was sensibly felt. After the Creation, there comes often the Deluge. Whoever wants a Revolution must be prepared to meet these difficulties in carrying it out!

However, when the week of looting and burning was over, all the dangers of anarchy melted away and the Revolution assumed some organised form in Allahabad. In that province, as in all places where a Revolution due to popular agitation takes place, the difficulty after the rising is that of finding capable leaders. This difficulty was soon got over in the city of Allahabad; for, an ardent lover of liberty, called Leakat Ali, soon became the leader of the Revolution. The only information we have about this extraordinary man is that he was a religious preacher among the weavers. Before the Rising, he had worked as a teacher in a school. He was adored by all people for the holy purity of his life. When the province of Allahabad became free, the Zemindars of the Chauvis Parganas brought this Moulvie in a few days to Allahabad and appointed him chief officer there. And he was proclaimed in great ceremony as the representative of the Emperor of Delhi. This Moulvie established his head-quarters in a fortified garden called Khusru Bagh and began the work of organising the Revolutionaries in the province. He soon put all the affairs of state in good order. He did not stop with merely saying that he was the Subahdar of the Emperor but he continued to send, to the last, reports of the events in Allahabad to the Emperor of Delhi.

The first thing that Moulvie Leakat Ali had to do was to capture the fort of Allahabad. He had begun the attempts to organise and prepare the army that collected under him and direct an attack on the fort, when the news came that General Neill was marching from Benares towards Allahabad. Even now, if the four hundred Sikhs in the fort had come to their senses, the whole fort, together with the guns, arms and ammunition, would have fallen to the Revolutionaries without a shot being fired ! General Neill was so afraid of this that he marched with his English troops in haste to Allahabad. Neill arrived there on the 11th of June. He had no hope that the Sikhs would protect the fort and its English occupants till his arrival. He was therefore, overjoyed when he saw the English flag still flying on the walls of the fort. He, immediately, kept the English soldiers to garrison the fort and sent the loyal Sikhs out to do the fighting. It is clearly seen from this how little faith Neill had in the Sikh Sepoys. Though Neill had no faith in the Sikhs, the Sikhs had complete faith in him; for, they refused to join the Revolutionaries even after this insult, and consented to burn the neighbouring villages. On the 17th of June, the English army began to push its way into the town. Describing the incidents, the Moulvie, in his report to the Emperor, says, 'Of the traitorous sinners who have joined the enemy, some have spread the rumour that the English are going to blow up the whole town. The people have left their homes and have announced that they are going away in order to save their lives! Therefore, the whole town is being deserted in spite of assurances of protection.' As this unfortunate report of the Moulvie had set out on its way to Delhi, the English attack on Khusru Bagh began. The Revolutionaries defended the place that day; but the Moulvie soon saw that it was madness to attempt to hold Allahabad from a dilapidated garden while the fort was in the hands of the enemy. So, on the night of the 17th he left for Cawnpore with all his followers. The next day, on the 18th, the English re-entered Allahabad together with the 'loyal Sikhs.'

Though Allahabad followed the example of Benares and fell in the English hands, the Revolutionaries did not lose courage at all. Seeing the enemy thus safely protected in the chief forts. the people of the province were all the more enraged and every village put up entrenchments and prepared to make a stand. The days were gone when such determined people could be seduced by bribery. The war was a war of principle, and though Neill offered rewards of thousands of Rupees for the heads of even minor leaders, the penurious peasants themselves were unwilling to help him. An English officer of the time has expressed his surprise at this noble stand for the sake of principle. He writes of one village : 'The magistrate offered a reward of one thousand rupees for the head or the person of the leader of rebels who is well-known to the natives; yet, such is their ha tred towards us that no one would give him up![15] Let alone betraying the leaders, it was considered, at that time, a great sin even to sell for money any commodity to the English. If anyone did commit that offence, he was immediately given a harsh punishment by the community. 'Anyone who had worked for the Europeans, these murderers killed. So, if the population is to a man against us, we should stand but a bad chance. A poor baker was found with his hand cut off and his nose slit, because he had sent in bread to us.' This is the report of the 23rd of June. Simply because the baker gave bread to the English, the villagers cut off his hands and nose. When the national and armed boycott was proclaimed, the misery of the Feringhis knew no bounds. It is true they had taken the fort of Allahabad. But, they found it impossible to move even a step one way or the other. They could get neither oxen, nor carts, nor even medicine! No *dolies* for sick soldiers and no men to lift them! There were sick men lying about in various places. Their shrill cries were so fearful that some English women died by hearing them. The days were hot. And the trick of the: Revolutionaries in rising in June, so that the Englismen might die- of heat also, now came to be understood. All Englishmen were busy bathing their heads in cold water? Besides, the provisions always fell short. Nobody could be found who would sell even a grain of corn to the English. 'Up to to-day,

15. Charles Ball's *Indian Mutiny*, Vol. I

we have had little to eat; indeed, I could not have fed a dog with my yesterday's breakfast!' So writes an officer from Allahabad! This heat and this starvation brought an cholera in the English camp. To add to the troubles, English soldiers regularly started getting drunk! All discipline was gone. These drunkards began to disobey Neill's orders to such an extent that he wrote to Canning that he had decided to hang a few of them! The English army, beset with these numerous difficulties, was chained to Allahabad city. Though urgent messages requesting help were coming frequently from the English of Cawnpore, a dashing warrior like General Neill, had to see the first of July dawn in Allahabad itself!

It is important to note that General Neill and his fusiliers had been brought from Madras. If, at this time, there had been even a slight tremor of a Revolution towards Madras, the English would have been unable to bear the strain even for a day. For, though the resolute Indians of Allahabad had all but succeeded in the cleverly organised plan of shutting up English soldiers in the forts, the English had no real reason to be disheartened. For Madras, Bombay, Rajputana, the Punjab, Nepal, and other parts were still lying dead weights hampering the national movement. When some of these parts did begin to move, they fell on their own countrymen, like demons. Were not thousands of Sikh Sepoys ready to help the English in Benares itself? However whatever the others might do, the Brahmin priests and Mullahs of Prayag, Talukdars and peasants, teachers and students, shopkeepers and customers-in spite of various difficulties, in spite of the want of a great military leader who could lead them to battle, in spite of defeat, discouragement, and anarchy—showed a confirmed and inveterate hatred of slavery. Of the great sacrifices, including the sacrifice of life itself, made by these noble patriots for the lofty ideals of Swaraj and freedom, History will ever be proud!

For, all these patriots were actually paying a very heavy

price for rising against English slavery. It is difficult to find a parallel, even in the history of savages, to the cruel brutality which Neill showed in the province of Benares and Allahabad!

We do not write this as a figure of speech; anyone will be convinced that what we have said is nothing but the bare truth, if he reads the accounts given by the English themselves. We had given some account of the inhuman conduct of the British in Benares. Here, we extract a letter of a brave and generous Briton to describe his achievements in Allahabad. 'One trip I enjoyed amazingly; we got on board a steamer with it gun, while the Sikhs and the fusiliers marched up to the city. We steamed up throwing shots right and left till we got up to the bad places, when we went on the shore and peppered away with our guns, myoid double-barrel bringing down several niggers. So thirsty for vengeance I was. We fired the places right and left and the flames shot up to the heavens as they spread, fanned by the breeze, showing that the day of vengeance had fallen on the treacherous villains. Every day, we had expeditions to burn and destroy disaffected villages and we have taken our revenge. I have been appointed the chief of a commission for the trial of all natives charged with offences against the government and persons. Day by day, we have strung up eight and ten men. We have the power of life in our hands and, I assure you, we spare not. A very summary trial is all that takes place. The condemned culprit is placed under a tree, with a rope round his neck, on the top of a carriage, and when it is pulled off he swings.'[16] Neill burnt old men; Neill burnt middle-aged men; Neill burnt young men; Neill burnt children; Neill burnt infants; Neill burnt babies in cradles; and Neill has burnt babies suckling at the breasts of their mothers! Kaye admits that six thousand Indians were

16. Charles Ball's *Indian Mutiny*, Vol. I, page 257.

done to death at the place above mentioned. Hundreds of women, young girls, mothers, and daughters have been burnt alive by Neill, without even counting their number. We make the statement in the presence of God and in the presence of all humanity! If anyone has the slightest proof against it, let him come forth boldly for a moment at least before the world and God!

And what was the crime all these had committed? The crime was that they were ready to bear all these for the sake of their country's freedom!

Still the massacre of Cawnpore has to come! Neill's barbarities were not a revenge of Cawnpore, but the Cawnpore bloodshed was the result of and revenge for Neill's inhuman brutalities!

Neill has killed as many people in Allahabad alone as all Englishmen, women and children who had been killed throughout India in the Revolution, put together! And tens of such Neills were conducting such massacres in hundreds of places! For every Englishman, a whole village has been burnt! God will not forget this and we will, also, never forget this!

And what do English historians say about this? They generally omit this, and that too, ostentatiously! If they do give some of the details, it is to prove how bold and brave Neill was. What greater mercifulness than such timely cruelty? Some say that this cruelty on his part shows the great love of humanity in Neill's heart! Kaye, no doubt, suspects that the Cawnpore massacre were a result of this barbarous revenge; but, he says, it is natural that the leonine qualities of the British people should come out on account of the insolence of the 'natives,' Kaye does not write a single word against Neill for this cruelty. But, instead of allowing man to discuss this question, he leaves it to God! When talking of Nana Sahib, his pen puts even Obscenity to shame! Charles Ball praises Neill inordinately. But what does Neill himself say?

He says, 'God grant I may have acted with justice! I know I have acted with severity but under all the circumstances, I trust for forgiveness. I have done all for the good of my country, to re-establish its prestige and power, and to put down this most barbarous, inhuman insurrection.' The definition of Patriotism in England is unique indeed!

Another historian, Holmes, says: 'Old men hid done us no harm; helpless women, with suckling infants at their breasts, I, felt the weight of our vengeance no less than the vilest malefactors. But, to the honour of Neill, let it be remembered that, to him, the infliction of punishment was not a delight but an awful duty.'[17]

We fervently hope that impartial history, by examining the above extracts, and the true God-not Neill' God-will look more sympathetically and forgivingly at the few massacres by the Revolutionaries than at these wholesale slaughterings by the English. Are massacres in the cause of freedom justified? This question 'should be left to God!' 'Let God forgive me, for what I am doing, I am doing to win national independence for my country!' —this sentence would fit the mouth of Nana far better than that of Neill! It was the Revolutionaries who were 'fighting for their country,' not Neill! And, if anyone performed a 'duty' in massacres, it was the Revolutionaries alone, fired with the desire of fighting for Swaraj and Swadharma and burning for vengeance for all the oppressions that the Motherland suffered for a hundred years!

But, of what use is all this philosophy now? Neill has sowed the seeds of cruelty and horror in Allahabad. Their abundant crops are already rising in the fields of Cawnpore. Let us, then, go towards Cawnpore to reap them in their full harvest!!

* * *

17. Holmes's *Sepoy War*, page 229-230

CHAPTER VIII

Cawnpore and Jhansi

LET us now leave aside, for a moment, the bloody stream of the Revolutionary Ganges flowing about violently on the fields of Northern India with the holy desire of saving our forefathers from the bottomless pit of slavery, and turn to the events happening at its source at Haridwar. About the time of the Meerut rising, there were assembled a larger number of Revolutionary leaders in the palace of Nana Sahib than could be found, at the time, in the palace of Lucknow, in the Subah at Bareilly, or even at the Dewan-i Khas palace at Delhi. The Revoiution of 1857 was conceived in the palace at Brahmavarta. It was there that the embryo also took a definite shape. And if the birth also had taken place at Brahmavarta, the Revolution would surely not have- been so short-lived. But, before complete development, the thunder at Meerut brought the Revolutionary child into being, unfortunately before its time; it was not, however left to its fate; but strenuous preparations were made in the palace at Brahmavarta to sustain and nourish it even under such adverse circumstances.

At the place of honour sat the proud and noble form of Nana Sahib, the very incarnation of the Revolutionary Spirit. His brothers, Baba Sahib and Bala Sahib, and his nephew Rao Sahib, were there, ready to sacrifice their lives, wealth, and comfort for the fulfilment of their leader's noble objects. Beside these sat the man who, from the low station of a menial servant, had risen in his master's favour by means of his industry and ability, the man who had studied the politics and warfare of Europe, determined to utilise that knowledge in the holy war of liberating his country from slavery. This was none other than Azimullah Khan. There also sat the lightning Queen of Jhansi, aiding now the experience of the Revolutionary leaders with her magnificent intuition and inspiring them with her own unbounded love of country and honour. But in this historical meeting, who is the warrior over there, sharpening his sword in the direction of the armoury ?

Readers, that hero in the armoury is the celebrated Mahratta Tatia Tope. He is the last valiant Mahratta warrior of the school of Shivaji. There are many people who are brave, but the valour of this last Mahratta hero was the sword incarnate drawn by the Mother herself for her freedom.

Tatia Tope was born in about 1814. His father's name was Pandurang Bhat. Pandurang Bhat had eight sons and of them, the second was called Raghunath. It is this Raghunath who shines as the brilliant star of liberty in the galaxy of the heroes of Hindusthan. Pandurang Rao Tope was a Deshasth Brahmin and was the head of the charity department under the late Bajirao , Peshwa at Brahmavarta. In the verandah, Nana Sahib, the Jhansi Ranee and Tatia Tope played the games of their childhood! Nana Sahib and Tatia Tope were intimate friends from childhood. In childhood, these two were trained in the same school, fitted to perform the heroic deeds which they did in the great event of their later life. They had read the Ramayana and the Mahabharata together; they had read together the accounts of the war-like deeds of the Mahrattas, and their young hearts had throbbed together at the noble inspiration which the stories of Hindu heroism awoke.

Towards the end of April, Nana Sahib and Azimulla Khan had travelled through all the chief towns in Northren India to give the necessary unity to the work of the secret organisation. They were now waiting for the appointed time. Suddenly on the 15th of May, the news of the rising at Meerut and the subsequent freedom of Delhi came to Cawnpore. At this news of the premature rising, there was not the least apparent agitation in the palace of Brahmavarta. In a Revolutionary organisation are bound up together thousands of separate parts; it is unavoidable that some should move too quickly and others too slowly; some at the appointed signal and others at the sudden impulse of the moment. The palace at Brahmavarta at once understood the situation and decided to turn the Meerut rising to advantage. But to take such an advantage, which was the better course? To follow Delhi at once or wait till the first week of June according to the original plan? Of these two alternatives, the latter seemed preferable and, accordingly, the machinery at Brahmavarta continued to work secretly.

Cawnpore was, for a long time, an important military station of the English. In Cawnpore, there were the 1st, 53rd and 56th Sepoy infantry, and a regiment of Sepoy cavalry—altogether three thousand Indian soldiers. The cavalry was wholly in the hands of the English and, besides, they had about a hundred English soldiers. The chief officer of the whole army was Sir Hugh Wheeler. Sir Hugh Wheeler was an old and very popular commander among the Sepoys. He had done good service in the Sikh and in the Afghan compaigns. The Government knew fully well that the Sepoys were very much attached to him and nobody entertained any serious suspicion that secret societies were working among the Sepoy lines at Cawnpore.

About the 15th of May, a peculiar agitation was to be seen in the whole of Cawnpore city. At the news of the doings of the Meerut Sepoys, their Cawnpore comrades had lost their usual stolidity and looked perturbed. But the English authorities heard the news only on the 18th. As the telegraph communication to Delhi was cut, Sir Hugh Wheeler sent scouts to obtain correct information as to the extent of the disaffection These scouts met on their way a Sepoy coming from Delhi, but he flatly refused to give any information to the Feringhis! It is a great mystery to English officers how, in 1857, the Sepoys quickly got from distant points news of which the English authorities, with their telegraph system, were ignorant.[1] The Sepoys had no necessity of learning of the Meerut rising after it took place; for, even a day before the events, human telegraphs had conveyed to them all detailed information! It is only after the English, at last, got the news of the Meerut rising that they began to think seriously about the secret agitation among the Cawnpore Sepoys. But Sir Hugh Wheeler was still confident that the agitation was due to the extraordinary nature of the news that arrived from Meerut and would gradually subside. But there in the city of Cawnpore and in the Sepoy lines, everyone saw clearly that the days of English rule were over. Hindus and Mahomedans held big meetings; the Sepoys held secret conferences; school-masters and students discussed the rising; and everyone in the shops of the bazaars openly thought out plans. The fire of popular indignation, so far kept secret, now burst forth openly. People openly discussed in the streets about driving out the English and the Sepoys refused to obey all orders except those given by their Swadeshi superiors.[2] When an English lady went to the bazaar to make purchases, in the usual proud and haughty manner, a passer-by came up to her and said with a frown, 'Enough of this haughtiness now! You should understand that you will soon be driven out of the bazaars of Hindusthan !' This was the rude awakening first experienced by the English. Seeing that it would be folly to keep quiet under these conditions, Sir Wheeler began to make preparations for the defence.

His first thought was to select a place of refuge in case of danger. He selected one near the Sepoy lines, to the south

1. 'Indeed one of the most remarkable features of the mutiny has been the certainty and the rapidity with which the natives were made aware of all important movements in distant places. The means of communication is chiefly by runners who forwarded messages from station to station with extraordinary celerity. '—*Narrative,* page 33.

2. Nanak Chand's Diary.

of the Ganges. He fortified it by entrenchments, erected places for mounting guns, and even ordered a supply of provisions to be stored there. But, it is said that the Indian contractor, without Sir Wheeler's knowledge, put a far smaller quantity of provisions than ordered for. Sir Wheeler and the English officers believed that, even if the Sepoys rose, this place would save them from any material damage. For they would follow the example of their camrades in other places and march towards Delhi and would leave the English quietly to go down the Ganges and join the army at Allahabad! Sir Wheeler did not rest with the preparation of this fortified place as a protection for the English in case of a rising but he also sent urgent letters to Sir Henry Lawrence at Lucknow to send reinforcements! But such was the strength of the Revolutionary propaganda at Lucknow that Lawrence was crying for reinforcements himself! However, he immediately sent towards Cawnpore eighty-four English soldiers, the English artillery under Lieutenant Ashe, and some cavalry. There was nothing special in these preparations which Sir Wheeler made for the defence of the English. But the third remedy which he sought for removing the danger to the English power was one which now appears very extraordinary and yet gives a true idea of the skill in the Revolutionary organisation of the time. This was the request made by Sir Wheeler to the Raja of Brahmavarta to come to save Cawnpore! The news of Meerut had produced an extraordinary agitation among the ranks of the Sepoys and the common people in the bazaars, but the palace of Brahmavarta appeared as quiet, peaceful, and unruffled as before. It was impossible to have discovered even a ruffle on its surface that would betray the tremendous internal agitation. The movement among the Cawnpore troops at least put Sir Wheeler on his guard. But, he never for a moment entertained any adequate suspicion that Raja of Brahmavarta would go against him. The man whose crown the English had trampled under foot only a short time before, the Naga snake whom they had only just before enraged by wilfully treading on his hood, from that man the English now asked for protection in their hour of need! The English were not altogether mistaken in this procedure. Nana Sahib was 'a gentle Hindu,' and how many cowardly Hindus are there not in India who are harmless and cringing even when trodden under foot by the English? In the pious belief that Nana Sahib was also one of them, Sir Wheeler invited his help. What better chance could there be for the Prince of Brahmavarta ! He entered Cawnpore on the 22nd with two guns, three hundred private Sepoys, infantry and cavalry! There was a large number of civil and military officers of the English at Cawnpore. Nana encamped the very midst of these English people. Now it was certain that, if there was a revolt at Cawnpore, the treasury would be attacked. How best to guard it ? Of course by entrusting it to Nana Sahib! Soon two hundred of Nana's Sepoys began to keep guard over it. Collector Hillersden profusely thanked Nana Sahib and Tatia Tope and it was even proposed that the English women and children should, if necessary, go for safety to the Nana's palace at Brahmavarta!

Here was Mahratta policy! That Nana should be invited with his troops to Cawnpore to 'protect' the English and to fight against his countrymen rising for freedom, that he should take his head-quarters in the English camp, that a treasure of lakhs of Rupees should be entrusted to him for better keeping and, above all this, that the English should thank him for his services! Here is Mahratta policy! Nana paid the English in their own coin. And all this, only a week before the great upheaval! From this it is evident how in 1857, the English were long left groping the dark and then pushed down the precipice! The knowledge that independence was the goal and War the means was clearly given to the general populace at that time; but, as to who were the leaders, what was the day of rising, what were the chief centres, all this was kept so secret that not only the English even the rank and file of the Revolutionary society knew not much about it. The heads of the Central Secret Society and their faithful servants were the only men who had detailed information. This brings out the meaning of what we have said before that there was a secret committee in every regiment. The letter which fell into English hands at Benares was signed only 'From a great leader.' The responsible leaders conducted themselves in a manner suited to the work of the Secret Society. Even on the day before the rising, the English had not any adequate inkling about the plans of Emperor Bahadur Shah, Nana Sahib, or the Queen of Jhansi! And, amongst all these, the palace of Brahmavarta kept the closest and strictest secrecy. The historian Kaye says: 'Nana had not studied in vain the history of Shivaji, the founder of Mahratta Kingdom!'

The chief the secret societies of Cawnpore was the house of Subahdar Tikka Singh. Another place of meeting for the secret societies was the house of the Sepoy leader Shams-ud-din Khan. At these secret meetings, two faithful servants of the Brahmavarta palace household, Jwala Prasad and Mahomed Ali, used to attend on behalf of Nana Sahib. Subahdar Tikka Singh and Jwala Prasad—both bold, freedom-loving, and passionately sincere patriots—soon got a hold on the assembly and the whole army had unanimously sworn to obey their orders. So, the voice of Subahdar Tikka Singh was the voice of the whole army. It was extremely necessary that such a leader and Nana Sahib should personally meet and settle important points. Besides, the settled programme had become useless on account of the Meerut rising and the consequent confusion. It was, therefore necessary to alter that programme to suit the changed circumstances, and for this it was decided that Tikka Singh and Nana should meet.[3] In their first meeting, a long discussion took place. The Subahdar gave assurances that

3. Forrest's *State Papers* and Trevelyan's *Cawnpore*

both Hindus and Mahomedans were ready to rise unanimously for Swadharma and Swaraj and were waiting only for Nana's orders. After this, it was settled that another meeting, more secret and of longer duration, should be arranged to settle the minor details, and the Subahdar returned. On the evening of the first of June, Nana Sahib, accompanied by his brother Bala Sahib and his minister Azimullah Khan, came down to the banks of the sacred Ganges. There stood Subahdar Tikka Singh and the heads of the Secret Society awating him. The whole company then got into a boat. They entered the waters of the holy Ganges; everyone there took an oath, with the holy water of the Ganges in his hands, that he would participate in the bloody war for his country's liberty. Then followed a deliberation of two hours in which the whole of the future programme was definitely decided upon, and the company returned. Their secrets were known to the sacred Ganges alone and in her hands they were safe! But this much is well know that on the following day, Shams-ud-din came to the house of his beloved Azizan and told her that within two days the Ferinighis would be destroyed and India would be free! Shams-ud-din did not give this news of freedom to her as empty bravado; for the heart of this beauty yearned as much for India's freedom as that of her brave lover. Azizan was a dancing girl very much loved by the Sepoys; she was not one, however, who sold her love for money in the ordinary market, but in the field of freedom it was given as a reward for the love of country. We will soon show further on how a delightful smile from her beautiful face encouraged fighting heroes and how a slight frown from her dark eyebrows hastily sent back to the field cowards who had come away.

While the plans of the Revolutionaries were thus ripening, the terror in the English camp was beyond all description! Sir Wheeler sighed with relief when he got reinforcements from Lucknow and when the treasure and the arsenal had been put under the charge of Nana Sahib. But the English population had lost all courage. The 24th of May was the great *Id* festival or the Mahomedans. The English in every town apprehended a rising on that day. But the leaders in 1857 were not such fools as to rise on such an easily marked day. To keep peace ostentatiously on a day when a rising is expected by the enemy as certain and to burst forth on a day when the enemy thinks there is no chance whatever of trouble, is one of the chief means of carrying a Revolution to success. Therefore, even in Cawnpore, on the day of the *Id* festival, there was not the slightest disorder. The English, were so much frightened that morning that Sir Wheeler telegraphed to Lucknow, 'There will be rising to-day inevitably'! But when, on the evening of the festival, the Mahomedans paid and received visits as usual, Sir Wheeler was reassured. On the day of the birth of Queen Victoria, the usual salute of guns was not fired in the apprehension that the Sepoys would be unnecessarily disturbed by the noise! Some English officers were heartily grieved that, on the birth-day of Victoria, a salute dared not be fired in her honour; but what could the poor fellows do? If we look at the place erected by the English as a refuge in case of a rising, as has been said before, we shall at once understand how helpless the condition of the English had become! Someone would purposely set up a rumour that the Sepoys had risen, as in the story of the wolf and the shepherd-boy, and caravans of the English would begin to run through the streets with all possible speed! An English officer writes: 'Whilst I was there, buggies" palkies, gharries and vehicles of all sorts drove up and discharged cargoes of writers, tradesmen, ladies, women suckling infants' ayahs and children—and officers too! —In short, if any insurrection took or takes place, we shall have no one to thank but ourselves, because we have shown to the natives how very easily we can be frightened and when frightened, utterly helpless!' The cowardice exhibited in this conduct of the English, as this officer says, was thoroughly understood by the populace. When the entrenched place was being erected, had not Azimullah said the same to a Lieutenant in a jocular vein? Azimullah Khan, in his usual sweet voice, asked the lieutenant, 'Well, Sahib, what are you going to call this new building which you are constructing here?' The lieutenant replied, 'Really, I have not yet thought about it.' The smart Azimullah, with a wink in his eye, retorted, "Well, you can just call it 'the castle of despair.'"

One day towards the evening, a young gallant Englishman, under the influence of drink, shot a Sepoy. The shot missed but the Sepoy brought a case against the culprit. According to usual custom, the soldier culprit was declared not guilty and released, the reason given being that the gun went off while the accused was intoxicated! This decision was the customary one, but alas! the times had changed![4]

At this insult, the whole Lashkar began to mutter among themselves, 'Alright, our guns will also soon go off!' This became an exciting catch-word among the Sepoys. When they saw each other, they would say, 'Well, now our guns are to go off, aren't they?' The sarcastic greeting became common in the army. However, they decided to suppress their anger for the time and not to be hastened into a premature rising as at Meerut.

To add fuel to the fire, the dead bodies of an Englishman and his wife were carried down the Ganges to Cawnpore, This testimony of the rising, in a city somewhere up the river, began to hold a terrible conversation with the city of Cawnpore. Oh! Ganges, how many more of the impure loads

---

4. Trevelyan says :— 'The Sepoys, familiar as they were with the brutality of low Europeans and the vagaries of military justice would at a less critical season have expressed small surprise either at the outrage or the decision. But, now, their blood was up and their pride awoke, and they were not inclined to overrate the privileges of an Anglo-Saxon or the sagacity of the military tribunal.'-*Cawnpore*, page 93.

have you to carry before you send them to their ocean home! The English had now been so often deceived by the cry of 'The wolf! the wolf!!' that they were frequently slumbering when the wolf was really to come. On the 1st of June, Sir Hugh Wheeler. wrote to Lord Canning, 'Unrest and danger are no more. Not only is Cawnpore safe, but I am soon going to send help to Lucknow!' And the white troops which had come from Allahabad actually started for Lucknow! And that, on the 3rd of June! What a wonder that the plot—in which three thousand Sepoys and the whole city of Cawnpore, not excluding the dancing-girls, participated—should be kept sealed from the English and their auxiliary dogs like Nanak Chand!

The seal was finally broken on the night of the 4th of June. According to the general programme, by dead of night, three shots were fired and the buildings already agreed upon were set fire to! This was the sign that the time for bloodshed, destruction, and death had begun. In the beginning, Tikka Singh's horse leapt forth and, immediately, thousands of horses started galloping at a smart pace. Some started to burn English houses and stables, some ran to fetch other regiments, and some went to capture the military flags and banners. When the old Indian, Subahdar-Major, in whose charge the flags were, began to dispute with the Revolutionaries, a blow of the sword on his head sent his corpse rolling on the ground.

'Subahdar Tikka Singh's Salaams to the Subahdar of the 1st infantry regiment. He asks the reason why the infantry is delaying when the cavalry had already risen against the Feringhis?' Two galloping cavalrymen gave this message, and the whole of the 1st regiment came out with cries of *Victory*! and *Country*!— *Din*! and *Desh*! At this, their officer, Colonel Ewart, said, 'Oh! my children (Babalog), what is this? This disgraces your loyal character! Wait, children, wait!' But the Sepoys did, not waste their time in listening to him. In a moment, the whole regiment marched in military order to join the cavalry, and then the whole army together marched to the music of war-songs to the Nana's camp at Nabobganj! Nana's Sepoys were ready at the Nabobganj treasury. They embraced their comrades and, at once, the enormous treasure and the great arsenal fell into the hands of the Revolutionaries! While this was going on at Nabobganj, there were still two regiments left behind at Cawnpore. The English immediately called them on parade in older to keep them in their hands. As the English had the artillery in their hands, the two regiments together with their officers stood in arms on the parade ground all night. At daybreak, the English officers satisfied themselves that these regiments at least were not rebellious. They were permitted to go back to their lines and the officers also began to leave. Now the Sepoys saw a good chance. A couple of officers whispered something from a corner, and suddenly, one of them rushed forward and shouted, 'God is on the side of Truth! Brethren, come arise!' At this order, swords began to flash on all sides, and, seeing the crisis coming, the English artillery opened fire. But the Sepoys had already gone beyond its range! It was quite possible for the Sepoys to have killed their officers at the time, but, without doing so, they went away to join their comrades at the first opportunity. Thus, three thousand Sepoys encamped near Nana Sahib at Nabobganj, on the 5th of June, Sir Wheeler had one satisfaction—that not a single Englishman was killed. He thought that the Sepoys would, as usual, march towards Delhi, and the danger to Cawnpore would be over.

And if there had been a lack of able leaders in Cawnpore as there was in other places, the Sepoys, would, indeed, have gone to Delhi as Sir Wheeler surmised. But, at Nabobganj, at the time, there was no such lack of bold and able leaders. Nana Sahib was there; his brothers, Bala Sahib, Baba Sahib, and his nephew Rao Sahib were there; Tatia Tope was there; and Azimullah Khan too was there. When such brilliant and intellectual leaders were there, what need had the Sepoys to go to Delhi to seek one? The best interests would not be served by shutting up all the available forces in Delhi alone. The successful plan would be to harass the English in various places. Above all, as Cawnpore to a great extent commanded the line of communications between the Punjab, Delhi, and Calcutta, it was necessary to strike a blow at Cawnpore and capture. When the Subahdar's and Nana's men had explained all this to the Sepoys, it was unanimously decided to turn back towards Cawnpore. The three thousand Sepoys elected Nana Sahib their King and expressed an ardent desire to see him. When he appeared, he was hailed with tremendous enthusiasm and they saluted him with all royal honours. When the election of the King was over, with his consent, the Sepoys proceeded to elect their officers; Subahdar Tikka Singh, the very life of the Revolutionary centre at Cawnpore, was elected the chief commander of the cavalry and was given the title of 'General.' New army regulations were issued. Jamadar Dalganjan Singh was made the colonel of the 53rd regiment, and Subahdar Ganga Din of the 56th regiment. Then, there was a grand procession of the flag of freedom on the back of an elephant, and on the same day it was proclaimed by beat of drum that Nana Sahib had commenced to reign.

After these elections, Nana Sahib did not waste even a second. When the English received the information that the Sepoys did not go to Delhi but had stopped on the way, they entrenched themselves in the new fort and had their artillery ready. Their number was about one thousand, men, women, and children all told. It was of the first importance to capture this fortified place, and Nana Sahib ordered the whole army to march thither. The English were not certain that the Revolutionaries would attack them; but, early on the morning of the 6th, Sir Wheeler received a note. It was from Nana Sahib and was couched in the following terms:— 'We are going to begin the attack. We want to warn you, and therefore send this previous notice to you.' When he received this invitation to fight, Sir Wheeler got ready all his officers and soldiers and artillery men, and made all necessary preparations for the fight.

The fact that, before beginning the battle, Nana Sahib gave a previous written notice to the English when it was in no way called for, is of the greatest importance. The English would certainly not have shown this generosity had they been in Nana's place. Those who always try to pour foul disgrace on Nana Sahib's name, should bend their heads with shame at this act of natural gallantry! If we remember these two facts, the saving of the lives of all English officers at the time of the rising and the twelve hours' previous written notice given by Nana Sahib, and then read the final scenes, we will appreciate better the real situation at Cawnpore.

Soon after sending the notice of battle to the English, Subahdar (now General) Tikka Singh went towards the arsenal and was busy, all the morning, arranging the arms etc. and sending them to the place of attack. Guns were pointed against the English fort from the side of the river as well as from land. The plan of the attack was formed with true military skill. At the same time, the Cawnpore town was also in a tumult! Spinners, sword-smiths, and pepole from the bazaar, Mussalmans, and the influential silver-merchants —everybody took anything that came to hand and were looking for Englishmen. Offices, courts, and all English records, old and new, were burnt and those Englishmen that forgot to betake themselves to the fort were killed. It was now mid-day. At about one the English fort began to be besieged, and, about evening, the guns began to boom and the attack commenced.

The English had about eight cannon and plenty of ammunition which they had already kept buried in the fort. The Revolutionaries, also, had captured the arsenal and the big guns and they too were not hard up for ammunition.

General Tikka Singh had from the first kept the artillery in excellent condition. Nana Sahib's guns played great havoc on the English buildings within the fort, When, on the 7th of June, the artillery of the Revolutionaries began to do its terrible work. English women and childrern, who had never been in such a plight before, began to run about here and there crying frantically. But habit took away the terror even of death, and balls flying over the heads created no greater surprise than birds flying in the air. Two days after the attack was commenced, the supply of water in the fort began to fall short. There was only one well within the fort which was of any use but the Revolutionaries had a keener eye on it than the English soldiers themselves. The heat of the sun was so strong that the solidiers would die of sunstroke. All hearts became hardened like stone. The difference between the sexes, and modesty, banished. Children died for want of milk and sorrow killed the mothers. Let alone burying the dead, but it even became impossible to inquire who was dead and who was alive. For even while making a list of the living, some name would have to be scored off. To draw a true picture of such situations, the best way is to describe the events of a typical hour. Captain Thomas; relating his experiences, says: 'While Armstrong was lying wounded, Lieutenant Prole came to see him. Just as he uttered a few words of consolation, a bullet from the Sepoys struck him in the thigh and he fell down. With his hand on my shoulder and mine round his waist, I began to lift him to take him to the sergeant. Before I had gone many steps, there was a buzzing noise and a bullet entered my shoulder. I and Prole both fell dying on the floor. Seeing this, Gilbert Bucks came running towards us. But the enemy's bullet came after him, pierced his body through, and he fell at once in the jaws of Death.' This account of one hour gives a good idea of the history of those twenty-one days! When Sir Wheeler's son was wounded, his two sisters and his mother were giving him medical assistance in a room But, before he could take the medicine, there was a fearful explosion and a cannon ball carried away the young man's head. While Magistrate Hillersden was talking to his wife in the verandah, a twenty pound cannon ball burst on his head and he was blown to pieces. A few days later, the wall on which the widow was leaning collapsed and she met her death. There were seven women in a ditch near the fort. A bomb exploded and not only killed them all, but it also killed the English soldier who, before the rising, had shot the Sepoy and had been acqitted as not guilty. So at last the guns of the Sepoys also went off! And when they did go off, it was in such a manner that succeeding English soldiers will remember it for ever, even when under the influence of drink!

In this terrible siege, there were also, some foolish Indians , who thought it their duty to be faithful to the English. They were there, in the jaws of death, simply for the sake of 'loyalty'! An Indian nurse in the employ of the English lost both her arms by a bomb explosion. Butlers running about here and there to give hot food to their masters also fell dead frequently by shells. Indian *bhishtis* often risked their lives to give water to the English. Water was so scarce that children would suck the leather bags containing water!' Cholera, dysentery, and typhoid also did not fail to take their revenge on the English. Sir George Parker, Colonel Williams, and Lieutenant Rooney died through illness. Those that did not succumb to shells or sickness went insane from the terrific fright of the ghastly living cemetery. Such was the pandemonium there. So, in return for the cruel wrongs of a century, Revenge incarnate was crushing everyone she found in her terrific jaws for twenty-one days, and was dancing with a ghastly smile!

While such was the state within the fort, the English guns placed outside did great service in the fight. Chief officers of the artillery, Ashe, Captain Moore, Captain Thomson, and other brave soldiers fought with a splendid valour. The English had great hopes of speedy succour from Lucknow or Allahabad. On account of the strict scouting of the Revolutionaries, it had become impossible to carry on correspondence. Still, an Indian messenger had carried as far as Lucknow a letter by Sir Wheeler, partly in Latin, partly in French, and partly in English, and packed in the quill of a bird. It said only, 'Help! Help!! Help l !! Send us help or we are dying! If we get help, we will come and save Lucknow!' But, the vigilance of the Revolutionaries was usually so good that hardly any such messenger from the English camp could get back there safe. The English often sent scouts, empowering them to promise lakhs of Rupees if they could find any traitors in the Revolutionary camp. But not one lived to return and give information! For example, we will give an account given by one of the scouts himself. 'When Mr. Shepherd lost his wife and daughter, he undertook the task of getting information from the Revolutionaries' camp and sowing dissensions in Cawnpore. He set out in the disguise of an Indian cook. Hardly had he gone a short distance when he was arrested and brought before Nana Sahib. When he was asked about the state of the English, he began to give false and glowing descriptions as agreed upon. But seeing that two women, captured just before he was caught, had told the true story of despair, he got confused. He was first put in a prison and, on the 12th of July, he was brought before a court and sentenced to three years' rigorous imprisonment.' From this will be seen the regard for justice which Nana had, even in the heat of the war. Though English scouts were thus baulked, the scouts of the Revolutionaries did their work exceedingly well. One day, a *bhishti* (water-carrier) stood, on a high piece of ground near the English fort and cried, 'Even disregarding the fear of death, since I love the English so much, I have come to convey to you a piece of joyful news. An English army with guns has come up on other bank of the Ganges. It will start to-morrow to receive you. This news has created a perfect consternation among the rascally rebels and we, all loyalists, have become ready to join the English!' At this news, the English imagined that their scouts must have successfully sowed discord among the Revolutionaries and, also, that the English army from Lucknow, must have arrived. On the next day, the same *bhishti* came up and cried, 'Victory to the English! The English army was late on account of floods in the Ganges; but, now, all is accomplished, and they are coming. Before the end of the day, my masters will be victorious.' That day passed, and so also the next; but the strained eyes of the English could see neither the army of succour nor the loyalist *bhishti*? Azimullah, now, knew enough of the misery of the English camp, and it was not again necessary for the *bhishti* to risk his life. The English were often taken in by such resourceful tricks of the Revolutionary scouts.

After giving notice of the siege on the 6th of June to the English, Nana Sahib had brought his camp close to the besieging armies and near by the tent of General Tikka Singh. When Cawnpore became free, the whole province became flooded by great wave of Revolution. Every day, new Zemindars and princes came with their retinues and joined Nana Sahib's camp. Nana had now about four thousand troops under him; but of these, the artillerymen were the most active in their duties. Here in one quarter Nanhi Nabob took his stand. When the rising began, his house and property were ordered to be confiscated for his fanatical Hindu hatred. But soon, a compromise took place and he joined that war of freedom. The artillery in Nana's charge were manned by the finest marksmen and old pensioners. While the Revolutionaries were making efforts to set fire to the English buildings within the fort, an amateur artillery man discovered a new explosive. The first experiment was so successful that the barracks, which were of immense value to the English and against which it was thrown, were soon burnt to ashes! There was so much competition amongst the people to join in firing the batteries that women helped men, and old men helped young men in the work. One quotation will show how, in that season of noble ideals and inspiration, the masses had risen up. A native Christian says, 'While I sat on a mat disguised as a Mahomedan, I saw men returning to supply waters to those who were fighting. Suddenly; one of them came up to me and said, 'While our countrymen are fighting there, it is a shame that a young Mahomedan like you should sit here killing flies! Come there to help at the artillery.' He also told me that the young son of the one-eyed pensioner Karim Ali had done a great deed that day. He had made some discovery and set fire to the English buildings. For this bravery, he was rewarded with ninety rupees and a shawl.' To sit idly, instead of fighting for the country, was considered a disgrace not only to a young man but even to woman; so, the women of Cawnpore had left their Zenanas and jumped into the battle-field. But all these young soldiers and heroic women put to shame by the ardour of a beauty which was no other than the dancing girl Azizan, above-mentioned. She had now put on a heroic garb. With her rosy cheeks and smiling lips, she was there on horseback, fully armed. And the artillery Sepoys would forget all their fatigue at the sight of her. Nanak Chand says, in his diary, 'Armed Azizan is flashing everywhere like lightning; often she stands in the streets giving milk and sweetmeats to tired and wounded Sepoys.'

Even while the fight was going on in this manner, Nana Sahib was making all possible arrangements for the civil administration. Though it is always a difficult task to introduce order in the revenue and police departments at a critical time like that of a Revolution, Nana Sahib first began the work of giving justice and protection to the inhabitants. The prominent citizens of Cawnpore were called together and the man elected by the majority of them, Holas Singh by name, Was given the office of chief magistrate. Nana Sahib gave strict orders that Holas Singh should protect the citizens from disorderly Sepoys or bandit villagers. The work of supplying provisions to the army was entrusted to a citzen, called Mullah. A court was appointed to settle civil and criminal disputes. Jwala Prasad, Azimullah Khan, and others were made judges and Baba Sahib was made the President. From few documents of this court that are extant, it is abundantly clear that those guilty of oppression or disorder were severely punished and that great care was bestowed on the maintenance of order. A man convicted of a very heinous theft had his right hand cut off. A Mahomedan butcher was given the same punishment for killing a cow. Vagabonds without any profession and people convicted of small thefts were publicly disgraced in the streets on the back of a donkey.[5] Like the Committee of Public Safety established during the French Revolution, this court gradually encroached upon all the other departments. To supply ammunition in case of shortage, to supply clothes to the army, to try the arrested English scouts, to punish rogues who wanted to escape all these were done by this court. It also gave rewards to those who discovered English refugees.

The attack of the Revolutionaries on the English fort took place on the 12th. Rather than take it by a general assault, the general plan of the Revolutionaries was to reduce it by harassing the English on all sides by artillery. They also directed assaults now and then. After both sides had lost some men the Revolutionaries would retire. The vigour and courage of the artillery was not equalled by the cavalry and the infantry. This fault will also be prominently noticed in the sieges of Delhi and Lucknow; but, in the siege of Cawnpore also, more importance was attached to the artillery than to hand-to-hand fight. Not that the Sepoys were, at all, afraid of death. The valour and bravery the Sepoys displayed in the assault, on the 18th of June, on the fort were remarkable. On this day, disregarding the cannon-fire of the

5. Thomson's *Cawnpore.*

enemy, they ran straight, like arrows, at the enemy's camp, mounted the walls, took an English gun, and turned its mouth, and it seemed for a moment that the flag of freedom would never be set back. Instead of helping such brave Sepoys, some had, on the other hand, sworn as it were to create disorder without reason and bring confusion in all the ranks. This weakness compelled the whole army to return. Like the brave Sepoys of Oudh, some brave hearts at Cawnpore did their duty, as heroes always do, without waiting to see what the others did. One day when the assaulting party was retiring, one Sepoy lay down there, pretending to be dead. When Captain Jenkins, renowned for his bravery and a bold fighter, came up there galloping confidently, the Sepoy jumped suddenly at his prey and shot him dead in the neck in an instant!

The 23rd of June came. One hundred years before, on this day, the English had laid the foundations of their power on the battle-field of Plassey. On that 23rd of June, the English got their first decisive victory in Hindusthan. The sting of the insult of that unfortunate day was burning in the heart of Hindusthan so much that, even after a hundred years, that evil day and its evil memory was fresh in the heart of all Indians. The terrible wound of slavery inflicted on that day had not been healed even after a hundred years. No balm had yet been found that could heal it ! What a righteous hatred was rankling in the heart even of the peaceful and forgiving India? In the last breath of every dying generation and in the first breath of every new one being born, she has been mixing in the spirit of revenge for Plassey! This went on for a hundred years, and the morning of the 23rd of June 1857, had risen. Astrologers had foretold that at last on this day the Mother would be avenged. Nana Sahib! Though the fulfilment of the prophecy is in the hands of God, you are to do your duty towards achieving the end!

And not to lose the chance of that auspicious day, the

23rd of June saw the whole of Nana Sahib's camp in a terrible commotion. All the divisions, if not every man of the army, had got ready to direct an assault as had never been directed before. The artillery, the cavalry, and the infantry—all, inspired by the memory of that historical day, came down into the battle-field. The bravest of them assembled together and took oaths—the Hindus with Ganges water and the Mahomedans on the Koran—that, on that day, they would either acquire freedom or die fighting! The cavalry rushed forward and came up to the walls without heeding the enemy's artillery. The infantry, under cover of big bags of cotton which they pushed along, showered bullets on the fort, from the other sides. People from the neighbouring villages had also come to join the Revolutionaries. From within the fort the English also kept up an incessant fire. Though they could not check the forward movement of the Revolutionists, they prevented them from breaking into the fort that day.

Nevertheless this last attack at Cawnpore did not go in vain. After that day's fight the English lost all hope. They were full of despair and saw clearly that it was thenceforth impossible to hold the fort against Nana Sahib. Though not on the 23rd, yet on the 25th of June, they hoisted on their wall the flag of truce! On seeing this flag, Nana Sahib ordered the fighting to stop[6] and sent to General Wheeler a letter by tile hand of a captive English woman. The note ran: 'To the subjects of Queen Victoria. Those who have had no connection with Dalbousie's policy and those who are ready to lay down arms and surrender will be safely conveyed to Allahabad.' This note was written by Azimullah Khan at the order of Nana Sahib.

When General Wheeler received the note, he gave authority to Captains Moore and Whiting to consider it and the two officers resolved upon a surrender to Nana Sahib.

---

6. Tatia Tope, in his statement, says:— 'The English general raised the flag of peace and the fighting ceased.'

The next morning, on the 26th Jwala Prasad and Azimullah Khan, on behalf of Nana Sahib, and Moore, Whiting, and Roche, on behalf of the English, met near the walls. First, the conversation began in English, but soon Jwala and Azim forced them to carry on the conversation in Hindusthani—the language of the nation. The terms settled were that the English should hand over all the artillery, arms and ammunition, and the treasure to Nana Sahib, and Nana Sahib should give provisions to and convey the party to Allababad.[7] The agreement was drawn up on paper and Azimullah Khan and others returned to get Nana Sahib's signature. In the afternoon there was some difference as to whether the English should start the same night or the next morning. However, a compromise was arrived at, and it was agreed that Nana Sahib should take charge of everything that night and the English should leave early the next morning. Mr. Todd (formerly English reader at Nana's palace) came to Nana Sahib with a copy of the treaty agreed upon by both parties. Nana showed great hospitality towards him and inquired as to his health, etc. The same evening, the English laid down their arms; the guns were handed over to Nana Sahib; and Brigadier Jwala Prasad, with two companions, came and took his quarters within the fort. The same night Holas Singh, the magistrate at Cawnpore, and Tatia Tope ordered boatmen to keep forty boats ready. The English officers who came on elephants to see them complained that the boats were rude and uncomfortable. So, one hundred labourers were employed immediately; bamboo coverings and canopies were erected, good seats were made, and corn and other provisions were also loaded on the boats.

The English now prepared to go out of Cawnpore. But we must also see who were now coming in there. Unless we take an account of the incomings as well as the outgoings, we shall not be able to understand later events. When the

7. *Red Pamphlet.*

news spread everywhere that Nana had raised the flag of freedom at Cawnpore, a constant flood of heroes was pouring in thither. Young national volunteers from every place were repairing towards Cawnpore. A town, which could not send men, sent money. But, alas! it was not only these volunteers that were now crowding into Cawnpore. Day and night helpless people, who had been unsuccessful in their efforts and who were tired of English slavery, also came to the camp in large numbers. Thousands of Sepoys from Allahabad and Kashi had come to Cawnpore in the preceding week with the news of the cruel vengeance which the English had taken on their comrades and their wives and children. Hundreds of young Indian sons, whose fathers had been hanged in shapes of the figures— '8' and '9', also had come there. Husbands whose wives and infant sons in the cradle had been burnt by Neill also came. Fathers whose daughters had their hair and clothes set fire to by English soldiers amid shouts of applause, also crowded the place. Men whose properties were burnt to ashes, men whose religion was trampled under foot, men whose nation had been enslaved, such men created a tumult round the banner of freedom with shouts of 'Revenge! Revenge!!' And when the day of victory had arrived, Nana Sahib's promise to convey the English to Allahabad dispelled all the hopes of the Sepoys and the people, and they began to grumble aloud. The English officers who came to look after the preparation of boats distinctly heard whispers of 'Massacre' (Katal) among the Sepoys lounging about on the banks of the Ganges! It is also said that a palace Pundit had explained to the Sepoys how, in tile eyes of religion, there was no sin in beheading men who had broken faith with a nation and had enslaved it![8]

On the 27th of June, the sun rose on this disturbed atmosphere. The English were to be seen off from the Sati Chowda Ghat. The cavalry and the infantry stood round the

8. Trevelyan's Cawnpore.

Ghat and the artillery was also in position. Thousands of the citizens of Cawnpore had also assembled at the Ghat, since the morning, to witness the scene on the banks of the Ganges, each with his own mental picture of it. Azimullah Khan, Bala Sahib, and the Commander Tatia Tope, also stood on the terrace of a temple near the Ghat. The name of the temple too was fitting to the occasion. Inside was the image of 'Har Dev' and it appeared as if the lordship of the whole region was vested for the time being solely in the hands of Shiva, the Terrible! Nana Sahib had sent the best conveyances to take the English from the fort to the Ganges bank. For Sir Wheeler, a beautifully decorated elephant, with Nana Sahib's own *mahut*, came and stood at the gate of the fort. Sir Wheeler did not like the idea of being taken in such a melancholy procession on an elephant; so, he seated his family on it and betook himself to a palanquin. The English women had also palkees allotted to them. The procession started. The English flag at the fort was hauled down and the flag of freedom and religion flew in its stead! Instead of having heart-burnings at this insult to English prestige, the prisoners expressed joy at being released from the jaws of death. In the flush of joy of a renewed life, they left the fort and proceeded hastily-but whither?

However, it is useless to discuss that question at this stage. The Ganges Ghat is still a mile and a half afar. When this procession, after going through the mile and a half, got down on the sands, the Sepoy lines closed from behind and guarded the way. While embarking on the boats from the palkees and elephants, no Indian came forth that day to help the English. Yes; but there were exceptions. In one or two cases, they did get help when they were getting down but, then, the Sepoys offered their swords, not their hands. The wounded Colonel Ewart had been put in a *doli*. A Sepoy stopped his *doli* and said: 'Well, Colonel, how do you like this parade? How are the regimental uniforms?' With these words, he dragged him down from the palkee and cut him to pieces. His wife was near by. Some said to her: 'You are a women and your life will be spared !' But, one frightful young man rushed forward, shouting, 'Get away! A woman? Yes, But she is a Feringhi! Cut her to pieces!' Before he finished the sentence, the thing was done!

The English committee itself has admitted after enquiry that all the boats on the river contained ample provisions on board. The English waded through the water and took their seats in them. Everywhere there was a dead silence and calm. The boats were almost crowded. The boatmen were ready with their oars. At last, Tatia Tope waved his hand backward and forward in the air as the sign for the boats to start. Suddenly, in one corner, some one blew a bugle to break the terrible silence. As soon as the shrill sound of the bugle was heard, a crashing noise- started-the noise of guns, rifles, swords, *kukris*, and bayonets. The boatmen jumped from the boats and came to the bank, and the Sepoys rushed into the water with a jump! No other sound was heard but t Maro Feringhi ko!'

Soon all the boats caught fire, and men and women and children all jumped hastily into the Ganges. Some began to swim, some were drowned, some were burnt and most succumbed to bullets sooner or later! Lumps of flesh, broken heads, severed hair, chopped-off arms and legs, and a stream of blood! The whole Ganges became red! As soon as anyone took up his head above water, he was shot by a bullet; if he kept it under water, he would die of asphyxia! Such was the wrath of Har Dev ! Such was the one hundredth anniversary of Plassey!

It was ten o'clock in the morning. It is said that, at this time, Nana Sahib was quietly pacing a hall in the palace. What wonder that he was uneasy in that palace, while an account of the century's wrongs was being settled! Such moments are epochs in history. They are the final strokes of a period, the summary of an age. Heaven knows his thoughts, at that time, when he was pacing the hall! But he was not allowed time to think much longer; for, a cavalryman came galloping fast and informed him that the Sepoys had commenced an indiscriminate massacre of the English on Sati Chowda Ghat. Hearing this, Nana Sahib remarked that there was no necessity of molesting the women and the children and made the same man gallop back fast with the stringent order, 'Kill the Englishmen! But no harm is to be done to the women and children!'[9] We must notice, while passing, that the second part of Nana Sahib's order is conspicuous by its absence in Neill's orders! When Nana Sahib s order reached Sati Chowda, the Sepoys were in the height of their dread work. Some Englishmen were burning in the heap of tottering boats, while some were attempting to swim across the river. The Sepoys also jumped into the water and followed them like wild dogs, shouting and foaming with rage. With their swords in the teeth and revolvers in the hand, the Sepoys began the terrible hunt in the water. General Wheeler was killed in the first rush. Henderson also fell. But it is easier to give a list of those that survived than of those that died! As soon as Nana Sahib's order arrived, the massacre was at once stopped and one hundred and twenty-five women and children were taken alive out of the water. They were taken as prisoners to Savda Kothi. The remaining Englishmen were made to stand in a line and the order for their execution was read to them. One of them asked to be given time to read to his comrades some sentences from a prayer-book, and the request was granted.[10] When the prayer was finished, the Sepoys quickly cut off their heads with swords! Out of the forty boats, only one boat escaped; and out of the Englishmen in it, only three or four were saved from the attacks of the villagers, and

---

9. Forrest's *State Papers*. Almost all English historians admit that Nana sent his order as soon as he heard the report. Also Kaye and: Malleson's *Indian Mutiny*, Vol, II, page 258.

10. Kaye and Malleson's *Indian Mutiny*, Vol. II, page 263.

that because a Zemindar, called Durvijay Singh, took pity on them! This Zemindar kept the naked and dying Englishmen for a month and then sent them down to Allahabad.

In short out of one thousand living Englishmen and women, on the 7th of June at Cawnpore, only four men and one hundred and twenty-five women and children survived on the 30th. The women and children were in the prisons of Nana Sahib and the four half-dead men were partaking of medicine and hospitality in the house of Durvijay Singh. It is here necessary to record briefly the arrangements made by Nana Sahib as regards the imprisoned women and children. We would have had no occasion to refer to this at all, had not English writers published a series of 'reliable information' and most shameless accusations that the women were violated, that they were insulted in the streets, that Nana Sahib himself attempted to violate them, etc. and had not the English nation been so blind and wicked as to believe these despicable and diabolical falsehoods! It is distinctly stated by the special commission appointed by the English in this behalf that all these accusations are false.[11] Still, this does not end the question. Not only did Nana Sahib save these women from massacre and thus put to shame Neill, Reynold, and Havelock, but, in that conflagration of 1857, Nana Sahib did not show to the treacherous enemy who ruined individuals, the nation, and, religion, even a hundredth part of the severity and cruelty which, in similar conditions and under similar provocations, England herself has shown to India, Austria to Italy, Spain to the Moors, or Greece to the Turks. And this is proved by the histories of the English themselves.

In the first confusion of the massacre at Cawnpore, four English women and some half-caste women had been taken away by some cavalrymen. At this news, Nana Sahib had

11. Muir's Report and Wilson's Report. See also, Kaye and Malleson's *Indian Mutiny*, Vol. II, page 267.

the Sepoys immediately arrested and disgraced. He compelled them to restore the women at once.[12] The prisoners were given *chapatees*, and meat occasionally.[13] They were not forced to do hard labour in any sense. The children were given milk. Over them was kept a chief wardress, called Begum. Since cholera and dysentery broke out in the prison. they were brought out to take fresh air, thrice every day.[14] It would not be here out of place to give a small anecdote to show how the people were furious even at the name, 'English'. One morning, a Brahmin peeped over the prison wall and saw English women, who would never go out except in a palanquin, wash their cloths. Moved at this sight, the Brahmin remarked to his neighbour, 'Why do they not allow them a washerman?' As a check to this excessive humanity, the neighbour slapped the Brahmin hard in the face. A few of the women in the prison used to grind corn and each of them was given flour for one *chapatee* free. This showed them what it meant to work for one's living! What was the end of this imprisonment and what was the reason for that end will appear at its proper time. We will leave the women and children in prison and now turn to more important matters.

When all the emblems of English rule had been wiped out of Cawnpore, Nana Sahib held a great Durbar, about five o'clock on the afternoon of the 28th. In honour of the Durbar, there was also a military parade of the whole army present. Six regiments of infantry, and two of cavalry, besides bands of Revolutionaries, with their banners, who had come from various places to join in the war, were present at the ceremony. The artillery by whose power Cawnpore was conquered was deservedly given the place of honour. Bala

12. Trevelyan's *Cawnpore*, page 299.
13. *Narrative*, page 113.
14. Neill himself says in his report: 'At first they were badly fed but afterwards they got better food and clean clothing and servants to wait upon.'

Sahib was, from the first, very popular in the army and got a splendid ovation when he arrived. At first, there was a salute of 101 guns in honour of the Emperor of Delhi which shows how, in 1857, Hindus and Mahomedans had forgotten all their animosities. Next when Nana Sahib arrived in the camp, he was acclaimed with shouts and received a salute of twenty-one guns. Some said the twenty-one guns represented the twenty-one days of the siege. Nana Sahib thanked the army for the great honour and said, 'This victory belongs to all of us. All have an equal glory therein.' It was then announced that Nana Sahib had ordered one lakh of Rupees to be distributed to the army as a reward for its victory and, when he presented himself on the parade, another salute of twenty-one guns was fired. Then, Nana's nephew-Rao Sahib, and brothers-Baba Sahib and Bala Sahib, each got a salute of seventeen guns in their honour. Brigadier Jwala Prasad and Commander Tatia Tope were given the honour of eleven guns each. In this manner, the evening sun heard the martial song of freedom through the din of cannon, and then the whole army returned to the camp. After the military review, Nana Sahib, in company with his brother Bala Sahib, proceeded to the historically famous palace of Brahmavarta. The 1st of July was fixed as the day of coronation. On that day, what splendour there was in the palace! The old historic throne of the Peshwas was brought with great ceremony into the Durbar Hall, and Nana Sahib, with the royal Tilaka on his forehead, amidst the booming of guns and the thundering applause of thousands, ascended the throne which was independent, earned by his prowess, supported by the populace, and blessed by religion. On that day, hundreds from Cawnpore sent presents to Nana Sahib.[15] The Mahratta throne which the English hurled down from Raigarh thus re-emerged out of the Ganges flowing red with English blood. The Hindus allover the land hailed it with 'Raja Ramachandra ki Jay!!!'

15. Trevelyan's *Cawnpore*, page 293.

But while Nana Sahib was straining every nerve to regain freedom in childhood, Rani Lakshmi Bai, a fellow competitor with him in childhood at Brahmavarta in horse-riding and elephant-riding, did not keep idle. When Nana Sahib cast the die on the battelfield for independence at Cawnpore, she did the same at Jhansi. She was as close an associate to him in the game of Revolution as she was in the games of childhood. On the 4th of June, on the same day that Cawnpore was suffused with the clouds of fiery fume of cannonade, the Rani of Jhansi too dashed out like lightning and joined the battle of freedom.

On the 4th of June, Jhansi rose. Before this rising, a few letters fell into the hands of the British commissioner at Jhansi from which it appeared that Lakshman Rao, a Brahmin in the Ranee's service, was organising a Revolution and, as a preliminary, intended to kill the British officers in command of the army. But while the English were discussing amongst themselves as to what precautions were to be taken, on the same day, the Revolutionists took possession of the fort. Finding this, the English went to take shelter in the city fort. The Revolutionaries made an attack upon that also, and took it. On the 7th Rasaldar Kala Khan and Tahasildar Mohomed Hussien of Jhansi and other valiant soldiers led the attack and tne flag of Revolution was hoisted on the fort of Jhansi. The English, on the other hand, hoisted the white flag and craved for peace. Hakim Salay Mahomed a prominent citizen of Jhansi, promised to spare the lives of the English, if they surrendered unconditionally. The English laid down their arms, and the doors of the fort were opened. But, when the English came out of the gates, the soldiers shouted, 'Maro Feringhi ko!' The Sepoys had known how the English had massacred their women and children and how Neill had burnt whole villages and were infuriated beyond measure. On the 8th, a procession was led through the city and the English were made to march in the procession as prisoners of war. The very English people, who were wielding the highest authority at Jhansi only a week before, were, to-day, parading as captives. As they were approaching Johan Bagh the Sepoys asked the general, 'Rasaldar Sahib, what further orders?' The Rasaldar ordered that the Feringhis who were guilty of treason in having dared to dethrone the Ranee and annex the country should not be spared and that, therefore, they should be drawn up in three separate rows of men, women and children and as soon as the jail Daroga decapitated the commissioner in the line of men, immediately the rest of the lines of men, women and children should be beheaded. In a second, blood began to flow in streams. Thus, they died as victims of the merciless annexation policy of Lord Dalhousie refusing to recognise the adoption made by the queen.

About seventy-five men, twelve women, and twenty-three children were decapitated by the Revolutionaries and, there being no legal or adopted heir of the English to represent them, the Revolutionaries annexed the Kingdom of Jhnsi to the Ranee's crown as the guardian of her son, Damodar Rao. They declared 'The Universe belongs to God, the country to the Emperor, and the authority to Ranee Lakshmi Bai!'[16]

* * *

16. There is an authoritative work on the life of the Queen of Jhansi by a well-known Marathi historian, and there the able author has established by an incontestable array of proofs that there was not the least incitement to this massacre from the young Queen. This work has a wide circulation and is translated in other vernaculars in India, and so we think it unnecessary to repeat the argument once more.

CHAPTER IX

Oudh

SINCE Dalhousie annexed Oudh, the people of that province had been sinking deeper and deeper in misery. After Oudh lost her independence, all the offices of honour, power, and wealth in the Nabob's Kingdom were given to Englishmen, and the Swadeshi men had to go to the wall. The Nabob's army was disbanded, his nobles were driven into poverty, his ministers and other officers lost their positions and were pushed to the low ranks of wage-earners; and all of them entertained a rankling hatred of the slavery which destroyed their country and reduced them to such a state. The sting of slavery was felt not alone in the capital and among the palace officials. The traditional rights of properties and Inams (fiefs) of the big Zemindars and Rajas were also confiscated by the English. So, all these Rajas and Zemindars saw how, between even a bad Swaraj (national rule) and subjection to a highly developed foreign rule, the former was to be preferred and was infinitely more agreeable and honourable. The increase in the land-tax produced discontent among the peasants. Most of the Hindusthanee Sepoys in the English army were from Oudh, and the misery and slavery of the place of their birth soon made them intensely disaffected. Everyone put his hand to the sword when he remembered how the English ruined Nabob Wajid Ali Shah with their cruel treachery and deceit. The big Zemindars of Oudh, were descendants of Rajput heroes. They were intensely excited when they heard of the perfidious cruelty of the English towards their King. After the annexation of Oudh, the English asked them to come and accept services under the new regime. Hundreds of the freedom-loving and valiant men replied, at that time : 'We have eaten the food of Swaraj! We will not touch the foreigner's food!'

Sir Henry Lawrence was made the chief officer of the

new Oudh province. He was the elder brother of Sir John Lawrence by whose alertness and statesmanship the seeds of the Revolution in the Punjab were smothered before taking root. Just as the chief commissioner of the Punjab had saved that province, so also his brother in Oudh had begun his preparations to save this. If anyone deserves the credit of having materially helped to perpetuate British power in India in this Revolution, it is the Lawrence family. Sir Henry Lawrence, as soon as he stepped into Oudh, really grasped the situation there and had expressed the fear of a Revolution, long before any other Englishman thought of it. Lucknow being the capital of Oudh province, Sir Henry had his headquarters there. He started the policy of pacifying disaffected Zemindars by sweet speeches. He took great pains in organising a Durbar at Lucknow and in giving various honours, titles, and rewards, in order to make the people forget their late Swaraj. He was not unwise enough to rest content merely with applying pacificatory means, but also began to think out various plans for opposing a possible popular rising. For, though Sir Henry Lawrence was a better officer than his predecessors, the people in Oudh were heartily disgusted with English rule as such, whether good or bad. Their ambition could be satisfied with nothing less than the restoration of Swaraj and the reinstallation of Wajid Ali Shah on the throne. They had no other desire but to break the English chains and make Hindusthan free again. Their religion was yesterday the religion of the free. Yesterday, it was the religion of the state and the king. But Today, it had fallen to a secondary and a servile place. These were their chief complaints, and the remedy was not good rule by the English but the end of all English rule. Powerful Hindu chiefs, like Man Singh, and leaders of Mahomedans, like Moulvie Ahmad Shah, resolved to sacrifice their all in this war for freedom and the Hindu and Islamic religions. Thousands of Moulvies and Pundits began to wander allover Oudh, preaching sacred war, openly and secretly. The army took the oath; the police took the oath; the Zemindars took the oath; almost the whole populace joined in a vast conspiracy to fight the English, and the fire of popular agitation spread everywhere. It has been already told how sparks of this agitation would come forth, now and then, unintentionally. Moulvie Ahmad Shah himself was convicted of sedition and was given the death sentence which was. later commuted. The 7th regiment was disarmed. Sir Henry Lawrence held a great Durbar on the 12th of May, in order to keep control over the Sepoys as far as possible. He then delivered there an eloquent oration in Hindusthanee. He fully dilated upon the importance of loyalty, the insults offered by Ranjit Singh to the Mahomedan religion, Aurangzeb's insults to Hinduism, and the protection accorded by the English to both Hindus and Mahomedans against mutual injury. He then personally presented swords, shawls, turbans, and other presents to those Sepoys who had shown their loyalty; while, on the other side, the 7th regiment was being disarmed and disbanded. What an irony time had in store for him! In a very short time, these loyalists who got rewards had to be- sentenced to be hanged on proof of their complicity with the Revolutionaries.

The loyal Durbar was held on the 12th. On the 13th, the news came that Meerut had risen and, on the 14th, the people heard the joyful news that Delhi had fallen into the hands of the Revolutionaries and that a proclamation had been issued of the freedom of Hindusthan.

Sir Henry Lawrence now selected two places near Lucknow city, Machi Bhawan and the Residency, and began the work of fortifying these as places of refuge. The English women and children were taken there and all Englishmen, clerks, civil officials, and merchants were taught military drill, discipline, and the use of the rifle. At Meerut too, after the rising, all the civil Englishmen there had been given such training and made ready for the field in ten days. Sir Henry Lawrence was made the chief military officer of the province. Oudh being close to Nepal, Sir Henry Lawrence sent a mission to Nepal requesting help from there. He asked Jung Bahadur to come down into Oudh with an army. While these precautions were being taken, Sir Henry would get reliable information every day that there would be a rising that day. Daily, on receipt of the news, he would take special precautions; but the day would pass and no rising would take place. He was often thus deceived. On the 30th of May also, an officer informed Sir Henry that there was to be a rising that evening at nine o'clock.

The sun set on the 30th. While Henry Lawrence was dining with his subordinates, the nine o'clock gun went off. Seeing that the man who had brought information this time was one who had proved a false prophet before, Henry Lawrence bent forward and said sarcastically, 'Your friends are not punctual!'

Not punctual! Hardly had he finished the sentence, when he heard the crashing noise of the rifles of the 71st regiment. As previously settled amongst themselves, at the nine o'clock gun, a detachment of this regiment attacked the bangalows of the English. The mess-house of the 71st regiment was set on fire and the English-men were fired at. Lieutenant Grant who was attempting to escape was hidden under a mattress by some one; but someone else gave the information to the Sepoys. He was dragged out and killed. While Lieutenant Hardings was guarding some streets with his cavalry, he also received a sword-cut. The cantonment was on fire. Brigadier Handscomb was also killed. The English soldier and a few Sepoys who stuck to the English flag were under arms all night, trying to check the spread of the rising as much as possible. On the morning of the 31st of May, Henry Lawrence marched on the Revolutionaries with the English soldiers under him and a few Sepoys who were still loyal to the English. But, on the way, the 7th cavalry regiment that was with him also rose. He left them to join the Revolutionaries and returned. Though the English had the whole of the 32nd regiment stationed at Lucknow, besides the artillery, before sunset, the 71st infantry, the 48th infantry, and the 7th cavalry regiment, together with the irregular troops, hoisted up the flag of freedom.

At a distance of fifty-one miles to the north-west of Lucknow is the town of Sitapur. There were stationed here the 41st infantry and the 9th and 10th irregular infantries. At Sitapur also stayed the commissioner of the province and other big officials. On the 27th of May, some English houses had been set fire to. But the English had not yet the experience to know that those fires were the premonitory symptoms of the rising. They, therefore, did not give any special attention to it, Nay, more, even the Sepoys made great efforts to put down the flames! This fire served two purposes. One was that the members of the secret society got notice that the time had come. The other was to test the credulity and confidence of the English. On the 2nd of June, an extarordinary incident occurred. The Sepoys complained that the flour bags given to them contained powder of bones and refused to take them. They also insisted that they should be instantly thrown into the Ganges. The English quietly threw the bags into the river! In the afternoon of the same day, the Sepoys suddenly rushed into the gardens of the English and everyone helped himself to whatever fruit he liked and as much as he liked. The English officers protested vehemently, but the Sepoys did not stop in their repast to listen to the remonstrance! After the terrible feast, they began an equally terrible exercise in order to digest the food! On the 3rd of June, a batch of Sepoys went up to the treasury and captured it, and the rest went and attacked the house of the Chief Commissioner. On the way, they met Colonel Birch and Lieutenant Graves and killed them. The 9th irregulars, also, killed their officers. All the Sepoys would shout, 'The

Feringhi rule is at an end!' and fall upon any Englishman they met. The commissioner and his wife were running towards the river. He, his wife, and a boy were killed while crossing the river. Thornhill and his wife, also, fell a prey to bullets. The Sepoys in their rage killed about twenty-four English. Many others among the English however, ran to the Zemindars of Ramkote, Mitavali, etc., enjoyed their hospitality for eight or ten months, and then were taken safely to Lucknow. All the Sepoys of Sitapur then went to Farrukabad. The fort there, in which the Englishmen had taken refuge, was taken after severe fighting and the Englishmen were massacred. Nabob Tafuzar Hossein Khan was re-established on the Gadi which had been wrested away from him by the English. The Nabob, also, caught and killed every Englishman in his state. Thus, on the 1st of July, there was not a single Englishman left in the province of Farrukabad. In the town of Malan, about forty-four miles to the north of Sitapur, the English officers had heard rumours of a conspiracy among the Sepoys and the people. When they also got the news of the rising at Sitapur, they ran away on their horses and, thus, the whole district became free without even a a drop of blood being shed.

The third district was Mahmadi. The English here had sent their families to the Raja of Mithavli. The Raja saw them and told them that they must live secretly in his jungles, as he had no power to protect them openly. For the Sepoys in the whole province of Oudh had taken oaths to rise. After sending away their wives to the Raja, the English officers at Mahmadi took themselves to the fort. On the same day, the English fugitives from Shahjahanpur in Rohilkhand arrived at Mahmadi. But there was not even a moment's safety at Mahmadi and the officers sent a message to Sitapur to help these helpless Englishmen. Sitapur had not yet risen then and some Sepoys were sent with carriages to Mahmadi to fetch the refugees. But, the Sitapur Sepoys brought with them the seeds of the Revolution. They put all the English in carriages and took them safely till half-way to Sitapur; but there, they suddenly told them to get down and killed them. In this massacre, there were eight women, four children, eight lieutenants, four captains, and many others. The officers remaining at Mahmadi immediately ran away and the whole district was. free from British rule on the 4th of June.

Another district near Sitapur is Barhaitch. The chief officer here was Commissioner Wingfield. There were four administrative centres-Sikrora, Gonda. Barhaitch, and Melapore. Out of these, at Sikrora were stationed the 2nd infanty regiment and a battery of artillery. When there were signs of a rising here, the English women and children were sent to Lucknow. On the morning of the 9th of June, many English officers voluntarily repaired to the Raja of Balarampur for refuge. Only the chief officer of the artillery, Bonham, retained his faith in the Sepoys and would not leave his post. But, in the evening, the Sepoys plainly told him that they did not wish to injure him personally but that they would not fight against their countrymen, because the English rule was at an end. At this, Bonham had to leave the station. The Sepoys showed him the safest way and he reached Lucknow safely. When the news of Sikrora's independence reached Gonda, that town also rose for freedom. Then the commissioner, Wingfield, together with all the Englishmen ran for safety to the Raja of Balarampur. This Raja protected nearly twenty-five English people and sent them to an English camp at a suitable opportunity.

The news of the liberty of Sikrora and Gonda soon reached Barhaitch. The English officers there, without waiting for a rising, left the chief town of the district and ran towards Lucknow, on the 10th of June. But, since the Revolutionaries had their outposts at various places all over the province of Oudh, they disguised themselves as Indians and tried to cross the river Gogra in a boat. First, they did not attract any attention; but when half-way, there was a sudden cry of 'Feringhi ! Feringhi !!' The boatmen jumped away out of the boats and the English officers were killed. With these officers vanished the British power in Barhaitch.

Though there was no military station at Melapore, still the popular outburst compelled the English officers to run away from the district. A Raja helped them as far as possible in their flight. But, soon, they fell victims partly to the swords of the Revolutionaries and partly to the hardships of the forest.

Fyzabad was the chief town of the Eastern part of Oudh and was also the residence of Commissioner Goldney of the province. In the province of Fyzabad, there were three districts, Sultanpur, Saloni, and Fyzabad. In the city of Fyzabad were stationed, at the time, the 22nd infantry, the 6th irregular infantry some cavalry, and some artillery, all under the command of Colonel Lennox. In the district of Fyzabad, the oppression of the English government was at its worst. Sir Henry Lawrence himself writes, 'The Talukdars have also, I fear, been hardly dealt with. At least in the Fyzabad district, they have lost half their villages, some Talukdars have lost all.'[1] Immediately after the news of Meerut, the English officers at Fyzabad were afraid that this oppression would soon be avenged, and anxiety to save themselves took possession of their minds. They could not send their families to Lucknow, because the road was thoroughly guarded by the Revolutionaries. They could not prepare to fight at Fyzabad, because the whole army there was composed of Indians. Finding themselves in this dilemma, these officers at last went to Raja Man Singh for protection. Raja Man Singh was the great leader of all the Hindus in the province of Oudh. His sword was always drawn to protect the Hindu religion under the Nabobs. In the May of 1857, this proud Raja had been imprisoned by the English for some begatelle about revenue. But, since the English had been

1. Kaye and Malleson's Indian Mutiny, Vol. III, page 266

weakened by the Meerut rising, they had released him in order to curry favour with him and gain him to their side.

With very great difficulty, he consented to give refuge to English women and children in his cattle. He still said that the people would not like his action and would not even scruple to attack his castle for it. On the 1st of June, however, the families of the English officers went to Man Singh for refuge and lived safely in his Shahganj Castle. While the English were taking these measures of precaution, the Revolutionary fire began to burn brighter at Fyzabad. Moulvie Ahmad Shah, a name which finds a place now in Indian history, was one of the several Talukdars whose property had been confiscated by the English. He had taken the vow not only to get his Talukdars back but to free his country. Since the English annexed the kingdom of Oudh, Talukdar Ahmad shah had given his all-in-all for the service of his country and religion. He became a Moulvie and set out on a tour through Hindusthan to preach Revolution. Wherever this political saint went, there was seen an extraordinary awakening amongest the people. He personally saw the great leaders of the Revolutionary party. His voice was law in the royal family of Oudh. He formed a branch of the Secret Society at Agra. At Lucknow, he openly preached the destruction of the British power. He was beloved by the masses in Oudh. With his body, his mind, his speech and his intelligence, he worked incessantly in preaching freedom and weaving a perfect net of secret societies. He then took up the pen also. He wrote Revolutionary pamphlets and began to spread them broadcost in the province of Oudh. In one hand the sword and in the other the pen! Seeing this, the English ordered his arrest. But the Oudh police did not help to arrest the popular leader! So, a military force was sent to fetch him! He was tried for sedition, sentenced to be hanged, and detained for a time in the Fyzabad prison.[2] The race began between the Moulvie and the English power to hang each other! While the Moulvie was preparing to hang the English power, the latter was hurrying to erect a scaffold to hang the Moulvie. But, in the hurry, they retained the Moulvie in the Fyzabad prison and thus erected scaffolds for themselves. For the Moulvie's arrest was the spark that set fire to and exploded the Revolutionary magazine at Fyzabad. The whole town, including the army, rose at once. When the English officers went to the parade ground to keep the Sepoys in order, the Sepoys on their part informed them boldly that thenceforth they would only obey the orders of Swadeshi officers and that their leader was the Subahdar Dhuleep Singh. Subahdar Dhuleep Singh then imprisoned the English officers; they were prohibited from going beyond a distance of twelve steps. Then, the townsmen and the Sepoys ran to the prison which had been sanctified by the feet of the popular hero. The door of the prison creaked and amidst the loving shouts of the populace, the Moulvie Ahmad Shah threw away the chains which had now been broken to pieces and walked up to the crowd! This was the Moulvie's rebirth! The English power which was about to hang him was itself hanged by him at last! As soon as he was released, he accepted the leadership of the Revolution at Fyzabad, and

---

2. 'Before the mutiny broke out, the Moulvie travelled through India, on a roving commission, to excite the minds of his compatriots to the steps then contemplated by the master spirits of the plot. Certain it is that, in 1857, he circulated seditious papers throughout Oudh; that the police did not arrest him; and, to obtain that end, armed force was required. He was then tried and condemned to death. But; before the sentence could be executed Oudh broke into revolt and, like many a political criminal in Europe, he stepped at once from the floor of a dungeon to the footsteps of a throne !'- Malleson, Vol. IV, page 379. Says Gubbins :- 'The Moulvie of Fyzabad was released from jail by the mutineers. He came from Madras and was of a respectable Mahomedan family and had traversed much of upper India, exciting the people to sedition. He had been expelled from Agra for preaching sedition.' Ete., etc.

the first thing which he did, in revenge for the sentence of death passed on him, was to send a message to Colonel Lennox, now kept under guard, thanking him for his permission to allow the use of a Hookah while he was in prison.[3]

After thanking for the gift of a Hookah the man who gave him the death sentence, the noble-souled Moulvie warned the English officers to leave Fyzabad immediately. To prevent looting and disorder at Fyzabad, as happened in some other places, detachments of Sepoys were sent out as guards. The arsenal and other public buildings were also guarded by Sepoys. The Sepoys of the 15th regiment elected a committee of war which resolved that the English officers should be killed. But the chief officers decided that the first promise should not be broken and so they let them go away alive. They were even informed that they might take with them all private property, but no public property as that belonged to the King of Oudh! Thereafter, the Revolutionaries themselves got boats ready for the English and gave them some money; then the officers took leave of all the Sepoys and went away along the Gogra in boats. On the morning of the 9th of June, a Proclamation was issued that Fyzabad had become independent, that the Company's rule was at an end, and Wajid Ali Shah had recommenced to rule!

While the English were floating along in the boats, the Sepoys of the 17th regiment saw them. They had received a letter from Fyzabad Sepoys asking them to kill all the Englishmen coming from there. The attack on the boats commenced. The chief commissioner, Goldney, was killed; so also Lieutenant Thomas, Ritchie, Mill, Edwardes, Currie and others. Those that went to the town of Mohadabad were killed by the police themselves. Only one boat and its occupants concealed themselves successfully till the end and

---

3. Charles Bali's *Indian Mutiny*, Vol. I, page 394.

reached the English camp safely with the help of the boatmen. While Raja Man Singh's household was anxious about the safety of English women and children given in his charge, many more men came there again for refuge. Man Singh was at the time, at the chief city of Oudh. He wrote home that he had just made an agreement with the Revolutionaries by which they allowed him to give shelter to women and children, provided that he did not take there any Englishmen, and that it had been decided that his house should be searched to see whether he observed the conditions. Therefore, the English-men in his fort, with their families, left to cross the river Gogra. They encountered many dangers and hardships on the way and those of them that survived arrived safely at the house of the Raja of Gopalpur. That Raja entertained the twenty-nine English with great hospitality, for some days, and then sent them safely to the English camp. Most of the Englishmen who escaped in the trials of 1857 have written long accounts of their experiences. They are all very instructive and are a living monument to the nobility of sentiment of the people of our nation. Though there was so much hatred all over Oudh against the English, they were entertained hospitably, when they surrendered even, in the houses of those Rajas who fought on the side of the Revolutionaries. And such examples are not isolated. Busher writes: 'Now, I alone remained. Running on, I came across a village on the way. The first man I saw there was a Brahmin. I asked of him some water to drink. He saw my misery and took pity on me and told me that that village consisted of Brahmins and that my life was safe... ...Buli Singh came up in pursuit. I ran into a gully when an old woman came up to me and pointed out a cottage. I went in and hid myself in the grass. Shortly after came Buli Singh's men and began to pierce everywhere with the ends of their swords to find me. They soon found me and dragged me out by my hair. The people in the village began to heap curses on the Feringhis ! Then, Buli Singh conducted me to another place, amidst the hootings of the village crowd. My execution was postponed everyday. I fell on my knees and craved for mercy. In this way, I was taken, at last, to Buli Singh's house.' After a long time he was sent away to the English Colonel Lennox writes: 'While we were running, the men of Nazim Hossein Khan caught us. One of them drew out his revolver, gnashed his teeth and said that his hands were throbbing to despatch the Feringhis away in an instant but that he could not do it! We were next taken up to Nazim. He was sitting in the Durbar leaning on a cushion. He told us to drink a little sherbet and rest, and not to be frightened. When the question arose as to what quarters should be given to us, an angry servant suggested the horse-stables near by. Nazim rebuked him for this, but immediately another broke forth, 'Why all this trouble? I will just kill these Feringhi dogs!' Nazim thundered against them all and promised us our lives. We hid near the Zenana through fear of the mutineers. We got good food, clothing and rest.' Then, Nazim disguised all these as Indians and sent them safely to the English camp.

As soon as the English officers left the city of Fyzabad the other districts in the province also hoisted the flag of freedom. Sultanpur rose on the same day, i. e. the 9th of June. The third district town, Saloni, rose on the 10th. The officers of the latter place were running for their lives. The Sirdar Rustom Shah saved some of them, and Raja Hanumant Singh also saved some. The gallant and brave princes of Oudh did not rest content merely by sparing the lives of those who Surrendered but also entertained the English most hospitably. As a matter of fact, the English had inflicted terrible losses on, and offered great insults to, almost all these Zemindars. Not that the Zemindars ever forgot that their Swaraj had been destroyed and their religion was trodden under foot. Followed by their Sepoys, they were openly warring against the English and many had taken oaths never to rest until the English were out of the country. But, to match this heroic-patriotism and love of freedom, they all showed equally heroic gallantry. While the common people were massacring the English in a fit of rage and revenge, they treated the English women and children hospitably and showed them clemency! Even those officers who had but now persecuted them were given their lives. when they came to surrender! Though the mass of the people insisted that it was not desirable to leave the officers, for they might again come to fight-as the officers did in the latter part of the war-they did not shrink from showing them generosity! In how many other countries except in India can be found, in Revolutionary times, this gallantry and this nobility of heart, even when it enraged the masses?

Raja Hanamant Singh was the chief of Kala and, though not behind anybody in his anxiety to fight in the cause of his nation, his nobility forced even his enemies to speak of him in the following terms: 'This noble Rajput had been dispossessed, by the action of the revenue system introduced by the British, of the greater part of his property. Keenly as he felt the tyranny and the disgrace, his noble nature yet declined to regard the fugitive chiefs of the nation which had nearly ruined him in any other light than as people in distress. He helped them in that distress; he saw them in safety to their own fortress. But when, on bidding him farewell, Captain Barrow expressed a hope that he would aid in suppressing the revolt, he stood erect, as he replied, 'Sahib, your countrymen came into our country and drove out our king. You sent your officers round the districts to examine the titles of the estates. At one blow, you took from me lands which, from time immemorial, had been in my family. I submitted. Suddenly misfortune fell upon you. You came to me whom you had despoiled. I have saved you. But now,– now I march at the head of my retainers to Lucknow to try and drive you from the country.'[4]

---

4. Malleson's *Indian Mutiny*, Vol. III, page 273 (foot-note).

This generosity on the part of the people of Oudh was not a sign of weakness. Between the 31st of May and the end of the first week of June, the whole province rose in Revolution like a big machine suddenly setting to work! In the whole province, the Zemindars, Jagirdars, and Rajas; the thousands of Sepoys under the British-infantry, cavalry, and artillery; all the servants of the civil departments; peasants, merchants, and students; in short, all, whether Hindu or Mahomedan, rose like one man for freeing their country. Private enmity, differences of religion and caste and rank were all forgotten. Everyone felt in his heart that he was jumping into the battefield for a war of justice. It was the masses who re-established Wajid Ali Shah on the throne of Oudh in ten days. What a statesmanlike answer this to Dalhousie's contention that he deposed Wajid Ali Shah for the good of the people! At the end of the first week of June, there was scarcely, a village in the whole Oudh province that had not given such a statesmanlike reply to Dalhousie, by tearing to pieces the, English flag!

After giving a true picture of this state of things, the famous historical researcher, Forrest, says in his preface, 'Thus in the course of ten days, the English administration in Oudh vanished like a dream and left not a wreck behind. The troops mutinied, the people threw off their allegiance. But there was no revenge, no cruelty. The brave and turbulent population, with a few exceptions, treated the fugitives of the ruling race with marked kindness, and the high courtesy and chivalry of the people of Oudh was conspicuous in their dealings with their fallen masters who, in the days of their power, had, from the best (?) of motives, inflicted on many of them a grave wrong.'[5] If the experienced and able English officers had not been thus spared by the heroic nobility of the people of Oudh, Oudh could not have been reconquered merely by the English novices! For, as we shall see later on

5. Forrest's *State Papers*, Vol. II, page 37.

these were English officers and were returned with the new forces sent by the English and wreaked terrible vengeance on the Revolutionary leaders and followers who had, through misplaced generosity saved their lives as shown above!

About the 10th of June, the whole province of Oudh became independent and all the Sepoys and volunteers marched towards Lucknow. In that city, the great English leader, Henry Lawrence, was moving heaven and earth to inspire life into the dying English power. Though he had lost the whole province, he had still kept his hold on the capital. He had smelt the Revolution from afar and had fortified the two places, Machi Bhawan and the Residency, as has been already mentioned, When the Sepoys revolted on 31st of May and went away, Lawrence formed a splendid regiment of Sikhs and another of the 'most loyal' Hindusthanees. The remaining division of the old Sepoy army had rebelled before the 12th of June. This revolt pleased Sir Henry in a way, for now he had with him a select and faithful army consisting of the English regiment and artillery and the two regiments of Sikhs and Hindusthanees, whose loyalty to the English had been proved by, severe tests. Sir Henry was now waiting, ready to give battle.

The Sepoys and young fighting men of the province of Oudh were collecting together around the city of Lucknow. Both sides, before commencing the fight, were awaiting the issue of another struggle. The siege of Cawnpore was at its height, and neither the English nor the Revolutionaries started the battle until the final news from Cawnpore came. Each party based its hopes. on the result of Cawnpore. Sir Henry wrote hopefully to Lord Canning, on the 23rd of June,'If Cawnpore stands, it is doubtful whether Lucknow will be besieged at all.' On the 28th, the news came to Lucknow that not a single Englishman was left alive at Cawnpore! The Revolutionaries were flushd with the victory and marched up to Chinhut to attack the English.

The terrible defeat of the English at Cawnpore shook the basis of English prestige everywhere. Sir Henry Lawrence thought that, unless this defeat were counteracted, not only the Residency at Lucknow but even Fort William of Calcutta would not be safe and resolved to wash away the insult of Cawnpore with the blood of the Revolutionaries. The English army assembled near the iron bridge, on the 29th of June. Sir Henry left Lucknow with four hundred English soldiers, four hundred traitor Sepoys and ten guns. He marched a long distance without seeing any sign or the enemy. At last, he came across the front ranks of the Revolutionaries. Sir Henry, then, ordered his sepoys to take a very important village on his right. The Sepoys attacked that village and it fell into the hands of the English. The English soldiers, also, took the village of Ismailganj on the left. The Indian and English officers of the guns rained such a fire against the guns of the Revolutionaries that the latter was silenced. The English almost won the day at Chinhut. But, suddenly the cry arose that the Revolutionaries had entered unobserved the village on the left; the English soldiers were suddenly attacked and driven out, and the village was captured by the Revolutionaries, who now attacked the English centre and rear. As the English soldiers retired, the Revolutionaries rushed on. There was confusion in the English ranks and Sir Henry, seeing that a further stand would result in the ruin of the whole army, sounded a retreat! During the retreat the English suffered excessive hardships; for, the Revolutionaries did not stop with the victory of Chinhut but started a hot pursuit. The Sepoys manning the English artillery now began to slack. But the rest of the Indian cavalry and artillery showed even greater bravery than the English soldiers and ably covered the retreat. But, in a short time, the retreat ended in a rout! The despairing English army began to run towards Lucknow. Out of the four hundred English soldiers, nearly one hundred and fifty died that day. We need not count the Indian loyalists! The

English left on the field two guns and a big howitzer. They had also to leave there the revenge of Cawnpore. Beaten in this manner, Sir Henry re-entered the Residency at Lucknow. Still, the Revolutionaries were following him. When the English and the Sikhs and other loyalists came within the shelter of the guns at the Residency, the battle of Chinhut came to an end, But, its results still remained. The Revolutionaries now surrounded both Machi Bhawan and the Residency. Sir Henry, therefore, decided to vacate Machi Bhavan in order to render his defence more effective. The arsenal there, containing a large quantity of ammunition, was blown up, and all the Englishmen now came into the Residency. This Residency had enough stores of provisions, arms, and ammunition to stand a siege. There were now, in the Residency, about a thousand Englishmen and eight hundred Indian sepoys. They prepared to defend themselves against the vast number of Revolutionaries collecting outside. Seeing the preparations of the English general to defend the Residency after the battle of Chinhut, the Revolutionaries commenced a regular siege. Thousands of the Revolutionaries were mustering strong and chafing to put an end to the slavery and foreign domination.

In this manner, the enraged Ayodhya beat and pursued and imprisoned the English Power in this little Residency of Lucknow.[6]

---

6. The well-known writer of the Red Pamphlet says :— 'All Oudh has been in arms against us. Not only the regular troops but sixty thousand men of the army of the ex-king, the Zemindars, and their retainers, the two hundred and fifty forts—most of them heavily armed with guns-have been working against us. They have balanced the rule of the company with the sovereignty of their own kings and have pronounced, almost unanimously, in favour of the latter. The very pensioners who have served in the army have declared against us and to a man joined in the insurrection.'

CHAPTER X

The Summing Up

WHAT effect had this spirit of freedom which inspired life in the dead or dying thrones of Delhi, Cawnpore, Lucknow and Bareilly or the other states which were still, more or less, living?

The mass of the people, in 1857, had thoroughly understood that, so long as foreign domination over Hindusthan remained, the living states were as useless as the dead ones were lifeless. 'The Revolution in 1857, inspired by the holiest and the highest ideal of freedom, was not fighting furiously for the sake of this king or that heir. Individuals—peasants or kings—may live or die, but the nation should not die, must not die. The ideal was the establishment of the country's freedom by breaking the dreadful chains of slavery, and the universal war was sounded for the attainment of this noble end, even though the way to it was over the ashes of cottages and of thrones. He is a king who would, free his country. The other kings were as well dead as alive.

The people in the states like Gwalior, Indore, Rajputana, and Bharatpur were, also, full of the spirit of the Revolutionary War, as much as those in territories which had completely lost their independence. None of them entertained the sordid idea of keeping away from risk and danger, because his own native state was safe; nor looked upon his own tiny state as the whole nation, and upon the annexed provinces as people having exclusive interests and belonging to a foreign system. Foreigner! One son of the Mother, a foreigner to another! No; 1857 has come and all India is one; one in life; one in destiny!

Now, then, you Scindia of Gwalior! Give us the order to fight against the English. Give us not only the order but come and be our leader; Raise the holy cry of 'Swadesh' and

'Swadharma' on the battlefield and march on with the army to complete the half-done work of Mahadaji. The whole country is hanging on the one word of Jayaji Scindia! Say 'War!', and Agra falls, Delhi is liberated, the Dekkan rises amidst thunder, the foreigner is expelled from the country, the land is free, and you are the man who shall give it the gift of freedom! The lives of two hundred millions of men depended on the tongue of one man. Such an occasion is verily Historical!

But, the one tongue of the Scindia first would not move at all and, when it did move, it said 'Friendship!' instead of 'War!' The Scindia resolved to preserve his friendship—not with the country but with the English! At this, the people rose in a fury. If the Scindia does not wish to fight, we shall fight! If you do not run to save the Motherland, we well run to liberate her without you, and if it comes to that, in spite of you. To-day is Sunday, the 14th of June. We have waited for the Scindia till to-day. We will only wait for the sun to set to-day; when the sun sets—*Har! Har, Mahadev!* Who is there driving in that carriage? Mr. and Mrs. Coopland. How dare anyone salaam to them? Salaam a Feringhi after the 14th of June? Not only this Feringhi but, see there, the brigadier is coming, and no one raises his hand or moves his head to salute him! Brigadier, indeed! But who made him brigadier? Is it not the Feringhis? A crow, though standing at the top of a palace, does not become an eagle. So, march on right in the face of the brigadier and pay no attention to him. And so, the Sepoys of the Gwalior contingent passed the brigadier without saluting him.[1] Still there was no disturbance till the evening. In the evening, one bungalow took fire. Yes; now comes the time of rising. Artillery! rise in revolt! Infantry! take burning torches in one hand and shining swords in the other and dance about in all directions,

1. Mrs. Coopland's *Narrative.*

roaring like lions. See the colour of every man you meet in the street; if he is dark, embrace him; if white, kill him.

Maro Feringhi ko! You are hiding in the house; all right, we will set fire to it ! Who is this running out of the bungalow to save himself from the fire? Is he a white man? Cut his head off ! Who is this again? A white woman. 'Mat Maro! Mat Maro!'. (Don't kill!) 'We do not want to kill women!'[2] The whole night, the ghostly dance is going on. 'There must be no English-man in Gwalior, not even in the Scindia's palace. The white men were driven out of the Scindia's dominions-right up to Agra. The white women were collected together and put in prison. But, it is improper not to speak to them. See there an English woman suffering in the sun. Let us speak to her. So, one man asks her, 'Well, madam, how do you like the sun of this place? Is it not too hot? You are feeling it very much just now—are you? If you had remained in your own cold country, there would have been no such difficulty for you!' After listening to this 'devilish' bit of advice given to this woman, listen to what another of them says: 'What, you want to be sent to Agra? Ha, ha! Your people have been killed long ago and Agra now belongs to the Revolutionaries. Do you still wish to go there? And so arose a wave of mirthful laughter. The Scindia was made lifeless like a dummy; the Gwalior contingent forces revolted, spilt the blood of their officers, drove out English women, the English flag, and English power out of the limits of Gwalior state and made Gwalior perfectly independent. They next began to order the Scindia : 'Come and be our leader; come out with the whole army towards Agra, Cawnpore, and Delhi to liberate Hindusthan!' Scindia kept them quiet for many days by constant promises. Until Tatia Tope comes secretly to Gwalior and leads them, the troops are to remain thus inactive.[3]

2. Mrs. Coopland's *Narrative.*

And, therefore, it is that the English at Agra have still some hope. For the Lieutenant Governor of the North-Western Province, Mr. Colvin, is at Agra, standing in terror of death every minute. He had previously delivered a lecture on 'loyalty' to Sepoys, agitated by the Meerut news. He had issued a proclamation of pardon! But there was not even a single Sepoy weak minded enough to come to beg his pardon; nay, more, as a reply to the proclamation of pardon, they attacked Agra on the 5th of July. The revolted regiments of Nasirabad and Neemuch marched on Agra; so, the 'loyal' troops of the rulers of Bitaoli and Bharatpur were sent against them! The troops sent by these states declared that though they would refrain from rising against the English, for such were the orders of their rulers, they would not lift their swords against their own countrymen!' The English were thus deceived and disappointed. The native states were 'loyal'; but their people and armies 'would not lift their swords against their countrymen!' So taking with him the English troops alone, Brigadier Polwhele marched upon the Revolutionaries coming to attack Agra. Both armies met near Sassiah and the battle lasted the whole day; at last, the English force found it impossible to stand the attack of the

3. 'It was a most favourable moment for recovering his lost authority. It was merely necessary to accede to the proposal of the mutinous contingents and to revenge himself on the British. Had he so acceded, had he put himself at their head and, accompanied likewise by his trusty Mahrattas, proceeded to the scene of action, the consequences would have been most disastrous to ourselves. He would have brought at least twenty thousand troops, one half of them drilled and disciplined by European officers, on our weak points. Agra and Lucknow would have at once fallen. Havelock would have been shut up in Allahabad; and either that fortress would have been besieged or the rebels, giving it a wide berth, would have marched through Benares on to Calcutta. There were no troops, no fortification to stop them.' *Red Pamphlet* page 194.

Revolutionaries, and retired. The Revolutionaries, flushed with victory, pursued them hotly. When the army entered Agra, the Revolutionaries were at their heels with shouts of victory. Agra got the opportunity it wanted. It was the 6th of July. The town of Agra rose in revolt, headed by the police! The police officers were all in concert with the Revolutionary society. The religious leaders of both Hindus and Mahomedans organised a great procession. The Kotwal and othe police officers walked in the front line. They raised shouts of victory for Swadharma and Swaraj and proclaimed that the English rule was at an end and that the authority had been transferred to the Emperor of Delhi!

When Agra thus became free, Mr. Colvin, together with all the English there—ashamed of the defeat and anxious for the future—retired into the fort. He had now one great fear, and that was about the side that the Scindia would take. The mere news that the Scindia had joined the Revolutionaries would have made Mr. Colvin surrender that impregnable fort! But as it was clear that the Scindia was not against him, as was proved by his 'loyal' letters and help, the English flag at Agra seemed to revive. But the weight of supporting it was too much and Mr. Colvin died on the 9th of September, 1857, to the deepest sorrow of the English government in India.

The Revolutionary spirit that exhibited itself among the masses and the Sepoys at Gwalior had also burst forth in a terrible manner at Indore. Secret communication was established between all the troops in the English camp at Mhow and the troops of Holkar, and a rebellion was ,decided upon. On the 1st of July, Saadat Khan, a Mahomedan nobleman at the Indore court. ordered the army to fall upon the English at the Residency. He declared that the Maharaja Holkar had given him the order. But the Indian troops did not need any such declaration, even. They raised the flag of freedom and, at once, marched with their guns on the Residency. The Indian troops at the Residency refused to fire on their countrymen on behalf of the English. The English lost all hope; they quietly packed their bag and baggage and fled from Indore. The Indian troops at the Residency had guaranteed them their lives and protected them till the end. English, authors always try hard to find out exactly whether the Maharaja Holkar sympathised with the English or with the Revolutionaries. But one who minutely studies the history and the conditions of 1857 would see at once that during the Revolution, most of the states had purposely observed a dubious attitude. The desire of freedom is innate in man. Most of the states intended to raise the flag of freedom as soon as there was reasonable prospect of the success of the Revolution. They did not join the English, because they did not want to aid in the failure of the Revolution. On the other hand, they did not want, by actively helping the Revolutionaries, to give a handle to the English, if they should be able to overpower the Revolutionaries, to confiscate their estates. Thus, they provided for the other alternative of the Company coming out victorious. Fools that they were, not to be able to see that, if they joined the Revolulionaries, there was absolutely no chance for the English to succeed; while, if they remained neutral, the chances of the success of the Revolution were greatly lessened! This is the real explanation of the conduct of most of the states in this critical period. If the people and the troops drove out the English from the Residencies, they were permitted to do so; because, it meant the freedom of the states. Nonwithstanding this, the rulers would continne to declare their friendship for the English, so that, in case of English success, they should not lose what they had. It would seem that Cutch, Gwalior, Indore, Bundela, Rajputana, and other states—all behaved in this manner.

And it was this selfish conduct on the part of the princes, which, in the end, strangled the Revolution. If they had boldly come forward, crying 'Freedom—or death', they would certainly have obtained freedom. But they played a double-game-the- result of mean selfishness. Their good intentions, being weak, achieved nothing and their baseness was conspicuous! They were not open and bare faced traitors to the country like Patiala and others; but they played, indirectly, the part of traitors they let base selfishness take possession of their souls, even while hoping for the noble goal of freedom and, hence, they are cursed for their sin. When will they wash it away?

But these selfish motives which mastered the minds of the princes did not enter for a single moment the hearts of the people. And it was by their glorious onslaughts from Peshawar up to Calcutta that the fire broke forth and blood began to flow, in order to reduce to ashes and wash away the terrible curse of slavery which had smitten the land. And it was by their united strength and unselfish fight that English power collapsed and was grounded into dust, for some time at least.[4]

How little Calcutta and England understood the nature of this terrible earthquake! In the opinion of the Government, there was perfect peace before the Meerut rising. Even when Meerut rose and the Proclamation of freedom was issued from Delhi, Calcutta would not understand the real meaning of the eruption. Seeing that no wave of the rising appeared

4. Wherever the chiefs of the native states hesitated to join the revolution, the people of the states became uncontrollable and tried to throw off the yoke even of their own chief, if he would not join the nation's war. Seeing this extraordinary upheaval of the populace, Malleson says: ' Here, too, as at Gwalior, as at Indore, it was plainly shown that, when the fanaticism of the oriental people is thoroughly roused, not even their king, their Raja-their father, as all consider him, their God, as some delight to style him not even their Raja can bend them against their convictions.' The Sepoys of the Rajas of Jaipur and Jodhpur refused point blank to raise their hands against their countrymen who were fighting for the nation, even when asked by their Raja to do so, Malleson's *Indian Mutiny*, Vol. III, page 172.

between the 10th and 31st of May. Calcutta was confirmed in its idea that there was no serious trouble in Hindusthan. On the 25th of May, the Home Secretary proclaimed openly: 'There is perfect peace within a radius of six hundred miles from Calcutta. The momentary and isolated danger is passed. And it is strongly hoped that in a few days, perfect peace and safety will reign.'

The few days passed; the 31st of May dawned. 'Peace and safety' reigned everywhere! Around the Lucknow Residency, in the Cawnpore Maidan, in the Jogan Bagh at Jhansi, in the bazaars of Allahabad, on the Ghats of Benares, everywhere 'peace and safety' reigned! Telegraph wires cut to pieces, railways and iron bridges smashed and mixed into dust, English corpses floating in the rivers, pools of blood in the streets—everywhere 'peace and safety!'

It was then, that the fog at Calcutta cleared. On the 12th of June, all the English residents began to organize a corps of volunteers. English shopkeepers, clerks, writers, civil officers, in short, all Englishmen were hastily enrolled in the military list; they were taught drill and rifle practice. The work was done so quickly and energetically that, in three weeks, a whole brigade of the newly-drilled volunteer recruits was formed. The brigade consisted of cavalry, infantry, and artillery; since they were thought capable of protecting Calcutta, that work was given to them; and the Government got the opportunity of sending the professional English soldiers to parts where the Revolution was in full swing.

On the 13th of June, Lord Canning called a meeting of the legislative council and got a law passed against newspapers. For as soon as the Revolution began, the Indian newspapers of Bengal had begun to write articles openly sympathising with and encouraging the Revolution.

On Sunday, the 14th of June, a carnival of 'peace and safety' was celebrated at Calcuttla, also. We shall describe that day's scenes best through an English pen. 'All was panic, disorder, and dismay. The wildest reports were in circulation. It was all but universally credited that the Barrackpore brigade was in full march on Calcutta, that the people in the Suburbs had already risen, that the king of Oudh with his followers was plundering Garden Reach. Those highest in office were the first to give the alarm. There were secretaries to Government, running over to Members of Council, loading their pistols, barricading the doors, sleeping on sofas; Members of Council abandoning their houses with their families, and taking refuge on board the ship; crowds of lesser celebrities impelled by these examples having hastily collected their valuables, were rushing to the fort, only too happy to be permitted to sleep under the fort guns. Horses, carriages, palanquins, vehicles of every sort and kind were put into requisition to convey panic-stricken fugitives out of the reach; of imaginary cut-throats. In the suburbs, almost every house belonging to the Christian population was abandoned. Half-a-dozen determined fanatics could have burned down three parts of the town......'[5]

In the very capital of the English, merely at a bazaar rumour. so much 'peace and safety' began to reign. Therefore, the Government prepared to destory the Barrackpore Sepoys and the Nabob of Oudh, who were the cause of so much 'peace and safety.' They got, from one amongst the Sepoys, the information that the Barrackpore Sepoys would rise on the night of the 14th. So, before they could rise, they were brought before the English artillery and disarmed. And, on the 15th of June, the Nabob Of Oudh and his minister were arrested for the 'safety of the realm,' and their houses, including the Zenana, were thoroughly searched. And, though nothing of an incriminating nature was found, the Nabob and his Vizier were incarcerated in the Calcutta fort. Thus, the gradually accumulating powder-magazine of the city of Calcutta itself was emptied, only

5. *Red Pamphlet,* part I, page 105.

just before the spark fell on it.

The Vizier Ali Nakkhi Khan was the man who, residing in a harmless garden-house at Calcutta, had set on foot the Revolutionary secret organisation among the Sepoys all over Bengal and had woven the terrible net in order to re-establish his master on the throne of Oudh. When be was imprisoned in the Calcutta fort, the Revolution lost as it were, its head. While in the fort, he once spoke plainly to the English who were cursing the Revolutionaries : 'The terrible Revolution created in India is in my opinion just. It is a proper revenge for the annexation of Oudh. You have consciously left the road of justice and have entered the thorny path of deceit and selfishness. What wonder, then that your feet are bleeding by the self-same thorns? You were laughing when you sowed the seeds of revenge; why do you, then, blame the people when the self-same seeds have borne fruit in due course?[6]

When Calcutta itself had such a hazy and misty idea of the extent of the Revolutionary movement, we can easily understand how England, which depended for its information solely on the mail news from India, at first slept the sleep of ignorance, and then, when suddenly awakened, became possessed by terror and behaved like a madman. When the news of Barrackpore, Berhampore, Dum-Dum, and other places reached England, all eyes were turned towards India. But soon, everything became quiet and all began to feel safe again. On the 11 th of June, the President of the Board of Trade said, in reply to a question in the House of commons, 'There is now no reason for anxiety as regards the late unrest in Bengal. For, by the dexterity, firmness, and quickness of my honourable and noble friend, Lord Canning, the seeds of unrest sown in the army have been completely rooted out.' These are the sentences which the Parliament heard on the 11th of June. On that date in India, eleven cavalry regiments,

6. *Red Pamphlet.*

five field-batteries of artillery, at least fifty regiments of infantry, and nearly all the sappers and miners had risen in open revolt! The whole of Oudh was in the hands of the Revolutionaries! Cawnpore and Lucknow were besieged! The Revolutionaries had taken more than ten millions of Rupees from Government treasuries; and all this, at the moment when, owing to the dexterity, firmness, and quickness of Lord Canning, 'the seeds of unrest had been completly rooted out.'

But soon, the news of the extraordinary and sudden growth of these seeds of Revolution again disturbed England's sleep. The news about the Cawnpore massacres somehow reached the people and on the 14th of August, 1857, the unhappy, terror-stricken, and agitated masses caused a question to be put in the Parliament. in the House of Lords, 'Is the rumour about Cawnpore true?' Earl Granville replied: 'I have received a personal letter from General Sir Patrick Grant that the rumour about the massacres at Cawnpore is altogether untrue and is a vile fabrication. A Sepoy first set up the rumour. Not only is his baseness discovered but he has been hanged for spreading the false rumour.'[7] While the rumour about Cawnpore was being discussed in the House of Lords, a month had already passed since the 'truth' had been written in grim letters of red blood! While English politicians were resting a little in safety, after hanging the Sepoys who started the rumour, the truth came in person to the shores of England. And the whole of England became mad and hysterical with anger, fury, wounded pride, and this malicious fury continues up to this day. And England is shouting, even to-day in every line of her own histories, that the massacres committed by the Revolutionaries are demoniacal in their cruelty and are a blot on the fair name of Humanity!

And this loud shouting by the English at the top of their

7. Charles Ball's Indian Mutiny.

voice has made the whole world deaf! The very name of 1857 brings a shiver and horrification and shame to everybody! The very mention of the name of the Revolutionaries of 1857 creates disgust and loathing in the minds not only of their enemies, not only of innocent and indifferent third parties, but even of those for whose sake the Martyrs shed their blood! Their enemies give them choice epithets like 'demons', 'goblins', 'blood-thirsty and hellish vermin.' The strangers call them savage, inhuman, cruel and barbarous. Their own countrymen are ashamed even to own them. Such is the cry everywhere even today. And this incessant cry has deafened the ears of the whole world so that they should not any more listen to the voice of truth! The Revolutionaries are demons, goblins, murderers of women and children, blood-thirsty vermin of hell, inhuman. Oh World! When will you forget this and understand the truth?

And why all this? Why? Because, the Revolutionaries rose against the English, rose for their country and religion, and, with shouts of 'Revenge!', massacred some of them. Indiscriminate massacre is a heinous sin. When Humanity will reach the goal of universal justice, of ultimate beatitude, when the millennium preached by the incarnations, by the Messiahs, and by religious preachers will be an accomplished fact on earth, when the resignation taught by Christ in the glorious words —'Whosoever shall smite thee on the right cheek, turn to him the other, also' will be impracticable, because, there will be no one to hit on the right cheek, in such a divine age if anyone revolts, if anyone sheds a drop of blood, if anyone even whispers the word 'revenge!', then, at once, the sinner, by his act, by his very utterance, would be eternally damned. For, when Truth reigns in every heart, revolt must be a heinous sin. When everyone abhors killing, to shed a drop of blood must be a sin. In a time of such unchallenged justice, to punish a man even for uttering a sinful word would be altogether blameless.

But so long as that divine age has not arrived, so long as the highly auspicious end remains only in the lines of saintly poets and in the prophecies of the divinely inspired, and so long as, even to make that state of universal justice possible, the human mind has to be busy eradicating sinful and aggressive tendencies, so long, rebellion, bloodshed, and revenge cannot be purely sinful. As long as the word 'rule' is used for 'authority' both just and unjust, so long its antonym 'rebellion' can, also, be just as well as unjust. And till then, before passing judgement on the history and the authors of any revolt, bloodshed, and revenge, there must be a full and minute inquiry of the circumstances under which they took place. Revolt, bloodshed and revenge have often been instruments created by nature to root out injustice and introduce an era of justice. And when Justice uses these terrible means for her salvation, the blame of it does not lie on Justice but on the preceding cruel Injustice, the power and insolence of which called forth the means. We do not hold the justice which gives the death sentence responsible for bloodshed but rather the injustice which is taken to the gallows, Therefore, the sword of Brutus is holy. Therefore, the *waghnakh* of Sivaji is sacred. Therefore, the bloodshed in the Revolutions in Italy is of fair fame. Therefore, the beheading of Charles I is a just deed. Therefore, the arrow of William Tell is divine. And the sin of brutality falls heavily on the heads of those who committed the provoking injustice.

Moreover, had the world no fear of revolt, bloodshed, and revenge, the earth would have bent under the devil-dance of unchecked robbery and oppression! If Oppression were to be secure from the fear that Nature would, sooner, or later, create the Avenger of Temporary Injustice, the whole world would have swarmed to-day with Tsars and robbers!

But because every Hiranya-Kashipu has his Narsimha; because every Dushshasna has his Bheema; because every evil-doer has his avenger, there is still some hope in the heart of the world that Injustice cannot last. Such a revenge, therefore, is nature's own reaction against Injustice. And, therefore, the sin of the cruelty of that revenge rebounds on the orginal evil-doers.

And it was the fire of such a divine vengeance that was burning in the heart of the sons of Hindusthan in 1857. Their thrones were broken, their crowns smashed, their country taken away, their religions trodden under foot, their lands confiscated, their properties robbed, and laws despised; they had been cheated with promises made only to be broken; insults and outrages had reached a climax. Life itself had lost all its charms for them on account of the dire dishonour in which they had sunk. Requests were in vain; so also, were petitions, complaints, wailings, and cries, all in vain. Then the natural reaction began and everywhere could be heard the whispers of 'Revenge!' India had been subjected to innumerable, cruel oppressions each of which, individually, would have justified the revenge. If there had been no revolution even after all this, we would have had to say 'India is dead!' That revenge, therefore, was only the inevitable reaction against the English injustice and oppression. And when once the whole nation rose up in a rage, we should wonder not that there were indiscriminate massacres in one or two places, but that there were not such massacres in every place! For, the excited logic of those who committed the massacres naturally began to say, 'Oppose illegal force by righteous force!' Before the Sepoys who were caught in the battle of the river Kali were mounted on the scaffold, the English asked them why they had massacred their women and children. They at once retorted, 'Sahib, does anyone kill a snake and let its offspring alone?' The Sepoys at Cawnpore used to say: 'to extinguish the fire and leave the spark, to kill a snake and preserve its young is not the wisdom of the wise.'

'Sahib, does anyone kill a snake and leave its offspring alive?' How are the Sahibs going to answer this blunt question asked by the Sepoys at Kali-nadi? And this blunt question has not been asked by the excited masses of India alone, or the masses of Asia alone, as some English writers have been charitable enough to suggest. Wherever national wars are proclaimed, national wrongs are avenged by national killing alone. When the Spainards won back their independence from the Moors, to what state did they reduce them? The Spanish are neither Indians nor Asiatics. Then, why did they fall on the Moors who had stayed in Spain for nearly five centuries, and why did they massacre indiscriminately whole helpless families—men, women and children simply for the fault of belonging to another race? Why did Greece in 1821, massacre twenty-one thousand Turkish peasants—men, women and children? The secret society, Hetairia, which is looked upon as patriotic and heroic in Europe—what explanation does it give of the massacre? It is only this, that the Turkish population in Greece was too small to be kept in the country and too big to be removed. outside and that, therefore, to kill them all was 'a necessary measure of wise policy.' Was this not their answer? The idea that no one kills a snake and leaves his off spiring alive, also, came into the minds of the Greeks and burnt away the natural feelings of mercy in their heart! And the whole of the responsibility rests on the black poison or the snake.

Indeed, if there was no propensity in human nature towards a terrible revenge for an horrible injustice suffered, the brute in man would have been still the dominating factor in human dealings. Is not one of the most important functions of law—the punishment of crime?[8]

History bears testimony to the fact that whenever, in the human mind, the passion of vengeance—as a consequence of injustice carried to a climax—rages with uncontrollable strength, wholesale massacres and other inhuman atrocities take place in the life-evolution of every nation. Instead, therefore, of being surprised at the cruelties and massacres in four or five places during the Indian Revolution, our wonder should be that such cruel massacres took place on such a modest scale and that this terrible vengeance did not run riot more extensively and in all places. All Hindusthan had been scorched to the bone by the 'terrible oppression of the English, and a most grim reprisal did Indian humanity

8. Sir W. Russell, the famous correspondent of the London Times. remarks: 'We who suffered from it think that there never was such wickedness in the world; and the incessant efforts of a gang of forgers and utterly base scoundrels have surrounded it with horrors that have been vainly invented in the hope of adding to the indignation and burning desire for vengeance which hatred failed to arouse. Helpless, garrisons surrendering without condition have been massacred are now. Risings, such as that of Pontus under Mithridates of the Irish Roman Catholics under protestant settlers in 1641, of the actors in the Sicilian Vespers, of the assassins who smote and spared none on the eve of St. Bartholomew, have been over and over again attended by inhuman- cruelties, violations, and tortures. The history of Mediaeval Europe affords many instances of crimes as great as those of Cawnpore. The. history of more civilised periods could afford some parallel to them in more modern times and amidst most civilised nations. In fact, the peculiar aggravation of the Cawnpore massacres was this—that the deed was done by a subject race, by black men who dared to shed the blood of their masters and that of poor helpless ladies and children. Here we had not only a Servile War and a sort of Jacquerie combined, but we had a war of religion, a war of race, and a war of revenge, of hope, of national determination to shake off the yoke of a stranger and to re-establish the full power of native chiefs and the full sway of native-religions.'-*Russell's Diary*, page 164.

take when the oppression became unbearable—so unbearable that the massacres became not more but rather much less than the necessities of national punishment would have required in any other country. But, Hindusthan did not, in 1857, —for the just removal of its wrongs—give that punishment, take that vengeance, cause that bloodshed of which the English nation, led by Cromwell, was guilty in the massacres in Ireland. Does not history record how he was very much enraged at the sturdy patriotism of the Irish, how his sword cut to pieces not only those who fought but also the helpless, impoverished masses, how rivers of blood flowed in that unfortunate country, how helpless women were butchered along with the infants in their arms and were weltering in pools of blood, and how, in this manner, Cromwell, for the guilty object of conquering and subduing Ireland, committed cruel oppression, took more cruel vengeance, and, cruellest of all, caused terrible bloodshed? But, in 1857, in Hindusthan, Nana Sahib and the Begum of Oudh, Bahadur Shah and Lakshmi Bai, tried to the last to save women and children, though the fierce Sepoys were wild with fury. But how did the English women reward Nana for saving their lives at Cawnpore? Why—by playing the spy on him! And—how did the European officers return the kindness of the Indians who spared their lives? History has to record with shame that they returned it by poison- ing the minds of the ignorant English soldiery with lying stories of vengeance, by marching at their head against the Revolutionaries, by betraying the strategic weakness of the Revolutionaries, and by butchering those very Sepoys and villagers who spared their lives. Strange indeed-immensely strange it is—that the Hindu people allowed not their constitutional magnanimity to be disturbed even by such gross ingratitude! What a number of roofs of the poor agriculturists have been instrumental in saving the lives of the hunted English! Many and many a woman and child amongst the English fugitives has been tenderly protected by village women, painting them black with their own hands and giving them Indian clothes. Raw English officers—insignificant English youths—have again and again been brought back to life by Brahmins giving them a sip of milk in time, while they lay by the roadside exhausted by running day and night! Read Forrest, and he acknowledges that Oudh—Oudh into whose body the knife of oppression had been driven most ruthlessly—treated with incomparable generosity the English while they were flying everywhere unprotected. Did not the leaders of the Revolution warn their followers bent on vengeance, again and again, by issuing proclamations in various places that their sacred cause would become unsuccessful through child-murder and woman-murder? The 'mutineers' of Neemuch and Nasirabad spared the lives of the whites. While some white people were running for very life everywhere, even the villagers on the way shouted, 'Feringhis, Feringhis, kill the Feringhis!' Then one family came forward and said that they had just dined with Rajputs, and to kill them, therefore, —heartless enemies though they were—was out of the question.[9] If the Hindusthanee who is by nature kind and magnanimous, whose villages, up to this very day, are full of humanity, respect, and regard for life-human and animal, sanctioned and took part in the massacres of 1857, then the cruelty of these massacres, instead of reflecting discredit on the morals of the nation, proves only the immense hideousness of the Alien oppression to which it was now intended to put an end. The famous truth enunciated by Macaulay is here well exemplified; 'The more violent the outrage, the more assured we feel that a Revolution is necessary.'

And who have the right of sitting in judgement on the people of Hindusthan for the offences they are alleged to have committed? The English? If there is anyone in this wide world who have the least right to condemn the conduct of

9. Charles Ball's *Indian Mutiny*, Vol. I

the Revolutianaries, it is these English! Is it England that is to declare to the world that Hindusthan was guilty of one or two massacres? the England which procduced Neill? Or the England which devastated by the sword and destroyed by fire villages after villages with the 'women and children in them? Or the England which bound to the stakes and burnt, actually burnt, those brave fellows with the spirit of Panday in them, fighting for their country-deeming hanging not a sufficient punishment? Or the England which seized 'the innocent Hindu villagers, sentenced them to be hanged, and then pierced them with bayonets, and then, Heavens! thrust beef dripping with blood—the blood of the cow—down their throats, at the point of the bayonet—a desecration to which they would have preferred being hanged and, even, being burnt alive? Or the England which ordered, under the very nose of the commander-in-chief, that the body of the Nabob of Farukabad should be smeared all over with the fat of the pig, before he was hanged ?[10] Or that England which sewed the follower of Islam in the skin of a pig before killing him?[11] Or the England which advocated these and hundreds of other similar crimes as *justifiable revenge* on the 'mutineers'? justifiable vengeance! Whose was the justifiable vengeance—that of the Panday party enraged and vowing vengeance because their mother—the country—was being ground down under oppression for a hundred years, or that of the Feringhi party which was guilty of that National oppression?

Not one individual, not one class, alone had been moved deeply by seeing the sufferings of their country. Hindu and Mahomedan, Brahmin and Sudra, Kshatriya and Vaisya, prince and pauper, men and women, Pundits and Moulvies, Sepoys and the police, townsmen and villagers, merchants and farmers—men of different religions, men of different

10. Forbes-Mitchell's *Reminiscences,*
11. Russel's *Diary.*

castes, people following widely different professions—not able any longer to bear the sight of the persecution of the Mother, brought about the avenging Revolution in an incredibly short time. So universal was the agitation! This fact alone shows that, at this time, the utmost had been done as far as oppression went. Not even the class of Government officers-the class that were individually benefited by the foreign domination—were on the side of the Government. An English writer says that to give the list of Government officers who were seduced would mean the drawing up a list of all the Government officers in the disaffected provinces. Exceptions were rare. He gives the following names as instances:— Kazi Abul Fazul, Chief Judge of the N. W. P., the Principal Sudder Amin of Agra, the Munsiff of Agra, the Principal Sudder Amin of Delhi, the ten Government Pleaders in the Sudder Dewani, the Chief Kotwal of Agra, two of the Munsiffs of Delhi, the Principal Sudder Amin of Calcutta, the Deputy Collector of Cawnpore, the Deputy Collector of Fatehpur—the man who killed Robert Tucker—the rest of the native officers of Fatehpur, the Munsiff of Allahabad, another Munsiff of the same province, the Principal Sudder Amin of Bareilly, the Deputy Collector of Azimgarh, the Principal Sudder Amin of J—, the Principal Sudder Amin of G—, this is only a select list![12] So all-embracing was the Revolutionary fire. The worst abuse that one could use towards another, in those days, was to call him 'loyal'! Anyone who showed such 'loyalty' and any who obtained service under Government were classed as traitors to their country and their religion! Those who persisted in Government service were excommunicated by their castes; no one would eat with them; no one would marry among them; the Brahmin refused to do Puja for him; none would set fire to his funeral pyre. The service of the foreigner, of the Feringhi, was considered as sinful as matricide! Are not these indications that the climax of oppression had been

12. Rev. Kennedy, M.A. page 43

reached? [13]

And hence this volcano—supremely quiet externally—was boiling inside and had reached the bursting point. On the back of this volcano, Oppression was stalking about reckless and without fear. But as soon as the psychological moment came and Tyranny stamped on the green surface with all the more reckless vehemence the Volcano burst! Behold, the Revolution in Eruption! fountains of fire are surging up—blood is raining upon her—piercing shrieks are mingled with the clashing of swords—ghosts are dancing—heroes are shouting! The cool green tract of the volcano has split in twain—now it bursts into a hundred parts—aye, it has burst in a thousand places—it has deluged the earth with fire and sword!

In Kathiawar, there is a curious kind of stream, known as the Vitharoo, in some places. The surface of the stream has the appearance of hard ground. Strangers, ignorant of this, step on to it confidently. When the hard layer moves a little, they try to steady themselves by firmly pressing on the surface. No sooner is this done than the surface yields and the poor wayfarer is drowned in the deep waters. The Revolutionary stream had spread over India like the Vitharoo. Oppression believed, deceived by the dark colour on the face, that it was only earth that suffers with- out complaint every wrong (as the Sanskrit name सर्वसहा for it signifies). Oppression stepped on it. The black surface showed

---

13. 'Revolt had, in consequence, swept before it, in many cases, all regard to personal interest and all attachment to the former master. The imputations of remaining faithful to the Government, in such circumstances has been intolerable. It is well known that the few Sepoys who have remained in our services are deemed outcastes, not only by their comrades but their caste people in general. These even say they cannot venture to go to their homes; for not only would they be reproached and denied brotherly offices, but their very lives would be in danger.'-Rev. Kennedy.

agitation. Then Oppression, in the pride of its power, pressed harder on this deceptive earth. But, behold! the ground has yielded and up surges the bottomless pit of blood, foaming and raging, waves on waves! Doomed Oppression! step where you will, no solid ground meets your feet! Know, now at least, and know well that below the dark face flow streams of blood, red blood. And hear, even yet, the deafening roar of the Volcano's Eruption!

THE END OF THE SECOND PART

PART III

The Conflagration

CHAPTER I

The Flight in Delhi

AFTER declaring her Independence on the 11 th of May, the city of Delhi had been busy in organising the wild storm that such a bold step had raised into a systematised revolution. By restoring the Emperor of Delhi to the ancient throne of the Moguls, the citizens of Delhi had already created a nucleus mighty enough, by the very prestige of its name; to sustain the struggle of a people's liberation. But this restoration of the old Mogul was a restoration, neither to the old power nor to the old prestige, nor to the old traditions. Though the raising of the old Bahadur Shah to the Emperorship of Hindusthan was, in a narrower sense, a restoration of him to his ancient throne, still in a wider and truer sense, it was no restoration at all. For, 'the Mogul dynasty of old was not chosen by the people of the land. It was thrust upon India by sheer force, dignified by the name of conquest, and upheld by a powerful pack of alien adventurers and native self- seekers. It was not this throne that was restored to Bahadur Shah today. No, that would have been impossible; for, such thrones are conquered and not received. That would have been suicidal; for, then, it would have been in vain that blood of hundreds of Hindu martyrs had been shed in the three or four centuries preceding. Ever since the rising power of Islam left its native wilds of Arabisthan and went conquering East and West, irresistible and unchallenged, country after country and people after people had been made to prostrate in submission to Islam. But the unopposed wave was opposed, for the first time in the land of Bharat, with such strenuous, uncompromising, and undaunted tenacity as could be found only very rarely in other histories. For more than five centuries the struggle continued; for more than five centuries the Hindu civilisation had been fighting a defensive war against the foreign encroachment on its birth-rights. From the death of Prithvi Raj right up to the death of Aurangzeb, the war was without a truce. And in the midst of this gory struggle of countless years, a Hindu power arose in the western mountains of Bharat Varsha which was destined to fulfil the mission of the innumerable dead, who fell fighting in protecting the honour of the race. From out of Poona, a Hindu prince Bhausahib—advanced with a mighty host, captured the throne of Delhi, and vindicated the honour of the Hindu civilisation; the conqueror was conquered and India was again free, the blot of slavery and defeat being wiped off. Hindus again were masters of the land of the Hindus.

So, in the truer sense, we said that the raising of Bahadur Shah to the throne of India was no restoration at all. But rather it was the declaration that the longstanding war between the Hindu and the Mahomedan had ended, that tyranny had ceased, and that the people of the soil were once more free to choose their own monarch. For, Bahadur Shah was raised by the free voice of the people, both Hindus and Mahomedans, civil and military, to be their Emperor and the head of the War of Independence. Therefore, on the 11th of May, this old venerable Bahadur Shah was not the old Mogul succeeding to the throne of Akbar or Aurangzeb—for that throne had already been smashed to pieces by the hammer of the Mahrattas—but he was freely chosen monarch of a people battling for freedom against a foreign intruder. Let, then, Hindus and Mahomedans send forth their hearty, conscientious, and most loyal homdge to this elected or freely accepted Emperor of their native soil on the 11th of May, 1857 !

And from far and near, the loyal homage did come to the Delhi monarch, from many Rajas, many regiments, and many of the chief cities of Hindusthan. The different regiments that had risen at different places in the Punjab, Ayodhya, Neemuch, Rohilkhand, and many other places, marched on to Delhi with their flags and banners, and tendered their services to the venerable Bahadur Shah as the accepted head of the Revolution. Many regiments again brought whatever treasuries they had looted from the possession of the English Government on their way to Delhi and faithfully handed them over to the treasury of the Emperor. A proclamation was at once issued, addressed to the whole of Hindusthan, declaring that the foreign domination and the rule of the Feringhis had come to an end and that the whole nation was free and liberated. It exhorted the people to rise to a man to complete this Revolution so promising, in its beginning and warned them that the sole motive that should dominate them in this fight should be a self-denying, spiritual fervour and a consciousness of a divine duty. 'Let it be known that the only inducement we can hold forth is that of Dharma alone. Let all those to whom God has granted determination and will, renounce the hope of property and of life and join us in this cause of ancient faith. If the people sacrifice their private interest for the public good, the Englishmen will be exterminated from our land. It should be known that no one dies before his time and, when his time comes, nothing can save him. Thousands of men are carried off by cholera and other disease; while, to be killed in a war of Dharma is martyrdom. And it is the duty of every man and woman to kill or expel every Feringhi from the land of Hindusthan. Let zeal for religious duty alone be the motive of those who join me, and not any worldly aspiration, though they who rise for the faith get happiness in this world too!'

These extracts are from the different, and sometimes

similar Proclamations published in Oudh and Delhi. Another Proclamation was issued from the throne itself and was most widely published allover India. Even in the farthest south were found copies passing from hand to hand, in the bazaars and in the army. It insisted: 'To all Hindus and Mahomedans! We, solely on account of religious duty, have joined with the people. Whoever shall, in these times, exhibit cowardice or credulously believe the promises of the English impostors, will be very shortly put to shame and receive the reward for their fidelity to England which the rulers of Lucknow got. It is further necessary that all, Hindus and Mahomedans, unite in this struggle and, following the instructions of some respectable leaders, conduct themselves in such a way that good order may be maintained, the poorer classes kept contented, and they themselves be exalted to rank and dignity. Let all, as far as it is possible, copy this Proclamation and fix it in some prominent place, escaping detection if prudence requires it, and strike a blow with the sword before!'

Soon after the general declaration of war against the English power, the Revolutionaries at Delhi began to manufacture the arms and ammunition necessary for its continuation. A big factory of cannon, guns, and small arms was started, and some Frenchmen were employed to supervise the manufacture. Two or three big ammunition depots were also opened and many maunds of gun-powder began to be prepared by people working day and night. A general order was issued prohibiting the slaughter of kine throughout the country and, when once some fanatic Mahomedans wanted to insult the Hindus by declaring *Jehad* against them, the old Emperor, seated on an elephant and with all his Imperial officers, went in a procession through all the city declaring that the *Jehad* was against the Feringhis alone! Anyone found killing a cow was to be blown up or his hand cut off. Different regiments were named after the different princes of the palace. Some Europeans, too, were to be seen fighting on the side of the Revolutionaries against the English power.

The position which the English had occupied after the battle of Bundel-ki-Serai was very nicely suited to their military operations. The long range of hills, styled by the English as the Ridge, which almost touched the fortifications of Delhi at one of its extremities and extended to the river Jumna four miles ahead, had, owing to its height, a special advantage from the military point of view. For the Ridge, being higher than the surrounding level by fifty or sixty feet, offered a fine position for the guns so as to keep up a continuous and effective cannonade. Again, this Ridge had at its back the wide canal of the Jumna which, owing to the heavy rains of the year, was copiously supplied with water even in this month of June. Being at their back, this canal was free from attacks of the enemies of the English power, and now especially so; for, the Punjab, which would have been the greatest terror to the English had it attacked them from their rear as Delhi had been doing from their front, had now declared in favour of the British. The Rajas of Nabha, Jhind, and Patiala rendered an immense service to the English people by guarding all the highways to the Punjab and, thus, facilitating the transport of corn, men, and ammunition from the Punjab into the English camp. This combination of circumstances, unfortunate for India, rendered the situation extremely favourable to the English. High and lowering hills, behind them a plain for the whole army to encamp beyond the range of the enemy's fire and at the same time, escape the detection of the enemy's scouts, water living and inexhaustible so closely running, the great highways to the Punjab all open, at hand, and protected, at the back guarded by the constant watch of the loyal Punjab states at their own cost-all these circumstances heightened the confidence of the British commander, Barnard, who along with his officers was of the opinion 'Now, to take Delhi is not the work of even a day!'

And if it is not even one day's work to take Delhi, then, why spend two for it? Why should we not reduce this sinful, treason-loving city to dust by ordering these English soldiers to pounce upon it just this very minute? The Punjab is the back-bone of our army and when that is so strong in loyalty, why should we try to take Delhi by these weak tactics of prolonged siege? Would it not be better and nobler to rush straightway against that wretched city and crush it at the very first onslaught? Let our army be divided, let one of these divisions blow up this Lahore gate, let another pull down that Kabul gate, let many others rush simultaneously into the streets of the city with a torrent-like rush and, taking post by post, let us all march on straight against the palace without the loss of a moment! Wilberforce Greathead and Hodson-warriors like these are longing for this bold and straight onrush, and have taken upon themselves even the entire responsibility of carrying it out to a successful termination. Then, there need be no hesitation at all. So, on the 12th of June, General Barnard issued secret orders for the assault. It was all settled who should gather, where the gathering should take place, and when and how the different divisions should start under the cover of night, who should command the right and who the left. All these and many other details of the attack were settled and fixed and, now at two o'clock in the morning, the English army began to debouch itself on the parade ground which was fixed as the secret rendezvous. When it is certain that to-morrow's night will give us the chance of sleeping in the royal palace itself, who is so foolish as to grudge, to-night, a few hours' loss of sleep? Unlikely, indeed, but unfortunately true! For it happened that, at the proper hour, some parts of the army were found missing, Brigadier Graves thinks it rashness to begin the assault on Delhi in this fashion and it is even suggested by many others that such a scheme would be fatal to the British power itself allover India. Therefore, the dreams of the quick success and straight attacks, indulged in by the British army, had to be realised that night not in the palace of Delhi but on the Campbeds alone.

The next morning, Wilberforce Greathead again drew up a scheme for the future attack and sent it to the commander, Barnard, for reconsideration of the same. General Barnard, though a famous warrior known much in the Crimean campaigns, yet had been suspected of a very halting and hesitating mind. He called a council of war, on the 14th of June, to consult his chief officers on the subject of the assault. Even after the bold and eloquent advocacy by Greathead of a straight assault, the other officers could not feel confident of its success, and they urged further that even assuming that the assault would result in success, still, it would be as much waste of energy and prestige as an actual defeat. The straight assault might carry Delhi—yet, how to hold it? How many English soldiers were likely to—survive the constant cannonade of the Revolutionaries from street to street and from house to house? Barnard himself was most diffident of the issues. After all this discussion, the war council agreed simply to disagree! And thus, even like the night dream of the 12th of June, passed away this day dream of the 15th or June, leaving 'the straight assault' and 'the bold rush' still in their theoretical existence and excellence. This council of war again sat, on the 16th of June; but that ended in a worse division of opinion and diffidence of mind. For, as the English commander was planning the bold and straight assault on the city of Delhi, there on the other side, into the city of Delhi were pouring fast new hearts, new treasuries, and new energy. And the Revolutionaries, leaving the defensive policy which they had up to this time observed, began to assume the offensive as well, made frequent sorties, and attacked the British army from different sides and with varying success.

The regiments that had risen all over India had been, all the while, pouring into Delhi with their treasuries, arms, and ammunition and left no anxiety in the Revolutionary camp as to the provisions of war or to the number of Sepoys. And so, it was quite natural that the Revolutionary army should assume the aggressive and pin the English army to its place by not allowing it to move onwards even by a single step. After making a bold attack, after a slight or even a bloody skirmish or encounter, without themselves suffering any heavy losses, the Indian army would retire into the city. By this harassing policy, the Revolutionary army kept the English in constant check and prevented them from assuming the offensive. On the 12th of June, they issued out of the city and, concealing themselves in trees and low grounds, advanced as far as within fifty yards of the English front and attacked them before they were aware of their presence. The English lost many artillerymen and Knox himself was killed by a Sepoy who deliberately aimed at and shot him. Simultaneously with this, another division of the Sepoys attacked the English rear, and there a hot encounter took place. Even on the right of the English army, the post called 'Hindu Rao's house' was most vigorously attacked by the Sepoys. A detachment of native irregular cavalry, on whose loyalty the English had relied, went over to the enemy. And so sudden was the retrograde movement that the greater number of them escaped from the fire of our guns which were turned upon them as soon as their treachery was disclosed.'[1] Major Reid who was in charge of this place says: 'They went to the front just as if they were going to charge; but no sooner had they closed than, to my horror, I saw them mix up with the enemy and walk off with them. Immediately I saw this, I ordered the guns to open upon them but the wretches were too far off and I don't think that more than half-a-dozen were killed.'

After this assault, every day saw the Revolutionaries issuing from out the city and every evening saw them retiring

1. Kaye's *Indian Mutiny*, Vol. II, page 411.

back into the city. Any regiment that newly came into the city had to go out and attack the enemy the very next day. On the 13th of June, Hindu Rao'a house was again attacked; the 60th regiment (the same that joined the Revolutionaries on the 12th) was conspicuous in the day's action. Major Reid writes that they 'marched up the Grand Trunk Road in columns of sections right in front and led the attack headed by the Sirdar Bahadur of the regiment, who made himself very conspicuous, calling out to the men to keep their distance as he intended to wheel to his left. They fought most desperately. The Sirdar Bahadur was killed by his orderly, Lall Singh. I took the riband of India from his breast and sent it to my wife.' On the 17th of June, the Indian army tried to erect a battery on the Idga building, which would have completely enfiladed the Ridge. Seeing this, Major Reid and Henry Tombs attacked the Revolutionaries from both sides and pressed upon them with irresistible force. But the handful of brave Revolutionaries who had been entrapped in this building did not surrender at all. When they could no longer discharge volleys of shots, they threw away their guns, drew out their swords, and fell fiercely on the British foe. They did not allow the enemy to occupy the Idga building, until everyone of them was killed and fell fighting at his post!

On the 18th of June, the Sepoys who had rebelled at Nasirabad came to Delhi, and delivered over the treasure that they had brought with them to the royal authorities; and their representatives were received by the Emperor himself in the palace; and they were treated with due honour and respect. At the Durbar, the representatives of the Sepoys of this regiment took oath to attack the English army on the 20th of June. Accordingly the morning of the 20th of June saw the hosts of Revolutionaries leaving the gates of the city and marching towards the foreign foe. In order to attack the English forces on their rear, the Sepoys stole forth through Sabzi Mundi and, taking the English by surprise, they opened fire with terrible effect and advanced against the English.

Scott, Money, Tombs, and other English officers tried their utmost by heavy cannonading to stop the onslaught, but the tenacity with which the Indian army pushed on was irresistible. The brigade from Nasirabad pushed on with such destructive force that the brave Tombs cried out, through supreme despondency, 'Run on, Daly, run on! or my cannon are lost to the enemies!' Daly did come on with the Indians of the Punjab but, in a short time, was sent back by the Revolutionaries with a bullet lodged in his shoulder. As the evening approached, the Revolutionaries decidedly got the upper hand. Again, they pressed on, nay almost captured the British guns. The 9th lancers and the loyal Punjabees, though they more than once came rushing against them, had to retire precipitately. The night set in, but the field was still hotly contested. The English did their best but could do nothing further than to save their cannon. Lord Roberts writes: 'The mutineers routed us.' Hope Grant had a horse killed under him, himself was terribly wounded, and, but for the loyalty of a Mahomedan horseman standing near by, would have been killed in a minute. Such fighting continued till the middle of the night, but still the advance of the Sepoys could not be checked, and so, at last, the English retired from the battlefield and left the Revolutionaries in complete and victorious possession of an important position at the rear of the British camp!

That night the British commander could not sleep for anxiety. For, had the Revolutionaries retained the possession they had so bravely won, they would have completely cut off the British communications with the Punjab. To avoid this evil, the British, early in the morning, were preparing to offer a further resistance to the victorious Swadeshi army. But owing to the want of ammunition and further additions to their numbers, the Sepoys retired into the city, leaving the English to take possession of the ground they had vacated. The news of this battle and the dogged march of the Sepoys had encouraged the Delhi people and, the cannon on the wall being of long range, they kept up a constant and unceasing fire on the British army. These onslaughts of the Delhi army effectively prevented the British army from assuming the offensive, by constantly compelling them to be themselves on the defensive. And the difficulty which the English found even in maintaining the ground they had occupied made it impossible for them to advance even a step further without receiving new succour from the Punjab. And, to add to all these difficulties rose to-day-the 23rd of June, 1857!

This 23rd of June of 1857 is the centenary of the battle or Plassey! It was on this day that, a hundred years ago, in the gamble for empires, the Indian dice proved unlucky on the battle-field of Plassey. One hundred years have passed, each adding flew insults and new shame to those previously inflicted! To settle this standing account of a century of degradation, to wash off these national insults and this national shame by torrents of blood this is the fierce desire that gleams in the eyes of all the Sepoys in the city of Delhi. Through every breeze of the wind and through every ray of the sun, through every thundering roar of the cannon and through every clashing or the sword, comes forth a deep rumbling voice, 'Plassey! The Vengeance of Plassey!' As soon as the dawn announced the hundredth anniversary of the woeful field of Plassey, the Revolutionary forces began to. pour out of the Lahore gates of the city. The English people, too well aware of the fact that this day would tax their energies to the utmost, were quite prepared and had already drawn up their soldiers in battle-array even before the day rose. Nay, through this very anxiety, they requested the Government of the Punjab to send them help, which, fortunately for them, did arrive on the eve of this day. This news of the arrival of fresh troops from the Punjab infused the English with great confidence. But, neither this news of the reinforcements which the English received nor the discovery of the fact that the British had already destroyed the bridges leading to their rear would stop the enthusiasm of the Revolutionaries. They rushed on through the Sabzi Mandi and began to open fire on the British. The British infantry led charge after charge, but the Revolutionists repulsed them as often as they sallied forth. The artillery from the walls of the city was doing its work with equal vigour. Hindu Rao's house, too, was receiving its share of attention from the Revolutionaries. At twelve in the noon, the battle was raging hottest. The Revolutionaries led attacks after attacks on the Punjabee division, the Gurkha battalion, and the white troops of the British. Major Reid says: 'The mutineers, about twelve o'clack, made a most desperate attack on the whole of my position. No man could have fought better. They charged the rifles, the guides, and my own men again and again and, at one time, I thought I must have lost the day.'[2]

That one of the bravest English officers, fighting on the-very spot, should write these words testifies to the fierceness and strength of the attacks of the Revolutionaries. Yet, they had no capable leader who would bring into a focus these scattered elements of fire and energy. The ardent desire to win back the liberty of the land and the remembrance of the national insult or Plassey were the only ties that could keep them coherent. Even the English artillery was in a great danger of being captured by the Indian army and, at last, the chief officer, Colonel Welshman, himself was shot dead while goading on his men! The whole- day, every man in the English camp was fighting hard and now it seemed that they could no longer hold on. But still the British commander need not lose hope! For thc fresh troops of the loyal Punjabees that had come this very morning are eager to try their chance! They were ordered to march on and, against this fresh attack of fresh soldiers, the Revolutionaries, who had unceasingly been fighting the whole day, had to enter into an, unequal contest. However, till the night set in, the Revolutionaries

2. Major Reid's *Siege of Delhi.*

fought on, greatly handicapped as they were, And then, the armies retired from the field, each party claiming the honour of a victory! So ended the centenary of Plassey in the defeat of neither, and both the arınies entered their respective camps, filled with respect for each other's courage and bravery.

Day after day, new troops were coming in on both sides. The English forces, after frequent reinforcements from the Punjab, had, by this time, risen to the number of seven thousand. On the other side, the regiments of Rohilkhand who had risen in revolt had reached Delhi, with Bakht Khan at their head. Lord Robert says: 'The Rohilkhand army, having crossed the bridge of boats, began to enter the city through the Calcutta gate. We could clearly see these thousands of Sepoys from the Ridge, entering the city with perfect discipline and drill, playing martial tunes, and waving variegated flags and banners.' The only force that was able to unite to some extent these different regiments in, Delhi was that of love of the principle alone. For, there could grow no organised and compact army from amongst these thousands of Sepoys of different castes and creeds who had never seen the faces of each other in their whole life and had been drifted together by a chance storm. In spite of the utmost efforts of the Emperor and his councillors to stop looting and anarchy in the city, no day would pass without some complaint or other of Sepoy lawlessness, or of looting, or of blackmail. In this state, the supreme need of the hour was a leader who could unite these innumerable and divergent forces into a unifying focus. The city of Delhi, in spite of the growth of the evil tendencies and vicious propensities in the men, so natural in an agitated time as this, had led attack after attack on the English army and had, at least, held them in fear and check. It was the ardent desire amongst the soldiery and the citizens to drive away the foreign foe, that enabled them to do this. But to ensure ultimate success, it was imperatively necessary that this love of the abstract principle must be united with, and concentrated in, the ability of a great personality. It was, therefore, thought to be a Godsend when the brave Bakht Khan of Rohilkhand entered Delhi with bis troops and treasury. The state of the Public mind at Delhi, at the time of the arrival of Bakht Khan, is well described in the diary of one who was then living in Delhi. This extract, though meagre and casual, is taken here not only to give some account of this particular day but to give a general idea of the state of Delhi and the course which events were taking. 'The bridge on the Jumna is repaired; for, the arrival of the Rohilkhand troops is expected. The Emperor with a telescope viewed the approaching army of Rohilkhand while it was still far away. On the morning of the 2nd of July, Nabob Ahmad Kuli Khan, with all other nobles and citizens, went forth to receive the army of Rohilkhand. Hakeem Ahsanullah Khan, General Sanad Khan, Ibrahim Ali Khan, Gulam Kuli Khan, and other leaders, too, were present. Mahamed Bakht Khan, the commander of the forces of Rohilkhand, requested the Emperor to accept his services. When Bakht Khan pressed his request to know the desire of the Emperor, the Emperor said: 'It is my ardent desire to see that the people are completely protected, that the security of life and property is maintained, and that the extermination of the British foe is triumphantly carried out.' The General then said that, if the Emperor wished, he was ready to act as the commander-in-chief of the Revolutionary forces. At this, the Emperor pressed the hand of the general with affection. Then, the different heads of the different regiments were called together and they were asked whether they would elect Bakht Khan as commander-in-chief. All of them voted 'aye' and took military oaths of obeying the general as their commander-in-chief. After the levee was over, the Emperor again granted a private interview to the general. All over the city, the order went forth that Bakht Khan would act as the commander-in-chief. He was presented with a shield, a sword, and the title of general. The Prince Mirza Mogul was appointed adjutant-general. Bakht Khan informed the Emperor that, even it any of the princes of royal blood would continue looting in the city, he would not hesitate to cut off his ear and nose at once. The Emperor replied, 'You are invested with supreme authority. Do whatever you think best, without the least hesitation.' The Kotwal of the city was ordered that if there was any row or looting through his negligence in the city he would be hanged. Bakht Khan reported that he had brought with him four infantry regiments, seven hundred cavalry, six horse guns, three field pieces, etc., etc. As this part of the army had been given its pay for six months in advance and as the general had with him four lakhs of Rupees in cash, the Emperor was assured that he need have no anxitey about money or pay. Not only this, the Emperor was informed that further captures of money would at once be sent to the Royal Treasury. The Emperor distributed sweet-meat worth four thousand Rupees amongst the Sepoys. The Sepoys of Agra, the regiments of Nasirabad, of Jallundhar, all are under the command of Bakht Khan. The general ordered that every citizen, in the city should be armed. All householders and shopkeepers should keep arms. And those who had none should, at once, ask for them at the Supreme Thana and they would be given them free. But none should be found without arms. Any Sepoy who would be found looting would be deprived of his hand. Bakht Khan went to the armoury and, after examining it, got the arms and powder-magazines properly arranged. At eight in the night, the general went to the palace. The Emperor, with Begum Zinat Mahal, Hakeem Ahsanullah Khan, and Ahmad Kuli Khan, discussed the state affairs. In the general parade on the 3rd of July. nearly twenty thousand Sepoys were present.'[3]

While the arrival of Bakht Khan was giving the

3. *Native Narratives* by Metcalfe, page 60.

Revolution in Delhi some sort of organisation, in the English camp too, men of energy and initiative were arriving from the Punjab and other places. The English government had very few men with them who could surpass, in energy or ability, the brave Brigadier General Chamberlain who had just arrived from Punjab. The famous, military engineer, Baird-Smith, too, came there. All the men who distinguished themselves in the Sikh War were sent from the Punjab by John Lawrence to help the English army at Delhi. Then, General Barnard decided to try once more the 'straight and bold' assault on Delhi which had been so many times thought of and given up in the past. Even as in the past, this assault too was perfectly planned. And on the 3rd of July, the English army all the while standing ready to march, did begin to move but, lo! someone has just brought the news that General Bakht Khan has spared them all the trouble of marching on Delhi; for he himself has marched upon them! On the 4th of July, Bakht Khan again came forth and passed on the English rear as far as Alipur itself!

That the city of Delhi, about which the English had been openly boasting before the siege began that to see it was to conquer it, should not allow him even to take one step further on in spite of new forces pouring from the Punjab to his help, even after the constant struggle of a complete month, was too much of an anxiety and shame to the sensitive nature of Barnard. The English were so eager to take Delhi and so confident of their ability to do so that, long before June had ended, the news of the fall of Delhi would reach Bombay, Calcutta, and Madras! And, no sooner did this usual news prove as usually groundless than the English people all over India would begin to ask each other, 'What are the English forces doing at Delhi, at all ?' This anxiety and shame were working on the mind of Barnard. And to this gloomy view of the past there could be seen nothing in the future but a still darker sequel! He was not allowed even a moment's rest by the constant attacks of the Sepoys; nor could he fail to see that every day that rose was lessening the hope of carrying any bold or straight assault on the city of the Revolutionaries. At last, Barnard, the commander of the British forccs, emaciated in body and eaten up in mind by this hopelessness and dark despair, fell an easy victim to cholera, on the 5th of July. This came up like a shock over the English forces in the camp. This was the second commander of the English forces who tried to enter the city of Delhi but succeeded only in entering the grave, instead! General Reed, now, took up the charge and became the third commander of the English forces!

While the British camp was busy in planning assaults, the people of Delhi were busy in actually carrying them out. All of them cannot be described here for want of space. Yet, the sortie of the 9th of July and again that of the 14th of July, and the doggedness with which the Revolutionaries fought, and the bravery with which the English and the revolutionaries fought are too important and inspiring to be omitted without any remark. On the first day, the English cavalry was actually routed and driven back. The English artillery was silenced. A brave Sepoy threw Hill and his horse down on the ground. Hill, recovering himself, drew his sword, while three Sepoys jumped upon him. Hill tried to shoot twice and twice he missed, while one of the Sepoys succeeded in snatching away his sword. They closed in hand-to-hand fight; they struggled; down they came. Hill was lying on the ground and the Sepoy was standing with one foot planted on Hill's breast and with sword drawn in his hand. Major Tombs saw this from a distance of nearly thirty feet; he aimed and shot at the Sepoy and killed him. Major Tombs raised Hill from the ground and began to move him off, but saw, to his utter dismay, that yet another Sepoy had picked up the pistol of Hill and was coming towards him. The Sepoy, single-handed, fought ,with two or three Englishmen, wounded one with the sword, killed the second, and was himself struck down by the sword of a third. Tombs and Hill, both of them got the

'Victoria Medal' for this brave encounter, and Sir John Kaye says that the brave Sepoy, too, ought to have got the 'Bahadur Shah Medal'! How many must have deserved the Bahadur Shah Medal for their brave martyrdom in that War of Independence! But this, too, is equally true, that those that are so brave and so self sacrificing get, if not the Bahadur Shah medal, yet the nobler one, the Duty medal of Martyrdom, even from the hands of Death himself! On this day, the English soldiers were disgracefully routed! But unable to avenge this on the Revolutionaries, these brave people went back to their camp and wreaked their vengeance on the poor innocent *bhishtis* (water-carriers) and other Indians in their service, by actually cutting them down to death in cold blood!'[4] And yet it was these *bhishtis* and others who had kept the English army in fighting condition! But the English were: worsted still more terribly in the attack of the 14th of July. For, on this day, the brave Chamberlain was shot dead by a Sepoy. The first warrior in our camp, the first in fame, the first in honour! Woeful the day when our Chamberlain was carried back to the camp wounded mortally! —' such is the language with which the English historians express the fullness of their grief at this their national loss.

Thus, the 15th of July passed off and still the proud towers of Delhi were carrying their flags and banners, resplendent in the rays of the sun, proclaiming to the world that the city had now become the abode of Freedom! At last, Reed himself resigned and retired to the Himalayan hills

4. 'It is related that, in the absence of tangible enemies, some of our soldiery, who turned out on this occasion, butchered a number of unoffending camp-followers, servants, and others who were huddling together, in vague alarm, near the Christian churchyard. No loyalty, no fidelity, no patient good service on the part of these good people could extinguish, for a moment, the fierce hatred which possessed our white soldiers against all who wore the dusky livery of the East.'— Kaye and Malleson's *Indian Mutiny*, Vol. II, p. 438.

to avoid a sure death! This was the third commander of the English forces. Two were put into the grave; the third could survive simply by resigning the charge still Delhi could not be taken! The chiefs of the staff, Quartermaster-General Becher and Adjutant-General Chamberlain were laid down in the camp expecting their death every moment still Delhi could not be taken! Nay, even the question of self-defence is getting more and more hopeless by the constant and harassing attacks of the Revolutionaries who numbered, by now, more than twenty thousand! Even if the Revolutionaries lost more men in the encounters, yet the English could reap absolutely no advantage. But the death of even a handful of their number perceptibly weakened their strength. For this reason, the English determined to remain only on the defensive. For, defeats in these assaults could neither weaken the Revolutionaries nor put a stop to their further assaults. But on the contrary, they grew more determined and fearless and did openly boast. 'Even a success is costing the English as much as a defeat!' Even the English people themselves all over India began to write and criticise and complain that the 'besiegers themselves are besieged!' And, when, in such straits, even the third commander retired, then, men like Greathead, Chamberlain and Rotton began to give up every hope of attacking Delhi and, in the headquarters itself, tile question of actually raising the siege of Delhi began to be discussed! This was the state of the siege of Delhi when the third commander Reid resigned and the fourth one, Brigadier-General Wilson, succeeded him in the command !

* * *

CHAPTER II

Havelock

WHEN the Sikh Sepoys delivered the Allahabad fort into the hands of the English, instead of into the hands of the Revolutionaries, the English made it a base of operations on their side. There was now no longer the danger of having to carry on all civil and military operations in the North of India from a distant centre like Calcutta. Lord Canning decided to shift the capital itself to Allahabad until the Revolution was suppressed and, accordingly, he came in a few days to reside at Allahabad. But in the meanwhile, came the news of the miserable plight of the English at Cawnpore and their piteous cries for help. General Neill, therefore, kept a small army for protection at Allahabad and sent the rest under Major Renaud to raise the siege of Cawnpore. This detachment marched on burning villages indiscriminately, on their way. Just then, Havelock was appointed to the command of the Cawnpore army in place of Neill. He arrived at Allahabad, towards the end of June. He was a trained and an experienced officer. Fortunately for the English, the war with Persia came to an end about the time when the Revolution actually broke out, and the whole English army, under good commanders like Havelock, arrived in India just at the time when they were very badly wanted. Though Neill was extremely chagrined to find that Havelock superseded him as the chief officer at Allahabad and that he had to be under him, he did not allow his private feelings to come in the way of the welfare of his country's rule in India. He made vigorous efforts towards the equipment of the army. He gave every help to the army which was to be commanded by Havelock, made all arrangements as to the commissariat, and quietly handed over the charge of the troops to Havelock when the latter officer arrived. This army was now fully prepared to go to the assistance of the English at Cawnpore. Havelock was eager to start, when suddenly news came that Sir Hugh Wheeler was defeated and had surrendered and that all the Englishmen, including him, had been massacred on the banks of the Ganges!

Havelock determined to revenge their death and set out in haste from Allahabad towards Cawnpore. He had with him one thousand select English infantry, one hundred and fifty Sikhs, a picked detachment of English cavalry, and six guns, all desperate with rage. There were, also, several civil and military officers going along with them, officers whose life had been saved consciously and deliberately by the revolted Sepoys and the people, out of mercy, or who had escaped their vigilance, and who now came to give information about the geography of the country to the new officers and men, to fight along with them and to wreak a terrible vengeance. And these brave Englishmen, whom one word of a Sepoy would have despatched from this earth, who would have been dead by now but for their mercy, now came together and started the campaign of burning villages wholesale.

When the news came to Cawnpore that a detachment under Major Renaud was marching towards Fattehgurh, Nana Sahib sent some troops in that quarter. Hoping to crush the small detachment in a short time. This army under Jwala Prasad and Tikha Singh reached Fattehgurh. But, by that time, Havelock's army had joined Major Renaud and the united English army fired their guns as soon as they heard that the Revolutionaries, had come. When the small Revolutionary force rushed into the field, confident of crushing Majar Renaud in no time, it found arrayed against it the whole army of Havelock, together with artillery and all necessaries, This was on the 12th of July. They were, thus, compeletely taken by surprise. The fight began and they had to retire from the field leaving their guns behind them. Pursuit was impossible and the English army gave up the idea and entered the town of Fattehpur. At the time of rising in Fattehpur, the leadership of the Revolution had been taken up by a deputy magistrate in the English employ, a Mahomedan named Hikmat Ullah, English officers had also been killed there. The sword of English revenge now fell on that town. The former magistrate of the town, Sherer, who had been spared his life by the Revolutionaries and let off, now came with the army and was now eager to exercise his power of magistracy, so long in abeyance. So, a looting by the military was ordered, first of all. When it was certain that nothing more remained in the town worth looting, the order was given to set fire to it; but the honour of this work was left to the Sikhs. So, when the English troops left, the Sikh troops performed their allotted task, set fire to the whole town and followed them.

When the English army burnt alive the whole town of Fattehpur, the fumes spread along and, at last, reached Cawnpore. The news reached Nana Sahib's camp that the detachment which attacked Major Renaud's force was suddenly set upon by Havelock's army and that, after routing them, the English had entered the town and destroyed the whole city by first looting the place and then, burning alive the people in it. The whole of the Cawnpore Durbar was excited with rage and fury. Just when it was decided to send another army under Nana Sahib himself to obstruct the English march on Cawnpore at the Pandu river, it was announced that some traitors who had deserted to the English had just been arrested.[1] At their trial, it was proved that some of them had carried letters from the women prisoners

1. .After the defeat of Nana Sahib's forces at Fattehpur, some reputed spies were brought to Nana Sahib. They were accused of being the bearers of letters supposed to have been written to distant stations by the helpless women in prison. In the correspondence some of the Mahajans and Baboos of the city were believed to be complicated. It was, therefore, resolved that

at Cawnpore to the English at Allahabad. When the news spread that those whom Nana had saved from massacre as 'women' were maintaining secret, treacherous correspondence with the English at Allahabad, the important question arose as to what should be done to them. As the English burnt Fattehpur, why not avenge it by destroying this 'Bibigarh' (Palace of Females) in return?

Though the prison was called Bibigarh, there were, also, some men in it saved by the intervention of Nana Sahib. After the unanimous resolution that these prisoners, along with the traitors who carried the correspondence, should all be killed, the dreadful meeting of the dreadful night adjourned. Next day, the spies and the Englishmen were dragged out of the prison and made to stand in a line. At first, the spies were decapitated with swords, in the presence of Nana Sahib himself; then the English-men were shot. When Nana Sahib left the place, people came up to the corpses and mocked, 'This is the Governor of Madras; this of Bombay, and this of Bengal.'

When this grim mockery was going on here, the order was sent to the Sepoys at Bibigarh to kill all the inmates. When the warders would not dare to do it, it was resolved to bring someone of greater mettle as regards, cruelty. The chief wardress of Bibigarh, Begum Sahib, sent a man to butcher quarter of the Cawnpore city. In the evening, some butchers brandishing naked swords and big knives in their hands, entered the prison gesticulating in rage. They entered about evening and came out when it was just beginning to be dark. But, in that short space of time, there was a regular stream of red blood within the prison! As soon as they

---

the said spies together with the women and children, as also the few gentlemen whose lives had been spared should all be put to death.'- *Narrative of the Revolt*, page 113. Qne of the Christain prisoners in the prison of Nana Sahib tells the same account and one of the Ayahs (nurses) deposes to the same effect.

entered, they stabbed right and left and killed about one hundred and fifty English women and children! The room was a lake of blood with pieces of human flesh swimming in it. When they went in, the butchers walked on the ground; but when they came out, they had to wade through blood. The night was wailing with the screams of the half-dead, the deep groans of the dying, and the piteous cries of a few children who escaped on account of their size in the general massacre. About dawn, the unfortunate creatures were dragged out of Bibigarh prison and pushed into a neighbouring well. A couple of children, so long crushed under the weight of the dead bodies, got out near the well and began running away. A blow threw them also dead on the heap of the dead. Men drank water so long from the well, but the well now drank! humanblood.[2] As the English had thrown to the skies the screams of brown women and children at Fattehpur, so, the Pandays threw the screams and the corpses of white women and children into the deep down! The account between the two races, extending over a hundred years, was thus being settled! Even the Bay of Bengal might, in ages, be filled up; but the yawning well of Cawnpore—never !

About the same time, Havelock was pushing forward after defeating the army sent by Nana Sahib at Pandu nadi. Commander Bala Sahib Peshwa, brother of Nana Sahib, was hit by a bullet in the shoulder, in a skirmish, and returned to Cawnpore. Nana Sahib called together a council of war to

---

2. ' The refinements of cruelty-the unutterable shame-with which,. in some chronicles of the day, this hideous massacre was attended, were but fictions of an excited imagination, too readily believed without inquiry. and circulated without thought. None was mutilated, none were dis- honoured. ...This is stated, in the most unqualified manner, by the official functionaries, who made the most .diligent enquiries into all tpe- circumstances of the massacres in June and in July. '-Kaye and MaUeson's Indian Mutiny, Vol, II, page 281.

settle the future plan of campaign. The question was discussed whether Cawnpore should be evacuated without fight or a strong resistance should be offered to the English advance; and, at last, after a long discussion, the latter alternation was decided upon. On the 10th July, the English army came near Cawnpore. The news of the Cawnpore well had not reached them. Though Wheeler's fort was gone, they had a strong intention of rescuing Bibigarh. With this desire, they did not rest a moment in spite of fatigue, sun, and strife. When the turrets of Cawnpore came into view, Havelock was inspired all the more by these hopes. He sent reconnoitring parties to spy the army of the Pandays. That army was so splendidly arranged on the field that the English warrior who had spent all his life on the battlefield perceived that there were some men, among the Revolutionaries, of extraodinary military skill. He called together his officers and drew out for them, with his sword, on the ground a map of his plan of attack. While Havelock was explaining to them that, instead of a front attack, the Revolutinary left wing should be attacked first, Nana Sahib, mounted on a white horse, joined the efficiently arranged troops of the Revolutionaries. From the English camp, the figure of Nana Sahib could be seen distinctly galloping into the different ranks and encouraging the soldiers. About noon, the English attack on Nana Sahib's left wing commenced. To check this fierce, sudden and unexpected attack on the left, the Revolutionary artillery began fire. As the English artillery was a little late in arriving, these guns did very effective work. But when Havelock, irritated, by the success of the Revolutionaries, began to push forward again in desperate vigour and when the Highlanders, with turned eyes, ran straight to the guns and when the English, without going back an inch, rushed forth with the cry, 'Death or Victory!', then, the left wing became quite unable to resist the united, sudden and orderly attack and retreated, leaving their guns behind. While the left was retreating, the English artillery had defeated the right wing. Seeing the English army victorious, the Revolutionaries began the retreat along the road to Cawnpore. But, with the courage of despair, Nana Sahib rallied them and, with the rest of the guns, renewed the fight. At this time, Nana Sahib made marvellous efforts to encourage and lead the Sepoys. 'Such was the battle of Cawnpore. The Revolutionaries fought very well. Some of them did not retire even when sword clashed with sword. They saved their guns with determination and the firing was, also, splendidly aimed.'[3] One more assault from the English side, and even this desperate resistance became in vain and the defeated Revolutionaries retreated towards Brahmavarta.

On the 17th of July, Havelock's victorious army entered the city of Cawnpore. Havelock and his army who had brought up to Cawnpore the first wave of victory, to revive the lost English prestige were blessed by Englishmen, both in India as in England. Everywhere in England, in the street. corners, on sign-boards or shops, on the walls of public-houses, Havelock's name was engraved!

When the permission to loot Cawnpore was given, hundreds of English officers and soldiers, along with the Sikhs, fell upon, Cawnpore like vultures on a wounded lion. At Bibigarh, the spot was clotted with blood and there was a suspicion that it was. English blood that had been spilt there. Therefore, a large number of Brahmins in Cawnpore were caught and those of them against whom there was any suspicion of complicity with the Revolution were sentenced to death. Not merely that, but, before being hanged, they were made to lick off, with their tongue, the blood spots and then wash away the stains, broom in hand. The reason of giving this unheard of punishment to those about to be hanged is thus given by an English officer: 'I know that the- act of touching Feringhi blood and washing it with a sweeper's broom degrades a high caste Hindu from his religion. Not

3. *Red Pamphlet*.

only this but I make them do it because I know it. We could not wreak a true revenge, unless we trample all their religious instincts under foot, before we hang them, so that they may not have the satisfaction of dying as Hindus.' In the massacres ordered by the Revolutionaries, not only no religious injuries were inflicted on the English, but they were always given time, when they requested so, to read the Bible before they were killed. But the English clean took away, so far as they could, from the Revolutionaries who were massacred at Cawnpore and Delhi, all consolations of religion. But many gallant men, even in this misery, embraced death with a smile for the sake of their principle and made sacred the gallows on which they were hanged. Charles Ball says: 'General Havelock began to wreak a terrible vengeance for the death of Sir Hugh Wheeler. Batch upon batch of natives mounted the scaffold. The calmness of mind and nobility of demean our which some of the Revolutionaries showed at the time of death was such as would do credit to those who martyred themselves for devotion to principle. One of them, who worked as a magistrate at Cawnpore under Nana Sahib, was arrested and put on his trial. But he seemed so indifferent to all the proceedings as if they all referred to someone else and not to him. After he was sentenced to death, he rose and turned his back to the judge and walked with a firm step to the scaffold erected for him; while the Maungs were making the final preparations, he was looking at their movements in an easy and natural manner. And without the least agitation, he mounted the scaffold even as a Yogi enters Samadhi! Fortified by the assurances of his creed, death to him was but a transition from the hated association of the infidel Feringhis to the blissful enjoyment of paradise.'[4]

While the British army entered Cawnpore and was taking revenge *ad libitum*, Havelock praised the small army

4. Charles Ball's *Indian Mutiny*, Vol. I, page 389.

consisting of English and Sikhs for having fought bravely in an orderly compact, and determined manner. Soon after this, General Neill also arrived at Cawnpore, having left a sufficient English garrison at Allahabad. When these two English officers of equal rank came together, each of them would have the desire of having all the troops under his control and there was a possibility of more disorder in the already disorderly English army. Seeing this, Havelock told Neill plainly on the latter's arrival, 'General Neill, it is better that we should understand each other clearly. So long as I am here, the whole command is mine and you should not give any orders.' In order that English interests might not suffer through the personal jealousy of the two officers. Neill remained to guard Cawnpore and Havelock marched towards Oudh at the head of the troops going for the relief of Lucknow. Neill hit upon a new plan for the defence of Cawnpore. He formed a corps of Mahars and gave the town in their charge. The trick of inciting these low class men against the higher classes succeeded wonderfully. When the division among the Hindus and Moslems vanished. this caste difference was thus made use of! After the defeat of Cawnpore, Nana Sahib Peshwa left Brahmavarta and crossed the Ganges with his treasure and his army. His first camp was at Fattehgarh; the English army under Havelock. not being able to ascertain Nana's whereabouts, marched towards Lucknow. By the end of June. the whole province of Oudh was a perfect beehive of the Revolutionaries, and it was not easy task to march through the province and to relieve Sir Henry Lawrence and raise the siege of Lucknow. Still. in the flush of victory, Havelock and his army thought lightly of the work of crossing the Ganges and relieving Lucknow. Just as the idea, 'to see Delhi was to conquer Delhi.' possessed the English army which descended from the Punjab. so, the idea that it was only necessary to cross the Ganges in order to take Lucknow now haunted Havelock's army going up from Cawnpore. It is true

Lucknow is not very far from Cawnpore. It is also true that the energy and quickness which was displayed by Havelock on his march from Allahabad to undertake stupendous task with a light heart. But now, there was not an inch of space in Oudh that was not involved in the flames of the national Revolution. Oudh being the cradle of the Purbhayya Sepoys who began the revolt in India, the parents. the children and relatives, and friends of these Sepoys in every hamlet and every cottage, were inevitably burning with Revolutionary spirit. Still, this terrible state of affairs did not daunt the English commander who was full of his victory. He was in such high spirits that he hoped to conquer Lucknow at the very sight thereof, then to march to Delhi and, after taking it, to go to Agra! With such confidence, Havelock, with two thousand English troops and ten guns, crossed the Ganges on the 25th of July. General Neill stayed at Cawnpore and Havelock marched towards Lucknow. Such was the disposition of the English troops at the end of July, 1857.

* * *

CHAPTER III

Behar

THE province of Behar and its capital, Patna, did not remain aloof from the wave of Revolution which was sweeping over the North-Western Provinces, Allahabad, Agra, and Bengal. Of the different districts in the province, the chief towns were Gaya, Arrah, Chapra, Motihari, and Muzzafferpore. The army to control the province was stationed near Patna, in the town of Danapur. There were the 7th, 8th, and 40th native infantry and, to keep these in check, there were the European artillery and a European regiment, all under the command of Major-General Lloyd;

besides, there was the 12th native cavalry regiment under Major Holmes stationed near by, at Sigwali.

The historical town of Patna was the centre of the powerful Wahabi sect of the Moslem religion. The English commissioner, Tayler, was certain that Patna would take part in the Revolution of 1857, and he, therefore, kept a close watch on the leaders of that sect. The town of Patna which thoroughly hated the English yoke had started a secret society with the object of overthrowing the English power as far back as 1852. This secret society had amongst its members influential and rich merchants, bankers and Zemindars, a fact which gave the society immense funds for its work. As prominent Moulvies accepted leading positions in the society, the work soon assumed a grave turn. They had correspondence and communication with the secret society at Lucknow as well as with the Sepoys at Danapur. The whole town of Patna, from the police officers down to humble booksellers, was anxious and eager for the moment when the first blow was to be struck against the English power.

Patna was the headquarters of the secret society and the orgainsation counted amongst its members representatives of all classes in the vast population of the town. To the mass of the people, the word 'Feringhi' itself was as gall and wormwood. They had no lack of funds and even sent some money to the distant frontier districts in the west to organise a Revolution against the English. Since the police had also joined, the nightly secret meetings went on without a hitch. The various members of the society employed hundreds of Revolutionaries in their service under various pretexts and paid them out of the funds of the society. While Patna was, thus, burning with the hatred of Feringhi rule, its flames were spreading in all directions in the vast province, giving secret inspiration to the people. Soon communication was established with the Sepoys stationed for the protection of the province, with the Zemindars, Rajas, with the chief towns in the various districts, and all were hand in glove with the secret society at Patna. The Sepoys in the camp at Danapur began to hold secret meetings and form plans at nights. under cover of the trees! And if they saw some Englishman. who might have discovered them on his patrol, they killed him! When the power of the people was thus organised and ready for Revolution, negotiations began with the secret societies at Delhi and at Lucknow.

When the final question was being discussed as to the time when they were to start the Revolution, the English commissioner. Mr. Tayler, got the news of Meerut. Following closely came the news that there was unrest among the Sepoys at Danapur. The commissioner was a clever man and thought the whole of India, was rising in Revolution. The Sikhs were yet confirmed traitors. Therefore, Tayler immediately sent two hundred Sikhs under Rattray for the defence of Patna, and the Sikhs, accordingly left for Patna. But, wherever they passed, all the way they were despised and cursed, day and night! They were accused of treachery (Nimak-haram) to the nation and, on the way, villagers. would ask them sarcastically, 'Are you true Sikhs or Feringhi converts?' They were advised, secretly and openly, to stand up for their country when the crucial moment came. When the Sikhs, with the curses of the whole province on their heads, began to enter the town of Patna, the popular fury became intense every:' where on seeing them every citizen of the proud city ostentatiously avoided the touch, even of their shadow. What more—the priest of the Sikh temple in that freedom-loving city curtly refused entry to these traitors within the temple! The belief that these Sikhs, were not real followers of Guru Govind Singh-a belief shared by the Sikh Guru, the Mahomedan Moulvie, and the Hindu Prayagwal—is an excellent proof how, in the town of Patna, the ideals of

Swadharma and Swaraj were really in unison.[1]

When the Sikh army came into Patna, Tayler proceeded to try and nip in the bud the Revolutionary activities in the province. The conduct of Waris Ali, the police Jamadar of the Tirhut district, appeared suspicious and the authorities suddenly surrounded his house and made him prisoner. This Jamadar in the English service was just then writing a letter to a Revolutionary leader at Gaya, called Ali Karim! On the evidence of the Revolutionary correspondence seized in his house, he was, soon after, sentenced to death. When he was brought to the scaffold, he shouted, 'If there is any real devotee of Swaraj here, let him liberate me!' But, before his request could be heard by the devotees, his lifeless body was hanging from the scaffold!

The Mahomedan leader, Ali Karim, was also ordered to, be arrested and a European detachment was sent for the task. When Mr. Lowis, the head of the detachment. came up to Alii Karim, the latter mounted his elephant and an exciting race began! But, the spectators soon dropped their impartiality and exceeded the bounds of fair play. The neighbouring villagers, seeing the, Feringhis chasing a countryman, began to harass the former, misdirected them on their way, and at last, even stole one of their ponies! The English officer 'irritated by fatigue and despair,' left it to his Indian servant to chase the swift Karim and returned the next day, not having achieved his task. The servant also. being an English-hater, let Karim alone and came back to his master with a sorry face.

While these arrests were going on in the province, Mr. Tayler came to know the names of several leaders in the city and he resolved to surprise them. The Revolutionary

1. 'As soon as the Sikhs entered the town, a wild Fakir rushed forward into the road and, with savage menaces and threatening gestures, reviled them as traitors and accursed... ..'-*Patna Crisis* by Tayler.

secret meetings used to take place in the house of the leaders at night and, though Tayler had no definite information about the names of the persons who were implicated in, or the general programme formed, still he had no doubt about the complicity of three most influential Mullahs of the place. He thought it necessary to arrest them .at once. However, there was the fear that an attempt to arrest them openly would, perhaps, precipitate the revolt he wanted to suppress. So, the honest officer struck upon a new plan. One day, select citizens were hospitably invited to Mr. Tayler's house to confer with him on important political matters. When all the guests had arrived, he came up with the Sikhs; and when after some conversation, the company were taking leave to depart, Tayler stopped the three Moulvies, who were also among the guests, and informed them smilingly that, as it was dangerous to leave them at liberty in the then troublous times, they were arrested! However, this act was applauded everywhere on the pretext that it was for the good of the English power and all admired Tayler's energetic action.

After having thus arrested the prominent Revolutionary leaders without shedding a drop of blood, Tayler decided to strike at the town of Patna, while it was still confused at the suddenness of the arrests. He, therefore, issued an order to disarm the town and prohibited the people from leaving their houses after 9 p. m. This order rendered the nightly meeting of secret societies impossible. The storing of arms, also, became difficult. So long, the Revolutionary society at Patna was awaiting the signal to rise from Danapur. But, when this life-killing procedure began, they resolved to rise suddenly and boldly rather than be crippled by it. On the 3rd of July, Mussalmans began to crowd towards the house of a leader, Peer Ali by name. They entered his house and settled their plans. In a short time, they came out one by one, with green flag and shouts of 'Din, Bolo! Din!' About two hundred *Jehadis* came out in procession and attacked the church. Just then, a white man, called Lyall, was seen coming with some troops, and Peer Ali shot him dead, and his infuriated followers hacked his body to pieces beyond recognition! But, Rattray came with his 'loyal' Sikhs and made a desperate attack on the Revolutionaries. When the Sikhs thrust their swords in the body of the Mother, when their bodies became red with her blood, then, the handful of Revolutionaries were soon broken up by the force of superior discipline and arms. The English arrested the Revolutionary leaders one after another, among them being Peer Ali who had shot Lyall.

Peer Ali was originally a resident of Lucknow but had lately established himself as a bookseller in Patna. He had imbibed the ideas of independence by reading the books which he used to sell. The conditions of dependence and slavery became unbeareble to him. He placed himself in communication with the Revolutionaries at Delhi and Lucknow. He imparted to others his passionate patriotism. Though he was onJy a humble bookseller, he had great influence in the Revolutionary councils of Patna. He collected together a large number of armed men with the help of the wealthy members of the secret society and they were all sworn to rise against the British power at a given signal. When the English officer at Patna, Mr. Tayler, began torture and oppression, Peer Ali's hot nature could not keep quiet. He was by nature stern, spirited, and brave. He could not bear to see the tortures of his countrymen, and therefore he, as he confessed later, 'rose prematurely.' Next, we see Peer Ali sentenced to death, severely hand-cuffed, his hands bleeding from his wounds. He stood before the scaffold, with a heroic smile on his face, defying the death that was awaiting him. There was only a slight sob when he took the name of his beloved son. Immediately, the English officer, to take advantage of his emotion, addressed him these words: Peer Ali, you might even now save your life by disclosing the names of the other leaders.' Turning calmly to the Feringhi, he replied in bold and noble words, 'There are some occasions in life when it is desireble to save one's life—but there are some others when it is more desirable to sacrifice it! This moment is one of the latter kind, when to embrace death at once is the means of eternal life !' Then, describing in plain language the numerous acts of injustice and oppression committed by the English, the martyr dying for his people said, 'You might hang me, you might hang other men like me; but, cannot hang our ideal. If I die, thousands of heros will rise out of my blood and will destory your kingdom.'

With these prophetic words, this hero, without casting the shadow of a shame on his country, entered by the door of death, into the circle of patriots of immortal memory![2]

'Out of my blood will rise thousands of heroes!' These last words of the noble martyr could not be falsified, were not falsified! At the news of his death, the 'most loyal' regiment at Danapur rose in revolt on the 25th of July. In spite of the presence of an English regiment and English artillery, the three Indian regiments, with their hands, tore away in disgust the Company's uniforms and marched away to the Shon river. On account of the fear and old age of Major-General Lloyd, the chief officer of the place, the English army did not dare to pursue the Sepoys. Though the English major-general was thus handicapped by old age, still in the direction in which the revolted regiments were marching, there in the palace of Jagdishpur, was an old hero who, in spite of age, had the spirit of youth in his arms and his sword, and who was proudly twirling his moustache. It is to his banner that the Sepoys were hurriedly flocking!

There was almost always one great defect which often nullified the efforts of the freedom-loving Sepoys and people, and that was the want of capable leaders. In the Shahabad district, at least, the Jagdishpur palace had removed this want, and therefore the Sepoys marched thither after crossing the Shon river. For, there the Sepoys could find a leader befitting the battle of Swaraj. A man of heroic spirit, of unconquerable valour, and born in a Rajput family of ancient fame, this leader of the Swaraj war graced the name of Kumar Singh by wearing it. His lordship over the extensive Shahabad lands had been established by the continuity of ages and the people there felt a natural love towards his ancient family. Storms of great empires rose and subsided in the land of Hindusthan from time to time; but, through all those cruel vicissitudes, this province was free under its beneficent Rajput princes and continuously enjoyed freedom and Swaraj. Through all the most oppressive seasons of a hundred Revolutions, the Banyan tree of the dynasty of Kumar Singh had been bearing all the inclemencies of heat and cold on its summit, but had never ceased to protect the humble birds that nestled in its branches. Summer heat might scorch the top; winter frost might bite the leaves; but, the birds enjoyed the quiet of eternal spring for endless generations. The dynasty loved the subjects like its own children; the subjects worshipped the dynasty as the representative of God upon earth. But, to the foreign despot, this reciprocal loyalty and kindness was a thorn in his side. He, therefore, determined to ruin this royal family! All of a sudden the chattra of Swaraj was broken and the province was laid bare; the tree was struck by the cruel lightning and the birds began to flutter about in helpless agony! And it was with a determination to avenge the wrongs of his dynasty and his country that the old youth was standing on the terrace of Jagdishpur palace, twirling his moustache!

An old youth!—yes, he was an old youth. For, nearly eighty winters had passed over his head and yet the fire in

2. The Commissioner Tayler himself says: 'Peer Ali himself was a model of a desperate and determined fanatic. Repulsive in appearance, with a brutal and sullen countenance, he was calm, self-possessed, almost dignified in language and demeanour. He is the type of the class of men whose unconquerable fanaticism renders them dangerous enemies and whose stern resolution entitles them, in some respects, to admiration and respect!'

his soul was as fierce as ever and the muscle in his arm was strong. A Kumar of eighty years and a Singh! How could he bear the sight of the spoliation of his country by the English! After Dalhousie swallowed the kingdom of Oudh, the English went about, throughout Hindusthan, digging up and demolishing all raised places in order to raze them all to the ground. It was in that campaign that Kumar Singh's country also fell a victim. Kumar Singh swore that he would shatter to pieces the English rule which had ruined his country and Swaraj in this inexcusable, cruel, and injust manner! And he began at once communications with Nana Sahib.

Commissioner Tayler of Patna had, for long, been receiving information that Kumar Singh was planning a Revolution, that he had established communications with Revolutionary societies throughout India, and that hundreds of Sepoys at Patna were secretly in league with him. The very idea, however, that this old man of eighty would run to the battle-field, instead of lying down for a peaceful death, appeared to his mind absolutely impossible. Besides, was not Kumar Singh always writing letters of loyalty, to him? Still, Tayler who was not an exception to the usual nobility of heart of Englishmen wrote to Kumar Singh: 'You are very old and your health is very bad! I feel great anxiety for your company for the rest of your days. I will feel very much obliged if you will do me the honour of accepting my hospitality. With the hope that this invitation will not be rejected, —I am yours etc., Tayler.' In the past Afzul Khan had sent a similar invitation to Shivaji ! The astute Rajput at once understood that the loving invitation of the commissioner meant only the quiet opening of the prison door! Therefore, he wrote back: 'Thanks awfully! It is true, as you say, that my health is very bad; and therefore it is that I cannot come to Patna just now. As soon as I feel better, I will start immediately.' O Kumar Singh! You are indeed, uneasy in mind and body! And it is also true that, when you feel better after shedding Feringhi blood, you are going to

Patna ! But, for what? That is a different question.

Just then came the revolted Danapur Sepoys with the medicine to cure Kumar Singh. 'Why do you wait now, on Kumar Singh! We bind you by the oath of the Motherland, by the oath of our religion, of your honour! Throwaway the sheath and draw your sword for Swaraj! You are our king, our leader, our general! You are an ornament to the Rajput race; you ought, at once, to jump into the battlefield!' Thus cried the Swaraj-loving Sepoys; thus advised the holy Brahmin priests; thus, also, whispered to him his sword, anxious to smite the enemy![3] Then, the hero of eighty, who was too weak to go on an elephant to Patna, was suddenly inspired and, from his sickly bed, he jumped right into the battlefield!

The Sepoys next hurried from Jagdishpur to Arrah, the-chief town of the Shahabad district, looted the treasury, and destroyed the English prisons, offices and flags. At last, they turned to a small fortress. The clever Englishmen of the place had stored in that fort arms, ammunition, and stores of provision in order to defend themselves in case of a rising. Besides, a detachment of fifty Sikhs had been sent from Patna to help the handful of Englishmen. While these men, about seventy-five in all, lay waiting in the fort fully prepared, the occasion for which they were waiting arrived and the Revolutionaries besieged the place.

While these twenty-five Englishmen and fifty Sikhs were trying to defend the fort obstinately, the Revoultionaries, instead of assaulting it, were busy in shutting them completely on all sides. It is probable that they considered the place almost in their hands and did not think it worth while to spend time and men in capturing it by general assault. They probably thought it more advantageous to look after the surrounding territory and other English camps. Partly

3. 'The Brahmins have incited him to mutiny and rebellion!'—Major Eyre's Official Despatch.

for this and partly for the fierce artillery of the besieged, the Sepoys brought up their guns and began to use them instead of ordering a general assault. In one or two places, mines were laid and blown up with dynamite. In a few days, the water-supply in the fort was exhausted. But the Sikhs were too valiant to bear to see the miseries of the English. In twenty-four hours, they dug a new well in the fort! And, while this work was going on, they were, at the same time, fighting like demons. The Europeans would not agree to a conditional surrender, thinking of the fate of their Cawnpore comrades. When the Sepoys discovered that there were Sikhs, besides Feringhis, fighting within the fort, they grew wild with indignation. Because, then it was not alone the Sepoys that were besieging the English but it was Kumar Singh besieging the followers of Guru Govind Singh. The Sikhs were extraordinarily brave but basely treacherous to their country. Every evening, efforts were made to bring them round to their duty. The messengers of the Revolutionaries would stand behind pillars and shout out to them words of advice: 'O Sikhs! What hell do you look forward to by thus helping the Feringhis ! They who have destroyed our kingdom, they who are violating our Mother-country, they who have insulted our religion! Fighting on their side, what hell do you look forward to ?' The Revolutionaries would bind them with oaths of religion, of country, of freedom. They shouted heart-rending implorations to leave the side of the Feringhi. They threatened to massacre them if they still persisted in acting treacherously and helping the foreign despots. Not only had all this no effect on the Sikhs, but the reply they would give was a shower of bullets, while the English clapped hands in applause shouting, 'Bhale ! Bhale!' (Well done!). Thus, the siege went on for three days. On the third night, on the 29th, the English force was suddenly awakened by the noise of distant guns. Their faces beamed with smiles. Was it not the English army, coming to kill the Revolutionaries and raise the siege? Yes, it was the English army. About two hundred and seventy Englishmen of the English regiments at Danapur and about one hundred Sikhs under the valiant Captain Dunbar had come to the banks of the Shon river to raise the siege. Never was the English army so jubilant and hopeful of victory. The Englishmen and women who had come to see them off bade farewell to them, all smiles. The boats sailed smoothly on the Shon and, about seven in the evening, the army reached the outskirts of Arrah. The bright orb of the waxing moon, also marched along with them to partake of their victory. Oh, Captain Dunbar! Arrange your troops properly while the moon is shining, for soon it will be dark. In this arrangement as usual, the 'loyal Sikhs' must be put in the front. They also stepped forward lightly. Where is the black guide who is to show the way in the thick jungles of Arrah? Put him forth, and then oh victorious warriors! march on brandishing your swords in the bright moonlight. Trees were left behind, the ground was being covered, mile after mile was being crossed, and even Arrah bridge is reached. But what is this? Where is the enemy? How is this, that not a single Revolutionary has yet fallen? The cowards have run away! They have run away at the bare news that Dunbar is coming! Even Alexander did not inspire his enemies with such terror! Oh Moon! You have so long waited in cold and wind to witness the raging battle, but you have only seen the cleverness of the retreat of the Revolutionaries. Go, then; do not stay any longer to be disappointed; draw the curtain of night over this universe and retire to your resting place! But, though the moon went away, you, Dunbar! do not return! Here now comes the mango-grove and there is no more chance of encountering the Pandays. But, oh! What is this sound? May it not be the leaves of the mango-trees shaking in the wind? Whiz! Whiz!! Beware, Englishmen! Beware! A deluge of bullets from all sides! Every tree of the mango-grove had as if guns in its branches, smiting the foreign

Feringhis! Kumar Singh is come? The English army is prepared to fight; but, with whom? Not one man on the enemy's side could be seen! In the thick mango-grove, in the weird darkness of the night, in the high and low places, Kumar Singh's soldiers were hidden and not one could be seen! Nothing was visible except the stars in the sky and the trees on the earth! And it was not possible to fire at both these and gain victory! The wind-god was enraged and sent red-hot shots from somewhere foaming, into the English army! Fire from the left, fire from the right, and fire in front! The clothes of the English army were white and easily distinguishable but Kumar Singh's men were dark, their clothes were dark, and the night was dark! If all the dark circumstances conspired together, how could the English hold to their feet? The white Englishmen and the dark Sikhs, both ran away from the field! Their commander, Dunbar, was one of the first to be killed. Running for life, the English army came into a ditch near by. There they tried to hold on for some time, but, about early morning, they left behind not only their dead but their wounded comrades on the field and commenced the flight to the Shon river, being thirsty, hungry, full of blood, and black with shame. But it was no easy matter to run away from Kumar Singh. At every step, blood began to flow. As a wild boar pierced by lances, dropping on this side and that through weakness, runs shedding streams of blood on the field-such was the English army when it came to the Shon river. But here, there was the climax of destruction. At first, they could not find their boats. After some time, they found that they had stuck in the sand. Those that there were not so stuck had been set fire to by the Pandays ! At last, a couple of boats were saved. When the white population of Danapur came to the bank expecting to greet a victorious army singing warsongs, and bringing with them the rescued men of Arrah, they did not hear a single shout of joy from the boats. No flag, no band, not a single face uplifted! All hearts began to beat in impatience, 'My son, my brother, my husband, my father left only yesterday for the field in all hopes; and to-day—God forbid the thought!' Before the prayer could reach Heaven, the unfortunate troops landed on the Ghat at Danapur, and soon the terrible news spread like lightning that, out of four hundred and fifteen men, only about fifty returned alive safe from the hands of Kumar Singh! An Englishman writes, 'He who had beard the heart-rending cries of those English women will not forget it to this day! Some began to beat their breasts crying piteously, some shouted hoarsely, and some began to pull away their hair. If they had seen General Lloyd, the originator of this destructive plan, there is not the least doubt that they would have lynched him!'

But while the sky was being rent by the cries of these women at Danapur, Major Eyre was marching towards Arrah to revenge the defeat and their sorrow. Though he had not yet heard of Dunbar's defeat, he had marched straight towards Arrah, on bearing that the English there were besieged. While Kumar Singh's Sepoys were returning after crushing Dunbar's army on the 29th and 30th of July, they got the news that Eyre was advancing towards Arrah. The old commander got together his troops without losing a moment. He made arrangements for fighting after taking advantage of every strategic position on the route, and gave the last desperate battle on the 2nd of August, near the village of Bibiganj. Both armies endeavoured to take possession of a thick forest near by. In this race between youth and age, the aged Kumar Singh arrived first and thus defeating Eyre's plans, he opened a terrible fire. Eyre had three excellent guns and he was continually advancing on the strength of these. Thrice Kumar Singh's men jumped at the guns. Thrice did they go almost near the mouth of the fire-spitting guns, but the English kept their artillery constantly firing. At that moment, Captain Hastings came up panting to the commander Eyre, and said, , Eyre, even the English infantry is being pushed back! Victory has slipped from us!' If this state had continued for half an hour more, the battle would have been Kumar Singh's. Now, as anyhow the victory was going, the English wanted to try a last desperate attack before leaving the field. In this, Eyre ordered the English force to charge with bayonets. Immediately, the English soldiers rushed like arrows on the Revolutionaries. It cannot be understood why the Sepoys who would bravely rush up to the mouths of guns could not stand a general charge with bayonets, but it is certain that they did not withstand it. Eyre drove them out of the thicket and pushed forward, marched up to the fortress at Arrah, and relieved the Englishmen besieged there. And the town of Arrah thus fell into English hands again.

The siege of Arrah lasted only for eight days. In these eight days, the brave Rajput had to maintain the siege as well as fight two battles. His extraordinary courage, spirit, and bravery were not matched by the bravery of his followers, and so, after suffering defeat at Eyre's hands, Kumar Singh had to retreat to Jagdishpur. But when he heard that the English army, reinforced by the lately besieged troops at Arrah, were swelling considerably, he began to collect together all the available fighting men at Jagdishpur. The English by this time had seen not a little of Kumar Singh's activity. Fearing that he might again march on Arrah, Eyre forestalled him and himself started towards Jagdishpur. Kumar Singh was greatly handicapped and recognised that it was impossible, with his disheartened followers, to oppose in open battle the English army, well-disciplined and victorious, and that, too, near a capital town. He, therefore, decided to use guerilla tactics and, after two sharp skirmishes, came out of Jagdishpur. And Eyre, with the English army, pitched his tent in Kumar Singh's palace on the 14th of August! Though the English destroyed the palace, the Hindu temples, and other buildings at Jagdishpur, still, the idol of the temples, the king of the palaces, and the owner of the buildings, Kumar Singh, was as unconquerable after the battle as before it. Other kings might be cowed down by the fall of their capitals, but the king of Jagdishpur was not of that sort. His motto was, 'Wherever I am, there is Jagdishpur!' So, to hold Jagdishpur without capturning him was only a vain endeavour. Now that his home was lost the battlefield itself had become his home.

* * *

CHAPTER IV

Delhi Falls

WHEN the third chief commander of the English army before Delhi became hopeless of taking the town and resigned, Brigadier General Wilson replaced him. At that time, in the camp of the English army maddened by the attacks of the Revolutionaries, it was seriously discussed, in despair, whether the siege should be, raised. It is difficult to say what would have been the course of the Revolution of 1857 if this plan had been resolved upon. Still, it is clear that this one moment on the part of the English would have harmed their cause more than many defeats at the hands of the Revolutionaries. The English had a strategic advantage in thus besieging the town of Delhi, because the Revolutianary army was shut up there in one place. If that vast host had spread over the province instead of being thus bottled up and had harassed the English after forming small detachments everywhere, this guerilla warfare would have soon reduced the small English force to impotence. But Delhi being besieged, the battlefield was restricted, the English force had not to put up with an unbearable strain, and the Revolutionaries were inconveniently huddled up together in one city and thus were more liable to attack. In these circumstances, to raise the siege of Delhi was to break the dam and let the Revolutionary forces inundate the whole country. Even if Delhi were captured, the Sepoys would no doubt have spread all round. But there was a vast difference between driving them out of Delhi, defeated and dejected, and making them elated by raising the siege and allowing them to fall upon the English. Though the English commander thoroughly understood this difference despair, discouragement, and the fierce onslaughts of the Revolutionaries made him think of raising the siege. At that moment, the English power in India hung in the balance It was, indeed, fortunate for the English that there was, at this time, a bold and desperately courageous officer like Baird-Smith in the English camp outside Delhi. When all other officers were thinking of a retreat, he said with determination, 'We must not release our hold of Delhi even by an inch! Our noose, fallen round her neck like cruel death, must be constant and thorough! If we raise the siege of Delhi, the Punjab will be out of hand, India will be gone, and the Empire ruined forever!'

Encouraged by the words of Baird-Smith, Brigadier Wilson determined not to turn back without taking Delhi. The Revolutionaries, on the other hand, sustained the siege with rare ability and courage. They would make a sudden sortie. attack either the right or the left wing, kill as many people as possible, and retreat quickly when the English rose vigorously to repeal the attack. When the English army would have been decoyed near the fort in pursuit of the Sepoys, the Revolutionary guns would at once open a tremendous fire. With these tactics, the Revolutionaries so often deceived the English and killed so many of their number that Brigadier Wilson had to issue a special order that on no account was a pursuit of the Sepoys to be attempted. As the English numbers began to dwindle by this new ruse of the Revolutionaries, their commander's eyes were turned towards the expected siege-train from the Punjab. All means of communication in North Hindusthan-telegraphs, railways and posts-were completely destroyed, and the English army at

Delhi was as much besieged as the Revolutionaries. The English had no adequate knowledge as to what was going on in the south of Delhi, or as to where the army sent from Calcutta had arrived, or as to the state of affairs in the towns of Lucknow, Cawnpore, Benares and other places. A month after Sir Hugh Wheeler was killed, the English army at Delhi got 'reliable' information that he was hastening to come to their help! There was no hope of getting any reinforcements from Calcutta and the whole strain fell upon the Punjab. Sir John Lawrence had borne his burden well and had often sent reinforcement of English as well as Sikh Soldiers. This time, too, he did not refuse the new request for a siege-train and more reinforcements but sent two thousand troops under the command of Nicholson. When the news of the arrival of this army reached the English camp at Delhi, every face beamed with joy, hope, and encouragement. The fact that Nicholson was the commander encouraged them more than that two thousand soldiers were coming. A leader like Nicholson is worth thousands of soldiers! In the dispirited English ranks, everyone would say, 'Now that Nicholson is coming, there is no doubt about the victory!'

As the acquisition of good leaders removed the doubts as to victory in the English camp, so the lack of good leaders among the Revolutionaries made their defeat more and more certain. The Emperor, whom they had set upon a rejuvenated throne, though of praiseworthy qualities of kindness and mercy fit for times of peace, was quite inexperienced in war and unequal to military leadership. There was no lack of brave Sepoys at Delhi. Those who had even surpassed English troops in warfare when fighting on their side, those who had learnt their drill and discipline under the English themselves, those whose swords had extended English rule right up to Afghanistan—there were fifty thousand of such heroes within the walls of Delhi. But there was wanted at least one capable head to command and lead to victory these fifty thousand men. All honour to these fifty thousand men who fought and failed. The wonder is that they held on for so long without a capable leader to lead them! Even the old Emperor whom they had placed on the throne was as anxious to find a good leader for them as they were themselves. He tried many experiments, but they did not work. He gave all the power in the hands of Bakht Khan. He appointed three generals to manage the army. He then ordered that a committee of six—three Delhi citizens and three Sepoy leaders—should together took after all the affairs of the army. And when this representative council also proved fruitless, the noble and patriotic Emperor fearing that, perhaps, the Revolution was being destroyed on acconnt of his fault and that capable men were leaving his side on account of his being at the head, announced publicly that he was ready to give up all his power and abdicate. Rather than India come back under the English, rather than the constantly wheeling vulture of foreign domination tear the entrails of long-suffering India, rather than India be always submerged in the mire of slavery, the old Mogul proclaimed that the rule of any man over Hindusthan who would give her freedom and Swaraj would be a hundred times more pleasing to him than the continuance of his own rule. He sent letters written in his own hand to the Rajas of Jaypore, Jodhpur, Bikaner, Alwar, etc. 'It is my ardent wish to see that the Feringhi is driven out of Hindusthan by all means and at any cost. It is my ardent wish that the whole of Hindusthan should be free. But the Revolutionary War that has been waged for this purpose cannot be crowned with success unless a man capable of sustaining the whole burden of the movement, who can organise and concentrate the different forces of the nation and will unify the whole people in himself, comes forward to guide this rising. I have no desire left in me of ruling over India, after the expulsion of the English, to my own personal aggrandisement. If all of you native Raj as are ready to unsheath your sword to drive away the enemy, then, I am willing to resign my Imperial powers and authority in the hands of any confederacy of the native princes who are chosen to exercise it.'[4]

This is the letter written by the leader of Indian Mahomedans, the Emperor of Delhi to the Hindu kings in India! This unique and typical letter shows how the noble words—Swatantrya, Swaraj, Swadesh, and Swadharma-were thoroughly understood in Hindusthan. Seeing the religious instincts of Hindus and Mahomedans thus completely united together in patriotic harmony, Charles Ball says, 'Such unexpected, surprising, and extraordinary transformation is rarely to be seen in the history of the world!'

But this extraordinary transformation had been completely effected only in one province of the vast land of Hindusthan, and the immediate result of the Proclamation was not a perfect success. Though it is in the main, and in this sense, true that, before the walls of Delhi, a fight was going on between freedom and slavery, in another and in an important sense, we can say that there never was a true fight there between Indians and Feringhis as such. The author of the famous work *The Siege of Delhi*, says, 'There were four times as many natives as Europeans in the artillery. For every European horseman there were two native horsemen. It was not possible to move a step without the help of the natives.' The vigorous life in one part of the country was killed by the treacherous activity in other parts. In spite of this even towards the end of August, the Revolutionaries gave the English no opportunity to attack, but always pursued the offensive and continuously directed attacks on the English camp. This is not a mean indication, of their devotion to the principle of Swaraj.

While all this heroic devotion on the part of the Revolutionaries was rendered powerless for want of a

4. The autograph letter :— *Native Narrative* by Metcalfe, p. 226.

capable leader, the camp of the enemy got the advantage of commander like Nicholson. Now was to be seen, for the first time, a shadow of despair in Delhi. The armies of Neemuch and Bareilly began to accuse each other for the present state of affairs; and riotous Sepoys, though regularly paid, clamoured for more pay and threatened to loot the rich men of the town if their demands were not satisfied. Then, at the command of the Emperor, Bakht Khan assembled together the Sepoy leaders, Sepoys, and prominent citizens and asked them the question, 'War or surrender!' At once, the cry went ringing up to the sky, 'War, war, war!' (Ladhai!) At this display of enthusiasm there was hope everywhere, and the Revolutionary army, not excepting the Bareilly and Neemuch Sepoys, marched towards Najafgarh to attack and carry the English siege- train. After reaching Najafgarh, the Neemuch army would not encamp where the Bareilly brigade was encamped; and, instead of preparing to fall together on the enemy, they disobeyed Bakht Khan's orders and encamped at a neighbouring village. When the English heard this news, the new commander, Nicholson, took a select and sufficient force and marched in all haste towards Najafgarh. He suddenly attacked the Neemuch brigade which had encamped at a distance disobeying the orders of Bakht Khan. The Revolutionaries were lying scattered, unprepared, and unformed—the attack was cautious and well-ordered and under the command of Nicholson! The destruction of the Neemuch Sepoys was complete. They fought; they fought with great courage; they fought with such bravery that the enemy applauded them. But this was vain bravery! The Revolutionaries had never suffered such a defeat since the battle of Bundel-ki-Serai. The whole Neemuch brigade fell this day on the field! This was the fruit of self-willed action and disobedience of the orders of their own elected commander! Undisciplined bravery is as useless as cowardice!

This victory of the 25th of August removed altogether

the cloud of despair in the English camp. This was their only real victory since the month of June. Everyone was anxious now to assault Delhi. Commander Wilson gave the order to Baird-Smith to prepare the plan of the final attack. This Baird-Smith who, by his persistence, had retained the English army at Delhi when it was thinking of raising the siege, prepared the map as ordered. The new siege-train from the punjab also arrived safely in the English camp. The English commander sent a massage to his troops in the following strain. 'This city of Delhi has baulked the English army and three generals' military skill for the last three months! The time has certainly come near your efforts upto now will be rewarded by the razing to dust of the city!'

After the arrival of reinforcements from the Punjab, the English army consisted of three thousand and five hundred English soldiers, five thousand Sikhs, punjabees, etc., two thousand and five hundred Kashmiris—altogether eleven thousand men. Besides the Raja of Jhind himself was there, with hundreds of his men to assist in the fall of Delhi. In the first half of September, the English commander assumed the offensive and began to construct new batteries. This produced consternation among the Delhi Sepoys. While, outside the walls, the English were steadily advancing in good order, inside there was a climax of disorder, anarchy, and disobedience among the Indian troops! The Indians on the English side worked so arduously in the work of constructing the battery, in spite of the artillery-fire of Delhi, that Forrest writes, 'The natives excelled in steady and unparalleled bravery. When man after man was being killed, they would keep their work. If the man in front was killed by a bomb, they would stop for a moment, shed a tear or two for the dead, put the new body in the line of corpses, and begin work again in that terrible place!' The Indians under the English worked with such discipline, while those in the town of Delhi shirked their work. From this difference, what a lesson has to be learnt! Honouring the officers and obeying their word of order is the very essence of discipline. But this principle was being trampled down everywhere at Delhi. Most of the fault lay on the incapaable officers and the rest on disorderly Sepoys, and, now, there was disheartening despair to crown all! The 14th of September came. The English army was divided into four columns—three under Nicholson stood on the left and the fourth under Major Reid stood on the right to force the Kabul gate and enter Delhi.

When the sun rose, the English guns which had been so long shattering the walls stopped suddenly. There was a dead silence for a moment in the English camp and immediately the force under Nicholson dashed against the wall. The first column went up to the breach which had been effected in the Kashmir Bastion. From within, the guns of the Revolutionaries kept up a hot fire. The English fell in heaps one upon another in the trenches but some reached the walls. A ladder was placed over the wall and the English army began to scale up the ladder. The Revolutinaries fought desperately and shot down hundreds after hundreds of the Feringhi army. But the English force pushed on in spite of the terrible onslaught. At last, the English effected a big breach and carried it. Delhi's walls yielded and the bugle of victory sounded!

In the same manner, near the breach at the Water-Bastion also, there was a terrible hand to hand fight, and the second column, killing and dying at every step, carried the breach and jumped inside the city.

The third column was marching towards the Kashmir gate. When Lieutenants Home and Salkeld came in front of the gate to blow it up with dynamite, from the walls, from the windows, from everywhere came a perfect shower of grape. The draw-bridge over the trench in front of the Kashmir gate is broken. Only one plank remains. Enough, march forward on it, one by one! The sergernt is killed, this Mahadoo has fallen-but, Home, rush forth. Home ran forth and placed the dynamite near the gate. Others then rushed forward on the plank to apply the fire to it. Lieutenant Salkeld has fallen, shot by a bullet; rush forth, you, Captain Burgess; why, you are also shot; never mind, the hero has set fire to it, even as he was dying! A terrible crash like thunder! The Kashmir gate was blown up by the terrific force of the dynamite. But even this sound was not heard, in the din of battle, by the English commander who was waiting for the Kashmir gate to open! Should he advance or should he not? But, though he had not heard the bugle of victory, he had not the slightest doubt about the success of the English heroes who had rushed forth. After waiting for a time, he marched forth. With absolute confidence in his soldiers, Campbell gave the order for an assault. The troops came near the ditches. They saw their victorious and dying comrades in the ditches, rushed through the breach in the Koshmir gate, and jumped into Delhi.

The forth column under Major Reid had started from the English right to take the Kabul gate. When it reached Sabzi Mandi, it met the Sepoys who had come out of Delhi to oppose it. Major Reid fell in the first encounter, the English advance was checked, there was confusion in the English camp, the Revolutionaries were elated, and it seemed that the English would be routed. But Hope Grant brought up the cavalry and the battle again became equal. Though the English artillery opened a terrible fire from every house and garden of Kishenganj, the Revolutionaries sent bullets flying and shed pools of blood. The English cavalry also found it impossible to advance. But it was also impossible to return for fear that the Revolutionaries might capture the guns. The English cavalry stuck to their posts to die. Not a man moved from his place, except by death. Of the grand bravery and discipline of the Indian cavalrymen, their commander, Hope Grant says: 'The native cavalrymen remained firm. Their valour is unparalleled. When I began to encourage them, they said : *Do not be anxious! We will stand this fire as long as you wish!'*

Equal bravery was shown by the Indians who were fighting for love of country and freedom. The infuriated Revolutionaries, fighting every inch of space, made a great effort near the Idgah; they made more and more desperate attacks, when the English force, trying to capture Idgarh, was wavering. The Revolutionaries delivered another fierce attack. The English retired. The Revolutionaries pursued, vigorously attacking them all the way, up to their guns and cavalry. Now, at last the English forces are leaving the fleld after abandoning the position which they held so long! Bravo, Revolutionaries bravo! You have shown a splendid fight! If all of you had been as brave, and as disciplined!—

While the forth column was being thus foiled, the three English columns that had entered Delhi waited for a short time at the Kashmir gate and then rushed forth to attack the town. The three chief commanders, Campbell, Jones and Nicholson, taking their followers, fought their way to the Kabul gate. The guns found in the way were captured; on every tower and pillar was placed a British flag, and the force went fighting right up to the Burn Bastion. But, from this place onwards, instead of empty guns, lifeless hillocks, and vacant fields, they encountered the fierce war-cry of the Revolutionary force. The Revolutionaries opened a terrible fire; fierce bloodshed and death marked every foot of ground they covered; the English army which had advanced far in heat of victory was forced back beaten. When thus the English force received this check, Nicholson dashed forth like a tiger. His motto was nothing is impossible, in this world, to a brave warrior. When the irritated Nicholson left the Water Bastion and again entered the *Gully*—the bloody battle was renewed. Whichever Englishman stepped forth was shot down by the Revolutionaries fiighting for freedom. From the roofs, from the windows, from the porches, from ths verandahs, this obstinate, freedom-loving

Gully began to pour forth fire and forced even Nicholson to retire. The brave Major Jacob also fell in it! Now, rush forth, Nicholson! All other English officers, except you, have been killed by this *Gully*! Oh! freedom-loving *Gully*! Nicholson himself is coming forth—now is the true test! The fight began in a dead encounter. Suddenly, there was a cry in the English army, as if it had been struck by lightning descending upon it! Nicholson, Nicholson! Where is he now? Some brave Sepoy had singled him out and hit him—and he was rolling on the ground! There was an uproar— 'Hato !' (Retire!) in the English army, and 'Chato' (Cut down!)' in the Sepoy ranks! The dreadful *Gully*! Every inch of her length was the grave of an Englishman!

Hardly did this column of the English army retreat through this heroic *Gully* and reach the Kashmir gate, when the bugle also sounded for the retreat of the column which had gone towards Jumma Musjid. Though there was no resistance till the mosque was reached, as soon as the troop came there, a terrible war-cry was heard and, in the subsequent fight, Campbell was wounded.

Thus ended the first day of the assault on Delhi. Of the four columns, three had their chief commanders wounded; sixty-six officers, and eleven hundred and four soldiers were killed! Reckoning in the evening the advantages gained at this expense, the English commander, Wilson, found that he had taken only one-forth of Delhi! Fear, despair, and anxiety maddened general Wilson and he said that an immediate retreat must be ordered. 'The town is yet unconquered; and thousands of the Revolutionaries are proudly inviting those that remain alive to come forth for battle. Shall we now sacrifice everyone of us or suffer the ignominy of defeat? We must now retreat! —such was the opinion of Wilson.

When the dying Nicholson who had been taken to the hospital heard the news, that hero said, 'Retreat! By God's grace, I have still strength enough in me to shoot the retreating

Wilson! All the living Englishmen agreed with this dying hero, and, on the night of the 14th of September, the English troops stuck to the posts they had conquered.

The English council of war overruled General Wilson's opinion as to retreat. The movements in the revolutionary camp itself that night showed that the force of the Revolutionaries was spent. One party declared that it was better to give up Delhi and renew the war in the province, and the other insisted that Delhi should never be surrendered even if everyone of them was killed. In the English camp, whatever the differences of opinion, the majorty was always respseted and the differences were merged in the unanimity of action. This virtue, however was conspicuous in the confused Sepoy ranks by its absence, and the two parties, instead of uniting to form a common plan of action, went each their own way. Some Sepoys left Delhi., but others resolved not to go back an inch till the end, stuck to Delhi, and came out on the battle-field ready. This party fought for Delhi from the 15th to the 24th of September! And that too, with such determination, such bravery and such steadiness that, when an Ehglish detachment would enter a mosque or a palace, a guardsman would stand with his hand on the trigger, would aim calmly when the English came near, and would fire the last shot for his country and religion when they approached him. After doing this last service for his motherland, he would court death!

When three fourths of Delhi fell into the hands of the English, the commander-in-chief at Delhi, Bakht Khan, went to the Emperor and said, 'Delhi has now slipped out of our hands. But this does not mean that all chances of victory are over. Even now, the plan of harassing the enemy in the open country ratber than protecting an enclosed place is certain to bring victory in the end. I am going to fight my way out of Delhi, after selecting the warriors who are ready to keep their swords drawn till the end in this war of liberty.

I think it more advisable to go out fighting rather than surrender to the enemy. At this time, you should also come with us, and under your banner, we will fight to the last for Swaraj.' If this old Mogul had even a hundredth part of the valour of Babar, Humayun or Akbar in him, he would have accepted this valiant invitation and would have marched out of Delhi with the valiant Bakht Khan. If he was to die, he should have died like a king. But despairing on account of old age, slow on account of long enjoyment of luxuries, and frightened by defeat, the Emperor Bahadur Shah maintained an undetermined and vacillating attitude till the end. On the last day he hid himself in Humayun's grave, and, after refusing Bakht Khan's invitation, began to decide upon surrender to the English, according to the advice of Ilahi Baksh Mirza. This Ilahi Baksh was a first-class traitor! He gave the news to the English, who immediately sent thither Captain Hodson. After a promise to spare his life, the Emperor surrendered, was brought to the palace by the English, and imprisoned. Just then, the traitorous dogs, Ilahi Baksh and Munshi Rajab Ali, came up running and said, 'But the princes are yet hiding in Humayun's tomb!' Again, Hodson ran; the princes surrendered to him, were put in a carriage, and taken to the town. As sooo as the cavalcade entered the town, Hodson ran up to the carriage and shouted out that those who killed English women and children deserved death alone. So saying, Hodson turned towards the surrendered princes, who were dragged out of the carriage, and robbed of all valuables on the person, and helpless stood before him. Three shots put an end to the lives of the three princes! Hodson cut away this last sprout of Timur's family! But his revenge was not satisfied by simply shooting dead these illustrious princes. It is only savages that wreak a vengeance till death. If Hodson had stopped there, where would be the humanity of civilised English vindictiveness? Therefore, the dead bodies of the princes were thrown right before the police station. When the vultures had fed on them for some time, the rotting bodies were dragged and thrown into the river. Oh Time! what changes are wrought by thee! that there should be no one to give the last burial rites to the descendants of the great Emperor Akbar! And now, the Sikhs thought that the prophecy in their books was fulfilled! But, in what way? By what means? to what end? For whose benefit?

Then began terrible looting and a general massacre at Delhi. After hearing the accounts, Lord Elphinstone writes to Sir John Lawrence, 'After the siege was over, the outrages committed by our army are simply heartrending. A wholesale vengeance is being taken without distinction of friend and foe. As regards the looting, we have indeed surpassed Nadir Shah!'[5] General Outram was of opinion that Delhi should be burnt!

The English army, both European and Indian, engaged at the siege of Delhi, was about ten thousand men. Of those, about four thousand fell on the field, killed and wounded. Such a terrible death-roll is not found even in a struggle like the Crimean war! Though it is impossible to form a reliable estimate of the losses of the Revolutionaries from English accounts, they must have been about five to six thousand.[6]

In this manner this historical town, inspired by the noble sentiments of Swadharma and Swaraj, fought with a powerful enemy like the English for a hundred and thirty-four days and nights. On the whole, the fight was one befitting a high and exalted principle! From the day on which Delhi threw away the Feringhi flag from her walls and proclaimed the establishment of Swaraj, from the day on which Delhi smashed the chains of slavery and established freedom, from the day on which Delhi first pronounced the formula of unity for the vast and extended continent of Hindusthan under a national banner, from that day onward, to the day on which

5. Life of Lawrence. Vot. II, page 262.
6. Rotton says: 'The casualties of the mutineers were often manifested beyond all due bounds.'—page 175.

English swords drank Swadeshi blood in the palace of Bahadur Shah, this town had done not a few deeds of noble and unselfish heroism befitting the holy war of freedom! Without a leader, without good organisation, having to fight a well-trained enemy like the English, and having to oppose Swadeshi swords no less brave,-why, braver than the Feringhi ones—ready to pronounce upon their compatriots—in spite of all these disadvantages, the Revolutionaries fought a splendid fight. But disunion and want of organisation—the result of the lack of a great leader filled their camp and greatly handicapped them. Despite all these enormous difficulties the Sepoys at Delhi fought like real national and religious martyrs. Their virtues and even their faults, will be looked upon with reverence by future generations! 'The elephant breaking his tusk, in trying to smash a mountain, is noble! Throughout all the faults and all the virtues lurks constantly the fire of the love of Swadharma and Swaraj and freedom and sacrifice for a noble principle. And so, both these are living sermons on moral herosim !

* * *

CHAPTER V

Lucknow

ON the day on which the Revolutionaries were successful in the battle of Chinhat, the English power in Oudh came to an end and the revolt had openly assumed the form of a national Revolution. The Sepoys, princes, and people began by establishing a ruler liked by them on the vacant throne of Lucknow. The anarchy which raged everywhere for the space of a week after the battle of Chinhat had to be first suppressed before preparations for war could be made. Therefore the Revolutionaries set themselves to the task of administration at Lucknow, though the week's interval gave an opportunity to the English of fortifying their defences. The late Nabob of Lucknow, Wajid Ali Shah, being a prisoner of the English at Calcutta, they unanimously elected and placed on the throne his son, Prince Birjis Kadar. This Birjis Kadar being a minor, the regency of the kingdom of Oudh was given in the hands of his mother, Queen Hazrat Mahal. As in the palace of Delhi, on account of the extreme old age of Emperor Bahadur Shah, the affairs of state were looked after by Begum Zinat Mahal in the Emperor's name, so in the palace at Lucknow, the Nabob being a minor, the Government depended on his mother, Begum Hazrat Mahal. This Begum of Oudh, though not quite another Lakshmi Bai, was undoubtedly a great organiser, full of love of liberty and the spirit of daring. She had perfect confidence in an Omrah (nobleman) of the court, called Mahbub Khan. She appointed various officers to the judical revenue, police, and military departments. These officers selected were such as were loved and honoured by the representatives of the Sepoys, by Mahbub Khan and other leading Sirdars, and also by the large numbers of the people who hurried from all parts of Oudh to Lucknow to join in the great War of Independence. Every day, a Durbar was held to discuss political affairs, and there, the Begum Sahiba exercised authority in the name of the Nabob. The news that Oudh was free and that not a trace of English rule remained there was sent to the Emperor of Delhi, under the Begum's seal, along with valuable presents. Letters were sent to all the neighbouring Zemindars and vassal Rajas to come to Lucknow with armed followers. From the appointment of the various civil officers; from the good order in all the departments of Government, from the daily Durbars, and other signs, it was apparent that the revolt had ended and constructive government had begun. But unfortunately, the Revolutionaries did not show as much zeal in obeying the officers appointed as they showed in participating in their appointment. In all Revolutions this common blunder is committed, and this sows the seeds of destruction of the Revolution in the very beginning. Every Revolution is started by cutting down the laws of existing authority by the sword. But when once the habit is formed of mowing down by the sword the unjust laws of unconstitutional authority, then in the heat of the moment, the vicious habit develops of setting at naught all laws at will. The sword used for destroying wicked and cruel laws tends to destroy all law. The heroes, who start out for overthrowing foreign rule, soon get into the habit of overthrowing all rule. In the excitement of breaking the bonds of foreign rule, they begin to dislike all bonds, even those of just and normal rule. And in this way, Revolution ends in Anarchy, virtue in vice, and what ought to be a great benefit ends in loss. The destruction of individuals, of society, and of kingdoms is caused as much by anarchy as by foreign rule, as much by the absence of any bond as by the presence of cruel bonds. If any Revolution forgets this sociological truth, it generally kills itself in the end. Just as a man who begins to take wine as a cure for some distemper does not get rid of the habit of drinking wine even after he is cured; similarly, the habit of breaking bonds, in order to remove bad rule, persists even after its work is done and makes men disorderly and anarchical. That Revolution which destroys injustice and oppression is holy. But when a Revolution roots out one kind of injustice and oppression but plants, at the same moment, the seeds of another kind, it becomes at once unholy, and the seeds of destruction accompanying that sin soon put an end to its life.

Therefore, those who want to take the wine of Revolution to cure the disease of foreign slavery must be on their guard not to get addicted to the vicious habit. The mind must be trained from the beginning to honour one's own rule as much as to hate foreign rule. In wiping out foreign misrule, care must be taken to discourage, by all possible means, internal disorder. In smiting down foreign rule and foreign authority, one's own rule and authority should be worshipped as sacred. The moment the foreign power is destroyed, in order to guard the country from the evils of anarchy, a constitution liked by the majority of the people should be at once established and that constitution should be obeyed with reverence by all. The orders of all officers thus appointed must be implicitly carried out, discipline must be observed, individual caprice must give way to devotion to the principle of the common good and, if any change in this constitution is thought desirable and just, it must be attempted only by means of the voice of the majority. In short, the rule should be Revolution outside and Constitution within, chaos outside abd cosmos within, sword outside and law within.

These elementary principles of all constitutions so necessary for the success of Revolutions were fairly well observed in the first half of the Rising. Immediately after the Revolution began, attention was given to organise administration with all possible speed at Delhi, Lucknow, Cawnpore, and other cities. In all these big towns, no impostor set himself up with the desire of individual aggrandisement. The undoubted hereditary and popular rulers were set up on the various thrones. These rulers did not even evince any desire to take advantage of the Revolution to further their own selfish ends and increase their power. Nay, more; written documents are published which prove that they were ready to relinquish all their rights if their persons were in the way of the country's independence.[1] Thus, in 1857, the first part of constructive administration was successfully achieved in a spirit of adorable nobility. But in this organisation, the importane and major section being composed of common sepoys, they began to feel all bonds unbearable when they had once removed the shackles of foreign rule. And, at the time of the crisis, all discipline became lax. Therefore, even those officers, whom they appointed at the first impulse of the ideal of Swaraj, they later on insulted, disobeyed, and mocked. And thus, the Revolution tended to end in anarchy. Under these circumstances, had there arisen a hero who, by his individual prowess and the might of his all-conquering sword, could have won the hearts or awe of those follwers who, incapable of being unified by an abstract ideal, could have still been bound together by a common hero-worship, the Revolution might have been crowned with success. But, in the absence of such a hero on the one side and the inherent tendency of an uncontrolled Revolution to lapse into anarchy on the other, there were more rabble than disciplined soldiers in the army of the kingdom of Oudh. The martyrs, by their undaunted, unconquered, and unconquerable determination to do and die, kept the field busy for three years! In the camp at Lucknow, the men of the first kind were much more numerous than those of the second, and the orders of several officers appointed by Begum Hazrat Mahal were never strictly obeyed. And the Sepoys became impudent, oppressive, disorderly, and self-willed.

But still some brave heroic spirits who were staying among them inspired the Sepoys with their bravery, noble ideas, and natural excellence of spirit. And as these valiant

---

1. See page 311.

men insisted, it was resolved to make the first great attack on the besieged Residency on the 20th of July.

On the morning of the 20th of July, the Revolutionary artillery which had been very active so long, suddenly stopped firing. About eight o'clock, the Revolutionary party laid some mines under the Residency walls and filled them with dynamite. The mines were blown up and the Sepoy ranks rushed forth after the explosion. At the same time, the guns again began a terrible fire on the English. The Revolutionary army fell upon the English from different directions—towards the Redan, on the house of of Innes, on the Cawnpore Battery. The part of the army which attacked the Cawnpore battery made a desperate rush on the English guns. Again and again, they rushed against the guns. Their heroic leader, fluttering the flag of Swaraj in his hand, jumped into the ditch and called upon the others to follow, shouting, 'Chalo. Bahadur! Chalo!' (Come, brave men, come!) He crossed the ditch and began to plant the Revolutionary flag on English guns![2] But this brave soldier was soon shot down by an English bullet. Instead of thousand rushing forth over his dead body at this time and avenging the death of the martyr the crowd of camp followers retreated instead of advancing. But, bravo! You ladder-men! You did not imitate the cowardly camp followers but rushed forth like real Sepoys. Plant the ladders in the ditch and mount up quickly in spite of the fire of the English! The first batch has fallen—but let the next one come. But where are the others who dare risk it ? This is the difference between the English army and the Revolutionaries! The English never allowed the blood of their comrades to be shed in vain; if one falls, ten rush forward in his place. We do not care where those who fled behind will go to; but you heroes you martyrs, you have reached Heaven! Those who took the flag of Swaraj in their own hands in order that it might not be polluted by the touch of

2. Gubbins's *Mutinies*, Page 218.

cowardly living corpses, those who went up to put that flag on the enemy's fire-spitting guns, by their glorious, holy blood—that flag will be eternally pure and shine with a divine splendour ! The flag of Swaraj looks its best only in such wounded and bleeding arms! One whose wrists are not bespattered with blood should not touch and pollute the holy flag of independence!

After this first assault was repulsed, the Revolutionaries had, daily, small skirmishes with the English. They did their best in dynamiting the houses in the Residency. From above the fire of terrible guns, and from below, dynamite explosions! No Englishman was sure when the ground beneath his feet would burst and swallow him. According to Brigadier Innes's calculation, the Revolutionaries dynamited the Residency thirty-seven times! The Revolutionary guns were, also, constantly active. The Sepoys would send splendidly aimed shots against the English and the English would reply to them. There were death-dealing fights between bands of scouts which set out at night to get secret information from the opposite camps. Often, the secret whispering of a group of men either within or without the walls were heard by the other party and nullified their plans. The Revolutionaries amused themselves often by aiming a ball exactly at the English flag and destroying it. And the English, also, unfailingly hauled up a new one at the Residency as soon as night fell. At such ghastly jokes, the battlefield of Lucknow would open her terrible jaws and smile a deathly smile! Every night the messengers of the Revolutionaries would go hiding near a part of the fort occupied by the Sikhs or other Indians and ask them, 'Why do you play the traitor (Nimak haram) with the nation and thrust the sword of the Feringhis into the bodies of your own brethren?' If any night these questions become persistent, the 'loyal' Sikhs, to have some fun, would ask them to come near in order to converse better and, as soon as they came, would make an Englishman who had hitherto kept himself concealed stand up before them! Seeing such treachery, the Revolutionaries would return cursing their baseness. Of all the splendid and untiring shouts among the Revolutiooaries, an African eunuch who had been in the service of the late Nabob spread terror in the English Residency. He was nicknamed 'Othello' by the English.

About this time, Major Banks who had taken charge of the office of chief commissioner of Oudh, after the death of Sir Henry Lawrence, also fell dead by the bullet of a Revolutionary. This was the second English chief commissioner killed during the siege! But on account of the fixed, regular, and orderly organisation of the English army, even during the uncertain terrors of a seige, the death of a commander had no more effect than the death of a common soldier as regards the efficiency of the army. When the second commissioner fell, Brigadier Inglis took charge as commissioner, and the work of defence went on as before. At this time, however, the losses, deaths, the removal of leaders, the scarcity of food, and the activity of the Revolutionaries had made the English at Lucknow fairly desperate, though not altogether hopeless.

Just then Angad returned from Cawnpore! This Angad was an Indian formerly empolyed in the English army and now a pensioner. Since the siege of Lucknow, it had become impossible for any white messenger to go out and return with information. His white skin, his yellowish hair, and his blue eyes could never escape the swords of the Revolutionaries. Therefore, it became necessary to employ brown men on the English messages, and thus, many 'loyal' brown messengers had been sent out from Lucknow. But, out of all these, only Angad returned alive! He did not bring any letter or anything else suspicious with him for fear of the Revolutionaries, but he gave commander Inglis the assurance that he had himself seen the English army set out from Cawnpore for the relief of Lucknow. Encouraged by this news, the English told Angad to go back and get a written reply. Angad left Lucknow on the 22nd and returned at eleven o'clock on the night of the 25th. With him was Havelock's letter, 'Havelock is coming with an army sufficient for all odds. Lucknow will be relieved in five or six days.' In order to furnish Havelock, who was coming to relieve them, with all information, the English gave military plans and maps to Angad and told him to go to Havelock again. That marvellous scout again went to Havelock's camp and delivered to him all the military maps of Lucknow. Now all English eyes were turned towards the direction from which they expected Havelock's victorious flag to march over the dead bodies of the Revolutionaries. They even heard some distant sounds of artillery-fire. Could they be Havelock's guns?

The English had not long been fondly hoping that Havelock was coming to help them when they discovered that it meant a second assault from the Revolutionary side! The Revolutionaries at first opened fire on the Cawnpore battery, Johannes' House, Begum Kothi, and other places. On that day, the Revolutionary dynamite did splendid work. There was a tremendously big breach in the English wall, enough for a whole regiment to march in good order. But where was the regiment that would go in? If the English had effected such a breach in the enemy's wall, they would have captured the place in half an hour. Some heroes among lhe Revolutionaries fought bravely till two in the afternoon. The Indians on the English side, however, excelled in bravery, discipline, and contempt of death! What a misfortune! This bravery in treachery and this cowardice in patriotism! What a contrast! Run up, some one, to remove this stain! It is now five and the attack is almost repulsed, but run up, someone, though not for immediate victory at least for ever-lasting glory! Captain Saunders, beware! The furious march ot heroes devoted to principle is coming! It is come; this band of infuriated heroes is marching straight on—they are obstructed by the English wall but they are trying bodily to push it away. The English, at this crisis, left their guns and took up their bayonets. Hail, Freedom! Some snatched away the bayonets with their own hands and at last, fallen a prey to an English bullet! But they have saved the disgrace of their country on the field and exhibited bravery admired even by enemies. The fight was such that the English themselves took photographs of these heroes who struggled to wrest away English bayonets from the walls and fought with the frenzy of lions till death !

On the 18th of August, the Revolutionaries made another attack on the English. On this day, as usual, a breach was first made by dynamite and, then, the Revolutionaries rushed forth. Malleson writes :— 'One of their officers, a very gallant fellow, sprang at once to the top of the breach and, waving his sword, called on his men to follow. Before, however, his summons was responded to, a bullet had laid him low. His place was instantly occupied by another, but he was as instantly killed. Etc, etc.'

The bravery of the three men, as described even by Feringhis, was a match to Nicholson's bravery at Delhi. But it went in vain on account of the timidity of their followers. Instead of pushing forth with redoubled vigour at the death of the three, the thousands behind them thought it prudent to retire. From this one event, what a lesson ought to be learnt?

These frequent attacks were not all. Before the terrible daily fire of artillery and guns, the English found it unbearable to hold out much longer in spite of the excellent assistance of the 'loyal' Indians. Just then, Angad again returned to Lucknow ! As the English commander was about to ask him, in eager joy, how far Havelock had marched according to his promise, the scout delivered to him Havelock's letter, 'I cannot come towards Lucknow for at least twenty-five days to come'! Nothing is more unbearable than despair following hope. Not only dying patients and emaciated women but soldiers and officers became extremely dispirited, sad, and frightened. A death-like shadow come over the whole English force. Food became dear and all were ordered to live on half ration! Why this delay? Why is a warrior like Havelock not coming to such an important work as the relief of Lucknow?

Without the delay of a moment, Havelock had left Cawnpore and crossed the Ganges as far back as the 29th of July, in order to save his comrades at Lucknow. He had a thousand and five hundred men and thirteen guns and had written a letter of assurance to them, promising to relieve them without fail within five or six days. But as soon as he crossed the Ganges and stepped into Ondh, the imaginary ease of the task began to melt away like a cloud! Every inch of the way through Oudh had risen in revolt! Every Zemindar had collected a few hundred men under him and had begun the fight for independence. Every village flew the national Revolutionary flag. Seeing this terrible state of affairs, Havelock became very much dejected in mind. He was dejected but he did not despair. He marched on. The Revolutionaries countered him first at Onao but flew away soon, After this skirmish at Onao, Havelock gave his soldiers only time for eating and, after that, the march continued. At Bashiratganj, a second skirmish took place with a similar result. Havelock's army fought two such skirmishes on the 29th and got the better of the Revolutionaries in both.

But, was this a real victory? In one day, the handful of his army lost one sixth of its number. And the Revolutionaries. were not in the least broken up. Nay, more; it is doubtful whether the Revolutionaries were really defeated and chased away or they had hit upon the new Plan of harassing the enemy considerably without suffering any losses themselves! And just then the news had come that the Danapur Sepoys had also joined the Revolution. This threatening state of affairs compelled Havelock to stop his forward march on the 30th and retire back to Mangalwar.

Hearing that Havelock's army had left Cawnpore, Nana Sahib Peshwa again resumed operations round about Cawnpore. While Havelock left Cawnpore and crossed the Ganges to enter Oudh, Nana Sahib left Oudh and was crossing the same river to re-enter Cawnpore! Not to be caught in this trap of Nana Sahib, Havelock had to remain encamped at Mangalwar till the 4th of August. Instead of Havelock driving the Revolutionaries within a week to the banks of the Gotami, Nana Sahib had made Havelock stick to the Ganges. Just then the Revolutionaries in his front came up again to Bashiratganj. Irritated by the persistent harassing Havelock became desperate and started towards Lucknow with his troops. At Bashiratganj he again gave battle to the Revolutionaries and drove them away. But here, also, the question was whether it was a victory or a defeat. For, in this fight, Have-lock lost three hundred men and his troops were so fatigued that instead of advancing towards Lucknow, he began to retire on the Ganges. On that day, out of the one thousand and five hundred men that started with him there remained only eight hundred and fifty!

Hearing that Havelock had again retreated to Mangalwar on the 5th of August, the Revolutionaries once more captured Bashiratganj and encamped there. In this army of the Revolutionaries, the greater number were well-to-do Zemindars. 'All the men killed yesterday were Zemindars.'[3] For the sake of their country, for the sake of their independence and Swaraj, those rich and happy men had discarded their soft beds and had resolved, to go to the battle-field and risk all its dangers and risks. Seeing this enthusiasm on their part, the English historian Innes says: , At least, the struggle of the Oudhians must be characterised as a war of independence.' The Revolutionary army was constantly hovering round Havelock's camp, destiny-like. As soon as Havelock retired to Mangalwar the Revolutionaries, as we

3. Kaye and Malleson's *Indian Mutiny,* Vol. III, page 340.

said before again encamped at Bashiratganj. Therefore, on the 11th of August, Havelock pushed forward to Bashiratganj for the third time—and for the third time there was a fight and the Revolutionaries fled away; but Havelock asked himself, for the third time, 'Is this victory or defeat?'

It was neither a victory nor a defeat. Therefore, instead of advancing, Havelock fell back on Mangalwar. In the meanwhile, Nana's plans were becoming ripe. The Revolutionaries of Sagar and of Gwalior and bands of volunteers came and joined him. Taking them with him, Nana marched to Bithoor and threatened to attack Cawnpore. General Neill had not enough troops to march against him and so he sent word to Havelock of his critical position. It was now impossible to think of proceeding to Lucknow. Therefore, on the 12th of August, Havelock had to recross the Ganges and go back to Cawnpore! When the English bands sounded the retreat, everywhere there were joyful shouts of acclamation as if the victorious drum of independence was being, beaten! You faithful Zemindars, you have served your country well in thus shedding your blood and driving away the foreign foe, who wanted to re-enter Oudh, away on the other side of the Ganges! Innes writes: 'This retirement from Oudh produced a result which he had, doubtless, never contemplated. The Talukdars openly construed it as the British evacuation of the province and now formally recognised the Durbar at Lucknow as the *de facto* government; and, though they refrained from supporting it by their own presence, they obeyed its orders which they had hitherto disregarded and sent to the scene of warfare the contingents which they had been called upon to provide.'[4]

The victory of the Revolutionaries was not a direct but an indirect one. If, in the above four or five skirmishes fought by Havelock, he had been defeated and driven away to

4. *The Sepoy Revolt*, page 174.

Cawnpore a greater self-confidence would have been seen in the Revolutionary ranks than was to be seen now by simply forcing him to retire by harassing his rear. And, proportionately, the English forces would have been more demoralised. The English army perceived that the retreat to Cawnpore was due not to lack of bravery but to lack of numbers and, though baulked of its fruits, its vigour, self-confidence, and pride were not a whit diminished by this indirect defeat. And, therefore, Havelock encamped .at Cawnpore with the full confidence that he would start again for Lucknow as soon as he got reinforcements.

At this time, there was a serious quarrel between Havelock and Neill on account of personal jealousy. This is clearly seen in the following letter written by Havelock to Neill: 'I wrote to you confidentially on the state of affairs. You send me back a letter of censure of my measures, reproof, and advice for the future. I do not want and will not receive any of them from an 'officer under my command, be his experience what it may. Understand this distinctly, and that a consideration of the obstruction that would arise to the public service at this moment alone prevents me from taking the stronger step of keeping you under-arrest. You now stand warned. Attempt no further dictation.'[5] In this letter, one sentence is an excellent indication of the sense of duty towards the nation, ingrained in the bones of all Englishmen. Even in the height of passion, Havelock says that, consideration of the obstruction that would arise to the public service alone prevented him from then and there avenging his personal insult! In this dispute between the two generals Neill and Havelock at this critical time, not only did both of them behave calmly in order that their national enemy might not take advantage of this division, but both helped each other, as far as possible, for their common end. In that society where, individualism is held in check by regard

5. Quoted by Malleson, *Indian Mutiny*, Vol. III, p. 837. note.

for public advantage, in that society alone can wealth and intellect, and fame and independence last long.

The first news that Havelock received when he came to. Cawnpore was that Nana Sahib's army had re-occupied the town of Brahmavarta. Seeing that the Revolutionaries had thus advanced again close to the Cawnpore army, Havelock marched against them at once. On this day, at the battle of Brahmavarta, when the English came up fighting within twenty yards of the Revolutionary ranks, the 42nd regiment on the Revolutionary side began to use their bayonets. The English so long used to think that, when all other means failed, bayonets would surely frighten away the Revolutionaries. But to-day the brave heroes of freedom, themselves, began to attack with bayonets. At the same time, the Revolutionary cavalry fell upon the English rear and carried off their provisions. Thus, the English army was attacked both in front and the rear by the gallant Revolutionaries. Even the English commander saw that the Revolutionaries were gradually becoming more and more valiant. But this bravery and heroism was not properly moulded by discipline as it was on the English side and, even after all this valour, the Revolutionaries were defeated and had to retire. When Havelock retired to Cawnpore on the 17th of August after inflicting this defeat on the Revolutionaries, he perceived that the whole army of Nana Sahib was not at Brahmavarta but that he had a vast and fully equipped force in the town of Kalpi, on the banks of the Jumna. Harassed from Kalpi, harassed from Brahmavarta, harassed from Oudh, harassed on both sides of the Ganges! Thus harassed on all sides, the , victorious' Havelock wrote to Calcutta: 'We are in a terrible fix. If new reinforcements do not arrive, the British army cannot escape the fate of abandoning Lucknow and retreating to Allahabad.' Havelock awaited a reply to this appeal, from Calcutta. He expected to receive reinforcements according to his request and hoped that he would crown all his victories and defeats by the relief of Lucknow. But, suddenly, he got an order that the command of the army to be sent to Lucknow was taken from him and given to Sir James Outram! English punishment is so severe! Even though victorious, Neill was a little late in going to Cawnpore; so, the command was taken from him and given to Havelock. And, though victorious, Havelock was inevitably late in going to Lucknow; so even an able general like him was removed, and Sir James Outram was made the commander! At this news, Havelock was extremely mortified. The glory for which he strove day and night, with his life in his hands, the glory of relieving Lucknow, would now fall into other hands. This insult grieved him very much. Still, Malleson writes, 'It is one of the glories of our countrymen that, however actually they may feel a disappoiment of this nature, it never affects their public conduct. It is this recognition of, and this devotion to duty, that stamp the Englishman. He subordinates to it all private feelings. He may be keenly sensible of the injustice perpetrated towards himself, but above himself is always his country, He may have his own views as to how that country may best be served; but, when the Government which represents it has other and different views, he feels bound to devote all his energies to make possible the success of the orders of the Government. Thus acted Neill And, now, thus also acted Havelock. Superseded, as he regarded himself to be, he was as active, as daring, as devoted, as when he ruled as the unfettered commander of an independent force.'[6]

While Havelock was working day and night for the victory which was to belong to another, Sir James Outram arrived at Cawnpore on the 15th of September. After the chief command was transferred from Havelock to Sir James Outram, the first order that Outram issued was to the following effect: 'He who so bravely has been keeping up

---

6. Malleson's *Indian Mutiny*, Vol. III, page 346

the struggle for the raising of the siege of Lucknow, he alone deserves the honour of accomplishing that task. For this reason, I have handed over all my authority as a commander to the brave Havelock, till the siege of Lucknow be raised, and have enlisted myself as a simple volunteer in the ranks.'

What a moral education this first noble order of the commander must have been to the English army! How the individual must bave been merged in the nation! With the first order, Outram gave tbe chief command to Havelock and showed unparalleled patriotism, generosity, and unselfishness.

Inspired by the moral lesson of this piece of heroic nobility, and reinforced by fresh English troops from Calcutta under officers, like Eyre, Outram and Cooper, the Cawnpore army, with redoubled vigour, again started to cross the Ganges on the 20th of September to march to the relief of Lucknow. The impatient Havelock of July 25th who started to 'relieve Lucknow in five or six days,' the Havelock of August 12th unfortunate in having to retreat to Cawnpore and who found it difficult to hold out at all in Oudh, and the resolute and hopeful Havelock of 20th of September! How different are these three pictures of Havelock? He had, now, two thousand five hundred English troops, and the whole army, including the Sikhs, numbered about three thousand two hundred and fifty. Select cavalry, excellent artillery, officers like Neill, Eyre, and Outram were with him. Now, he did not pay any heed to the Oudh Revolutionaries. Every Zemindar who came to the field to save his country from the polluting touch of the Feringhi was killed. Every proud village that stood up to fight, unable to bear a sight of Feringhi horsemen galloping in the mother-country, was burnt to ashes! Every road, every field, every river on the way was reddened with Swadeshi blood! Thus, the powerful English army began to push its way into Oudh with violence. Fighting skirmish after skirmish and routing the ill-trained Revolutionaries,

Havelock arrived at Alam Bagh on the 23rd of September. A Revolutionary force was encamped there. The two forces met. The whole day the terrible battle was raging near Alam Bagh. The enemy captured five of the guns of the Revolutionaries, 'One of which the Revolutionaries recaptured. Both sides determined to spend the night on the field. But when the army of the enemy began to rest at night in the muddy and swampy ground, the Revolutionaries forswore all rest and started the fight again. That night rain was falling in showers. But the waves of enthusiasm in the English army were stronger even than the showers of rain, for the electrifying news of the fall of Delhi had reached them that night!

At last, the critical day of the 25th dawned. Seeing that Havelock's army, avoiding the regular roads leading to Lucknow city, was marching to the Residency by an odd road, the Revolutionaries opened a terrible fire. Bearing this artillery fire bravely, the English came up from Alam Bagh right up to the bridge at Char Bagh. To cross this bridge was to enter Lucknow, and, therefore, an obstinate fight began on this most strategic point. Captain Maude directed a heavy fire for half an hour on that bridge, but neither the bridge was emptied nor were the guns on it silenced. Nay more, the English had lost already twenty-one killed near the Yellow House and more on the bridge. Was the whole English army to be checked by this one defiant bridge? So, Maude said to Havelock's young son standing near by. 'Young hero, find out some remedy for this!' At this, young Havelock came to Neill and told him that the Revolutionaries could not be driven away by the artillery, and requested him to give the order to lead an assault on that bridge. But General Neill said that he could not give such an order without consulting Havelock. What was to be done next? Young Havelock at once found out the answer to this question. He spurred his horse and galloped a little in the direction where the general-in-chief, Havelock, was and, pretending to have seen him, returned to Neill. He humbly saluted Neill and said: 'The commander-in-chief has ordered the assault on the bridge.' Hearing this, the general gave the order to assault. Young Havelock himself rushed to the bridge with the first batch of twenty-five Englishmen. The fire was terrible. In one or two minutes, which of the twenty-five remained alive? And the young Havelock himself beware! beware—a brave and fearless hero has jumped upon the bridge and is taking aim straight at you! The brave Sepoy came up to within ten yards of young Havelock, stood there coolly before all the English host and quietly aimed at Havelock; the bullet went-but there was a difference of only half an inch! Instead of entering the head, it entered Havelock's helmet. Still the dauntless Sepoy stood there calmly while several English guns, were aimed at him and began loading his gun again! At last, you have been shot by Havelock, but bravo! you have died killing like a hero in this battle for independence! In a few moments, the vast English army rushed upon the bridge which began to shake with their weight. The Revolutionaries had to retire and the English advanced. The bridge fell; the first road to Lucknow fell; then, the second fell; then, the third-the English army pushed onward, victorious. Every few steps, swords would clash with swords and guns with guns. When a copious lake of blood accumulated there, the living Battle would advance again. In the evening, Outram said that the night should be spent outside. But no, no! How could the brave Havelock bear even to hear the name of rest? To those countrymen of theirs, crushed in the very jaws of death in that Residency, one night would be like an age. Therefore, Havelock advanced-Neill advanced. The English army missed the road fixed upon and came nearer and nearer into the line of fire of the Revolutionaries-still Neill advanced. When he entered the great arch of Khas Bazaar, he saw that the English artillery had slacked a little behind. Therefore, he drew up his horse and turned his head to look back. Now is the time!

This is the time for the country's revenge! O you Revolutionary hero on the arch, even if you lose your life, you must make use of this opportunity. In a moment, a Sepoy who was lying in wait on the arch took aim and lodged a bullet straight into the very neck of General Neill and he dropped down dead! In the whole English army, it was very difficult to find another man so brave and so cruel, so insolent and so undaunted, so patient and so heartless, by the good luck and ill-luck of humanity.

But it is the peculiarity of the English army that the continuance of its work does not depend upon an individual—even an uncommon general like Neill. Neill's death did not create the slightest confusion; the English army continued its march to the Residency all the same. In that Khas Bazaar where Neill fell with his neck broken, even if there had flowed an ocean of English blood, the English army would have marched in the same manner. When they went through the bazaars, they heard the joyous hurrahs from the Residency. They also shouted 'Hurrah' in reply. Havelock had relieved his compatriots from the very jaws of Death! That scene can best be described in the pen of Captain Wilson who was present there. 'In spite of deaths that were diminishing their ranks at every step, the white army approached the Residency, and at their sight all fear and doubt vanished away from the besieged garrison. They showered their congratulations and blessings on the advancing deliverers, the sick! and the wounded crept out of the hospitals, and continuous cheers and welcomes pealed forth in succession. Very soon the deliverers met the delivered. The occasion defies description. Those who had heard of the death of their husbands found themselves in the arms of their living husbands, to the unbounded joy of both. And those who were looking forward to the cherished embrace of their beloved ones learned for the first time that death had left no hope of seeing them any longer!'

In the Residency of Lucknow, fighting without intermission for eighty-seven days, seven hundred men had fallen. About five hundred Europeans and four hundred Indians were alive, wounded as well as whole. And in the army of Havelock, which set out for their relief, seven hundred and twenty-two men were killed before the Residency was reached! It was at the cost of so many brave men's lives that the victory of Lucknow was achieved.

But you cruel Despair! You are still as invincible as ever! Havclock has harassed the Revolutionaries so much, but you still do not leave him! For, when he entered the Residency he had thought that after all the victories, all the bloodshed, all the fighting, he had, at last, relieved the English power from the grip of the Revolutionaries. But, now, his delusion is being dispelled and he asks himself, after reaching the Lucknow Residency, the same question as he did when he was on the banks of the Ganges, 'What I brought to the Residency is it complete relief or mere help?' Instead of the siege being raised by Havelock's coming to the Residency, the Revolutionaries now besieged the old army as well as the new! And therefore, everyone began to ask, 'What has Havelock brought us, relief or mere help?'

It was only help! The army, which the two great English generals, Havelock and Outram, brought, after fighting many battles, to relieve the English at Lucknow from the grip of the Pandays, instead of raising the siege, went in and was besieged itself along with the other. The English hoped that the army of the Pandays would disperse as soon as Havelock's army entered the Residency. All India soon saw that these hopes were completely dashed to the ground. Instead of giving up Lucknow or opening negotiations for peace with the English, the Pan day host, infuriated by the progress of the War of Independence, took up its former position round the Residency as soon as Havelock entered it. While entering the Residency, one part of the English army had been left behind at Alam Bagh. This part was not allowed a chance to join the main army. And before the pools of blood accumulated in the streets in the course of the day's fight had dried up, the freedom-loving city of Lucknow, discarding the discouragement and despair caused by their defeat and the victory of the English, again besieged and bottled up the English power in Oudh.

It was not only the English army at Lucknow that was placed in a fix by this firm determined stand of the Pandays in the War of Independence. The whole English army from Peshawar up to Aligarh had to suffer a severe strain. All the troops had been despatched under the command of Havelock to fall upon 'Lucknow; and when, in spite of the help of these troops, not only the besieged army in the Residency was not set free but the army was beleaguered there, then, the English power in the provinces below Lucknow became considerably enfeebled. Though, just then, Delhi had fallen and the English army there was free, it had enough work on its hands in 'restoring order' in the provinces around Delhi. In these circumstances, the English Commander-in-Chief left the armies at Lucknow and Alam Bagh to fight it out themselves for the present with the Revolutionaries, and began to attend to the lightening of the strain on the British power as the more important task.

The new English Commander-in-Chief, Sir Colin Campbell, had arrived at Calcutta on the 13th of August. From that day till the 27th of October, he was straining every nerve to prepare for the vast campaign to reconquer Hindusthan from the hands of the Revolutionaries. He portioned out the English army as it arrived from Madras, Ceylon, and China. He cast new guns in the Cassim Bazaar arsenal. He made excellent arrangements as far as possible for arms and ammunition, provision, clothes, and transport. He spent two months in these preparations for the next great campaign when the news arrived that Havelock and Outram were still shut up in the Residency at Lucknow. Therefore, with the resolve to deal personally with the obstinate town of Lucknow which fell but rose again, he set out from Calcutta on the 27th of October.

About the same time, a naval brigade had been formed under Colonel Powell and Captain William Peel and sent up the river to Allahabad. From Calcutta right up to Allahabad and Cawnpore, near all the big roads, small bands of Revolutionaries were constantly harassing the English army. If these bands had been found together, the English could have possibly attacked them all; but the Panday forces, trained in the school of Kumar Singh, hovered round the English army, always avoided battle, never gave the English any indication of their existence except when attacking them and by these guerilla tactics, had created consternation in the English camp in the whole province. While trying to drive away such a band from the Kajva river, the colonel of the naval brigade was killed. On the day on which the Panday sword drank the blood of Powell, the Commander- in-Chief arrived at Cawnpore. The Commander-in-Chief had himself had a terrible experience as to how the Revolutionary bands harassed the armies on their march.

Sir Colin Campbell was driving in a carriage from Allahabad to Cawnpore. Though the English had tremendous difficulties in obtaining transport and the Commander-in-Chief had to sit in a third-class cart, on the same road was marching a detachment of a Revolutionary regiment of infantry mounted on about a dozen elephants. There were, also, twently-five horsemen accompanying them. Sir Colin was alone. When the driver of the cart came near Sher Ghati, he saw the Revolutionary band coming to the same place by another road. Though the Pandays did not pay any attention to the freight on the cart, because they had no idea of it, still, the freight itself was considerably anxious! The Commander-in-Chief going towards Cawnpore to conquer the whole of India saw standing before him, suddenly, the terrible Revolutionary band. He gave up the route and turned back immediately. A word would have done him! A sign from the cartman would have been enough! And the man who could not have been caught even after killing thousands of Englishmen would have been made a prisoner by an ordinary cartmau. It was the difference of a moment. Sir Colin would have been arrested and taken before Kumar Singh or sent at once before the Angel of Death!

After escaping from this danger, Sir Colin arrived at Cawnpore on the 3rd of November. As large a force as possible had already been assembled there under Brigadier Grant. The naval brigade mentioned before also arrived there along with the new English troops. Greathead also, with the Delhi army, came there having routed the Revolutionaries of the province of Delhi on the way. After the fall of Delhi, the bravery which Greathead exhibited in restoring 'peace' in the province around Delhi absolutely surpassed that of Neill at Allahabad. It is unparalleled. Since the beginning of the Revolution, up till November, this province was in the hands of the Revolutionaries. But the people in the province were so little harassed that the English themselves write: 'The people not only cultivated but in many districts as extensively as ever. In fact, beyond supplying their necessity, the rebels did not venture to assume the character of tyrants of the country.'[7] The Pandays had treated this province as was proper for volunteers fighting for the freedom of their country—and the British who had set out to crush its spirit of independence, destroyed it completely as befitted the proclaimers of slavery! And all this, to restore peace! Burning village after village, hanging on the gallows any robust man found on the way, and killing the village inhabitants *en route* with more recklessness than if they were wild birds, Greathead's army came from Delhi to Cawnpore! That army and the naval brigade effected a junction with

7. *Narrative of the Indian Mutiny.*

the other white troops there, and Brigadier Grant began to go down the Ganges. O Ganges! How many English armies have come to thy shores to proceed to relieve Lucknow! And O you proud Ayodhya, are you not now at least going to release the English army from the dungeons of Lucknow when this new force has come to terrorise you?

Brigadier Grant had about five thousand English troops besides hundreds of camels, etc. He had also taken with him plenty of provisions for the Lucknow army. When the news came that this army of Grant had fought its way up to Alam Bagh, Sir Colin Campbell left Cawnpore and crossed the Ganges. To guard his rear, he left a select English and Sikh army with a number of guns at Cawnpore, under the command of Wyndham who had Won fame in several European wars. Sir Colin joined the chief army at Alam Bagh on the 9th of November. He reviewed the Alam Bagh forces and planned a combined attack by the various regiments. He now gave the order to make an assault on. Lucknow on the 14th of November. Before this, a daring Englishman, called Cavenagh, had entered tbe Residency in company with an Indian at night, evading the Sepoy guards by blackening his face and putting on Indian garb. He was sent there to get information about the state of defences of the Residency and to discuss plans about the coming attack. He had before this time delivered the messages of Colin and Outram to each other. In the Residency and in the English camp at Alam Bagh, everyone was waiting anxiously for the 14th of November. Havelock and Outram were to come out of the Residency to attack the Revolutionaries from inside and Sir Colin was to press them on the- other side! At this time, in the English camp were to be found most of the eminent generals and warriors that made their name in 1857. Havelock, Outram, Peel (of the naval brigade), Greathead Hodson of Delhi, Brigadier Hope Grant, Eyre, and the Commander-in-Chief Sir Colin himself—all were there. There were fresh, Highlanders, Outram's Europeans anxious to jump into the field from within the besieged fort, 'loyal' Punjabee youths and still more loyal Sikhs with their swords still bespattered with the blood of the Motherland shed at Delhi!

Such was the English army that started towards Lucknow on the 14th of November. The whole day was spent in skirmishes between the English and the Revolutionarjes. About the evening, the English army had advanced fighting up to Dilkhwush Bagh. Sir Colin decided to spend the night there and encamped in the garden. Tbough the Revolutionaries led intermittent attacks even, that night, the English army did not heed them and spent the night there. Next morning, Sir Colin arrayed all his troops and gave the order to attack Lucknow again on the 16th. Then, the English army advanced like a tidal wave and fell upon Sikandar Bagh. Till it reached this place, it had not met with serious resistance from the Revolutionaries. But, whoever was the leader or the Revolutionaries there, he did show some splendid fighting. When the Highlanders, under Ewart, and the Sikhs, under Powell, fell upon Sikandar Bagh yelling fiercely, it seemed as if the un-daunted dash of the English force would sweep everything before it. The Sikh Subahdar, Gukul Singh, waved his sword in the air and tried his utmost not to let the Highlanders go before his own fellows. Oh! Unfortunate Lucknow! With the cruel, emulation as to who will drink her blood most, Sikh and Highlander swords began grim work. But the strong boulders of Sikandar Bagh would not move on any account. And when the Stones were destroyed, the heroes there would not move back at all! For, when some stones of the wall fell, the English troops rushed there like arrows. Who goes first, Sikh or Higilander ? Both are trying hard. But, at last, the man who first reached the breach is a Sikh. To reward this traitor's valour, a bullet entered right in his breast! He fell and immediately Cooper rushed in, and behind him Ewart and Captain John Lumsden,—and then Sikh and Highlanders all quickly rushed in. The Sepoys within were staggered for a moment on seeing the whole army entering so quickly. But the hero who led the Revolutionaries that day at Sikander Bagh was no ordinary leader. He does not think of retreat!

Victory or Death! Death or Victory!! This cry fits only the mouths of those who fight for freedom. Cooper is the first man who has rushed into the Bagh; therefore, the Sepoy must try to kill him first. This cannot be done except by the brave Sepoy officer of the regiment which revolted at Ludhiana. He looked out for Cooper and ran straight at him. Clang! Clang! Clang of swords! A deep thrust, both simultaneously cut each other and both fell dead! Lumsden began to wave about his sword in the air and shouted, 'Come on, men for the honour of Scotland!' How insolent! For the honour of Scotland! And has Hindustan no honour? Before any white man came up for the honour of Scotland, a brown hero rushed forth for the honour of Hindusthan—and blood began to gush out of Lumsden's lifeless corpse! While such a terrible hand to hand fight was going on here, the English army broke the wall on another side and rushed in from also. Now this Bagh had no hope of victory. Then, O Sikander Bagh, are you going to fight even after victory is gone? Fight on, fight on! Let victory go but do not lose honour, do not lose fame, jump into the battle as a duty! On every door, on every step, in every quadrangle, sword clashed with sword! Blood was shed everywhere. Malleson says, 'The fight for the possession of the enclosure was bloody and desperate, the rebels fighting with all the energy of despair. Nor did the struggle end when our men forced their way inside. Every room, every staircase, every corner of the towers was contested. Quarter was neither given nor asked for; and, when at last the assailants were masters of the place more than two thousand rebel corpses lay heaped around them. It is said that, of all who garrisoned it, only four men escaped, but even the escape of four is doubtful.'[8]

Oh, you two thousand martyrs that died fighting for independence in Sikandar Bagh, let this grateful history be dedicated to your memory! The blood of two thousand patriots! This history is dedicated to that blood! Who were you that started to fight thus for the country? What were your names? Who was the brave leader that led you to the fatal battle? The good fortune of relating all this, the good fortune of pronouncing the names of you who sacrificed your bodies in the hope of serving humanity, has not fallen to our lot! Let, then, this history be dedicated to your nameless memory alone! Victory was gone, but you did not allow your fame to be tarnished! Let your blood and bravery purify and adorn the Past and incite and inspire the Future!

You did not soil your fames, O Heroes of Independence. but if your self-sacrifice in Sikandar Bagh had begun at its proper time, victory also would have been yours! Now, the might of your enemy has increased manifold. Thousands of new soldiers have come to fight on their side, their strain has become less after the fall of Delhi, their moral strength has augmented by victory and yours has diminished by defeat. Such a dry and lifeless soil, even the blood of two thousand men will not fertilise. If, however, as soon as the Revolution began, at the first onslaught on the feeble Residency, you had rushed up with the cry of 'Victory or Death!' — then, in half an hour's time, the crown of independence would have shone on the forehead of Hindusthan. You died as you should die but the auspicious moment was gone! Time and opportunity were gone. In a war of Revolution, what is lost by a minute, sometimes, cannot be regained in an epoch. A drop of blood could have given you victory then, but now, even fountains of blood will give you only fame, but victory is difficult. In the whirlwind of Revolutions, the loss of a single moment spoils the whole plan. One step back means disaster. The momentary hankering after life is sure to bring

8. Malleson's *Indian Mutiny*, Vol. IV, page 132.

permanent death to the cause!

Blood was abundantly shed in other places also than in Sikandar Bagh. Dilkhwush, Alam Bagh, and Shah Najaf were giving a terrible battle to the enemy that day and that night. In the early morning, all the bells of Lucknow city began to peal, drums began to beat, and again the wounded city began to give a fierce battle to the enemy. The fight at Moti Mahal to-day is not a whit less fierce than that at Shah Najaf yesterday. But, in the end, the English got decidedly the upper hand and the English army was enabled to relieve its compatriots so long shut up in the Residency. On the 17th, 18th, 19th, right up to 23rd, the battle raged at Lucknow and, at last, the besieged army and the relieving army met each other. The Residency, over which so long hung the shadow of death, now assumed a pleasant smile. But even now, the Revolutionaries did not heed the English victory. Though the two armies had united and whole city of Lucknow was swimming in a sea of blood, they would talk neither of surrender nor of retreat! On account of this obstinate courage on their part, it was always uncertain when the fighting would be over. So, Sir Colin began again to reform the British army. He evacuated the Residency and collected all the troops in Dilkhwush Bagh. He kept four thousand men and twenty-five guns in Alam Bagh under the command of Outram. He made all arrangements necessary for the future struggle. And for the victory that had been gained, he very properly praised the army for its bravery, discipline, and obedience. Of this praise, the greatest portion was deservedly given to Havelock.

But while the English army was rightly exulting over its victory, Havelock who had the chief share in it suddenly died!! By the exertions of the terrible battle-field of Lucknow, by care and despair, the brave Havelock had been sinking slowly. And he succumbed at the very moment of victory. This death poisoned the joy of the English on the 24th.

However, it was not the time for brooding in sorrow over the dead, but for carrying out their uncompleted task. If Havelock fell while taking Lucknow, to take Lucknow was the best way to remember and do honour to his memory.

But before starting to conquer Lucknow, why these sudden shocks of artillery near Cawnpore? Oh, they might be nothing! So long as the brave Wyndham, with fame in European wars, is there, the noise need not materially disturb Sir Colin. Who is the Revolutionary that would dare to face an English warrior like Wyndham?

But these messengers say that Tatia Tope is also there! Tatia Tope at Cawnpore! Sir Colin at once understood the meaning of the news of the cannonade he had heard; he sent Outram with the greatest haste against Lucknow and marched at once towards Cawnpore to see what Tatia Tope was doing there!

* * *

CHAPTER VI

Tatia Tope

WHEN the army of the 'mutineers' had been defeated at Cawnpore on the 16th of July, Srimant Nana left Cawnpore and proceeded to Brahmavarta. That night—the 16th of July—was spent by Nana in his palace there, in deliberation as to his future plans; and the very next morning saw Nana Sahib approaching the boats waiting on the river Ganges with his youngest brother Bala Sahib, his nephew Rao Sahib, his aide-de-camp Tatia Tope, with all the ladies belonging to the royal household, and with his treasure and a few supplies. Nana was going to Fatehpur in the Lucknow province. Chowdhuri Bhopal Singh, an intimate friend of Nana Sahib, received them there very cordially and entertained them in his house. While Havelock with all his army was besieging Cawnpore and was thinking of pressing on to Lucknow, Nana also was deliberating in full Durbar as to the best means of opposing Havelock.

To find a satisfactory solution to this problem, one person in this Durbar was eminently fitted by his extraordinary intellect. His subtle intellect seemed to be ever on the look-out for difficult problems which awaited solution. So far, Tatia Tope had done nothing higher than the work of a clerk; but then, there was nothing beyond the work of the clerk, so far, to be done at Nana's Durbar. But one glimpse of the spirit of liberty—and the Durbar of Nana, too, showed the characteristic intelligence, alertness, and brilliance of the old Raigarh Durbar. New aspirations were now struggling for fulfilment, fresh thrones had to be established, new armies had to be formed, fresh battlefields had to be fought and won. Now, the joy of victory had gladdened the Durbar but, then, the grief consequent on defeat produced a reaction. But, in close succession comes a profound calm; for, vengeance for past insults is being planned; and this calm is being disturbed alone by the still and silent deliberations in the Durbar as to the future plan of the Revolutionary party. It was but natural that the ability, so long latent for lack of scope, should now step forward boldly, that clever schemes, so long only suggested to the mind, should now be readily formulated for action. And it must be admitted that for clever, deep-laid, successful scheming, an equal of Tatia Tope would be hard, indeed, to find.

Tatia's idea was to reorganise the bands disorganised on account of the defeat at Cawnpore. The splendid logic, the intimate acquaintance with the most secret springs of human nature, and the undaunted daring of this extraordinary man were so superb that whole regiments of rude Sepoys would be ready to rise in his favour with one mind in the course of a single day. When the necessity for reinforcements arose, Tatia had gone straight to Sheorajpur and enlisted the 42nd regiment—lately risen—for the new cause. Meanwhile, Havelock had been preparing to cross the Ganges and advance on Lucknow; so, Tatia decided to harass his rear. How the English commander was, thus dragged back to Cawnpore, how on his return he saw, to his surprise, the extraordinary Mahratta ruling in his palace at Brahmavarta, how the English army was forced to give battle at this place, and how, in the encounter, the army of the Revolutionaries was defeated on the 16th of August—all this has been described in a previous chapter. After the defeat, Tatia swam the Ganges with his whole army and joined Nana at Fatehpur. Reinforcements were again necessary. The same problem rose again. But why need Nana worry about reinforcements so long as Tatia Tope was there? The army in the cantonments of Gwalior—anxious to meet the Feringhi in battle—had so far been obliged to keep quiet, because of the 'loyalty' of the Scindia. To Gawalior, then, someone must be sent—and who fitter than the wily Mahratta who, like the magician who weaves a spell round his audience, had seduced and kept within the hollow of his land whole regiments of Sepoys? Tatia, then, went to Gwalior incognito. And shortly after, he had seduced the whole army—infantry, cavalry, artillery and all—at Morar, and had even brought them as far as Kalpi. From a military point of view, Kalpi would have been of great help to the Revolutionaries. As the river Jumna flowed between Kalpi and Cawnpore, it could serve as a cover against the English army. Tatia realised, then, that after Cawnpore no better base could be secured than the fort of Kalpi and so he took the fort. When Nana heard that he had got a good army and the fort of Kalpi, he consented to make Kalpi his base and sent Shrimant Bala Sahib, as his representative, to occupy the fort and look after it. While Bala Sahib was holding the fort, Tatia began to think of attacking the English army.

At this time, General Wyndham who had earned fame

on the battle-fields of Europe was the chief commander of the Cawnpore regiments. Sir Colin had gone towards Lucknow leaving this small army to protect Cawnpore. Tatia, then, had got his opportunity. The Revolutionaries of Lucknow were engaging the huge army of Sir Colin and keeping it busy; it would be difficult for general Wyndham to get help from outside; and hence, this was the time to surprise him, engage him, and, if possible, to get rid of him. Such was the plan of Tatia. Bala Sahib thought well of this plan and Tatia himself was made commander of the forces. A mere clerk yesterday, this poor Brahmin of the Durbar of Nana was the commander of to-day. He crossed the Jumna and engaged openly in battle with General Wyndham who had spent a lifetime on the battlefields of Europe! And with what means? With the recently risen unorganised Sepoy mass and with the peasant rabble who had accompained them! He stood face to face with the English army which had all the advantages that organisation, military training, and discipline could give. It was instructive to watch such an encounter, to see how the spirit of independence could meet all the overwhelming advantages on the opposite side. It was a living example and lesson showing to what extent an army without the advantages of discipline but with the spirit of liberty could fight, illustrating with what success it might have fought had it all the advantages of discipline. With the troops of Gwalior which had joined him, Tatia had reached Kalpi on the 9th of November. Kalpi is situated about forty-six miles from Cawnpore. Having accurately ascertained the exact whereabouts of the English army, he left Kalpi, crossed, the Jumna, entered the Doab, and, leaving all his treasure and, other things at Jalna, occupied some villages adjoining Cawnnpore. He was playing a deep game in not rushing on to Cawnpore immediately after crossing the Jumna. He did not want to annoy Wyndham until news came that Sir Colin had begun to engage in the fight at Lucknow. When that news did reach him, he advanced on Sheorajpur, occupying important positions on the way. About the 19th of November, Tatia, by these clever tactics, was able to cut off all supplies from the British army. Meanwhile, the famous commander of the English forces was certainly not idle at Cawnpore. The stream of the English army flowing from Calcutta was stopped at Cawnpore, and Carthew was sent with a division to establish himself on the road to Kalpi. Wyndham coolly awaited Tatia's movements. Would Tatia go on to Ayodhya to cut off the rear of Sir Colin's battalions or would he attack him in Cawnpore itself?

But Wyndham was not a commander who would wait for ever. His daring nature ever pressed him forward. Moreover, he thoroughly believed in the superstition that English troops were superior not only to Indian troops but all Asiatic troops in general and that the best means of defeating Asiatics was to attack them boldly on the front with one heavy charge. 'Strong though you may be, the least hesitation on your part to attack, the least delay, and the Asiatic becomes proud and conscious of power, and, becomes aggressive. Thus, even if you are weak, hesitate not, but charge boldly with one united charge, and the Asiatics would be bewildered and fly before you through mere fright.' Such was the thorough belief of the English and, out of the many occasions on which they had acted on this belief, they had been successful on most. It was considered, therefore, quite a rule well-established by experiment, that it was not proportion of numbers but bluff and bullying that was the sure road to victory; hence, the advisability of a handful of European troops charging a large mass of Asiatics straight like an arrow! Every English soldier coming out to India was made to learn this rule by heart and every English historian who worte a book brought this fact prominently before all. General Wyndham, trained as he was in such warfare and with such ideas, was not likely to allow Tatia to make his movements unhampered. He left Cawnpore immediately and moved towards the bridge over the canal near Kalpi.

Tatia, meanwhile, moved from Srikhandi to the river Pandu on the 25th of November. When the daring enemy approached so near, the English army prepared for battle and the thoroughly tried antidote against Asiatic courage just referred to was used on the 26th. On that date, Wyndham started his straight-as-an-arrow attack. The Revolutionaries were ambushed in a thick jungle and they began their cannonade on the English army. After a good deal of exchange of shots, the English took three of the guns of Tatia and Wyndham almost believed that, once again, owing to his bold charge, his army was successful. His army, too, felt the assurance of victory. But it was a vain hope. For, soon the English troops were forced to retire steadily. In an instant, the hope of victory was changed into certain defeat and Tatia pursued him until he had retreated up to Cawnpore. The Revolutionary cavalry at their back would neither attack them nor leave them! They wheeled round and round the enemy, forced the enemy back, and themselves reached the gates of Cawnpore: Instead of taking fright at the charge of Wyndham, Tatia himself began the aggressive, meeting charge with charge.

Says Malleson : 'The leader of the rebel army was no fool. The blow dealt by Wyndham, far from frightening him, had disclosed to his mind the weakness of the British leader. Tatia Tope read, then, the necessities of Wyndham's position as he would have read an open book and, with the instincts of a real general, he resolved to take advantage of them.'[1]

Tatia ordered his army which had fought Wyndham for twenty-four hours without a minute's rest that they were to be ready by the morning to march against the enemy. But they were not to start the attack until another contingent of the Revolutionaries coming from Shewoli and Sheorajpur opened fire on the right flank of the English army. As soon

1. Malleson's *Indian Mutiny*, Vol. IV, page 167.

as that began, however, they were to begin the attack in right earnest. Wyndham meanwhile had led forth his army ready for battle; but when, even after nine, the army of the Revolutionaries did not begin the attack, and not a sign of them was visible, the English army returned to camp for breakfast. At eleven, the army was made ready for battle. A vague uncertainty as to the real intention of Tatia pervaded the atmosphere.

This was soon made known, however, in a terrible manner; for cannon-balls were sent flying from the Revolutionary guns against the right wing of the English. The vanguard, too, was attacked by Tatia. Directly after this, Wyndham sent Carthew with six guns to the road to Brahmavarta to protect that part of Cawnpore. And now a regular cannonade began. Soon it appeared that the English artillery-men were falling back. Tatia had arranged his army in a semi-circle and his game was to close on the enemy from the front and the flanks. Wyndham tried his best to break through the circle but the guns of Tatia would not allow him to advance even a step. It seemed they could not even maintain their position, and the English, within a short time, began to show signs of retiring. Seeing that the left wing had retired leaving their guns behind, the right wing held on for a time and tried to keep the guns. But they could not hold much longer. As they too retreated, the semicircle of the Revolutionaries closed on them more tightly. By six in the evening, the English army was thoroughly demoralised. A short while more and the rout was complete. Thousands of tents and oxen, a great quantity of provisions and clothing fell into the hands of the Revolutionaries. Half of Cawnpore was now in the hands of Tatia. Thus, the second crown of victory crowned this brave and stalwart Mahratta. Yesterday's battle gave him a victory which was but indirect and partial, but to-day's victory was complete and direct. For he had not merely defeated the clever and famous commander of the English in a battle which lasted a whole day, but he had routed the English army thoroughly; he had captured the whole camp, tents and all; he had driven them out of a portion of Cawnpore and himself taken the city. Even English historians admit that, if his army had been as disciplined as he was capable, he would have been able to destroy Wyndham's army completely.

And now the cannonade of Tatia had reached Sir Colin's ears. When Tatia came to Cawnpore, he believed as certain that Sir Colin would be engaged at Lucknow at least for a month. But soon, Tatia heard that, in some unforeseen way, the Revolutionaries had been got rid of by Sir Colin and it seemed now pretty certain that Sir Colin would attack him, and try to close him in by attacking him from both the side of the Ganges. Tatia's face clouded with anxiety at this news. Wyndham felt very hopeful. That very night, Wyndham resolved to win back the glory he had lost during the day. But his men were all tired and therefore, giving up the idea of the night attack, he began to prepare for giving another battle the next morning. He tried to repair the mistakes of the previous day and determined on an attack. The fight began early in the morning. The Revolutionaries aimed their artillery on both flanks of the enemy. The fight went on as on the previous day till midday. But this day, the English did not retire. They assumed the aggressive and began a determined, united, formidable and, as they thought, irresistible, charge.

Irresistible indeed! The right wing is absolutely shattered! Brigadier Wilson is down! Captain M'Crea is no more! Morphy, Major Stirling, Lieutenant Gibbins, all are down! Aye, Asiatics can produce a Tatia, after all! The third day, then, saw a victory for Tatia and his followers, for they fought hotly and well till late in the evening and they had routed what remained of the English army. The English army was more completely routed than even on the day before, both the wings having been actually driven from the field on this last day. And Tatia had now captured the whole of Cawnpore and thus the third crown was shining on the sword of the brave Mahratta.[2]

Just when the English army was being routed, the commander-in-chief, Sir Colin, arrived in their camp. He realised the extent of the injury done to British prestige by Tatia; he saw, with his own eyes, the English troops flying for their very life and the victorious troops of the Revolutionaries pursuing them: and he heard, with his own ears, the trumpets and drums proclaiming the victory of the Revolutionaries. He saw the importance of the struggle Tatia was carrying on at Cawnpore.

Tatia on his part realised that Sir Colin was enabled to march back to Cawnpore, just at this juncture, to the help of the English army, only through the utter failure of the Revolutionary party to hold their own at Lucknow. But he did not get disheartened. He smashed the bridge near Ayodhya to render it impossible for the English army to cross the Ganges; he also stationed guns near the place. But the enemy understood his game and, in the face of the fire, crossed from Ayodhya to Cawnpore before the 30th of November. In the camp of Tatia, Nana Sahib and Kumar Singh had also arrived. These leaders determined that, instead of leaving Cawnpore, it would on the whole be more creditable to meet the commander-in-chief in battle,

---

2. The following graphic picture is given of the defeat by an English officer: 'You will read the account of this day's fighting with astonishment; for it tells how English troops, with their trophies and their mottoes and their far-famed bravery, were repulsed, and they lost their camp, their baggage and position to the scouted and despised natives of India! The beaten Feringhis, as the enemy has now a right to call them, have retreated to their entrenchments amidst overturned tents, pillaged baggage, men's kits, fleeing camels, elephants and horses, and servants. All this is most melancholy and disgraceful.'—Charles Ball's *Indian Mutiny*, Vol. II, page 190.

especially as they had, as their leader, a man of very great natural ability.'[3]

Tatia stationed his left wing in a well-protected position between Cawnpore and the Ganges. His centre was right in Cawnpore city. And his right extended behind the Ganges canal and held a bridge over it. In his army, there were ten thousand trained Sepoys. With these he kept Sir Colin busy on the 1st and 2nd of December. On the 2nd, he actually opened fire on Sir Colin's tent. On the 6th, Sir Colin was forced to accept the open challenge of the Revolutionaries. Consolidating, therefore, his army of seven thousand in an admirable manner, he began his attack on these insolent 'mutineers' who could dare to attack! the camp of the commander-in-chief himself. Seeing the right wing of the Revolutionaries unprotected, Sir Colin determined to charge on the right.

But in order to draw off their attention from the right and direct it towards the wrong direction, the English opened fire early in the morning of the 6th on the left wing of the enemy, who were soon engaged in repelling the attack. A mock charge was meanwhile made on the centre, too, by Greathead. So believing that the enemy's objective was the left and the centre, the Revolutionaries began to concentrate their strength on these. While the left was seriously suffering from the artillery of the British, the English began suddenly to turn to the right of the Revolutionary army. But the Gwalior contingent stationed on the right by Tatia began a furious cannonade on the Sikhs and the English who were charging. The rifles of the Panday army, too, were very active. But the Sikhs made 'double march' and rushed forward, being backed up by Peel's white troops and the Gwalior army, under this double fire, showed signs of retiring. As soon as that was apparent, the fire of the enemy was

3. Malleson's Indian Mutiny, Vol. IV, page 186.

reduced and soon the Gwalior army was scattered completely. All their guns were captured and a furious pursuit of them began on the kalpi road. A complete victory was thus obtained by Sir Colin so far as the right wing was concerned; but he was not satisfied with that. He had an idea of blocking completely the road to Brahmavarta on the left, as he had blocked the road to Kalpi on the right, and thus, of capturing Tatia with his whole army. So he despatched Mansfield to the road leading to Brahmavarta. On this day, the well-established proposition about Asiatics, referred to above, seemed to have been confirmed both positively and negatively. The feigned attack on the left made by Greathead was so weak that, had the Pandays made but one attempt to repel it, not only would Greathead have been punished in a way he would have remembered to the end of his life, but the very fortunes of the day would have been changed as it was, the Revolutionaries began to give way under the straight attack of the English. While this affirmative part of the proposition, viz., that at a good charge and at a show of audacity, the Asiatics lose heart, was being confirmed on the centre emphatically; on the left, the negative part too was being realised in an unmistakably clear way. For when the Revolutionaries saw Mansfield coming, crouching in a round about and concealed manner, they attacked him even though he had a large division. Nana himself commanded the left. He took full advantage of the slow movements of Mansfield. When Sir Colin was inquiring whether Tatia had been hemmed in or not. he heard with regret that through the dilatory movements of Mansfield, he had been foiled in his desire. He did not succeed in capturing Tatia Tope!

For, that Mahratta general had pressed Mansfield and pressed him as far as Brahmavarta. He had broken through the network of the English army and had gone off with his army and with all his guns. How many more networks the English general would have to spread before they could succeed in capturing the Mahratta tiger will appear in a future chapter.

Though Tatia was able to escape, on this day, with all his men and all his guns; Hope Grant was pursuing him closely and, on the 9th of December, a running fight ensued between Tatia and the English near Sheorajpur; and though Tatia did break through this time too, most of his guns fell into the hands of the enemy. Thus, in an interval of two days between the 6th and the 9th, Sir Colin was able to repair the defeat of Wyndham, to capture thirty-two of the Revolutionary guns, and to break up their army forcing some towards Kalpi and the rest on to Ayodhya. After obtaining these big victories, he thought that minor victories were surely within reach. So, he marched on to Brahmavarta, looted the property there razed the palace to the ground, and to crown all his triumph, demolished the sacred temples of that city.

It was in this palace that the brightest gems of India, Nana and Tatia, Bala and Rao and the 'Chhabeli' of Jhansi had been bred and brought up. It was this palace that first conceived the War of Independence of that glorious year. The temples of that city had blessed the birth of the ideal. When the throne of Raigarh which had been snatched from the Mahrattas had been re-established again in this palace washed by a free flow of the stream of English blood the palace and these temples had been illuminated.

That very fire which could produce all the illuminations had been instrumental in reducing them to-day to ashes. But history need not drop a tear on these sacred ashes. For this palace and these temples had been burnt down only after they had accomplished their task. The very extinction of such structures is more life-giving than the existence of hundreds of other structures which are but manument of slavery; for these have attempted to give birth to independence; and they have died in that attempt. Far more profitable is death through the attempt to establish Swaraj than life in slavery. The sacred fuel burning in the sacrificial fire is a thousand times more life-giving than the log of wood burning in the funeral pyre.

* * *

CHAPTER VII

The Fall of Lucknow

AFTER thus stemming the fierce tide of Tatia's progress at Cawnpore, Sir Colin started re-conquering the other portions of the country that had risen. Seaton had been marching slowly, 'pacifying' province on the way, and had now come down to Aligarh. So now Walpole was sent by Kalpi road to accomplish the same task for all the territory from Aligarh to Cawnpore. Walpole was to march upwards from Cawnpore and Seaton was to go downwards from Aligarh; they were to meet at Minpuri; and thus, all the tract of the Doab along the Jumna was to be reconquered. While this was being done, Sir Colin was to march towards Fatehgarh from Cawnpore. Such was the plan of operations. It was thought that the Doab Revolutionaries would be pressed back by the English army and would eventually enter Fatehgarh. And hence it was decided that the closing finale of the operations should be conducted and a great battle should be fought near Fatehgarh, where the three armies of Walpole, Seaton, and Campbell were to meet after the close of their individual operations.

According to this plan, on the 18th of December, Walpole, with all his guns and his army, began his upward march from Cawnpore on the Kalpi road. After fighting one or two skirmishes with scattered Revolutionary bands all along the way, wreaking cruel vengeance—the well-known and customary Feringhi vengeance—on all persons indiscriminately, innocent people as well as those who actually fought against England, and on the villages which had sheltered the Pandays: and by such means, trying to bring back the territory under British allegiance, this Walpole came as far as Itawa and, of course, he would have gone further. But, though the Revolutionaries in Itawa had all left, he had still to stop, with all his army, in that city. What could be the reason of this extraordinary necessity? What could stop this march of the English army? Was is that Revolutionary troops, in large numbers had attacked him? Or could it be infantry or the cavalry? Or was it by any chance the artillery with the fierce fire playing all round?

No, none of these things were happening in Itawa. Neither the infantry nor the cavalry, nor the fire of the artillery was stopping the English at Itawa. Only twenty or twenty-five Indian heroes are making a stand from yonder building. That building has a roof and its walls have holes made in them for fixing the muskets. It is these twenty-five men, standing with a musket in their hand and a burning fire in their heart, that have made the fully-equipped English stop at the door of Itawa. Itawa blocked the passage of the English army notwithstanding the guns and cannon that it carried, because Itawa had not yet received its usual toll due to it as of right. That toll was that everyone who dared enter the threshold of Itawa against its wishes should fight first. The challenge was 'Fight first!' These twenty-five men had determined to sell their lives dear, though escape was easy. They stood determined there and only asked for a fight. What battle could be given to these handful of people in this building? If probably they waited for a few minutes, these mad people would come to their senses and make their escape, which was open to them—so thought the English. But though they waited long, there seemed no possible chance of the 'mutineers' coming to their senses. So, an engagement was at last decided upon. The mere show of the artillery would, it was thought, be sufficient to make them fly. The English, therefore, exhibited their artillery and tried to frighten the Revolutionaries.

But, fear could exist only in the hearts of ordinary mortals. Those who, charmed by the ideal of independence, welcomed death as the only means of achieving the ideal—who could succeed in frightening these? Who fights for victory fears; who battles for glory, even, may fear; but who could frighten him who fights for death alone? The utmost one can be afraid of is death! But he who has overstepped those limits and who smiles on death, what could frighten him? What could come in the way of such a man? Not all the thunders and all the lightnings or dread heaven could stop his progress; for his progress is towards death and those elements are only rendering his task easier. He who hopes for death alone has no room for despair. These national heroes of Itawa who courted death in battle with the ardour of a lover for his love, what could frighten them then?

And so they willingly relinquished all the ways and means of escape they had. They had not the slightest hope of victory and yet they defied the English army and loudly called on them to join battle. That army of the English which did not stop for the ramparts of Delhi nor for the walls of Cawnpore nor for the siege of Lucknow. now had to stop before this insignificant-looking building!

Malleson says: 'Few in number, armed only with muskets, they were animated by a spirit fiercer even than the spirit of despair—by a determination to die martyrs to their cause. Walpole reconnoitred the place. It was, for a place to stop an army insignificant. It could easily be stormed. Yet to storm it in the face of its occupants would cost valuable life and it seemed that easier and less costly means were available. These easy means were at first tried. Hand-grenades were thrown in; an attempt was made to smoke out the occupants with burning straw. But all in vain. Through their loop-holes, the rebels poured in a constant and effcctive fire on the assailants and, for three hours, kept them at bay. At last, it was resolved to blow up that place. For this purpose,

Bourchier, aided by Scralchley of the Engineers, made a mine with a number of his gun cartridges. The explosion of this conferred upon the defenders the martyr's honours they coveted. It buried them in the ruins.'

The dynamite exploded the building. The highly coveted honour of martyrdom was, thus, gained by these heroes who longed for it. They died on the spot and were buried in the ruins. And this sacred mausoleum of Itawa, since that day, has been preaching a silent and terrible sermon, by day and by night, on *How to die* in defence of a Noble cause!!

Brave Itawa ! Glorious for ever! What better, what holier inspiration could one find in the pass of Thermopylae, the ramparts of Breccia, or the stand of De Reuter in the Netherlands! All glory to Itawa ! Itawa for ever!

When Walpole reached Itawa, Seaton too had passed Aligarh, Kashgunj, and Minpuri, and was engaging in small skirmishes with the Revolutionary bands. The two armies met at Minpuri on the 8th of January, 1858. In accordance with their previous plans, the banks of the Jumna, near the Doab, had been re-conquered by the British army from Delhi and Meerut as far as Allahabad. Meanwhile, Sir Colin had been marching along the Ganges. He had crushed the Nawab of Fatehgarh and had thus destroyed the last resort of the Doab Revolutionaries, and he was now going towards Fatehgarh from Cawnpore, bent on clearing the territory of the Doab, as far as the Ganges and the Jumna on either side, of the enemy altogether. The Nawab of Farrukabad, as has been already told, had declared his independence at Fatehgarh. The Doab Revolutionaries had flocked into Fatehgarh from all the adjoining parts. Sir Colin had many small engagements with these. As these Revolutionary troops were mostly composed of undisciplined people who had been defeated at Delhi and Cawnpore and had run away from the battle-field in those places, they used to fly before the English, before the engagement had even begun, just to save their lives. But did they succeed in saving their lives by these dastardly means? Not at all. The English pursued them hard and, at times, would kill 600 or 700, sometimes even a thousand of the fleeing enemy. What a world of difference between the dying of those Itawa heroes and these! And the Nawab of Farrukabad had soon to suffer the consequences of this dastardly conduct of these bands. His capital, his forts, and his military supplies fell into the hands of the British and all the Revolutionaries were driven across the Ganges and into Rohilkhand. With the military supplies that were captured, Nadir Khan, the avowed enemy of the British. also fell into their hands. This Nadir Khan had fought the English on several occasions with credit under the flag of Nana Sahib at Cawnpore. As soon as such a formidable opponent fell into their hands, they hanged him. This Nadir Khan at the point of death, swore a terrible oath 'calling upon the people of India to draw their swords and assert their independence by the extermination of the English.'[1] This was the burning message delivered with his last dying breath by this glorious patriot, Nadir Khan.

On the 4th of January 1858, at the time when Sir Colin entered Fatehgarh in triumph, all the Doab and all the country from Benares upwards as far as Meerut had been reconquered by the British. So, now, the question was what was to be the future plan of operations of the British army? The hope of the British, that, when the flames of rebellion had been extinguished in the Doab, the insurrections in other parts would quietly settle down, now proved absolutely futile. Experts in political astrology had prophesied that, within eight days of the fall of Delhi, the 'mutiny' would be no more. As a matter of fact, the Revolution did not perish by the fall of Delhi, and all these prophecies had proved false. For the huge mass of the Revolutionary army, so far confined to

1. Charles Ball's Indian Mutiny, Vol. II, page 232.

Delhi, spread tumultuously all over the country like a river overflowing its banks. The troops of Rohilkhand under Bakht Khan, of Neemuch under Veer Singh, and other armies under their various Subahdars, instead of surrendering to the English, continued the war from other parts of the country. Once. right in Delhi itself, there seemed signs of another insurrection of the populace. For, a rumour had spread all over the city that Nana, after his victory at Cawnpore, had marched on to effect the release of the Emperor whom the English had imprisoned. Secret orders were immediately given to the military authorities that, should Nana really come to Delhi, the guards should rush in and shoot down the old Emperor like a rabbit![2] Since the fall of Delhi, the Revolutionaries had become even fiercer than before. They did not mind defeat now. The first ebullitions due to their victory had settled down by this time. A stoical calmness had now come over their hearts. Their one thought was that whatever happened they were to go on fighting. Either the Feringhis or they must be exterminated. They had determined, once for all, that, so long as neither of these was accomplished, they would continue the war to the end. They were quarrelling amongst themselves; some, for personal gain, were getting lawless; but no one was willing to give up the fight against the English. And, if ever this determination—never to keep down the sword until either the Feringhi or themselves had become extinct—appeared clearer than ever on the firmly set jaws, the contracted eyebrows, or the stern eye of the Revolutionaries, it was after the defeat in the Doab. Before the Sepoys who were captured in battle were hanged, they were usually questioned by the English why they joined in the war, and the Revolutionaries would answer clearly and sternly, 'It is the command of religion that Feringhis should be killed!' And the end? The extermination of the English and of the Sepoys!

2. Charles Ball's *Indian Mutiny*, Vol. II, page 184.

And then? What God wills, will be done![3]

Thus, after the fall of Delhi, the desire of liberty, instead of dying out, took only more fire. And to avenge Delhi, they continued the fight in Lucknow and Bareilly. For when the Doab bad fallen to the English, the territories of Ayodhya and Rohilkhand were under the complete control of the Revolutionaries. Therefore, Sir Colin's idea was to conquer Rohilkhand first and then to proceed to Lucknow. Lord Canning urged that, once the focus of the operations of the Mutineers, namely Lucknow, was destroyed, the smaller places would surrender easily. In deference, therefore, to the orders of Lord Canning, Sir Colin determined first to attened to Lucknow. As previously agreed, Seaton, Walpole, and the commander-in-chief had brought together at Fatehgarh about ten or eleven thousand troops. In all the strategic positions of the Doab, small garrisons were stationed for keeping the province in hand. The army was reinforced by a fresh batch of troops sent from Agra. With their larger reinforcements, Sir Colin started from Fatehgarh. English historians thus describe the magnitude of the English forces at this time : 'Onao and Bunni deserts had probably never witnessed such big armies, engineers, artillery, horses, infantry, carriages full of supplies, camp-followers, tents big and small; all arrangements were complete in every particular. Seventeen battalions of infantry (of which fifteen were English), twenty-eight squadrons of cavalry (which included four European regiments), fifty-four light guns, and eighty big guns were included!' Thus, on the 23rd of February 1858, Sir Colin Campbell left Cawnpore, and crossed the Ganges again with such a splendidly equipped and large army in order to punish Lucknow.

Oh Ganga, witness these strong English troops coming

3. 'The slaughter of the English is required by our religion. The end will be the destruction of all the English and all the Sepoys,—and then, God knows!'-Charles Balls's *Indian Mutiny*, Vol. II, page 242.

to destroy Ayodhya! And, O proud Ayodhya, are you at least now going to humble yourself to the dust frightened by these odds?

Ayodhya must have felt that the crossing of the Ganges by the English was to destroy her. She must have felt for the reduction to dust of her villages and for the destruction of her temples and images by dynamite;[4] but not so much for all these things as for the fact that the Nepalese troops of Jung Bahadur were advancing on her. It was this that brought tears to the melancholy eyes of Ayodhya; it was the advancing of this army that cast a shadow upon her face. Ayodhya was not a coward to fear the advance of the English army; for, if she had been, she would not have attempted to cast off the hated yoke of England. The very day that Ayodhya drove away from her domain the English authority by force, that very day, she was aware that an English army would soon advance on her; and aware of this, this brave Ayodhya had already stepped forth on the battle, with her thousand arms. But Ayodhya was not aware that on her would advance the Nepalese army of Jung Bahadur also. That the enemy would try to massacre her, she knew; but she did not know that her friends, her brothers, too, would raise the axe of destruction against her. She was ready to wrestle with the English, but she was ignorant of the shameful fact that she would have to wage war with a portion of Hindusthan herself, for the liberty or Hindusthan. And thus, when, as if to mock at poor Ayodhya, Jung Bahadur started with the Nepalese troops to advance on her, Ayodhya looked in the direction of those troops only and began to shed tears of grief.

For, at the very time when the huge British army was crossing the Ganges with Sir Colin at the head, Jung Bahadur too with the Nepalese was advancing on Lucknow to help his friends, the English! The English were his friends and

4. Russell's *Diary*, page 218.

the Hindusthanees were his enemies! Those who greased the cartridges with the fat of the cow were his confederates, and those who refused to bite them were his enemies! This Jung Bahadur, this blot on Indian history, brought eternal disgrace on himself and his family by joining the English as soon as he heard that the fight for Swaraj had begun. A little before 1857 he had visited England, and English historians assert that it was because he had seen with his own eyes the might aud the glory of the English that he did not dare to fight against them! Was the glory and might of England indeed so awe-inspiring? If Jung Bahadur had been to England, Azimullah, the minister of Nana, too, had been there; and so, also, Rango Bapuij; and history clearly records how this might have affected them, and how for every indication of that power, they only formed a fresh resolve to shatter it to pieces. The might of England alone would not explain the conduct of Jung Bahadur. The English glory only gave an additional stimulus to the patriotic hearts of Azimullah and Rango to make their Mother-country a crowned queen with the *tilaka* of Independence adorning her brow. On the other hand, the sight of. English power whispered to snake-like Treachery that, if it helped, to keep the Mother a slave of this might, perhaps two more crumbs would fall to its lot.

And this Jung Bahadur, ready to sell his Mother for a mess of pottage, sent his Nepalese to the English, first three thousand Gurkhas from Khatmandu, in the beginning of August 1857, descended on Azimgarh and Jawanpur to the east of Ayodhya. Mahomed Hussein, the leader of the Gorakhpur Revolutionaries, was ready to meet them on the field. When the English were fighting in the Doab, Veni Madhav, Mahomed Hussein and Raja Nadir Khan had, with credit to themselves, reconquered completely the parts round Benares and to the east of Ayodhya. Even before the English troops had time to look to Oudh, the Nepalese had pressed back the Revolutionaries towards Oudh. Within a few more days, Jung Bahadur and the British, came to a definite agreement and three armies were ready to advance on this province. On the 23rd of December 1857, Jung Bahadur started with his nine thousand Gurkhas; General Franks and Rowcroft started each with a large division of the British army. And, crushing the Revolutionary armies on the way, on the north of Benares and to the east of Oudh, these three armies began to enter Oudh.

About the 25th of February, 1858, the Nepalese and the English crossed the Ghogra and marched toward Ambarpur. On, the way, there was a strong fort in a very thick jungle, possessing great strategic advantages. It would not have been safe for the English army to proceed onwards without taking this fort. Hence the Nepalese were directed to attack this fort. The fort engaged in fight and continued it very vigorously in the face of this well-equipped enemy. The reader may inquire the strength of the army inside the fort which dared to stop this huge army on its way. It was an army composed of thirty-four persons only! But the minds of all of them were filled with the inspiring ideal of independence and it is this which gave them the strength to fight the enemies of the country in spite of such odds. The Nepalese fought with determination. Their opponents fought with still greater vigour. Patriotism maintained its fight with Treachery. Everyone kept and maintained his place fighting, struggling, hard. The name Ambarpur (Heavenly City) was eminently fitting to this fort; Ambarpur fought so well that it killed seven of the enemy and wounded forty-three. It fought so well that thirty- three, out of the thirty-four who defended it, were killed without moving from their posts, and still the thirty-fourth did not cease from the fight! And it was only when the thirty-fourth was killed, after maintaining the fight to the very end, that the enemy could enter the fort. The fort of Ambarpur fought as Delhi could not fight, as Lucknow could not fight![5]

After Ambarpur had been taken, the united forces of the Gurkhas and the English marched on reducing the country all the way. After them was also coming General Franks who, after engaging with Nazim Mahomed Hussein and Commander Banda Hussein at Sultan pur, Budayan, and other places, was advancing upwards towards Oudh. In order to repair the loss of prestige caused by the recent defeats and to regain the authority till recently maintained in that part of eastern Oudh, the Lucknow Durbar sent Gaffoor Beg, who was chief of the artillery under Wajid Ali shah, to drive back Franks. But in the important battle of Sultan pur which took place on the 3rd of February he was defeated and, at the end of that month, there was no enemy left for the army of General Franks to encounter with in those parts.

All these armies were approaching Lucknow to join Sir Colin. General Franks turned towards Daurara with the intention, of taking the fort there; but, as the defenders of the fort maintained the fight in spite of the loss of their guns, General Franks had to acknowlege his defeat and retire. As a matter of fact, Franks had engaged in many a battle and been successful in most; nor could any harm have come through this small and unexpected defeat. But discipline and responsibility were maintained so well and vigorously in the English army at that time that, in spite of the innumerable victories of Franks, Sir Colin struck his name out from the list of the officers who were to command the English divisions in the important battle that was soon to take place.

Now, the several portions of the British army advancing. on Lucknow began to approach nearer and nearer to one another. While Sir Colin's huge army starting from Cawnpore

5. 'It was defended with so much vigour and resolution that the assailants lost seven men killed and forty-three wounded before they gained possession of it. The defenders died all at their posts. Mallesonts *Indian Mutiny*, Vol. IV, page 227.

was approaching from the west, the armies of Franks and Jung Bahadur were advancing from the east. Before the 11th of March, these two armies met together and their swords were out to massacre the 'sinful' city.

Sinful? Not sinful but only unfortunate! While the swords of fellow-countrymen and foreigners were smiting hard, was. Lucknow doing anything, to meet them? Since the time—in the, November of the previous year—when Sir Colin hurried towards Cawnpore to watch Tatia's movements, till March, every patriot who was in Lucknow was trying his best, each in his own way, to protect Lucknow and destory the enemy. In honour of the flag of Swaraj which was floating high in Lucknow, everyone from the Rajas to the poverty-stricken peasant, took his life in his hands and began the fight. Some of these Rajas and Zemindars had personally and individually lost nothing by the advent of English rule; nay, some of them had actually been benefited by it. But the noble principle that what cannot benefit the country cannot in the end benefit individuals, the noble determination not to give up duty at any time through love of personal gain, the Rajput feeling that death is preferable to loss of honour, and the, realisation of the truth that there can be no self-respect, no manhood, without liberty-all these noble ideas filled and pervaded the aristocracy of Lucknow. The Zemindars of Lucknow did not rise merely because they had suffered through the revenue assessment of the English but because they hated foreign rule! This is not merely our opinion but the deliberate opinion of the then Governor-General, as will be seen from the following extracts: 'You seem to think that the Rajas and Zemindars of Oudh have risen because they have personally suffered by our land-revenue assessment. But, in the opinion of the Gevernor-General, this requires some more thought. More thorough-going hatred could hardly have been shown by any feudatories than was shown by the Rajas of Chanda. Bhinja, and Gonda, Not a single village of the first of these had been taken by us. Not only that but even his tribute had been reduced. The second one also was treated as generously. Of the four hundred villages of the third, only three had been taken and, in exchange for that, his tribute had been reduced by ten thousand Rupees.

'By the change of rulers, no one had gained more than the youthful Raja of Nowpara. As soon as the English government came in, we gave him one thousand villages and, setting aside all other claimants, we appointed his mother as his guardian. But from the first, her army has been fighting us at Lucknow. The Raja of Dhura, too, gained enormously by the changes. But his own men attacked Captain Hursey, captured his wife, and sent her to prison in Lucknow.

'Asharaf Baksh Khan, the Talukdar persecuted by his late master, was made at once sole owner of all his property. But, from the beginning, his hatred of us has been most keen. These and other similar examples go to show very clearly that not mere personal loss, due to our rule, has been responsible for the rising of the Zemindars and Rajas against us.'[6]

And so the English historian, Holmes, frankly admits that several of the Rajas and Zemindars who had begun and maintained the War of Independence were inspired by a nobler idea than mere personal gain. 'There were numerous Rajas and petty chiefs who without any substantial grievance to brood over, were always fretting against the restraints of the Government, the very existence of which was always reminding them of the fact that they belonged to a conquered nation. ...Among all these millions, there was no real loyalty towards the alien government which had been forced to impose itself upon them. In trying to estimate the conduct of the people of India during the mutiny, it is important to bear in mind that it would have been unnatural for them to feel towards an alien government like ours, the loyalty that can

6. Lord Canning's Reply to the letter of Sir James Outram. (Re-translated from the Marathi translation in the original).

only co-exist with patriotism. Those of them who regarded our rule beneficial helped us or, at least, left us free to help ourselves. But there was not one of them who would not have turned against us, if he had once cottle to believe that we could be overthrown!'[7]

Those whose blood boiled at the very name of foreign domination, those who had stepped forth into the battlefield leaving their all to unfurl the honoured flag of Swaraj, Rajas, Maharajas, Zemindars, and Talukdars had, be it remembered, one amongst them, at this, time who was the first in the field to protect the revered throne of Lucknow and who was, at the same time, the ablest in the council. This extraordinary man had been for four months moving here and there with lightning-like activity, inspiring by his presence both the battle-field and the council-hall.

Readers, this hero is none other than the Patriot of Fyzabad, Ahmad Shah Moulvie! With the burning torch of the Revolutionary War in his hand, he had been setting the whole country aflame, when the English authorities at Lucknow captured him and ordered him to be hanged. But, before being executed, he was taken to the prison at Fyzabad and there the storm of 1857 raised him from his cell in the alien's prison to the leadership of the Revolution. This national hero, Ahmad Shah Moulvie, was on the battlefield for the freedom of his country and the protection of his Dharma. He inspired by his tongue thousands of his countrymen on the platfrom and, on the field of battle, by his valour he earned the admiration of friends as well as foes.

When Sir Colin went to fight with Tatia, he had left Outram in Alam Bagh with four thousand troops. Since that day, the Moulvie was working day and night to take advantage of this weakening of the enemy's forces. Many a

7. Sepoy War by Holmes. (Re-translated from the Marathi translation in the original).

time, before this, had Lucknow been protected by the diplomacy and diversions created by Nana near Cawnpore. The isolated army at Lucknow had been brought under the complete control of the Pandays. When the British army crossed the Ganges to capture Lucknow, Nana had pressed on Cawnpore and dragged the forces of the enemy back into Doab. But Lucknow had not taken full and determined advantage of this diversion. The Moulvie tried his best not to let go the other chance which had fallen in his way through the ability of Tatia. Though the Begum of Oudh was the chief authority in the palace, it seemed that her efforts could not succeed in uniting and concentrating the Revolutionaries, Rajas, and Maharajas; internal disorganisation and carelessness had rendered useless many fine opportunities of destroying the handful of .he British army by a good determined charge. Delhi had fallen; Cawnpore, also, had fallen; Fatehgarh had shared the same fate; and thousands of defeated Revolutionaries from the neighbouring parts had come to Lucknow. But, instead of helping Oudh, they become a source of mischief by disobedience to authority. It appeared certain that this last attack of the British who were flushed with their victories and well reinforced by numberless new troops would carry everything before them. But the Moulvie turned darkness into light. This patriotic Moulvie inspired with high patriotism many an Indian heart by his eloquence and the force of his personality. He showed that it was possible still to beat the English, if attempts were made to act with one mind and make concentrated charges against them. He inspired the Durbar with the confidence that he possessed and evoked some order out of the chaos in the army. He had great difficulties to cope with. Some incapables grew jealous of his growing influence in the Durbar and so brought about his arrest and imprisonment. But as the Moulvie had more influence over the Sepoys than the Begum herself, and as, further, the troops from Delhi trusted and obeyed him implicitly, pressure was brought to bear upon the Begum by these people and the Moulvie was released and his influence restored. After he was released he was asked his opinion about the military situation. He replied, "The auspicious moment has passed. Things are out of joint. Now, we should fight only because it is our duty." His influencc over the populace of Lucknow was as great as ever. And he ended the petty quarrels amongst the troops and created in their minds a fresh inspiration and enthusiasm and desire to take up their swords for the destruction of the enemy knocking at their gates.

But he did not stop with this activity alone. Very often he himself would personally lead them to the battles. Whenever Hindusthanees attacked Alam Bagh, the Moulvie was always to be seen in the very forefront of battle. On the 22nd of December, he had made a clever plan of deceiving the English army at Alam Bagh and hemming them in. He gave the slip to the English and marched on the road to Cawnpore with his troops. He had given orders that, as soon as he was behind the English army, a charge was to be made against the front of the English army by the division of the Revolutionaries that was at Alam Bagh. The plan was admirable and bound to have succeeded but for the other division. The leader of the other division could not maintain discipline among his followers. Everyone wanted to go by his own counsel, conscious of his own wisdom and, before the first charge had even commenced, they turned their back on the enemy instead of meeting the charge. On account of such cowardice and want of discipline, the Revolutionaries were defeated even though the Moulvie had carried out his part of the scheme most admirably.

But the Moulvie did not cease in his attempts to destroy the English army. On the 15th of January, the Revolutionaries received news that the English army was advancing from Cawnpore, carrying provisions and help to the British troops at Alam Bagh. They began to discuss the best means of stopping those supplies. But only discussions went on. No scheme was decided upon, no arrangement adopted. Disgusted at the cowardice of the rest, the noble Moulvie swore before all that he would enter Lucknow right through the British army after having captured the convoy of the enemy. With this resolve, keeping his movements as far as possible concealed from the enemy, the Moulvie marched with his men on to the road towards Cawnpore. But through Indian spies, Outram was already informed of this and he had already sent a party to attack the Moulvie's men. The battle began. The Moulvie, in order to encourage his men to do their utmost, himself fought in the front and did his very best. In the course of the engagement he was shot in the hand and fell down. The English had been most anxious for a long time to capture him. But the Revolutionaries skilfully placed him in a *doli* and brought him to Lucknow in great haste. When it was known that the Moulvie had been wounded, everybody was anxious about his condition. But they felt that the best way of showing their regard and respect for him was to complete the work that he had begun; and, therefore, without a moment's rest, Videhi Hanuman—a brave Brahmin—started on the 17th of January and made a desperate charge on the English troops. From ten in the morning to six in the evening, this brave man was fighting in the front ranks. In the evening, however, he was dangerously wounded and captured. The Revolutionaries were disorganised and ran away completely routed. These defeats increased the disorganisation in the Revolutionary camp. Characterless Sepoys demanded pay before fighting. Though their pay had been given them in advance, they demanded more before they would consent to take the field. That the resolute, daring, and capable Begum still maintained, in spite of all these disorders, the whole administration intact is a sure indication of her grit.[8] While these defeats were following one upon another, the chief minister of revenue of the Begum, Raja Balkrishna Singh died. Hardly was this wound healed when the Moulvie again rushed into the field—on the 15th of February. He was anxious to finish Outram before Sir Colin was able to return from Cawnpore. But, day by day, the cowardice of the Sepoys was increasing beyond measure. All the Moulvie's efforts were thus baffled and on that day too, the Revolutionaries were defeated. But he went on fighting still. Amazed at the bravery of this man, the historian Holmes records in his book; 'If, however, the mass of the rebels were cowards, their leader was a man fitted both by his spirit and his capacity to support a great cause and to command a great army. This was Ammadullah-the Moulvie of Fyzabad.[9] All those who were fighting with the incomparable strength of calm philosophy fought bravely. The brave Subahdar of the 60th regiment swore to drive

8. Sir W. Russell says about this Begum: 'The great bulk of the Sepoy army is supposed to be inside Lucknow, but they will not fight as well as the match-lock-men of Oudh who have followed their chiefs to maintain the cause of their young king, Birjis Kadir, and who may be fairly regarded as engaged in a patriotic war for their country and their sovereign. The Sepoys during the siege of the Residency never came on as boldly as the Zemindari levies and Nuieibs. The Begum exhibits great energy and ability. She has excited all Oudh to take up the interests of her son and the chiefs have sworn to be faithful to him. We affect to disbelieve his legitimacy but the Zemindars who ought to be better judges of the fact accept Birjis Kadir without hesitation. Will Government treat these men as rebels or as honourable enemies? The Begum declares undying war against us. It appears from the energetic characters of these Ranees and Begums that they acquire in their Zenanas and harems a considerable amount of actual mental power and at all events, become able *intrigantes*. Their contests for the ascendency over the minds of men give vigour and acuteness to their intellect. *Russell's Dairy*, page 275.

9. *Sepoy War* by Holmes.

away the English from Alam Bagh in eight days and worked hard in the field to effect his purpose. One day, the Begum herself came on the field with all the army. But the unfortunate Lucknow could not get any victory.

At last, Sir Colin joined the English troops before Alam Bagh. The English were straining every nerve to take Lucknow. But despite their innumerable attacks, that town had proudly stood so far under the flag of Swaraj. But now the English had determined not to move without taking it. As the English had concentrated all their forces at this place, so the Revolutionaries, too, were straining every nerve to give a good fight. All the fighting force of Oudh was there. From every village and every field came the patriotic rural population, with determination to drive away the Feringhis or die in the attempt. Charles Ball writes, 'The whole country was swarming with armed vagabonds hastening to Lucknow to meet their common doom and die in the last grand struggle with the Feringhis.'[10] There were thirty thousand Sepoys and fifty thousand volunteers gathered together in that city. All those who had taken the oath before the Revolutionary war, all those who had eaten the chapatee, all those who had smelt the red lotus flower, all those to whom had come the sacred messenger of the Revolution, all these patriots swarmed into Lucknow armed to the teeth with the object of fighting for their country and for their king. At least eighty thousand men were armed in that city.[11] In street and lane, barricades and entrenchments were erected; houses had

10. Charles Ball's *Indian Mutiny*, Vol. II, page 241.

11. How the imagination is relied upon in giving the exaggerated numbers of the Revolutionaries will be best seen from the following example. Sir H&pe Grant says that there were' thirty thousand Sepoys and fifty thousand volunteers' at Lucknow. Colonel Malleson records: , The total army of the mutineers was one hundred and twenty-one thousandj' and thz civil commissioner who accompanied Sir Colin says: , Their army was exactly two lakhs.' Poor Holmes is simply bewildered at these amazing contradictions.

ramparts made and holes bored in the walls for muskets or guns to be mounted; heroic spirits were posted on every wall; to the east, large canals were dug from the Gautami river and guns were stationed to command them; huge ramparts, three in one row, were erected right from Dilkhwush Bagh to Kaisar Bagh; the palace itself was reinforced with armed Sepoys and mounted with guns. In short, all parts except the northern portion of the city were fortified admirably by the Revolutionaries.

Sir Colin recognised the weakness of the northern side, and from this very side, he began the attack. Before this, neither Havelock, nor Outram, nor Colin himself had attacked Lucknow from that side and, as the Gautami was on that side, the Revolutionaries naturally thought that the north needed no protection. But Outram took full advantage of this weak link to the chain of their defences and as this point gave way under the charge of Outram, the other defences were rendered useless. On the 6th of March, the British began their operations on the north of Lucknow. Soon after, the troops under Sir Colin had increased to nearly thirty thousand, and so the English attacked simultaneously from the north and the East. Sir Colin had so divided his army that not a single Revolutionary should escape alive from Lucknow. Though all the plans of the Pandays had been upset on account of the attack on the quarter least expected namely, the northern side, they carried on their struggle, day and night from the 6th to the 15th of March. For the third time in a single year, blood flowed freely in this unfortunate city. The British troops stormed one fort after another—Dilkhwush Bagh, Kadam Rasool, Shah Najeef, Begum Kothi, and others—and continued their advance. On the 10th, Hudson was killed by the Revolutionaries. It was this man that had shot down in cold blood the surrendered innocent, unarmed Mughal princes of Delhi. Lucknow then avenged Delhi by killing this wicked criminal. On the 14th, the British army entered right into the Palace. Giving a description of this triumph, Malleson writes: 'Its greatness and magnificence were due mainly to the Sikhs and the 10th foot!'

But, while Sir Colin was overjoyed at this unique triumph in Kaisar Bagh, the news from Outram's side disconcerted him not a little. For, though Lucknow had fallen, its thousands of Revolutionaries did not surrender or give up the fight; but, with their king and with the resourceful Begum, they had broken through the troops which tried to hem them in.

And while, in Lucknow, streams of blood are flowing profusely on every side, while the triumphant British army is looting the palace, secure from danger, and while the Queen-mother and the King have left Lucknow, where, the reader asks, is Ahmad Shah?

Let everyone bow down his head to do honour to this hero of heroes! The proud Moulvie is making his entrance again into the city, with his handful of followers. His proud heart hates like poison the idea that Lucknow should fall, and that right in Lucknow English bayonets should cause bloodshed; he wants that, though Lucknow should fall, its name should not lie low; and so he leaves his post outside the city—and, while the Feringhis are laughing and joking and talking in the streets of Lucknow attempts an entry into Lucknow! Annoyed by insults offered to his king, careless of his life, mad with devotion to his country, this Ahmad Shah Moulvie, only in order that history should record that Lucknow did not fall without a glorious fighting, entered a small part of the town, known as Shahdat Ganj, and there began to fight the enemy with his handful of followers. As Mazzini had clung to Rome, all alone, though the enemy had entered it and taken complete possession of it, so this Moulvie too, when all the other Revolutionaries had left Lucknow, when thousands of British troops were in it, continued the fight with the strength that despair gives! He thrust his hand right into the jaws of this Feringhi serpent, for it had swallowed

Lucknow, and he wanted to snatch it back!

Malleson writes : 'Something remained to be effected even in the city itself. The Moulvie, the most obstinate of the rebel leaders, had returned to Lucknow, he was still there, at Shahdat Ganj, in its very heart, occupying, with two guns, a strongly fortified building whence he bade defiance to the British. To dislodge him, Lugard was detached, on the 21st with a portion of the division which had conquered the Begum Kothi, the first day of the attack. The troops employed were the 93rd Highlanders and the 4th Punjab Rifles. Seldom did the rebels display so much pertinacity and resolution as on this occasion. They defended themselves most bravely and were not driven out until they had killed several men and severely wounded many others on our side.'[12]

That was the last fight of Lucknow!

When the heroic impulse of this struggle and those who carried it on had calmed down, they felt that the flag of Swaraj for which they were fighting, was no more at Lucknow but that it was awaiting their uplifted swords in the wilds of Hindusthan. So, they moved away from the building. The enemy pursued them for six miles. But the Moulvie again effected his escape.

Now, Lucknow had completely fallen into the hands of the English. One must really dip one's pen in blood to write the history of the vengeance that they wreaked on Lucknow! How the palace and the city were looted, how the citizens were massacred wholesale, how even dead bodies were insulted is a sad, sad story to tell. If, while reading the description of the atrocities given by men like Russell, we bear in mind that this description is given by Englishmen, we would be able to have some faint notion or the terrible vengeance that was taken by the English. How different was the conduct of the Revolutionaries! We give below two

12. Kaye and Malleson, Vol. IV, page 286

extracts, both from English writers, so that the reader might judge for himself the difference between Indian and English vengeance.

In the prisons at Lucknow, there were several English women and officers. For six months, there lives were spared. But when the English army entered the city at the first onslaught of Sir Colin, massacring all—innocent and guilty alike, the angered Revolutionaries went to the palace and wanted to take vengeance on some of the English prisoners. Accordingly, Lieutenant Orr, Sir Mount Stuart, and five or six other Englishmen were given over and they were immediately shot down. But when they insisted that the English women-prisoners also should be killed, 'to the honour of womanhood, the demand was imperatively refused by the Begum so far as the females were concerned, and they were immediately taken under her care in the Zenana of the palace.'[13]

We give below, for comparison and contrast, one or two examples of the vengeance of the English. These have been given by Russell himself, the famous correspondent of the London Times. 'While the massacre was going on in the palace, a frightened child was leading an old man. The old man came before the English authorities and prostrating himself before them, asked that their lives should be spared. As if in answer to this wailing request, the English officer took out his pistol and shot him on the temple! Again, he pressed the trigger but the shot missed. He pressed again but the shot again refused to kill the innocent boy. The forth time—thrice he had time to repent—the gallant officer succeeded and the boy's life-blood flowed at his feet![14]

This incident has come out, becasue there was someone who *would* write about it. Many an other incident has not come to light, because there was no pen to record these.

13. Charles Ball's Indian Mutiny, Vol. II, page 94.
14. Russell's Dairy, page 384.

These atrocities were going on to such an extent that distinctions were actually drawn up between a merciful death and a cruel death! A murder, such as the one above was a *merciful* death. The cruel death which rendered even cold-blooded murder merciful meant something like the following: 'Some of the Sepoys were still alive and they were mercifully killed; but one of their number was dragged out to the sandy plain outside the house; he was pulled by his legs to a convenient place, when he was held down, pricked in the face and body by the bayonets of some of the soldiery, while others collected fuel for a small pyre; and when everything was ready—the man was roasted alive! These were Englishmen, and more than one officer saw it; no one offered to interfere! The horrors of this internal cruelty were aggravated by the attempt of the miserable wretch to escape when half-burned to death. By a sudden effort he leaped away and, with the flesh of his body: hanging from his bones, ran for a few yards before he was caught, brought back, put on the fire again, and held there by bayonets, till his remains were consumed!'[15]

Delhi has fallen. Lucknow, too has fallen. But the War of independence did not flag. Seeing this unexpected result, the English were convinced fully that they had made a mistake in imagining that this Revolution was caused by the Sepoys and only for one or two grievances. This was no mutiny, it was a War of Independence! One or two grievances are not responsible for this rising, but political slavery, the source of all the innumerable grievances suffered—that alone was the cause. The selfishness of personal gain lay not at its root, but the sacred flame of liberty, the glorious ideal of Swaraj and Swadharma, it is these that were burning there. Not only had the Sepoy risen to give his life's blood with almost selfish eagerness to this sacred principle of Liberty, but the whole civil population all

15. Russell's *Diary*, page 302.

over the country, from villages as much as from towns, had also risen. Without that, this strength, this resolution, this selflessness, this grit would not have been displayed. For Lord Canning had now issued a proclamation that those who would join the Revolution thereafter, would see their lands and estates confiscated, while those who surrendered at once would be forgiven. Yet the Revolutionary would not lay down his sword. Still Oudh persisted in her fight. Lucknow had fallen. But Sepoy and shopkeeper, Brahmin and Moulvie, Rajas, Zemindars, and Talukdars, villagers and agriculturists-all Oudh was still making a rush forward! Dr. Duff writes about this terrible popular rising : 'Why, if it had been a merely military mutiny, in the midst of an unsympathetic, unaiding population, a few decisive victories, such as we have already had might quash it or, as the phrase goes, stamp it out. But so far from being quashed or stamped out it seems, still as rampant and, in some respects, more wide-spread and formidable than ever. And, it is a fact that it is not a mere military revolt, but a rebellion, a revolution, which alone can account for the little progress hitherto made in extinguishing it and, at the same time, precludes any reasonable hope of its early suppression. That it is a rebellion, and a rebellion, too, of no recent or mushroom growth, every fresh revelation tends more and more to confirm. And a rebellion, long and deliberately concocted, a rebellion which had been able to carry the Hindu and Mahomedan in an unnatural confederacy, a rebellion which is now manifestly nurtured and sustained by the whole population of Oudh and, directly, or indirectly, sympathised with and assisted by well-nigh half of the neighbouring provinces—is not to be put down by a few victories over mutinous Sepoys, however decisive and brilliant.

'From the very outset, it has been gradually assuming more and more the character of a rebellion-a rebellion on the part of vast multitudes beyond the Sepoy army, against British supremacy and sovereignty. Our real contest was never wholly, and now less than ever, with mutinous Sepoys. Had we only Sepoys for our foes, the country might soon have been pacified.

'Never has the enemy been met without being routed, scattered, and his guns taken. But though constantly beaten, he evermore rallies and appears again, ready for a fresh encounter. No sooner is one city taken or relieved than some other one is threatened. No sooner is one district pronounced safe through, the influx of British troops than another is disturbed and convulsed. No sooner is a highway reopened between places of importance than it is again closed and all communication is for a season cut-off. No sooner are the mutineers scored out of one locality than they reappear with double or treble force in another locality. No sooner does a moveable column force its way through hostile ranks than these reoccupy the territory behind it. All gaps in the number of the foe seem to be instantaneously filled up and no permanent clearance or impression seems to be made anywhere. The passage of our brave little armies through these swarming myriads, instead of leaving the deep traces of a mighty ploughshare through a roughened field, seems more to resemble that of the. eagle through the elastic air or a stately vessel through the unfurrowed ocean!'[16]

The truth described so picturesquely by Duff was realised by the English only at the end; but every individual of the Panday party had thoroughly realised it long, long before. Those who died on the field for their country and their king were, of course, giving expression to such thoughts; but, even their women showed an equal determination. When the 'brave' English attacked the Zenana of Lucknow, some Zenana ladies fell into their hands. Feringhi soldiers opened fire as soon as the door was forced and some of these ladies were killed! Those who survived were put in prison. Lucknow city was soon razed to the ground. The English were

16. Dr. Duff's *Indian Rebellion*, Pages 241-243.

overjoyed at the prospect, as they thought, of the early surrender of the Revolutionaries. The jailors of these Ranees, sharing to the full the general feeling of joy of their compatriots, asked them mockingly, 'Do you not think that the struggle has come to an end?' 'On the contrary,' replied the Ranees, 'we are sure that in the long run you will be beaten.'[17]

* * *

CHAPTER VIII

Kumar Singh and Amar Singh

HUNTED out of the valleys of Jagdishpur by General Eyre, Kumar Singh, the old but energetic lion of the territory of Shahabad, was roaming restlessly but always on the alert for every chance to spring at the neck of those who had deprived him of his liberty. Under his banner had united his brother Amar Singh and two other chiefs, Nisswar Singh and Jawan Singh. They were now lying in wait in the forests. With them were their beloved wives, heroic women, but ready to join in the fight, combing their hair not with the delicate combs of the Zenana but with sharp arrows, flourishing in their delicately fashioned hands, 'tenderer than the very flower,' the flashing Damascus blade, 'harder than adamant.' They were, also, waiting to drink the blood of the enemy! To, drink the blood of the enemy, we say again; for old as Kumar Singh was and proudly insolent as his opponent was, the ambition of Kumar Singh was nothing short of drinking the enemy's blood! For, though 'reduced to extremities with hunger, besieged by, age,—a picture of hard misery, with no

17. *Narrative of the Indian Mutiny*, page 338. *Russell's Diary*, page 400.

position, and courting death,' as the lion of the famous poem, our Kumar was still the king of the forest! And, therefore, whatever the reverses, how would he eat the dead grass of slavery? His ambition was—one ambition alone could be the ambition of the lion of the poem referred to—to break open, with his steel-claws, the skull of the elephant!

With the land belonging to his family for generations as far as your memory could go, now usurped by the stranger, with his very palace of Jagdishpur in the hands of the foreigner, and his temples and images pulled down by the desecrating hands of the enemy, Kumar Singh did not show any excitement. He did not make a dash for Jagdishpur nor did he persist in holding Shahabad. His capital was strictly guarded by the English and his army was small—only a thousand and two hundred Sepoys and five hundred untrained volunteers. He did not show, therefore, the least anxiety to recover his capital immediately. But his great desire was to hold aloft the bright golden banner of the War of Independence! The very day that he gave up Jagdishpur without serious resistance—that very day he had made up his mind to take to a different mode of warfare altogether. That mode of war-fare is the one mode that goes farthest to secure success in any War of Independence. It is guerilla warfare.

Therefore, enraged as he was at the loss of his capital, Kumar Singh sent not his army against the enemy, for then his soldiers would have perished like moths before the rushing enemy; but he moved quickly into the forest of West Behar and along the river Shon, carefully noting the weak points of the enemy. In the meanwhile, news reached him that troops, Nepalese and English, were being sent from Azimgarh into Oudh to destroy Lucknow. As soon as with his keen scent he scented the prey, the lion of Jagdishpur took one leap out of the forest. Unlike those who would still, in fallen days, hover round their capital without the least chance, and unlike those weak persons who give way completely to passion and emotion to console themselves, our Kumar Singh was the very genius of guerilla warfare. Though the British army was marching on to Lucknow, they still had an eye on Jagdishpur, where his activities might be expected to be centred. Kumar Singh, therefore, postponed indefinitely his operation there and started for eastern Oudh, to make one spring for that part where the British army was weakest, hoping to surprise Azimgarh by uniting together all the Revolutionaries that were scattered in eastern Oudh, and then to make a dash, if victorious, on Benares or even Allahabad and thus, to avenge the Jagdishpur insult. On the 18th of March 1858, even the Revoltionaries of Beeva joined him; and the united armies encamped near the fort in Atrolia.

Azimgarh is twenty-five miles' run from Atrolia. Learning Kumar Singh was so near, Milman marched on Atrolia with three hundred infantry and horse and two guns. Before the morning rays of the sun of the 22nd of March had lighted the field on Atrolia, the vanguards of Milman and of the Revolutionaries were within sight of each other. Milman gave them not even a moment's time to recover themselves, taken aback as they seemed to be by the sudden appearance of the British troops. He began the fight at once. But, of course, how long could the Revolution aries fight against the British? They were soon totally defeated. What an ending to the vain glorious boast of Kumar Singh! All glory to the British army which showed such fine front even af the all-night march of the previous day. Ye have earned your breakfast, British soldiers, by the sweat of your brow, nay, by the free flow of blood from your bodies; so enjoy your breakfast, with your commanders, in the cool shade of the mango groves! The rays of the morning sun are welcoming you, gay because of the great victory earned so lately. Arms were arranged all round, breakfast was ready, the hungry mouths were chewing the first morsel; the cups of drink were filled ready, —and then!

Boom boom! What is up ? The cups are dashed down from the lips, the morsels of foold have slipped off the mouths, the breakfast dishes are shattered and, instead, the army has to take up the arms only this hour laid down with a sense of relief! Has Kumar Singh come after all? Yes, yes! Kumar Singh has descended like a thunderbolt upon the English, who had been contemplating with delight their supposed victory. As soon as the Milman was completely enticed into the security of a false victory, the hero—old in age but youthful in spirit—came out of the fort of Atrolia and smiled with contempt at the prey, now completely his. Malleson says: 'What more could a general long for? Everything was in his favour, Kumar Singh, then, marched to a victory which he deemed assured. The imagination can almost picture him making to the confident by his side an exclamation near akin of that which burst from the lips of Wellington when he noticed the false movement of Marmont which brought on the battle of Salamanca! *Mon cher Alva, Marmont est perdu*![1] Still Milman struggled to escape and marched on with boldness, hoping to frighten Kumar Singh by keeping up a good and steady attack. But a regular shower of bullets was kept on from the avenues of sugarcane, from the trees of the mango grove, and from the mud-banks everywhere. The army of Kumar Singh numbered five or six times that of Milman and seeing that his enemy threatened to surround him completely, Milman was obliged to stop weakly in the midst of his bold attack. This weakness increased the determination of Kumar Singh to surround him. Now the British army, frightened and almost suffocated began to fall back. Now began the wolf-like warfare of Kumar Singh's troops, moving forward to shoot at stray soldiers and the flanks of the enemy. The temporary triumph did not turn Kumar Singh's head. He did not attack unitedly the retreating troops of the enemy; for, he knew well the nature of the troops under him. He could not be sure how long they would

1. Malleson's *Indian Mutiny*, Vol. IV, page 319.

have held on in a hand to hand fight. Hence, shrewd as he was, he determined only to continue the guerilla tactics. He drove the army of the enemy, hunting them from Atrolia straight to their camp at Kosilla.

But the British army was destined not to get a safe refuge even in the Kosilla camp. Already the news of the defeat of the army had reached there and the Indian servants had left with their oxen and everything else that was in their keeping. No servants ahead, no provisions near, with Kumar Singh's army preying on the stray unfortunates like wolves, Milman began his retreat leaving the camp behind him. Kumar Singh pursued—pursued even after he had taken complete possession of everything the enemy had, and hunted the British army and the miserable Milman from Kosilla right up to Azimgarh. At Azimgarh, Milman's hopes revived again! for, there he had aid of three hundred and fifty fresh forces from Benares and Ghazipur, who had come in response to his express message. Colonel Dames was the commander of the united forces. With a strong base like Azimgarh, with the British army reinforced to double the former number, with Colonel Dames to lead them -they determined to take revenge for the temporary defeat come what might!

So, Colonel Dames set out from Azimgarh resolving to revenge himself on Kumar Singh on the 28th of March. He thought he had his revenge, for he was victorious over Kumar Singh; but it was only to find the old game repeated again, perhaps better than before. The fresh soldiers with their fresh commander got such a sound beating that Colonel Dames ran from the field right to Azimgarh and took refuge within the fortification of the city. No one now even spoke of attacking Kumar afresh. Kumar now entered Azimgarh and leaving the work of annihilating the few Englishmen in the fortifications to a few of his followers—and to famine—he pushed on triumphant to Benares!

The governor-general who, as we have said before, was

now at Allahabad, was filled with terror, now that the lion had opened wide his jaws. 'Knowing what sort of a man Kumar Singh was, that he possessed audacity and courage, and that he knew the value of time in military operations, Lord Canning realised at once the danger of the situation.'[2] He who had just imprisoned the English forces at Azimgarh and, having marched with wonderful rapidity the eighty-one miles of the way, had threatened to cut off Allahabad from Calcutta by attacking the city of Benares, he—the Rana Kumar Singh, reinforced as he now was by the Sepoys flying away after the defeat at Lucknow and knowing full well the art of keeping together and in discipline even such demoralised forces as he had, was not to be lightly treated by Lord Canning. It was owing to the firm grip on the cities of Allahabad and Benares which the English could maintain through the loyalty of the Sikhs in the first part of the mutiny, that the rebellion was nipped in the bud in the provinces round Calcutta; and when it seemed the design of Kumar Singh to catch again the lost opportunity by dashing on Benares and Allahabad, Lord Canning ordered Lord Mark Kerr himself to march on this 'rebel' chief in all haste.

Lord Mark Kerr, well known in the Crimean campaigns and well experienced in Indian military matters, marched off at once with five hundred men and eight guns and arrived within eight miles of Azimgarh. After a little rest, he started onwards on the morning of the 6th of April. At about six o'clock in the morning, he learnt that Kumar Singh's men had been watching his progress. But pretending ignorance of this fact, he ordered his army to advance in readiness and at once commenced the attack on Kumar's left flank. No sooner did the English commence the attack than Kumar's left began a veritable shower of bullets on the enemy. On that day, the old Kumar was seen fighting lightning-like in the thick of the battle, seated on his favourite

2. Malleson's *Indian Mutiny*, Vol. IV, page 321.

white horse. Knowing full well that the strength of his army was not so much in their number which was simply swelled as a threat to the enemy by allowing all sorts of camp followers to enter the fighting ranks, Kumar Singh solely relied upon his own skill and courage and intrepidity.

He spread out his force to attack Lord Mark Kerr on his flanks. The guns of the enemy were vomiting fire upon him and he had no guns to silence them. Still did he succeed in bringing his army right to the rear of Lord Mark! This movement upset the plan of the enemy so totally that their guns had to fall back; and this was the signal for the Revolutionaries to rush forward with a triumphant war-cry. Kumar Singh had, by this time, tightened his grip on the English rear so firmly that the English elephants began to run amock, the conductors on them lost all hope of life and clung round their necks with both hands, and the servants and all began to run wheresoever they found a way. Yet Mark Kerr said 'Let us hold on for a while-victory might still be ours!' He had captured some houses on the Revolutionaries' front, while they had totally routed his rear.

Thus was this strange battle fought. In the beginning, the front of Kumar was opposed to the front of the English army and now the rear of the British army is opposed to the front or Kumar; now he has even set the rear of the enemy on fire! When Mark Kerr saw the rear surrounded in flames of fire, he determined to leave the battlefield and began to press on to Azimgarh. For, if not victory, at least the secondary purpose of carrying: succour to Azimgarh should be accomplished if possible. His guns did him a splendid service, especially as Kumar Singh had none with him. At midnight, Lord Mark brought his army to Azimgarh. About this battle and the strategic movements and errors of Kumar Singh and the difficulties under which he laboured, Malleson says :- 'That leader had showed himself greater as a strategist than a tactician. His plan of campaign was admirable but, in carrying it into execution, he committed many serious errors. Milman gave him a great, an unexpected opportunity. He had that officer at his mercy. When Milman's men were waiting for their breakfast in the mango grove near Atrolia, it was in the power of Kumar Singh to cut them off from Azimgarh. He preferred to attack them in front. Then, when he had forced him to fall back, he did not press the pursuit with sufficient vigour. A capable commander would still have cut them oft: Once having seen them housed in Azimgarh, he should have left a portion of his force to blockade them, pressed on with the remainder towards Benares, and occupied a position in which he could have engaged Lord Mark Kerr with advantage. He had at his disposal, it subsequently transpired, about twelve thousand men. To oppose these the few men led by Lord Mark were alone available. Everything was within his grasp had he dared to stretch out his hand. The chances are that, capable man as he was, he saw all this. But he was not supreme master of the situation. Every petty leader who had brought his contingent to serve under him wished to dictate a programme. The counsels of the rebels, tended, then almost always to a compromise.'[3]

But Lord Mark Kerr was baulked not only of his victory but even of this secondary purpose of relieving Azimgarh, For still the whole city was in the hands of the Revolutionaries who- had also a perfect hold of the whole surrounding province. A born commander is he who knows exactly the nature and capacities of his forces. Few men could have excelled Kumar Singh in this necessary quality of a commander. As he had correctly gauged the power and strength of his enemy, even so he measured the merits and demerits of his own followers. Therefore is it that he did not try at all to attack and carry the fortress in which the English had taken refuge. He had closely observed the fact that the Sepoys, for whatever reasons or panic it might be, were

8. Malleson's *Indian Mutiny*, Vol. IV, page 826-827.

ready to undergo any other ordeal but that of facing the English bayonets—a fact which had been clearly demonstrated in both the sieges of Arrah and Lucknow. Therefore, having rendered it difficult for the English forces to come out of the besieged fortress, he began to plan in his daring heart quite another scheme of worsting his enemy. In the forces of the Revolutionaries that had entered the field in 1857, it was clearly seen that there were men of two different temperaments—the one class, who would throw themselves right in the jaws of death with unflinching and firm and disciplined resistance on the battle-field, whether opposed to the cannon or the bayonet of the foe; the other who possessing the will to die for the nation but lacking in the courage to carry it jnto effect, would flinch back and get routed at the very moment when they ought to have stood unmoved. Out of these two sorts of men, Kumar Singh collected those who belonged to the first sort and had proved immoveable in the field, and organised them into a separate band of chosen veterans. Having made this selection and created a body on whom he could depend for any adventure however difficult, Kumar Singh became ready to put into execution the daring scheme which he had set his heart upon, and ordered his newly selected veteran band to stand on the bridge of the Tanu river.

For, it was by this little bridge that a British general. named Lugard, was marching ahead to relieve the English forces at Azimgarh. Lugard first, and most naturally, thought that the object of this Revolutionary band in contesting the passage of the bridge was simply to preserve the grip of the Revolutionaries on the city of Azimgarh. 'But,'says Malleson, 'the wily chieftain had matured plans far deeper than even those about him could fathom.' This unfathomable plan of the wily chieftain was to deceive the enemy by a false show of holding Azimgarh at any cost, to fix their whole attention there on that spot and, while they were thus completely beguiled there, to march off straight on to Jagdishpur. This scheme was matchless in its military wisdom. To march off from Azimgarh to Ghazipur, thence to jump into the Ganges, to cross it, to press on, to reconquer Jagdishpur–all this in spite of the pursuing force of Lugard at the rear and in the face of the deluded English force of Arrah in front! It was for the execution of this very bold plan that he ordered his veteran band to guard the bridge of the river Tanu. His orders to those veterans were to hold the bridge against the attacks of Lugard till the other division of his forces had time to leave Azimgarh and escaping the vigilance of the English, to take the road leading to Ghazipur. If once he reached Ghazipur and crossed the Ganges, the lion would be back again into his native forests of Jagdishpur, and the English must reenact the whole drama right anew, as all that they had done during the previous twelve months would be as if not done at all.

But to succeed in all these plans depends upon your bravery, O soldiers on the bridge of the Tanu! You must not allow the British forces under Lugard to step upon this bridge till the whole army of Kumar Singh has gone out of the range of the enemy's sight! You have been selected by your chief in the belief that you alone would rise equal to the occasion. May your bravery not belie his confidence! Let one thought, one determination, one vow alone be yours, namely, not to let the enemy capture this bridge till Kumar Singh had led off in safety his whole force out of the sight of the duped enemy! As Baji Deshpande, the Mahratta soldier, held out in the famous gorge of Pavankhind till Shri Shivaji could reach the fort of Rangana in safety, even so fight on hard and hot till Kumar's order is carried out to the letter, too, led assaults after assaults on this handful of the Revolutionary band as often as Fazul did against the Mahratta, but he could not gain a foot-hold on the bridge even for a second. Every charge of the English was firmly and vigorously repulsed by the Revolutionary forces who were defending it. Till Kumar

Singh signalled to them his safe departure from Azimgarh and his successful march on the way to Ghazipur, the veteran band held this bridge, contesting it inch by inch! Col. Malleson says,'They held the bridge of boats with a resolution and perseverance, worthy of veterans, and it was not until they had by their long resistance ensured the safety of their comrades, that they fell back.'[4] Thus, the brave band accomplished its mission, fell back with perfect order, and, as settled, succeeded in rejoining their chief, Raja Kumar Singh.

Seeing the sudden evacuation of the bridge, Lugard rushed on, but found, to his utter dismay, the magic like disappearance of the whole army of Kumar Singh, as if it never was there? So to pursue and find out this invisible force, he despatched a detachment of European cavalry and a horse battery. Twelve miles did the gallop on; yet, Kumar Singh could not be found—and when found at last, he was found in such a strong position as to make it impossible to distinguish who was the pursuer and who the pursued! It was not the Revolutionaries who were frightened at the sight of the foe but it was the english forces who seemed to have lost their balance at the sight of the Revolutionaries. Kumar Singh's army was drawn up in battle array, with their swords unsheathed and with their guns pointed at the enemy. One of the English officers engaged in this fight says,'It was all we could do to hold our own against such odds. Immediately our cavalry charged, they stood and formed square and used to abuse and tell us to come on.' And, when the English did so on, they received them with such a hot welcome that many soldiers and even officers on the side of the English fell dead. The squares of Kumar's forces remained impenetrable, and the English were completely thrown on the defensive. After this engagement, Kumar Singh pursued his march and was approaching nearer and nearer to the banks of the Ganges!

4. Malleson's *Indian Mutiny*, Vol. IV, page 330.

News of the ill-success of the English pursuing force reached Azimgarh. The British general, Douglas, started with five or six more guns and came to their aid. Douglas had already tasted the sharpness of Kumar's sword, and so he came on with circumspect steps as far as the village Nagbai, in pursuit of the Raja. Tbere also the Raja was quite ready. When the forces were within striking distance, Kumar Singh led on his veteran band to face the foe and again ordered them to fight on till the signal should come, and, dividing the remaining forces into two parts, he despatched them onwards by two different routes to the banks or the Ganges. While these movements were secretly being carried out, the veteran band kept up a vigorous fight with the enemy, in spite of the lack of guns to reply to the hot fire of the enemy's artillery which was mowing them down like grass. They wavered not, nor did their ranks break up, nor did their charge flag in the least! For four miles this living battle pressed on! At last, when the army of the enemy showed signs of exhaustion, the two divisions of Kumar Singh's army, until now going by different routes, united together and the whole force marched unhampered, and Raja Kumar Singh was again marching nearer and nearer towards the banks of the Ganges!

This exhausted British force passed the night of the 17th of April near the village Athusi. Early in the morning, Douglas, thinking he had given no start to the Revolutionary forces, ordered a march again—only to find that Kumar Singh was already thirteen miles ahead of him. The whole of the British horse and the British artillery had been pursuing Kumar Singh; but as the British infantry, through total exhaustion, were unable to proceed further, they were given rest for another night. The scouts of Kumar Singh were matchless in bringing him all detailed information about the enemy's plans and whereabouts. They did not fail to inform him of their exhausted condition. At this, the old general stood up, determined to take full advantage of this chance and, with his force, the octogenarian chief recommenced the march in the midnight and came straightway to Sikandarpur, reached the river Ghogra, crossed it, and entered the province of Ghazipur. He pressed on right up to the village of Manohar, and there ordered a temporary rest to the now tired, worn-out and hungry forces which had so bravely responded to the intrepid will of their patriotic chief. It was humanly impossible to avoid stopping here, though Kumar Singh knew full well that the position was rather a weak one. When Douglas heard that Kumar bad gained a start over him, he started in hot pursuit and eventually reached Manohar soon after Kumar Sing. He began the attack immediately and, as the Revolutionaries were tired on account of their long and continuous marching, their stand was feeble and they lost the battle, losing also many elephants and ammunition and food supplies. But Kumar Singh's heart and will remained as much unconquered and unconquerable as ever. For, no sooner he saw the signs of a crushing defeat than he put into execution the same tactics that he had hitherto been pursuing. He divided his troops into small bands and, as each division effected its retreat from the losing battle-field by a different route, the pursuit of the enemy was frustrated. Kumar had given the captains of the different bands definite instructions to meet at a pre-arranged place at a fixed hour, and lo, when the hour struck, Kumar Singh's forces had come together and were ready for their march. This place where they met was so completely hidden from the enemy that the victory of the English was altogether barren of any result, and so the English commander had to stop at the village of Manohar itself to ascertain the whereabouts of Kumar Singh's army, while Kumar Singh and his forces were all the while marching nearer and nearer to the banks of the Ganges!

Nearer and nearer to the banks of the Ganges! Nay, now he has won the terrible race and actually reached the banks of the Ganges. The English forces were also close upon his rear. But, as his forces were now greatly reduced, he decided that it was not wise to fight the enemy and so he now pursued quite different tactics. He spread a rumour all over the province that, owing to the scarcity of boats, his forces were going to cross the Ganges on the backs of elepants somewhere near a place called Balila. The English scouts brought the news to the general who must have felt triumphant of the efficiency of his intelligence department! How can now this rebel chief succeed in crossing the Ganges when my scouts have enabled me to know the exact place where he intends to cross the river? He is doommed to be drowned along with his elephants! So, the British general, with his white forces, went to Balila and kept himself in concealment, expecting, every moment, to pounce upon the unwieldy elephants of Kumar Singh as soon as they would appear. Brave soldiers! Enjoying all the while the sweet prospects of success, conceal yourselves near Balila till the looked-for enemy comes! There, seven miles below this very spot, is Kumar Singh actually crossing the river Ganges! Having duped the English by the story of the elephants and Balila, the Raja got together as many boats its he wanted and, from the Ghat of Shivapur, he began to cross the sacred Bhagirathi at night. The duped foe, awaked to this fact, got extremely irritated and, hurriedly marching from Balila, reached, Shivapur and even succeeded in capturing a boat belonging to the, Raja—but that was the last boat! The whole army had already been sent on the other side and in a minute or two the chieftain too, having supervised the crossing of the army, would have crossed the river himself. But, alas! What a calamity this one moment has brought with it! While this hero of the nation, the pride of chivalry, the sword of Liberty-Rana Kumar Singh was in the middle of the stream, a bullet shot from the enemy's gun entered his wrist! But old as he was, the octogenarian leader did not mind it at all! And when amputation was deemed necessary, with his own hand—the hand that was not wounded—Kumar Singh unsheathed his sword, lopped off the wounded arm at the elbow, and threw it into the sacred Ganges saying, 'Accept thou, Mother, this last sacrifice of a loving son!'

Though innumerable are the people who have addressed the Ganges as Mother, it is Kumar—this brave son of Ganga, and such as he, that make the motherhood of the sacred Ganges fruitful and glorious. As the poet says, innumerable are the stars that are in the sky; but it is the moon alone that adorns it and makes it lovely!

After offering this sacrifice to the Mother Ganges, this dlstinguished son succeeded in crossing the river without further trouble from the English army. The enemy, on the other hand, like a hunter whose prey is escaped out of his reach, unable to cross the river, stopped there with their pride wounded and mission unaccomplished. The lion, now triumphant by freeing itself from the hunter's nets and lances, again rushed into his native forests of Shahabad, came to Jagdishpur and, on the 22nd April, re-entered this his old capital. It was from this capital that he was hunted out eight months back. Once more now, in the palace of Jagdishpur is ruling the prince of Jagdishpur. His brother, Amar Singh, who had collected together a force of patriotic peasants and villagers even before Kumar Singh had crossed the Ganges, now joined him. The brave Kumar ordered out in divisions these united forces to guard the capital on all sides, while he too, as intrepid and unexhausted as ever, took again to war-fare.

That entrance into Jagdishpur was so sudden and dashing that the British forces at Arrah which had been kept there for the express purpose of watching Jagdishpur had no notice of Kumar Singh's descent on Arrah. Thus outwitted, Le Grand, the British general at Arrah, became wild at the discovery of this enemy's triumph. What audacity that this rebel chief should give the slip to all the British forces in East Oudh, should enter Jagdishpur, and even begin to rule with all the pomp of an independent prince here, under the very nose of the British general? It is not even eight months since Sir Eyre had chased this rebel out of these forests:—well, even like that will this Le Grand rush in the Jagdishpur wilds to hunt down this marauding chief. With this hope, the brave general, with four hundred British troops and two guns, marched on the doomed city of Jagdishpur on the 23rd of April. How, now, is it possible that this field should be contested by Kumar Singh? During all these months, the old warrior had been fighting incessantly and without a moment's rest; his forces had never been able to snatch a hearty meal or an undisturbed sleep; but yesterday had he come to Jagdishpur after the death dealing struggle in East Oudh, and he and his forces had not even taken one day's rest. According to the English official report itself his forces were 'disjointed, badly armed, and without guns,' numbering at the most to a thousand, with very few trained soldiers amongst them, and the octogenarian chief himself was wounded mortally in his hand! Against this army was marching the fresh, the vigorous, the disciplined forces of the British, well armed with guns and led by General Le Grand. The issue of the battle was, then, a foregone conclusion.! And with this full confidence, the English army entered the forest which, was about one mile and half from the town. The English guns began to thunder forth unchallenged, for Kumar Singh had no guns to oppose them. But, still, it seems that he means to smother us in this thickly grown jungle by stretching out his forces round us;—well then, let the all unfailing stroke be given. Let that straight and bold front attack of the Europeans, which had always been the terror of the Asiatics, be ordered! It was ordered; the Europeans rushed forth irresistible; the army of Kumar Singh, too, began to contest ; and none knows how, but in a moment, the brave Briton got confused and struck with terror and sounded the retreat. But, though the bands sounded the retreat, as Kumar Singh held the British force in his grip, it was more dangerous to attempt a retreat than even to try to make a stand. But, if retreat is as ruinous as a stand, then, O brave Briton, why not make a stand to prove that unflinching courage of your people which so many times you have boasted that you possess? Matters not whether it is proved or disproved, he alone lived who ran! And run they did; all the British forces, like hunted deer, left the jungle and began to fly wherever the way led, while Kumar Singh's army pursued them hot and the rout was complete! One of the men who himself was present in this rout, writes to this effect of his experience, in a letter written at the time:- 'Indeed, it makes me extremely ashamed to write what followed. We began flying out of the jungles, leaving the battle-field and being constantly beaten by the enemy. Our people, dying of thirst, rushed forth at the sight of a wretched, dirty pool of water, in the most confused manner possible. Just then, the horses of Kumar Singh closed upon our rear. Henceforth, there was no limit to our disgrace,and the disaster was complete. No sense of shame was left in anyone of us. Everyman ran wherever he thought his safety lay. Orders were thrown to the winds. Discipline and drill were dead. In all directions, nothing could be heard but sighs, curses and wailings. Bands of Europeans dropped dead in the flight by sunstroke. Nor was it possible to ask for medicine; for, the dispensary was already captured by Kumar Singh. Some died there and then; the rest were cut down by the enemy; the carriers dropped the *dolis* and fled; all was confusion—all terror! Sixteen elephants were all full-laden with the burden of the wounded. General Le Grand himself was shot dead by a bullet in his breast! Soldiers running for their lives for five miles and more had now no strength, even for lifting up their guns. The Sikhs, accustomed to the heat of the sun, took off the elephants and fled away ahead of all. None would be with the white. Out of a hundred and ninety-nine whites, about eighty alone could survive this terrible massacre! We were led into this jungle like cattle into the slaughterhouse, simply to be killed!'[5]

The forces of Kumar Singh were thus completely successful. They had, in spite of the fact that they had no artillery to speak of on their side, routed the British forces with a terrible loss and slaughter, and had captured even the two guns which the British had so proudly brought.[6]

But, one fact is most significant in this pursuit: the number of Sikhs that fell on that day was only nine. It substantiates most thoroughly the tradition that Kumar Singh was in the habit of issuing strict injunctions to spare as many lives as could be spared of the Indian people even though they were on the enemy's side, while there should be no mistaken mercy shown to the foreign foe. In the first outbreak of the Revolution, many of the Babus of Bengal were made prisoners, for joining the English side, by Kumar's men; but he not only released them but sent them without harm on elephants to the city of Patna where they wished to go.[7] When the Sepoys determined to burn down all government papers written in English, it was Kumar who stopped them from doing so, as 'otherwise, after the English were driven out of the country, there would be no proof of the people, and no evidence to determine the amount due from one party to the other.'

Having vanquished his foe thus completely and thoroughly, the old chief, Rana Kumar Singh, entered again his palace of Jagdishpur on the 23rd of April, crowned with fresh laurels and a fresh fame!

This was his last entrance, for no more will Kumar Singh re-enter on the stage of the world. The wound caused by the amputation of his hand proved mortal and, on the 26th day of April, the third day after his latest victory, the great

5. Charles Ball's *Indian Mutiny*, Vol. II, page 288.
6. 'The English sustained on this occasion a complete defeat of the worst kind.' *White's History of the Indian Mutiny*.
7. *Arya Kirti* by Rajani Kanta Gupta of Bengal.

Rana died in his own palace. He died on an independent throne and under the flag of freedom. The day he died, it was not the Union Jack of the British Isles but the Golden Banner of a free and liberated nation, the triumphant symbol of his Desh and Dharma, that was waving radiant over the palace of Jagdishpur. It was under the cool shade of this banner that he died. What nobler death can a Rajput long for?[8]

He had avenged his wrongs ; he had, with poor means, worsted a mighty foe more than once in a battlefield ; he had not proved a traitor to the nation or a renegade to his Dharma but had broken the chains that bound his land and made her free so far as one man could do it, and to-day, in a noble field, he had been crowned by Victory's own hands with a wreath of laurels. Then, this is the auspicious day:this is the supreme moment for you, O great Rajput, to close your eyes for ever, to lay down your body—not through disease, but even as a worthy sacrifice to the cause of your Mother's freedom, by the wounds received on the battle-field! Let your death be as noble and as matchless as was your life!

The personality of Shrimant Kumar Singh is striking in more than one respect. His personal dash and high character had naturally infused in his army the two indispensable virtues of discipline and bravery. It is rarely the case that persons who are called upon to lead a nation's regeneration are in their private morals as unimpeachable as they are unchallengeable in their public ability. This rare consistency of character was conspicuous in great degree in the life of this great Indian. Such was the influence of his pure conduct on his people that none would dare even to smoke openly in their verandahs for fear of being seen by him. Amongst all

8. The English historian, Holmes says : 'The old Rajput who had fought so honourably and so bravely against the British power died on April, 26, 1858'—*History of the Sepoy War.*

the leaders of the Revolutionaries in 1857, there was none who could surpass Kumar Singh in military ability. It was he who at once grasped the utility of guerilla warfare in the War of Independence and it was he alone who could imitate the masterful tactics of a veteran guerilla leader like Shivaji. If we compare the two great generals that 1857 brought to the front, Tatia Tope and Kumar Singh, in their military achievements as guerilla leaders, we shall be struck with one distinguishing point. To Tatia Tope may be at once assigned a very high place in the negative side of guerilla warfare, while Kumar Singh holds the position with equal eminence in the positive as well as in the negative side of it. Tatia Tope did not allow the enemy to completely crush his forces or his power to raise them, but Kumar Singh, while succeeding in doing this, could even succeed in crushing the enemy's forces by severe defeats. To ensure ultimate success, it is imperatively necessary in guerilla warfare to prevent the demoralisation of one's followers which the constant fights from the field or avoidance of battles against a mightier foe do inevitably tend to beget. The defeats which are suffered intentionally by the leader, and the flights which he finds it necessary to effect, ought not to be allowed to create domoralisation or diffidence in the minds of his followers. The constant avoidance of battles ought not to be allowed to create in the followers a fear for battle itself. The skilful avoidance of a battle and a panic-stricken flight in the course of the battle are two very different things. So it is most important in guerilla tactics never to leave the field through cowardice ; but whenever a battle is decided to be given, it should be given so sternly and dashingly as to strike a sudden terror into the heart of the enemy and to infuse an overwhemlming confidence into the heart of one's own followers. The main skill lies in taking care never to be forced to give battle where the chances are of an unequal contest. But once the die is cast, such must be the tenacity and desperation in contesting the field as was shown by Baji in the Pawankhind or by Kumar Singh on the Tanu Nadi. In short, if the strength is unequal, the leader should not get entgangled into a battle ; if the chances are equal, he should cast the die; but, in either case of a forced or voluntary contest, never should a battle once begun be left, through fear or want of discipline, but, on the contrary, it should be fought on so desperately and so bravely, in spite of an assured defeat or of an immediate death, as never to lose, fame, though success be lost in the field. Thus attacked, the enemy is struck with terror, the followers do not get demoralised, discipline is not slackened, and inspiration increases by stories of martyrdom; bravery begets bravery, and victory becomes insured. The guerilla general and his forces should never give the least chance to create an impression that their foe conquered them through superiority in bravery. This is the key to guerilla warfare.

But Tatia Tope could not follow this positive side of this warfare. Tatia's campaigns when trying to cross the Narbada and Kumar's campaigns when trying to cross the Ganges demonstrate this difference. Tatia suffered many a defeat. Though this was due entirely to the panicky and sometimes even cowardly conduct of the Sepoys he had to lead, and could not be attributed to any inferiority in his capacity. Kumar Singh while marching off, had all the while kept up such a bold front and, whenever opportunity offered, had hit his pursuing foe so hard, that all the while his forces were full of self-confidence and high inspiration in spite of the fact that they were retreating before pursuing enemy. Now, it ought not to be forgotten that Tatia had to take up to guerilla tactics when his forces were already completely demoralised by previous defeats and when all the veterans had been either killed or disabled in the earlier stages of the war, and so it was quite natural that, in spite of his skill and insight into the guerilla's art, he should not be able to put them in practice owing to the lack of materials. Whatever the reason, one thing is clear that, more than once, Tatia had during his wonderful career as a general to leave the field through panic and fear striking his ranks; while Kumar Singh, like his prototype, the great Mahartta Shivaji, never allowed his army to become diffident, but created in them absolute confidence in themselves as well as in himself, their leader, by his personal valour and intrepidity and discipline; and he, also, exhibited matchless skill both in giving battle and in avoiding it—in both the positive and the negative sides of guerilla warfare; and therefore it is that, having trampled his foe into dust, in the midst of a proud victory, on an independent throne, and under the banner of freedom—the old, the brave, the great Indian could die an honourable death!

On the 26th of April, 1858, Kumar Singh died. No sooner did this actor pass off from the stage than another—equally brave, equally noble, and equally patriotic—appeared on the scene. This new general was no other than the younger brother of Kumar Singh. Raja Amar Singh, without allowing a moment's slackening in the vigour of the war, without taking a rest of even four days, marched straight on to knock at the gates of Arrah itself! Having heard of the defeat of Le Grand of Arrah, the British forces which had stopped on the other side of the Ganges had by this time crossed it; and the two generals, Brigadier Douglas and general Lugard, marched on Raja Amar Singh on the 3rd of May. At Bihiya, Hatampur, Dalilpur, and several other places, each alternate day, the English forces attacked the Revolutionaries. Therefore, now Amar Singh resorted to different tactics. If he saw that the enemy was gaining the upper hand, he would order his forces to divide themselves into small bands, to retire in divers but well-mapped-out directions and, thus rendering pursuit by the enemy hopelessly impossible, to get united again at the appointed signal. How, now, to fight with this invisible army was the chief question before the British. Every battle seemed to them quite decisive, but the very next moment the army of Amar Singh was as strong and as active at some other place as ever! No sooner he was driven from one end of the jungle then he appeared again in the second, and as soon as he was driven from that, he would wheel round and reign supreme in the first. At last, worn out, disgraced, and disappointed—the British general, Lugard, resigned on the 15th of June and returned to England to rest. His army, too, left the field and entered the camp.

And this was the signal for Amar Singh to reunite his bands, and to appear on the battle-field with the pomp of a victorious general. Now the police of Gaya were won over to fight for the freedom of the nation. Then, sending the English forces on a wrong scent, Amar Singh attacked Arrah itself and entered it. Nay, now he is actually entering back into that capital of Jagdishpur. July passed; August and September also passed ;-yet the banner of a free people was flashing forth from the towers of Jagdishpur and the Rana Amar Singh was reigning, the beloved monarch of a liberated people! Brigadier Douglas and his seven thousand English forces were sworn to finish him. Nay, they had even offered prizes-to anyone who would bring the head of Amar Singh by hook or crook. They had, by this time, cleared the jungles and made roads; from post to post, the British bands were constantly advancing; but nothing availed against the worthy successor of Kumar Singh. It is not possible for want of space to enumerate his different activities. Suffice it to say that the Rana Amar Singh fought in such a manner as to make his whole people think that Kumar Singh died not at all!

At last, the English decided to end the whole campaign by a supreme effort and seven different armies advanced from seven different directions on Jagdishpur. All the roads leading to Jagdishpur were thus closed up and the Rana was caught as if in a trap. The cordon slowly began to close round Amar Singh and, last, on the 17th of October, it tightened its grip on the capital itself. Alas! it is in this net that the liberty-loving lion is to be captured and killed! At the appointed time, all these forces rushed simultaneously from all directions into Jagdishpur and the helpless lion was hit—but, well done, Amar Singh, well done! It was the cage that was hit, and the lion had already escaped all unscathed!

For, though six divisions had advanced and fallen on the town as ordered, yet the seventh one was late by five hours and the shrewd Amar Singh, with all his forces, vanished by this very side, taking full advantage of the delay of that division of the foe.

Therefore, abandoning the plan which had proved so ineffectual as regards the crushing of the Behar Revolutionaries, the English government sent a division of mounted infantry to pursue them. This ever-increasing and ever-pursuing force of the enemy left not one moment of rest to Amar Singh. The new rifles that were introduced into the enemy's camp at this time had made the matchlocks of the Revolutionary forces almost useless, and the infantry found it impossible to outrun the horsemen's pursuit. Still Amar Singh talked not of surrender! On the 19th of October the English forces shut up the Revolutionaries, first in the village of Nonadi and , out of four hundred of them, they cut off three hundred! The remaining one hundred dashed out desperately into the field outside, like infuriated tigers, and fought a bloody battle with the new division of British forces that had just arrived. It was found in the end that out of these only three escaped—and one out of the three was the Rana Amar Singh who had been fighting all the while incognito. Many were the bloody encounters and many the pools of blood through which the Panday army had to swim across. But, still, the flag of liberty was unbent! So narrow were their escapes that, once, the very elephant of the Rana was captured; but the Rana jumped off from it and vanished. In this way, the Revolutionaries contested every inch of their ground, while being pressed onwards and onwards out of their ground, while being pressed onwards and onwards out of their province ; and now they had reached the hills of Kaimur, for 'the whole population of the district constantly and systematically misled the British pursuers by false information.'[9]

With this sympathy of the populace, the patriotic chief entered the Kaimur hills but was soon followed by the relentless foe pursuing in his track. Still there was no talk of surrender. Every hill and every dale, every hillock and every rock, fought on with the alien till the whole of the Panday army died fighting for the liberty of the land, for the honour of their Dharma! Died fighting, yes, for not only the men but even the women of that patriotic band did not return back to their homes as captives and slaves! The hundred and fifty ladies of the Royal palace of Raja Shrimant Kumar Singh, seeing that no hope or chance of success remained to them in this world, stood before the guns, set fire to the fuse with their own hands, and got themselves blown up into the—immortality!

Thus fought Behar for its birthrights against the foreign foe!

But Rana Amar Singh did not fall into the hands of the enemy. Fortune left him, but his unconquerable soul could never! But what became of him? —Where did he end his days? Bewildered History echoes back, 'where?'

* * *

---

9. Malleson's *Indian Mutiny*, Vol. IV, page 344.

CHAPTER IX

Moulvie Ahmad Shah

AFTER the fall of Lucknow, there remained no powerful nucleus to concentrate the forces of the Revolutionaries in the provinces of Rohilkhand and Oudh. The tide of British conquest that had been sweeping over the Doab and Behar had driven all the Revolutionaries from these provinces into the ever-narrowing circle of Oudh and Rohilkhand. By this irresistible pressure on all sides and by want o£ powerful stronghold the Revolutionaries had to give up the old system of open warfare and pitched battles and to take to guerilla tactics. Had they done so at the very start the chances of success had been overwhelmingly innumerable. But, better late than never! For though success was rendered extremely difficult, yet there was not the least suggestion in the Revolutionary camp of surrender or desertion. So, the leaders of Oudh and Rohilkhand decided to continue the War of Independence by pursuing guerilla tactics, and issued the following Proclamation and military order allover the provinces: 'Do not attempt to meet the regular columns of the infidels in open battle. because they are superior to you in discipline and they have big guns. But watch their movements, guard all the Ghats on the rivers, intercept their communications, stop their supplies, cut up their daks and posts, and keep constant hanging about their camp. Give the Feringhi no rest!'[1] Moulvie Ahmad Shah at once began to put into execution these orders. He began to hang about the camp of the British forces which were at Lucknow and camped at Bari, a place twenty-nine miles away from the Englsh camp. The Begum Hazrat Mahal was encamped at Bitaoli with six thousand men. In order to break both these forces, Hope Grant started from Lucknow with a strong force

---

1. Russel says : 'This general order bears marks of sagacity and points out the most formidable war we would encounter.'—*Diary*, page 276.

of three-thousand soldiers and a powerful artillery, first in the direction of Bari. The next day brought with it an incident which showed the wonderful courage and cleverness of the Revolutiunary scouts. The Moulvie had sent out some of his scouts to get correct information about the British force. On the same night they entered the camp of the English with perfect nonchalance. The English watchmen stopped them and asked, 'Who goes there?' We are the men of the 12th regiment!' was the answer. This answer was literally true, for all of them had indeed belonged to the 12th regiment. But how were the poor watchmen to know that this 12th regiment was one of those which rose in rebellion as far back as July of the previous year and had killed their English officer? The steady and firm step of these men, that resolute answer, and that fearless simplicity of behaviour drove away all suspicion about them, and the watchmen replied 'Alright!' The daring band entered unopposed into the English camp, obtained all the information that they wanted, and came out all unscathed to report it to their master!

Having thus informed himself of the exact situation and the plan of the British camp, the Moulvie quickly formed his plans, marched ahead, and took possession of a village four miles from Bari. The plan of the Moulvie was that, while his infantry should hold this village against the enemy, his cavalry should march ahead by a secret route and should wheel round and attack the rear of the British forces. He knew it for certain that the next morning the British general was coming to that very place, suspecting no harm and in a perfect sense of security. As soon as this unwary prey came into the trap, the Moulvie's infantry was to attack him from the front, while his cavalry was to fall on the enemy's flanks on rear. Malleson says: 'It was really a brilliant idea and did credit to his tactical skill.'

There were two things most necessary for the success

of this brilliant design. The one thing was to keep perfect secrecy about the forces of the Moulvie in the village; and the other was that the cavalry that was to make a flank attack should not rally forth and put the enemy on his guard before the front attack should be begun. The Moulvie did whatever he had to do. He sent his cavalry from Bari that same night by the route agreed on; he quietly took possession of the village and succeeded in concealing himself there, and so cleverly that the next morning actually saw the unsuspecting British general approaching the banks of the river. Half an hour more and the Britsh forces would be done for!

But in that half an hour, the splendid plan of the Moulvie was shattered to pieces by the impetuosity of the cavalry men. They had already occupied a very convenient place on the flank of the British forces and had been holding themselves ready to pounce upon the foe. But their leader, while lying in ambush, saw some guns unprotected in front of them and, forgetting the strict orders of the Moulvie, made for them with the intention of capturing them, and even captured and obtained possession of them for a while; but soon, the English woke to their danger, the guns were recaptured, and the whole plan of the Moulvie was shattered. For, this fighting at the rear opened the languid eyes of the English commander and he saw the danger in his rear as well as in his front. Seeing his plan thus nullified by the rashness of his cavalry, the Moulvie who was holding the village left it after a skirmish and marched off—to find another opportunity and to mature another design.

While Hope Grant was pressing the Revolutionaries upwards, and upwards, from Bari to Bitaoli, with a view to drive them out of Oudh, there on the other side, on the 15th of April, was being fought a hotly contested battle, near the fort of Ruiya. We have seen how, sometime before this, in the province of the Doab, the English army, being divided into separate divisions and marching by separate routes, pressed on the Revolutionaries simultaneously and systematically, sweeping off the whole province, till they drove them all into the town of Fatehgarh. In the same manner, a campaign had been organised and put into execution to sweep the Revolutionaries off the whole province of Oudh, by different British forces, from all possible quarters, pressing them onwards and upwards towards the northern frontier of Oudh. About the 1st of April, 1858, the total number of the white forces in India had risen to ninety-six thousand soldiers, besides which there were the loyal armies of the Sikhs. The brigades consisting of the Pathans, Pariahs, and other raw recruits, though originally raised in haste, had by this time become quite like veterans through constant experience on the field. Again, the contingent forces of the native princes which had been sent forth to the assistance of the English, were also busy in the field. The pick of these innumerable brown and white troops were now engaged in the supreme effort of reconquering Oudh. As described in the last chapter, Lugard and Douglas were sent into Behar. Sir Hope Grant was sent towards Bari and Bitaoli, and Walpole was ordered to march up from the banks of the Ganges. Thus, these different forces, including those of the commander-in-chief and others, were marching in a line to drive out the Revolutionaries to a man further and further to the north till they were pushed into Rohilkhand; and then, the idea was to annihilate them by one supreme effort. With this intention, Walpole too had started to do his own part on the 9th of April, 1858; and now, on the 15th of April, he was busy in attacking the fort of Ruiya which is fifty-one miles from Lucknow.

It was not that either the fort of Ruiya was very strong or that its owner Narapat Singh was a very big and rightly chieftain. But small Zemindar though he was, ever since this great sacrificial fire was lighted up on the field of liberty, this Narapat Singh had offered himself with his all-in-all, as a willing victim for the regeneration of his nation. The 15th of April saw a mighty English army, armed with the most modern artillery, attacking this little chief in his tiny fort. As he had not even two hundred and fifty men with him in the fort, the English naturally expected that the chief must have already evacuated the place. But, on that very morning, one of the white prisoners whom Narapat Singh had released came to the English camp and informed the general that he had heard Narapat Singh say that he would evacuate the fort but not until he had had his vengeance. —Not until a gory fight, not until one bloody defeat is inflicted will Narapt leave his fort!

What! This little chief is to inflict a bloody defeat? And then alone is he to evacuate the fort? Walpole was furious and ordered his men to attack the fort. The English forces, as usual, circulated a rumour that the forces of Narapat Singh numbered about two thousand! When we are sure of crushing this Narapat Singh, what other way of magnifying our sure victory than of exaggerating the strength of the adversary? So even Walpole agreed that the forces with Narapat must be at least a thousand and five hundred. This released English captive who attests to the fact of only two hundred and fifty men defending the fort, though an eye-witness, might be a mad man! The English forces advanced—and that too, not on the weak side of the fort though its weakness was well-known to them, but the brave general would insist on marching against the strongest face of the fort! The defender of the fort began to pour a shower of bullets as soon as they saw the British attacking the fort from among the trees in front of it. The shower grew hottest when the enemy approached the ditch. Out of a hundred and fifty who marched, forty-six English soldiers were killed on the spot. Grove could not move one step forward on account of the fire of the Pandays. Now then, the skilful Walpole, seeing this crisis at the strong face of the fort, took his guns and rushed against the weak side of it; and with such accuracy he aimed his guns, that the English cannon balls sent from this side crossed over the fort and fell right amidst the English forces on the other side! Many are the generals who fight with their enemies, but matchless and the first without a second is General Walpole, who would fight with both friend and foe with equal skill and bravery! At the sight of this matchless skill of the veteran gemeral, another general Hope, came forth to save the day-but alas! he is killed by the unbearable fire of the Revolutionaries. Even Grove is retiring—confusion worse confounded! The confused British army left the field and fell back, disgracefully repulsed!

The death of this brave general, Hope, came as a shock over all Englishmen resident in India. Lord Canning and Sir Colin, why, all England was overwhelmed with grief. Not even the death of hundreds of soldiers would have inflicted such a sorrow and mourning on the English nation as did the death of this Hope one of the bravest and most energetic of the English officers of that period. The tiny chieftain, Narapat Singh, had done what he said, 'he had his vengeance,' and then left the fort with his handful of men, and went on fighting with the unsullied banner of liberty in his hand!

After these different divisions had swept off the Revolutionaries from the province of Oudh towards the north and then to Rohilkhand, the commander-in-chief got all the forces united and marched on to Rohilkhand in person. All the leaders of the Revolutionaries had now assembled in Shahjahanpur. There was Nana Sahib of Cawnpore and Molvie Ahmad Shah. These two men had baffled all the innumerable attempts of the British generals to get hold of them and were still as energetic and un-conquered as ever. So, when the news was brought to Sir Colin that these two leaders of the Revolutionaries were within his reach in the same place and perhaps ignorant of his movements, Sir Colin formed the shrewd plan of closing the town from all sides. He marched and closed on Shahjahanpur—but only to find that the birds had flown away! It was but natural that Sir Colin should be extremely piqued at this, as he had ordered four different forces to guard all the four sides, and the Revolutionary leaders escaped by the side guarded by the commander-in-chief himself!

Now that the plan of Shahjahanpur was frustrated, Sir Colin was desirous of reducing at least the city of Bareilly. So, leaving a division of his forces with four guns in Shahjahanpur, he started and arrived on the 14th of May within a day's distance of Bareilly. The Rohilla, Khan Bahadur Khan was still holding out in this city. After the fall of Delhi and Lucknow, the Revolutionaries had been pouring into this still independent town of their party. Mirza Feroz Shah, the brave prince of the Delhi dynasty, Shrimant Nana Sahib, Moulvie Ahmad Shah, Shrimant Bala Sahib, Begum Hazrat Mahal, Raja Teja Singh, and many of the lesser leaders, had retreated into Rohilkhand and Bareilly, its capital, where still was waving the flag of a free people. And it was for this very reason that Sir Colin had vowed vengeance against this city. But in the Indian camp there was no talk of making any stand at the city itself, as the leaders of the Revolution had determined, even according to the general order they had just issued, to resist the enemy by guerilla tactics. Their plan was to evacuate the city and get scattered all over the fields of Rohilkhand. All preparations had been made for leaving the city and only the last order of evacuation remained to be given. But when the brave Rohilas actually saw the hated Feringhi just near the town, the majority of them refused to evacuate the city without first tasting the steel of the foe-until, once at least, they had given proof of their readiness to die for the cause of their nation and their faith.

The English forces that had surrounded that city were exceedingly strong. Their artillery was well-equipped and they had numerous guns; their cavalry and their infantry were well-armed and well-disciplined; and the command was in the hands of no less a general than the commander-in-chief Sir Colin Campbell himself. Against these, the guns of Khan Bahadur Khan could make no impression, and so, on that 5th of May, the Revolutionary guns had to be silent and the Revolutionary sword flashed forth. The sword belonged to the martyr-spirits who, in spite of the hopelessness of success, nay, in virtue of the hopelessness of success, instead of leaving the battle-field, preferred to embrace death with a smile on their lips and the unconquered and unconquerable faith in the holiness of their cause in their heart. To die while fighting in a good cause is the key to the gates of Heaven, that was their belief; and they knew that the cause of the freedom of a people was one of the best causes for the sake of which one could lay down one's life. So they unsheathed their swords and dashed like thunderbolt on the English forces. With green turbans on their heads, with a Kummerbund girded round their loins, and a silver ring inscribed with chosen sentences of the Koran in their finger, these terrible-looking Ghazis rushed up from the right, holding their head behind their shields, with their swords shining aloft in the sun, and shouting wildly their war-cry of 'Din, Din! They closed with the British troops with a tremendous shock, and, at this desperate attack though they were very few, the British soldiers were startled and confused and swept away; the 42nd Highlanders tried to check their onrush-but the death-dealing Ghazis still advanced, while some of them even succeeded in reaching to the rear of the British forces! Not one of them returned back—all of them fell while fighting and mowed down the English soldiery like sheaves before the scythe! They fell; they fell like lions, despising even the thought of retreat or surrender; one only fell without being bayoneted by the enemy. Why? Wait a minute and the anwer comes; for, there is coming up to this spot the Commander-in-Chief of the British forces; nay, he has come here! And just then this martyr, who had been pretending death, jumps up from among the corpses and falls on the commander, but, alas! a loyal Sikh standing by the commander scents this danger and cuts the Ghazi off![2]

Of the few instances of the immortal bravery of martyrdom in the history of the world, none can be greater than this!

Next day, having baftled the attack of the British to capture them, the Revolutionaries, with Khan Bahadur Khan at their head, marched out of Bareilly on the 7th of may, 1858, and the English forces took possession of the evacuated capital of Rohil-khand.

Disappointed on account of the safe escape of Khan Bahadur Khan out of his clutches, but still feeling triumphant for the capture of Bareilly, Sir Colin was standing in his mighty camp. Just then, there rose one deafening cry allover the camp—the cry of 'The Moulvie! the Moulvie!! the Moulvie, again!!!'

It was an extermely surprising design that the Moulvie was hatching there at the town of Shahjahanpur. Having batlled Sir Colin, it was not simply to avoid a fight that Nana Sahib and the Moulvie had left Shahajahanpur. All the government buildings in the town had been demolished by the order of Nana Sahib even before they left the town. The keen-sighted leaders had rightly gussed that the English commander would leave only a few troops in Shahajahanpur, and would proceed to Bareilly; and they had decided that, when he was thus away, the Moulvie should wheel round and fall on the city, crush the English forces there, and thus avenge the loss of Bareilly by the sack of Shahjahanpur. This was their plan and all things turned up as they guessed. For the British commander did go to Bareilly, leaving only a small detachment, though with a strong complement of artillery composed of four field-pieces. And the English

2. *Russel's Diary.*

detachment had to encamp on a plain, unprotected and open, as Nana Sahib had already caused all fortified places to be pulled down. On the 22nd of May, Moulvie Ahmad Shah started for Shahjahanpur by rapid marches, while his prey was indulging in false security. But, after midnight, the forces of the Moulvie—none can say by whose foolish obstinacy—stopped for a while within four miles of the town. This stay made the excellent plan barren of fruits, as, 'native spies employed by the British were on the alert, and one of them flew with the intelligence of his dangerous vicinity to Colonel Hale at Shahjahanpur.' As soon as this traitorous spy brought the news, the British commander moved in the newly-built fortified position with his soldiers. The Moulvie pressed on though now his prey was awake and occupying a strong position. He attacked and occupied the town, captured the fort, and levied a tax on the rich inhabitants of the place for the supplies of his forces. Even Malleson admits that, 'in acting thus, he simply conformed to the custom of war in Europe.' Not only this; but in a war of independence, when a handful of noble spirits offer their fresh blood to wipe off the shame and slavery of a whole nation, it is the duty of the people to support them voluntarily. After taking possession of the town the Moulvie brought eight guns, and began a cannonade on the fortified place where his foe was under shelter.

When this news reached Sir Colin at Bareilly on the 7th of May though he was surprised, his joy knew no bounds. The lost opportunity, which had worried the Commander-in-Chief so much ever since the escape of the Moulvie some days before, seemed now about to be restored by the action of the Moulvie himself. And therefore, taking the utmost precaution possible, Sir Colin started by forced marches to pounce upon his prey. Now, it was clear that there was no loop-hole whatsoever left through which the Moulvie Ahmad Shah could escape. From the 11th of May, for three days, there was a continuous fight. It was, indeed, impossible for the Moulvie to escape. So from all sides the different Revolutionary leaders brought all their forces together, in order to save this most popular and most energetic of patriots. The Begum of Ayodhya, Mayyan Sahib, the king of Mahmadi, the Prince Feroze Shah of Delhi, Nana Sahib of Cawnpore—all these leaders poured in with their forces, before the 15th of May, to help the flag of liberty, now in such immediate danger in Shabjahanpur. Thus reinforced, the Moulvie marched out of Shahjahanpur, warring night and day with his now discomfited foe, and again escaped the coils that the commander-in-chief had prepared for him. So sure was Sir Colin of capturing the Moulvie that, in view of the certainty of the ruin of the Revolutionary party at Shahjahanpur, he had already issued orders for dividing his forces again and sending them to different directions. And, having dashed to pieces these orders and hopes of the enemy, where did the Moulvie go? He entered Oudh—the very province which the English had, after a year's trouble and bloodshed and with the greatest difficulty, succeeded in sweeping clear of the Revolutionaries. Sir Colin conquered Ayodhya—the Moulvie occupied Rohilkhand; now Sir Colin comes and conquers Rohilkhand-the Moulvie wheels back and again occupies Oudh!

In such a dogged manner and with such bravery did the Moulvie fight with the foreign foe.

The British power is now bent on crushing him and putting an end to his dangerous activities. Is there anyone who would assist them in this plight? Whose sword is mighty enough to kill this powerful head of the Revolution, whom the sword of Sir Colin has proved too blunt to cut? What is the best way to accomplish this end?

What is the best way? There need not be any such anxiety in the English camp. Is it not true that the British sword had. many a time before the present, proved equally helpless and unsuccessful in eradicating the enemies of

British power in India? Well then, those who could and did save England in all those periods of danger and despair would come forward to save her once more. If the English sword is too blunt to cut to pieces this Indian patriot, let the dagger of treachery accomplish the task!

After his re-entry into Oudh, while trying to offer as much and dogged a resistance to the foreigner as he could, the Moulvie thought it would be a great help to the new storm that he was preparing to raise in Oudh if the Raja of Powen would lend the little might he possessed to drive out the alien from the land. With this purpose, he sent a request sealed with the Royal seal of the Begum to this Raja at Powen. This tiny Raja was quite shocked at the mere mention of war and battlefield. Yet, as treacherous as he was cowardly, he wrote back that he would like to see the Moulvie personally. In answer to this invitation, the Moulvie started to see this Raja, But, to the Moulvie's great surprise, he found the gates of the town closed and the walls of it guarded by armed men; and in the midst of them, he found standing the Raja Jagannath Singh himself, with his brother by his side. Though the Moulvie knew the meaning of this sight, still undaunted, he began to hold a parley with the Raja. The wretch on the walls of the town was naturally the last man to appreciate his eloquence. When it became clear that the crowd was not going to open the gates willingly, the Moulvie ordered his *Mahut* to goad on the elephant on which he was sitting to break open the gates of the fort. One storke more of the mighty animal's head—and the gates would have been forced. But, the brother of the Raja took aim and Moulvie Ahmad Shah was shot dead by the hand of that wretched coward? The fat Raja and his brother at once came out of the gate, severed the head of the Moulvie from his body and, covering it up in a cloth, ran forth to the nearest British *Thana*, thirteen miles from the place, to the city of Shahjahanpur. Here, the British officers were at their table in the dining-room. The Raja came in, unpacked the burden which he had held forth as a trophy, and let roll on the ground, by the feet of the officers, the head of the Moulvie still gushing with blood! Next day, the civilised Britishers hung on the *kotwali* the head of an enemy who had fought against them so bravely and so honourably, and the fat brute of Powen was rewarded with fifty thousand Rupees for this, his nefarious act or treachery!

As soon as the news of his death reached England, the relieved Englishmen felt that '*the most formidable enemy*' of the British in Northern India was no more![3] In person, the Moulvie was tall, lean and muscular, with large deep-set eyes, beetle brows, a high aquiline nose, and lantern jaws. The life of this brave Mahomedan shows that a rational faith in the doctrines of Islam is in no way inconsistent with, or antagonistic to, a deep and, all powerful love of the Indian soil; and that the true believer in Islam will feel it a pride to belong to, and a privilege to die for, his mother-country! Even the English historian Malleson, in no way inclined to assess rightly-far less to exaggerate-the virtues of the Revolutionist leaders, is carried off by his inner feelings and, forgetting for the moment that he is an Englishman, remarks : 'The Moulvie was a very remarkable man of his capacity as a military leader many proofs were given during the revolt, but none more decisive than those recorded in this chapter. No other man could boast that he had twice foiled Sir Colin Campbell in the field! .....Thus died the Moulvie Ahmad'allah (*sic*) of Fyzabad. If a patriot is a man who plots and fights for the independence, wrongfully destroyed, of his native country, then most certainly the Moulvie was a true patriot. He had not stained his sword by assassination; he had connived at no murders; he had fought manfully, honourably, and stubbornly in the field against the strangers who had seized his country; and, his memory is entitled to the respect

3. Holmes's History of the *Indian Mutiny*, page 539.

of the brave and true-hearted of all nations.'[4]

* * *

CHAPTER X

Ranee Lakshmi Bai

GIVE up my Jhansi? I will not. Let him try to take who dares! With this challenge the heroic Ranee of Jhansi rose against the British and as it is recorded in previous parts of this History she assumed the leadership of the Revolution, drove the English and began to rule at Jhansi as the Queen of the province. The forces of the Revolution wreaked a bloody vengeance on the English people and army and left not a trace of their rule at Sagar, Naogaon, Banda, Banapur, Shabgarh and Karki. The people everywhere hailed the Queen as their own. She then busied herself-in restoring order and peace in her liberated province.

The Ranee's daily life at this period has been described as follows :— 'The Bai got up at five in the morning and took a bath with fragrant *attar*. After dressing and she generally wore a *Chanderi Saree* of faultless white—she would sit for her daily prayers. First, she dropped the necessary water as a *prayaschitta* for keeping hair on her head after her husband's death; then, she used to worship the *Tulsi* in the *Tulsi* grove. Then began the *Parthiva Puja* at which the Durbar musicians would sing in choir. *Puraniks* would then start reading the *Puran*. Then, Sirdars and dependants came and she returned their usual salutes. Being very keen of memory, even if a single man among the seven hundred and fifty who paid their respects to her in the morning was not present, the very next day, the Bai would not fail to inquire why he did not come the previous day.

---

4. Malleson's *Indian Mutiny*, Vol. IV, page 381.

After the worship of God began the dinner. After dinner, she would. take an hour's siesta unless there was urgent work to do. Then she would order the presents of the morning to be brought before her, which was done on silver trays covered over with silk cloths. those things that she liked, she accepted; the others were given over to the *Kothiwalla* (minister of the presents department) for distribution amongst her servants. At three she went to the Durbar, when she usually put on male attire. She wore a *pyjama* a coat of dark blue, a cap on the head, and a beautiful turban on the top of it, a *dupeta* of embroidered cloth round the slender waist, and the sword decked with gems by her side. Attired in this wise, this fair woman looked like Gauri herself. Sometimes, she wore the female dress. After her husband's death, she never wore *nath* or similar ornaments. Her hands had round them bangles of diamond; she wore a small necklace of pearls round her neck and a diamond ring on her little finger. These were the only jewels worn by the Bai Sahib. Her hair was gathered up to-gether behind. She wore a white *saree* and a plain bodice. Thus sometimes in male attire and sometimes in female, the Bai Sahib used to honour the Durbar by her presence. Those assembled in Durbar never used to see her person. For the room in which she sat was separate from, and only opened into, the Durbar hall. Gold carving adorned the doors. and over these fell gracefully the *chintz* curtain, embroidered with gold cloths. In this room sat the Bai Sahib on a *gadi* of soft down, leaning on a soft pillow. Outside the door, two pages with maces of silver and gold always attended. Opposite the room, Lakshman Rao Dewanji stood with a bundle of important documents in his hand, and beyond him sat the Registrars of the Durbar. Being very keen and intelligent, the Bai quickly grasped every matter brought before her, and her orders were clear and definite and to the point. Sometimes she wrote her orders out herself. She was very careful in affairs of justice, and decided civil and criminal cases alike with great ability.

Ranee Sahib worshipped Mahalakshmi devoutly. The temple of that Goddess was situated on the banks of a lake filled with lotus flowers, and every Friday and Tuesday the Bai visited the temple. One day, it so happened that after the Bai had returned from the temple and was passing through the south gate, she saw thousands of beggars blocking the passage and creating a disturbance. So, she inquired of the Minister, Lakshman Rao Pande, the reason of this. He inquired and informed her that the people were very poor, and that they suffered immensely on account of excessive cold, and that, therefore, they requested that the Bai would kindly consider their condition. The Bai felt very grieved for these poor people, and she at once issued orders kind-hearted that she was—that, on the fourth day from thence, a gathering of beggars should take place, where everyone should be provided with a thick coat and a cap and a blanket either white or black. The very next day, all the tailors of the town were given orders to make caps and coats. On the day appointed, it was proclaimed that all the beggars were to gather in front of the palace. Poor people, too, had been included in this gathering. All were given clothes by the Bai and they went away satisfied. ...In the fight with Nathe Khan when the wounded men. were brought into the city, the Bai herself would insist on being present when their wounds were being dressed. Her very presence soothed their pain, and they felt themselves sufficiently rewarded, by the kind and sympathetic interest she took in their well being. The Ranee grieved at their grief, gave them ornaments and medals, patted them, and showed such sympathy that others, in-stead of being disheartened at the sight of these wounded soldiers felt that they could even give up their lives for the sake of the Ranee. The grandeur of the Bai's processions passes description. On the occasions of the visits to the temple of Mahalakshmi, she started sometimes in a palanquin, and sometimes on horseback. When in the palanquin, the palanquin would be covered with curtains of gold embroidered cloths tied with golden ribbon. When she was on horseback, in male attire, the end of a thin and beautiful batti floated on her back and it fitted her admirably. The national flag of freedom was carried before her, with the band playing military music. Two hundred Europeans followed, the flag and a hundred horsemen rode before and behind her. With the palanquin came the *karbharies*, ministers, feudatories and other officers like Bhayya Sahib Upasane; and others either rode or followed on foot. Sometimes troops accompanied the procession. When the Bai started from the palace, the *choughada* on the fort made sweet music. The *choughada* of the *nagarkhana* of Mahalaksmi started at the same time![1]

And thus, from the Vindhyas to the Jumna, there was not a vestige of British authority left. Brahmins, Moulvies, Sirdars, Dorakdars, Sepoys, the police, Rajas, Raos, bankers, villagers, all were desirous fighting for only one thing, and that was Independence! And to unite together these thousand voices in one harmonious whole, the Lakshmi of Jhansi declared with her sweet but firm voice, 'None can have my Jhansi; he who dares may try!'

Very rarely had the world heard such a firm 'No!' Generous and liberal to a fault India has always been pronouncing and swearing by 'I shall give !', 'I shall give!' so far, But here was a strange phenomenon today — a set face and a stern voice which said I will not give! I will not give up my Jhansi!' Would to heaven, O Mother, that everyone, of thy sons and daughters had said the same! The Feringhi was taken aback at this unexpected assertion;'and Sir Hugh Rose was sent with five thousand armed 'men and a considerable number of guns to gauge the extent of the disturbance and to quell it.

In the beginning of 1858, the English had drawn up a

1. D. B. Parasnis's *Life of Lakshmi Bai*, Pages 147-151.

complete military plan for the reconquest of all the territory, from the Himalayas to the Vindhyas, which was under the Revolutionaries, The whole territory was divided into two portions, and to each of them a huge army was sent to subdue it, We have in an earlier chapter described how commander-in-chief Sir Colin Campbell marched upwards from Allahabad to the north of the Ganges and the Jumna and with his big army, conquered the Doab, and crossed the Ganges and marched on Lucknow; how after destroying Lucknow, he extinguished the flames of insurrection raging in Behar, in Benares and round it, and in Oudh; how he forced all the Revolutionaries into Rohilkhand, where the final engagement took place, and how, thus, the northern portion of the territory which was in the hands of the Revolutionaries was reconquered by the English. While Sir Colin was advancing from the north of the Jumna towards the Himalayas, Sir Hugh Rose advanced to conquer the southern portion lying between the Jumna and the Vindhyas, In the north, the Sikhs, the Gurkhas, and other Indian troops and feudatories had joined Sir Colin; so also in the south, Sir Hugh Rose had on his side the help of the princes of Hyderabad, Bhopal and other states. He had in addition, got the valuable assitance of the troops of Madras and Bombay and the Hyderabad contingent, To mention specially that the Indian troops had joined Sir Hugh Rose is unnecessary. For, to mention that Sir Hugh Rose was successful would imply the first proposition. For the English to obtain a victory, of themselves, is as impossible as the most impossible thing in the world. The traitorous Indian troops thus collected together for conquring the southern parts were divided into two divisions. One was under the command of Brigadier Whitlock who was to start from Jubbulpore and, subduing the provinces on the way, was eventually to join Sir Hugh Rose. The other was under Sir Hugh Rose himself. As soon as Whitlock started from Jubbulpore, Sir Hugh was also to start from Mhow; he was to advance through Jhansi on Kalpi. According to the plan of campaign, Sir Hugh started from Mhow on the 6th of January 1858 and, after a fight, he captured the fort of Raigarh. From thence, he advanced to Sagar, released the prisoners kept there by the Revolutionaries, advanced further south, reducing various positions of the enemy on the way, captured Banapur on the 10th of March, and reconquered the famous fort of Chanderi. On the 20th of march, the triumphant English army encamped about fourteen miles from Jhansi. By these many struggles, bands of Revolutionaries distributed all-over the country from the banks of the Narbada upwards, now crowded into Jhansi; and that is why Sir Hugh advanced with great dispatch on Jhansi to reduce this stronghold of the Revolutionaries. But Lord Canning and Sir Colin both issued orders to Sir Hugh first to relieve the Raja of Charkhari who was being besieged by Tatia. This order, if he obeyed it, would have spoiled Sir Hugh's plan of reducing Jhansi. What was he to do? He could neither disobey nor find his way to obey the orders. As, in these trying circumstances, the best interest of the British government lay in advancing on Jhansi, Sir Robert Hamilton took upon himself the whole responsibility of disobeying the orders of the two highest authorities in Hindusthan; and the British army, emboldened by the high national feeling, advanced towards Jhansi, hopeful of victory. But the English army suffered enormously as soon as they set foot on the soil of Jhansi. For they found, to their great surprise, that all the tract of land surrounding Jhansi had been laid waste by order of the Queen in order that the enemy should have no supplies of any sort. Not a blade of corn in the fields, not a vestige of grass on the meadows, not a tree which could afford shelter; So had william of Orange, when there appeared to be a possibility of the Netherlands falling into the hands of the Spanish tyrant and invader, ordered that the dykes be opened and the sea let in, rather than that the country should fall in the hands of the enemy. And this day Jhansi had adopted a similar course.

The same terrible thunder is in her voice; her eyes are spouting forth the red flames of anger! Mardan Singh, Raja of Banapur, the enraged chief of Shahagarh, the brave Thakurs, with their lives in their hands, Sirdars of Bundelkhand, resolute as ever, with their many followers—all these hot incendiary elements in the interior of Jhansi are burning and flame-red. The flames leap up even as the *Jaripatka*; and look, the central figure of the whole fight is there, shining above all! Aye, she is the central idea, the flashing impersonation of Swaraj ! She is the inspiration, she is the incarnation of Liberty!

In spite of the barrenness of the country around, the English approached Jhansi. For, thanks to the loyalty of the Scindia and the Raja of Tehri, the force was throughout the operations abundantly supplied with grass, firewood, and vegetables.[2] As the Scindia and the Raja of Tehri are helping the Feringhis, surrounded as you are by treachery and disloyalty, betrayed by relations as by strangers, you have not the slightest hope of success. Why not then avoid extinction by surrendering to the English? But, surrender? And for the Ranee of Jhansi ? Dewan Lakshman Rao. Moro Punt Tambe, brave *Thakurs* and Sirdars, all heroes of Liberty, if you surrender, you will be saved; if you fight, you will die. Which will you choose?

Jhansi answered from her thousand mouths, sternly, in the words of the Scripture, 'As everyone who is born must die, why sully fair fame uselessly?'

So, it was determined to give battle to the English for the honour of the country. And Jhansi was busy by night and by day preparing for the fight. Brave men, there were many in her army; but trained men, there were very few. Want of discipline was very apparent. The Queen herself, however, led the whole army. On every rampart and every gate, she was moving about actively; she was standing where

2. Malleson's *Indian Mutiny*, Vol. V, page 110.

guns were being planted and moved into position; she was busy selecting clever gunners; and she was to be found everywhere inspiring heroism even in the coldest hearts. The learned Brahmins of Jhansi were praying for the success of the country. Its temples blessed the soldier who went to the field, and tended the wounded who returned from battle; its workmen wery busy preparing ammunition and other necessaries for war. The men of Jhansi manned their guns, loaded the muskets; its women carried ammunition, built *Top Khanas*, supplied provisions.[3] When the night of the 23rd fell, sounds of battle-drums were heard throughout the town and lighted torches shone forth at frequent intervals from the fort. The guards fired a few shots too. The morning of the 24th approached. No more delay now! The *Ghanagarj* (thunder clap) gun began its work. The noise made by that gun was terrific.

We shall quote an eye witness's account of the early stages of the siege.

'From the 25th, the engagement began in right earnest. The enemy poured in a heavy fire all day and night. In the night came cannon-balls on the fort and the city. The sight was terrible to see. A cannon-ball of fifty or sixty pounds weight would look as small as a tennis ball but red like live charcoal. During the day one could not see these balls clearly for daylight, but in the night, they were clearly visible and gave a weird appearance to the night. On the 26th, at midday, the English silenced the guns on the southern gate, and not a man could make a stand there. All men in the field were nearly disheartened at this. Then, the gunner on the western gate moved the gun round and fired at the enemy; the third shot killed the best gunner in the English army, and the English gun was silenced in its turn. At this the Bai Sahib

3. 'The women were seen working in the batteries and carrying ammunition, etc.'- Sir Hugh Rose.

was very pleased and presented the gunner with a silver anklet. The name of the brave gunner was Gulam Ghose Khan. He had displayed similar skill in the engagement with Nathe Khan also.

'On the fifth or the sixth day, the same sort of engagement took place. For four or five hours, the Bai's guns were working wonders and the English lost heavily. Many of their guns, too, were silenced for some time. Then again, the English guns would be more vigorous, and the Jhansi troops would be disheartened and their guns silenced. On the seventh day, at sunset, the gun to the left was disabled. None could stand there. The battlement was destroyed owing to the enemy's fire. But in the night, eleven masons were brought under cover of blankets to the walls of the fort, and the work was completed before the day dawned. Thus, the battlement was repaired, and the English, to their great surprise, found the Jhansi gun in working order. At this time, the English were careless. They suffered considerably and their guns were disabled for quite a long time.

'On the morning of the eighth day, the English army went for Shankar Killa. The English had very expensive and modern telescopes and with their aid, they began to pour a heavy fire on the reservoir of water within the fort. Of the six or seven who approached near for taking water, four were killed; the others ran leaving their vessels there. As they could not get water for nearly four hours, even baths and other ordinary functions could not be carried on. Now, the gunners on the western and southem gates stopped the guns of the English attacking the Shankar Killa, by a contiuned fire on them. Then it became possible to get water from the reservoir for bath and dinner. There was a powder factory in the tamarind grove. As soon as two mounds of powder were prepared, it was taken to the sellers to be stocked. A cannon-ball fell on the factory, and thirty men and eight women were killed. On the same day, there was a great turmoil. There was a terrible fight. The fighters were shouting loudly. There was a terrific noise from muskets, and guns fighting heavily. Trumpets and bugles were sounding everywhere. Dust and smoke filled the air. Many gunners on the ramparts and a number of Sepoys were killed. Others were appointed in their place. The Bai Sahib was working very hard. She looked to everything, issued the necessary orders, and repaired every point of weakness. By this, the men in the army were very much encouraged and fought continually. On account of this determined resistance, the English, in spite of all their powder and ammunition, could not enter the fort till the 31st of March.[4]

But pressed as she is by this constant succession of disasters, why is Queen Lakshmi looking so earnestly in that particular direction? And see, she is smiling too! Be ready now and fire your salutes; let triumphal drums beat loudly; let war-cries rend the air! For there is Tatia Tope advancing with his army to aid Jhansi !

Tatia Tope has come with his army to dishearten the English army and to give courage to Jhansi. After the defeat of Wyndham at Cawnpore and Sir Colin's victory, Tatia crossed the Ganges and joined Shrimant Nana. Then, leaving Nana, he crossed the Jumna near Kalpi. As the Raja of Charkhari refused to help in the war for the country started by the Peshwa, Tatia, as representative of the Peshwa, attacked his capital, punished the traitor well, captured twenty-four of his guns, and took from him a contribution of three lacs of Rupees. And then Tatia turned towards Kalpi. There, he received a letter from Ranee Lakshmi Bai requesting him to come to Jhansi and relieve the siege. He sent the note to the Rao Sahib Peshwa, the chief in authority; and as soon as he got the orders, he charged the rear of the Engiish army. It is on seeing him that a smile of hope has

4. D. B. Parasnis's Lile of Lakshmi Bai, page 187- 193.

come to the lips of Lakshmi. These two had played together as children in the palace at Brahmavarta, without anyone noticing them particularly. To-day they are playing on the battle-field; the one, on the fortifications of Jhansi, is standing amidst rings of flaming fire, the other is approaching close to the Betwa, with his twenty-two thousand troops. While playing as children, people hardly noticed them; to-day, the whole world is looking on their game!

Tatia had under him, now, the largest number of troops he ever had, and hence the English were not a little disconcerted. They would have been completely so in the battle too, handful as they were. For, in front of them was the Ranee Lakshmi Bai; behind them was this Mahratta tiger, with his twenty-two thousand claws. Why should he not, then, tear Sir Hugh to pieces and eat him up? He advanced to do this, but his twenty-two thousand claws seemed all of a sudden disabled, they could hardly be lifted. And what could even a tiger do without his claws? Alas! A most shameful poltroonish cowardice was exhibited by the Revolutionary troops on the river Betwa. The army of Jhansi was to attack the rear, and Tatia was to attack the front; the plan was admirable. But the English, with the dash of despair, advanced on Tatia and opened fire on Jhansi. This nullified the two attacks of the aggressive party. One determined attack, like that of the Mawalas of Shivaji or the select band of Kumar, and vultures had fed upon the Union Jack and its followers. But the English charged straight on the enemy. The cowards did not even offer fight, and-was it treachery or terror-not a cannon shot from Jhansi was heard. So, the army and its commander were routed and ran away. Plentiful military supplies were captured by the English, Tatia's guns fell into their hands, and one thousand and five hundred of the Revolutionaries were killed in the pursuit. Fifteen hundred people killed in the flight! Mad men and fools! Instead of dying the death of cowards while fleeing, if you had only attacked Sir Hugh Rose, you would have died the death of the Ghazis of Bareilly, you would have destroyed the whole army with Sir Hugh Rose, and your name would have lived for ever! Yet God forgive you! If not our respect, you deserve at least our sympathy. For, howsoever you died, you died for the liberty of your country! May my country learn from your death at least the lesson that soldiers who fly to live, die, and that those who fight to die, live!

And for death was Ranee Lakshmi Bai fighting! Why then, this hopelessness on the part of Sirdars, Thakurs, and Sepoys? For nine days and nine nights, you stood the deadly charge of gun-fire in the hope that Tatia Tope would soon come to your aid. When he came, you shouted for delight; by the defeat of Tatia on the 1st of April, not only that joy but the very hope of victory is dashed to pieces; and those supplies, to deprive the the enemy of which thousands of lives had been sacrificed, have fallen with ease into the enemy's hands. Tatia's ammunition and guns also have fallen into their hands. All this is certainly true. But, why this despair? The enemy may render it impossible for you to live victorious, but he cannot deprive you of glory. There is nothing to despair for, then! And stop, hear the steady, firm, courageous voice of Ranee Lakshmi.

'It was not relying on the Peshwa that Jhansi fought so long nor does she require his help to continue her fight in the future. So far, your self-respect, your daring, your determination and your bravery have been exhibited by you most admirably. I urge to do the same now and to fight with courage and desperation.'

Aye, fight with desperation, be ready, let the battle-drums beat, and the trumpets sound! Let war-cries rend the air and let big guns thunder forth! The 3rd of April has dawned and the last assault of the English on Jhansi has begun. They are coming from all sides and pressing bard. Start, then, in right. good, deadly earnest! See how tbe goddess of war has taken the sword and see how she is making her way through the troops. She is moving about with lightning rapidity, presenting some with golden bracelets, some with dresses; some she is touching with sacred touch to pat, to some she is offering her sweet smile; others she is encouraging with her heroic words. So now! Gulam Ghose Khan and Kuar Khuda Bhaksh,'let the fire be most deadly! The enemy is storming the main gate and the fortifications, ladders have been planted at eight different places. 'Har, Har, Mahadev!' From the fort, from ramparts, and from houses came a perfect shower of bullets, a constant succession of shots. The deep-mouthed cannon are vomiting forth burning red hot balls. 'Maro Feringhiko!' Lieutenant Dick and Lieutenant Meiklejohn have mounted the ladders and are calling upon their men to follow them. Boom, boom! Instantly, the daring Englishmen fell in the jaws of death! Anyone coming behind? Lieutenant Bonus and heroic Lieutenant Fox, you seem anxious for death—your desire shall be accomplished;—die, then! Seeing these four heroes who had scaled with the greatest difficulty shot down, the ladders trembled. They swayed and broke under the weight of the English troops. The English sounded the bugle to retire; the army began to go back—it went back, the soldiers concealing themselves behind every stray stone![5]

A strong defence was thus offered at the principal gate.

5. 'No sooner did we turn into the road leading towards the gate, than the enemy's bugle sounded, and a fire of indescribable fierceness opened upon us from the whole line of the walls and from the tower of the fort overlooking this site. For a time it appeared like a sheet of fire, out of which burst a store of bullets, round shots, and rockets destined for our annihilation... .But the fire of the enemy waxed stronger, and amidst the chaos of sounds, of volleys of musccketry and roaring of cannon, hissing and bursting rockets, stink-pots, infernal machines, huge stones, blocks of wood, and trees, all hurled upon our heads, it seemed as though Pluto and the Furies had been loosened upon us, carrying death amongst us fast. At this instant a bugle sounded on our right for the Europeans to retire.'—Lowe's *Central India*, page 254.

But who is giving forth that tragic wail near the southern ramparts? May it be that mean treachery has lost the Morcha gate? Yes, unfortunately yes; the English have captured the gate, with the aid of treachery—so it is said—and they have mounted the ramparts, and are advancing rapidly on. There was no other thought that day but to kill or be killed! Once within the city, the English gave no quarter and streams of blood flowed freely. The English, taking one position after another, massacring, firing, destroying—came right up to the palace. As soon as the palace was forced, thousands of Rupees were looted, guards were massacred, and buildings were destroyed. At last, alas! Jhansi had fallen into the enemy's hands!

Standing on the ramparts, the Ranee looked back for one moment at Jhansi. Before her rose the hideous picture of the terrible disaster that had happened near the south gate. The enemy had, after all, defiled her Jhansi! Her eyes were ablaze with anger; she was almost mad with rage. She took up her sword and, with her small force of a thousand or fifteen hundred men, she marched down the fort. The tigress to avenge her cubs runs not so fleetingly. As soon as she saw the white troops near the southern gate, she rushed for them, and then, 'swords crossed, the two armies were mixed up before you could count even fifty; swords flourished and dealt hard blows. Many Englishmen were killed. The rest ran towards the town and began to fire shots from under cover!' By this sight of Feringhi blood, the anger of this Kali was a little appeased, and now she saw that it was foolhardy to fight alone so far from the fort. But echoes of such daring heroism were now to be heard in every street in the city. Fifty stablemen in the palace, while the whole town and the palace itself was bathed in blood shed by English swords, refused to give up the stables!' 'Surrender' was word not to be found in their dictionary. Everyone of these men cut down the enemy as hard as he could, and it was only when everyone of them was killed that the *paga* fell into the enemy's hands! The English had by now, rendered the whole town desolate. Everyone who fell into their hands from children of five to old men of eighty, was massacred; the whole city was set fire to; wailings from the wounded and the dying, and the cries of those who were killed, filled the air. A huge wail rose from the whole town!

When the Queen stood on the walls of the fortress (which the enemy had decided to storm only the next day on account or its strength), looking at this sad, sad picture, she was smitten with grief and tears started to her eyes! The Queen of Jhansi wept! Those beautiful eyes were red with weeping! Her Jhansi to be reduced to this! Then she looked up and saw the flag of the Feringhi flying over the walls of Jhansi, and a strange fire shone from those weeping eyes! All glory to her courage! But why is this messenger running hard towards her? He said, 'Your Majesty, the pre-eminenty brave Sirdar who guarded the chief gate of the fort, Sirdar Kuar Khuda Buksh, and Gulam Ghose Khan, the chief gunner of the artillery, have both been shot down by the English!' What a blow this to the already afflicted Queen! What a succession of disasters this! What is your next plan, then Queen? Aye, one and one alone! She said to the messenger, who was no other than an old Sirdar, 'I have determined to blow myself up with the fort, setting fire to the ammunition with my own hands.' With her *Jaripatka* she must be—if not on the throne, at least on the pyre!

Hearing this, the old Sirdar calmly replied, 'Your Majesty, as it is not safe to be in this neighbourhood now, your Majesty should leave the fort to-night breaking through the enemy's camp, and should join the Pesbwa's forces. If death comes on the way, the conquest of heaven by a dip in the sacred waters of the battle-field is always at hand!' Lakshmi said, 'I should choose to die on the battle-field, but, being a woman, I fear that the enemy might insult my person!' To this the whole Durbar answered with one voice: 'Insult! So long as there is life in the body of the least among us, our sword shall cut to pieces the enemy who would dare so much as touch your sacred person!'

Well then, the night had fallen; Lakshmi greeted all her dear subjects and gave them her blessings for the last time! Her subjects were full of tears at the thought that she was leaving Jhansi, perhaps for ever. She took a select number of horsemen with her. An elephant with jewels on him was placed in the middle and Ranee lakshmi descended the fort amidst cries of 'Har, Har, Mahadev !' She put on male apparel a steel armour covered her person, a *Jammia* was in her girdle; a fine sword hung from her belt, a silver cup was in her *Pudder*, and her adopted child Damodar was on her back, tied in a silk *Dhoti*. Thus accoutred, riding on a noble white steed, this queen, Lakshmi looked like the goddess of war. When the north gate came, the sentry who belonged to the traitor army of the Tehri State asked, 'Who goes there?' 'The army of Tehri is going to the aid of Sir Hugh Rose,' was the answer. The sentry was satisfied and the Ranee advanced, evading the English sentry too in a similar manner. One maid, one *bargeer,* and ten or fifteen horsemen formed her body-guard, and marched through the camp of the enemy. But her other horsemen were stopped by the English on suspicion and had to fight hard. Moro Pant Tambe, wounded though he was, was able to run as far as Datia. But the traitor Dewan of that State captured him and gave him over to tho English, who later on hanged him.

But, Lakshmi, put your horse now in a gallop. For Lieutenant Bowker is galloping behind, followed by select horsemen, in order to capture you. And you, O horse, fortunate on account of the sacred treasure you carry, gallop on! Let the men of Bharata be traitors, but, ye animals, ye at least be faithful! O Night, drop the curtain of darkness between Queen Lakshmi and her enemies! O horse, fleeting as you are, 'quicker than the wind, balance Lakshmi lightly!

Ye paths, do not obstruct the horses onward march! O ye stars, shine not for the enemy, but just shine so that this tender beauty, delicate as a flower, should be encouraged on the way by your rays, cool as nectar! The dawn has now broken; so, heroic Queen, flying all night on the wings of the wind, rest thee near the village of Bhandeir. The *Mahalkuree*; of the village will feed your darling Damodar.

As soon as breakfast was over, she again started on her journey on the Kalpi road. But what is this dust behind? Spur your horses on! Lakshmi, keep Damodar safe on the back and gallop on. Take out your sword! There, Bowker is pressing close! Here is the reward for your wicked pursuit! Dare you hold back the lightning? A long sweep of her sword, and Bowker was violently thrown off bis horse. A deadly fight took place between her fifteen or twenty horsemen and the English pursuers; those who were alive advanced forward to protect Lakshmi Bai. Wounded Bowker and his handful of men gave up the pursuit. The sword of the Mother advanced triumphant, shining. The sun in the heaven above, Ranee Lakshmi Bai on earth—both were marching forward. Morning was gone and mid-day came, but the Ranee did not stop. Afternoon came, the shades of evening began to fall, the sun went down the horizon—but the Ranee still would not stop. The stars rose. They saw her just as they had seen her the night before—marching, marching in hot haste. At last, at midnight, Ranee Lakshmi entered Kalpi. A ride of a hundred and two miles she accomplished, and that, fighting with Lieutenant Bowker and his soldiers and with the burden of a child on her back. That horse just lived, it so seemed, to carry her to Kalpi. For, as soon as he saw the rider safe in Kalpi. be fell down on the ground all in a heap. Six men were immediately ordered to attend to the horse. The Ranee loved the horse which carried safe such a person with such faithfulness deserves to be remembered, and his memory will be loved for all time.

The Ranee slept till dawn. In the morning, the touching meeting between the Ranee and Shri Rao Sahib Peshwa took place. Both remembered their ancestors—the thought that they were descended from those who had done such seemingly impossible deeds inspired them both. They realised that the flag of the Mahratta empire waved as far as Attock because men like the Scindia and the Holkar, the Gaekwar and Bundela and Patwardhan were ready to give up their lives for Swaraj. And for that very flag, for that very Swaraj for which their fathers and grandfathers had bled, they resolved to continue uninterrupted, to the very last breath of their lives, the war already begun against those who attempted to enslave their motherland.

While these arrangements are going on there, we shall take a rapid glance at the activities of Brigadier Whitelock whom we had left sometime back. To reconquer the tract between the Narbada and the Ganges and the Jumna, two armies had started and, of these, the one under Sir Hugh Rose, as we had already seen, had taken Jhansi. When Jhansi was taken, the British indulged in the wholesale looting such as Nadir Shah had accomplished before, defiling of temples and polluting of images, and massacring terribly all alike. That finished the army continued the campaign. The last part of the compaign had been appointed for Brigadier Whitlock to accomplish. Accordingly, Brigadier Whitlock started on the 17th of February from Jubbulpur, with all his army—European regiments, Indian regiments from Madras, 'black' and white cavalry, and splendid artillery. He entered Sagar in triumph, where the loyal Raja of Oorcha joined him. Then, the English army began to advance on the Nabob of Banda, the chief leader of the Revolutionaries in that province. In the beginning of the Revolution at Jhansi, Sagar and other places, cruel msssacres had taken place and the Europeons from those places ran wherever they could to save their lives. The Nabob had brought them to his palace and was looking after them well. But, at the same time, he was as busy in trying to throw off the British yoke already tottering through the shocks of the Revolution as he was in saving the lives of these Englishmen. From the very beginning, the symbols of slavery in his kingdom had been smashed and he was ruling as an indenpendent prince. Seeing the English army coming to deprive him of his liberty, the Nabob, urged and aided by the whole populace, was ready for battle. Several engagements, took place between the two parties, but being defeated in them, the Nabob started for Kalpi with his army, and Whitlock entered Banda in triumph on the 19th of April. The next march was to be on the Rao of Kirwi.

Rao Madhav Rao of Kirwi was a child of ten and his guardianship was in the hands of the English. The Rao of Kirwi was a near relation of Baji Rao Peshwa. In 1827, Anant Rao, the then ruler of Kirwi, deposited two lakhs of Rupees with the English Government for some charities in connection with the temples of Benares. As soon as he died, the English swallowed the whole amount. More than that, they took unlawful possession of a further sum of several lakhs of Rupees foolishly deposited with them by Anant Rao's son, Vinayak Rao, in spite of the lesson he had already received. This was soon after Vinayak Rao's death. Rao Madhav, the adopted son of Vinayak Rao, being a minor, as the supervision of the whole state was in the hands of the English, and Ramachandra Rao, the chief *Karbhari,* had been appointed by the English, there was every reason to suppose that there would not be much fear of revolt in the Kirwi State. But, in 1857, whatever the Raos and Maharaos did was not quietly acquiesced in by the people. Sometimes obscurely and sometimes clearly, the power of the people, the strength or the real nation, was slowly struggling into prominence. The Zemindars, the priests, the merchants of Kirwi, nay, even the common people, inspired by the strong ideal of liberty, hailed with joy the news which one day proclaimed Delhi free and the next day Lucknow and the third that Jhansi had uprooted the, flags of the Feringhi. Encouraged by these hopeful incidents, they proclaimed the independence of Kirwi and the destruction of the alien yoke, not waiting for the opinion of the Rao or the sanction of his ministers. Now, while this proclamation was being loudly celebrated by the populace, the Rao, a boy of nine or ten, had not done even a single thing against the English! Nay, when the English army returned to Bundelkhand, he went forward to receive them and invited them into the city. According to his invitation, the English army entered the city silently, but they entered to, imprison this little Rao, to destroy his capital and to pull down, his palace! Dreadful looting,[6] wholesale burning, and a vengeance of wickedness took place. And the State was annexed.

Whitlock now encamped at Mahoba, in order to 'pacify' the conquered provinces. As a matter of fact, he had now completed his compaign. He had conquered all the eastern part of Bundelkhand and he had sent small expeditions to 'pacify' one or two places. So now, leaving Whitlock let us again follow the sacred steps of the gallant Queen of Jhansi.

The Ranee, now again full of hope, made an advance on. Kunchgaon, forty-two miles from Kalpi, with the army of the Peshwa. But the Rao Sahib, it would appear, had not arranged the forces as she would have liked him to. It must be borne in mind, however, that it was not possible to make

---

6. 'With regard to this injustice done to Rao, Malleson has to confess: 'Not a shot had been fired against him (Whitlock), but he resolved nevertheless to treat the young Rao as though he had actually opposed the forces. The reason for this perversion of honest dealing lay in the fact that in the palace of Kirwi was stored the wherewithal to compensate soldiers for many a hard fight and many a broiling sun. In its vaults and strong rooms were specie, jewels, and diomonds of of priceless value. ...The wealth was coveted.' Kaye and Malleson's. *Indian Mutiny*, Vol. V, page 140, 141.

effective arrangements, either for Rao Sahib or Tatia Tope. Though in that place, the Nabob of Banda, the Raja of Shahgarh, and the Raja of Banapur had all gathered together under the same flag, they had not gathered together as the organised and disciplined parts of a grand military force, moved by oneness of heart, with a unity of plan and constitution, sustained by strict military discipline and subordination. No one could get his ideas carried out. But, in the opposing army, there was no such conflict amongst leaders. It seemed that the whole organisation was perfect and well controlled. Before Sir Hugh Rose was appointed commander, there was heated discussion and difference of opinion; but once he was the commander, his opinion was the opinion of all. Whatever orders he issued were right; and even if they were not right, they must be obeyed. And even mistaken orders of a weak general carried out by the obedient and unanimous bravery of the troops under him, become successful—are bound to become successful. On the other hand, even well-planned orders of a capable general lead to disaster and defeat, through the self-willed behaviour of the troops and the lack of oneness in command and proper subordination.

Otherwise the rout at Kunchgaon could never have taken place. As soon as Sir Hugh Rose came from Jhansi, the Revolutionaries met him at Kunchgaon. Knowing that the mid-day sun was unbearable to the English, the Revolutionaries had ordered in one of their commands, 'None should engage in the fight with the Feringhis before ten in the morning. The fight should begin always after ten.' This very clever rule was put into practice this day. Much havoc was thereby created in the English army as happened on many other occasions where the fight took place after ten. But, inspite of this, the Revolutionaries were defeated at Kunchgaon and retired towards Kalpi. The admirable way in which they retired, the organised manner in which the fell back has been praised very much even by the enemy.[7] But then this excellent organisation came after and not before the engagement. With this defeat, the Revolutionaries came on to Kalpi. There they begun to make up for the defeat by wrangling against and abusing one another, the infantry laid the defeat at the door of the cavalry, the cavaly blamed the Jhansi troops, and all together blamed the general Tatia.

But, Tatia Tope is not going to come any more to Kalpi to hear these wranglings. He has gone at present to the village of Charkhi, near Jalwan, to see his father. No one knows definitely where he is going after that, or whether he is going there at all. Let us remember that Gwalior lies in the direction of his road! May the meeting between this extraordinary son and his fortunate father be full of love! And after that loving visit, may this great messenger of the Revolution go with despatch to carry out whatever designs he might have set his heart on!

While Tatia was going on this journey, Rannee Lakshmi went to the royal tent of the Peshwa. The heroic Lakshmi relieved him of his dejection after the defeat of Kunchgaon and said to him that, if the army was properly organised, the enemy should never again be victorious. The Nabob of Banda was inspired by her speech. Proclamations in spirited lauguage were again published in the Revolutionary army.

7. 'Then was witnessed action on the part of the rebels which impelled admiration from their enemies. The manner in which they conducted their retreat could not be surpassed. They remembered the lessons which the European officers had well taught them. There was no hurry, no disorder, no rushing to the rear. All was orderly as on a field-day. Though their line of skirmishers was two miles in length, it never waved in a single point. The men fired then ran behind the relieving men, and loaded. The relieving men then fired, and ran back in their turn. They even attempted, when they thought the pursuit was too rash, to take up a position, so as to bring on it an enfilading fire.' —Malleson's *Indian Mutiny*, Vol. V, page 124, This praise by the enemy does credit to the Panday party.

And to-day, on the banks of the Jumna, crowds are gathering. Swords and guns, angry Sepoys invoking the Jumna to bless the cause of the independence of their soil-such a Revolutionary pilgrimage the banks of the Jumna had probably never before seen. These banks are simply echoing forth the triumphant cries for the Mother and for Dharma! Jai Jumna ! With this thy sacred water in our hands we swear that the Feringhis shall be extinct, that Swadesh shall be independent, and that Swadharma shall be reestablished! Jai Jumna! If all this is accomplished, then alone we will live. If not, we will die this day on the field of battle. We swear, by thee O Kalindi three times!'

Heroes, thrice bound by this oath, come on then to the field. Rao Sahib will lead the whole army. Drive away this 25th infantry under Sir Hugh Rose. They are all Indians—drive these traitors before you! Major Orr advances—make him share the same defeat! In this *maidan* before Kalpi, our position—with this undulatory part to cover—is almost impregnable. But look the vanguard, is falling back! It went too far, and being not well covered, has to retreat. Run then, Lakshmi, run to protect them. She rushed forward sword in her hand with lightning-like rapidity and fell on the right wing of the English, with her red-uniformed cavalry. The triumphant right stopped dead, so sudden was the attack; stopped dead, and then retired back helpless. This rapid onslaught of the girl of twenty-one, her horse at full speed, her sword cutting men down to the right and to the left,-seeing this, who would not fight for her? Who would not be inspired by her? All the Revolutionaries were inspired by her strength; the battle raged bloody and hot. The Feringhi gunners of the light field artillery began to die one after another. The Ranee and her cavalry, then, advanced right on the guns which were spitting deadly fire, and attacked the artillery. English gunners left the guns; the horse artillery was routed; the heroes of the Revolution advanced on and on, from all sides, overjoyed at the prospect of crushing the

Feringhis who had so long escaped them and before them all fought Lakshmi!

Sir Hugh Rose, taken aback by this terrible onslaught, then advanced with his reserve camels, and the English saved their own lives, simply because of the camels. An English writer says, 'Fifteen minutes more, and the mutineers would have cut us down! Fresh camels, one hundred and fifty in number, changed the fortunes of the day. Ever since that day, I have looked on the 'camel with eyes of affection.' By the strength of the camelmen alone, on the 22nd of May, the Feringhis succceded in forcing the Peshwa's army to retire towards Kalpi. After another complete defeat of the Peshwa's troops and after a few skirmishes, Sir Hugh entered Kalpi on the 24th of May. In the fort of Kalpi, the English captured a very considerable amount of military supplies which Shri Rao Sahib Peshwa and Tatia Tope had, with great trouble, gathered together in one year. Sixty thousand pounds of gunpowder were found buried under the ground; muskets beautifully made, brass balls of the latest type for the guns factories for making and repairing cannon-balls, heaps of military uniforms, flags, drums, French trumpets, Howitzer guns manufactured in Europe, and arms of various kinds—such was the very useful find that the English army came upon!

What they did not capture was brave and ever-memorable leaders of the Revolutionaries. For, when Kalpi fell after a week; Rao Sahib, the Nabob of Banda, Ranee Lakshmi Bai, and other leaders had left Kalpi and gone—nobody knew where. But now these unfortunate, helpless people, without an army and without arms, could do nothing beyond falling into the jaws of death, either by privations, or by capture, or by suicide!

Thus Sir Colin had begun the reconquest from the northern bank of the Jumna, and went on conquering as far as the Himalayas. Sir Hugh Rose and Whitlock began from the

Narbada, and conquered all the country as far as the south bank of the Jumna. The English had now every reason to congratulate themselves that they had destroyed the Revolution completely. Sir Hugh Rose congratulated his army in these eloquent words :—Soldiers, you have marched one thousand miles, captured one hundred guns, swam rivers, crossed mountains, marched through jungles, defeated big armies, reconquered extensive tracts, and re-established the glory of your country! Brave you are; and you have also observed the strictest discipline; for courage without discipline is nought. In the midst of difficulties temptations, and trouble, you have obeyed strictly the orders of your general, and have never showed even a single sign of insubordination. From the waters of the Narbada to the waters of the Jumna, this, your success, bas come to you through your splendid discipline!'

After publishing this glorifying proclamation, Sir Hugh resigned his charge for the sake of his health. And the triumphant English army, having destroyed the enemy completely, sighed the sigh of relief and wished to rest.

But how dare you rest yet? While Tatia and Ranee Lakshmi Bai are alive, there is no rest possible for the British troops. Come, stand up ! And if you would not stand of your own accord, here is the whole force of Gwalior, ready to goad you on! After escaping from Kalpi, the Revolutionary leaders went to Gopalpur to discues their future plans. Practically, at this time, there was not a sign of hope. From the Narbada to the Jumna, and from Jumna to the Himalayas, the English had conquered back the whole territory. The Revolutionaries were without an army, without a fort, without any hope of getting fresh force—defeated as they were again and again. But Tatia Tope was still alive, and that was enough! Tatia, too, had returned to Gopalpur. People say he had returned after visiting his father. Whatever people say, history does not say so. It was when Sir Hugh tried his deep-laid game at Kalpi that Tatia had a sudden fit of fondness for his father—a fondness, by-the-bye, which seemed to exceed even his fondness for fight; and, no longer able to control his filial feelings, he went to Charkhi to see his father. What was the secret of this sudden passion? The secret was that, as soon as Kalpi fell, it was absolutely necessary to get hold of some other strong position, some strong fortress, and some new army And, therefore, this Mcssenger of the Revolution had escaped from Kalpi secretly to enter Gwalior, and see how the Revolutionary idea was progressing there! He accepted the promises of the chief officers of the army, and created a new army for the Revolution, by secretly winning over the Durbar functionaries, Sirdars, and others. They promised to give him all the aid they could, and in one month he had the whole of Gwalior in the hollow of his hand. He then collected every information about the military position of Gwalior and, thus, after underminig the throne of the Scindia, Tatia returned to Rao Sahib at Gopalpur. He had 'seen his father !'

Learning the glad news, that Tatia had come back from Gwalior having successfully won over the people to the side of the Revolution, Ranee Lakshmi urged the Peshwa to advance straight towards Gwalior. On the 28th of May, the Revolutionaries came to Amin Mahal. The Mahalkars tried to stop them. They were answered, Who are you to obstruct us? We are the Peshwa and his forces and we are fighting for Swaraj and Swadharma.

These words of Rao Sahib silenced the cowards, and thousands of patriots in that part welcomed the Revolutionaries heartily, and thus the army of the Peshwa pressed right on the walls of the city of Gwalior. They had written to the Scindia. 'We are coming to you in a friendly spirit. Remember our former relations. We expect help from you, so that we shall be enabled to proceed towards the south.' But this ungrateful man had forgotten the former relations. Well then, remember the former and the present relations too!' The ancestors of the Scindia were our servants, our *Hujres*—that was the former relation. And, the present relation? The whole army of the present Scindia has joined us. Tatia had gone to Gwalior, seen the leaders, and gained all necessary information!' But still, forgetting all this, the Scindia, with all his army and all his guns, advanced on the Peshwa on the 1st of June, near Gwalior. The Shrimant who deserves the respect of the whole country thought for a moment that the Scindia had repented and was coming forward to salute the flag of Swadesh. But, Lakshmi said that he was coming, not to salute, but to smash that golden flag. She came forward with her three hundred horsemen and advanced right on the guns of the Scindia. Soon, she caught the view of Jayaji Rao Scindia and his personal guard the brave 'Bhaleghate' troops. The cobra shows not such rage when it is trodden upon as Lakshmi showed at the sight of this traitor! Like an arrow she dashed at his troops. Behold, you Bahadur—descendant of Mahadaji, this helpless girl of twenty-two, brought up in the Zenana, is inviting you for a trial of strength of the sword! Let us all see now how much of the prowess of Mahadaji, the devoted lover of his country, has descended upon this Jayaji the devoted slave of the Feringhi! As soon as this angry lightning struck him hard on the front, his personal guards wavered and the Scindia, with all his 'Bhaleghate' troops, was routed. But, at least, there was hope that his huge army and terrible artillery would do their best—and they did do their best! As soon as they saw Tatia, these troops which had been bound over by secret oaths to Tatia refused, point-blank, to fight against the Peshwa. As previously arranged, they joined the Peshwa with all their officers; the guns were silent and everyone in Gwalior honoured the flag of the Peshwa. The throne of the Scindia thus crumbled to pieces at the touch of the Revolutionary magician.

And so, Jayaji Rao Scindia, coward as he was, and his

minister, Dinkar Rao, fled not only from the field, but from Gwalior itself, and ran to Agra!

Gwalior was now mad with joy. The army fired salutes in honour of the Shrimant. The Finance Minister, Amar Chand Bhatia, surrendered the whole treasury of the Scindia, to the last pie, to Shrimant. Those few patriots who were in prison under thr old regime for having shown sympathy with the Revolutionaries were released from their prisons amidst the joyous cries of the populace. The traitors who had advised the Scindia to join the English had fled, but their mansions and their property were destroyed so that not a vestige of them remained. The black charge that the Asiatics do not understand the true relation between a ruler and his subjects, was washed away completely by Gwalior. For, how can he who goes against his own country and against his own Dharma be a ruler? Poona had been in 1818 guilty of being a traitor to the motherland in not having dragged Rao Baji from his Peshwai in right time. Gwalior was not guilty of that! And therefore, this Revolution of 1857 must be recorded in history as the first indication in modern India of the omnipotence of the *vox populi*, the power of the people. If Scindia joins not his country, the country shall not aid him either. Swords and guns, infantry and cavalry, Durbar and *Sirdars, Mankarees* and citizens, temples and Images—all are for the country, alone; and if the Scindia is not for the country, drag him down from his throne; and outside the palace, outside the capital, outside the borders of the kingdom let him be driven out! Hereafter, according to the Scriptures, 'The king receives his power only by pleasing the people!'

And now, we must not let this auspicious day, the 3rd of June, slip by uselessly. And so 'a big Durbar was held in Phul Bagh. All *Sirdars*, statesmen, noblemen, *Shiledars*, and cavalry officers, who had joined the Shrimant, took their seats according to their rank. Tatia Tope and the Arabs,

Rohillas, Pathans, Rajputs, Rangdes, Pardeshis, and others under him came to the Durbar in their military uniform and with swords by their side. The Shrimant himself was dressed in the Peshwa's uniform *Shirpana* and *Kalgitura* on head, pearls in his ears, and pearl and diamond necklaces, round his neck. Thus, with all the paraphernalia of the Peshwai, *Bhaldars* and *Chobdars* making way for him, and *Mourchas* flying, the Shrimant came to the Durbar. Then, as usual, all stood up in reverence, salutes were received, and the Shrimant ascended the throne. With tears of joy in his eyes, he congratulated all the noblemen with great eloquence. Ram Rao Govind was appointed Chief Minister. Tatia Tope was made general and a sword studded with precious stones was presented to him. The eight ministers were elected. Twenty lakhs of Rupees were distributed to the army. The Durbar was a complete success. Joy was on every face and salutes of guns were fired.'[7]

Shrimant Rao Sahib, representative of Nana Sahib Peshwa, had thus established a new throne, infusing a new hope and a new life into the Revolutionary party, and had created a centre, a basis, round which might be attracted the scattered forces of the Revolution. Tatia Tope was not mad in busying himself with this coronation and giving salutes after salutes just in the midst of the war. The whole world had seen the dead body of the Revolution which by this means alone he now lifted from the grave of despair. The world—some with pleasure and others with despair—had cried: 'That is a dead body, there is no life in it!' But what wonderful magic this! Tatia took the dead earth at Gopalpur, he breathed on it thus, and—wonderful!—the whole world saw with the dumbness of surprise, a throne rising from the thimbleful of earth, jingling with lakhs of Rupees! Wonder of wonders! See the thousands of swordsmen advancing; hear the salutes thundering forth from the guns! A new army

7. *Life of Lakshmi Bai*, by D. B. Parasnis, page 309.

is up, new guns are up, Tatia has captured a new kingdom! Tatia has done all this not merely to strike the world dumb with his splendid triumph. He knew that the Revolutionaries who had spread far and wide would, on hearing the salutes proclaiming the Shrimant as the Peshwa of the Mahratta empire, get a concentrated inspiration, vigour, and hope. He knew that the sight of the triumphant flag of the nation, thus unfurled at Gwalior, would infuse an uncontrollable enthusiasm and dash. He knew that the lawlessness which had set in owing to the want of a rallying point, would now make way for discipline, thorough respect for the new-established throne. All this Tatia saw. And what he foresaw soon came to pass. For the body of the Panday party was soon instinct with life. While thus, on the one hand, his countrymen were encouraged, the English army, which just gave a sigh of relief, was on the other hand, again disheartened. It was for this that the coronation was proclaimed loudly by Tatia and other leaders of the Revolution. Their deep-laid game was successful. For, by this very thunder of Tatia's cannon, Sir Hugh Rose's idea of the rest was rudely shattered to pieces![8]

---

8. Malleson, writing about the cleverness and diplomacy which Tatia and Lakshmi Bai showed in taking Gwalior, says :- 'How the 'impossible' happened has been told. ...He (Sir Hugh Rose) realised, moreover, the great danger which would inevitably be caused by delay. No one could foresee the extent of evil possible if Gwalior were not promptly wrested from rebel hands. Grant them delay, and Tatia Tope, with the immense acquisition of political and military strength secured by the possession of Gwalior, and with all its resources in men, money and material at his disposal, would be able to form a new army on the fragments of that beaten at Kalpi, and to provoke a Mahratta rising throughout India. It might be possible for him, using the dexterity of which he was a master, to unfurl the Peshwa's banner in the southern Mahratta districts. Those districts were denuded of troops, and a striking success in Central India would probably decide their inhabitants to pronounce in favour of the cause for which their fathers had fought and bled.' —Mallesonts *Indian Mutiny*, Vol. V, page 149-150

So far so good; but once having shocked Sir Hugh Rose and disheartened him, woe betide him who listened not to the words of Ranee Lakshmi Bai; All other functions but the one great function of war must be stopped. But it seemed that, as ill-luck would have it, the intoxication of the Revolutionaries. would make them blind to the necessity of keeping the army in complete readiness. They were all immersed in luxury, good dinners, and fatal dilatoriness—they thought, perhaps, that this. was the sole end of Swaraj!

They were only losing Swaraj. For, the surprised Sir Hugh Rose marched rapidly on Gwalior with his excellent army under him. He brought with him the renegade Scindia and proclaimed to all that the English were going to fight only for the Scindia's sake! It was a trick to deceive the simple men of Gwalior, who had the slavish and discreditable merit of blind loyalty, and it was calculated to prevent these from fighting against the Scindia. But the old world had changed, giving place to the new. Tatia, so far successful in awakening the Revolutionaries, rushed forward to meet the English. The English had already defeated the Morar contingents. Now, with the shadow of defeat on them. there began some excited movements among the Revolutionary leaders. Rao Sahib was hastening towards the house of the Nabob of Banda and the Nabob of Banda was rushing towards the house of Rao Sahib. But, in the midst of all this confusion, the Ranee alone was calm and was ready. Her sword was out. What need she fear now? Hope as well as despair she had trampled under foot; she treated with contempt the things on this earth; she had one aspiration alone, namely, that the flag of liberty should stand proudly erect until she gave up her last breath! Neither of them were to be in the dust; they were to lie in battle alone. So she gave Rao Sahib a word of courage, rearranged the undisciplined troops as far as she could, and took upon herself the task of guarding the eastern gate. She only demanded, 'I am ready with all my soul to do my duty; mind, you do yours!'

She donned her usual military uniform, rode a noble steed, ctook out her gem-bestudded sword from the sheath, and ordered the army under her to march on. She made ready all the posts near Kotaki Serai which had been given to her care and when the English army was in sight, everywhere, trumpets and pipes, drums and *nagaras* rent the air. If only she had an army, equal in courage and daring to herself! Even the insubordinate and hesitating felt heroic under her influence and, with them and her select band of horsemen, she charged hard the English army! Her two female friends, Mandar and Kashi, also fought bravely by her side. May the sweet memory of these two patriotic girls—beautiful in appearance, with male attire put on, taking pleasure in fight—live in history along with that of their mistress as long as history lives! A general like Smith was charging the Ranee's army, but to-day the Ranee's bravery and daring were a sight to see. Like lightning, she moved about all day. The English attacked the solid phalanx a number of times. On every occasion she maintained her hold firm. Her army occasionally felt enthusiastic and attacked the British and cut down many of them. At last, Smith was forced to retire; he gave up the attempt of breaking the mass and began to turn to another side, leaving the nest of the cobra alone!

Thus closed the day and thus rose the 18th of the month! This day, the English had resolved to make desperate charges From all directions, they advanced on the fort, and tried their utmost. General Smith, forced to retire the day before, was very determined to-day and, aided by re-inforcements, he charged the same Jhansi side he had gone for the day before. Sir Hugh Rose thought that his presence was also absolutely necessary and so he was personally present with the force attacking the Jhansi side. The Ranee too was ready for him with all her forces. 'She was ready with all her soul to do her duty.' That day, she wore a *Chanderi* turban embroidered allover, a *tamamee* cloak, and *pyjamas*. A pearl necklace was round her neck. Her famous steed being tired that day, anew, fresh-looking horse was made ready for her, fully caparisoned. While her two beautiful maids were taking sherbet, news came that the English were advancing. Lakshmi immediately darted forward from her tent. The arrow flies not so rapidly, the lightning flashes not forth with such force from the clouds, a lioness leaves not her lair so quickly to fall upon the approaching elephant! She rode her horse, lifted her sword, and charged the enemy with her army. An English writer says, 'Immediately, the beautiful Ranee went over the field and made a firm stand against the array of Sir Hugh Rose. She led her troops to repeated and fierce attacks and, though her ranks were pierced through and were gradually becoming thinner and thinner, the Ranee was seen in the foremost rank, rallying her shattered troops and performing prodigies of valour. But all was of no avail. The camel corps, pushed up by Sir Hugh Rose in person, broke her last line. Still the dauntless and heroic Ranee held her own.'

But while her side was fighting with such unexampled bravery, she saw the English army advancing on her rear—for they had broken through the ranks of Revolutionaries who were holding the posts behind her!

The artillery dumb, the main army routed, the victorious. English army closing on her from all sides, with only fifteen or twenty horsemen with her, Ranee Lakshmi, accompanied by her maids, put her horse to a gallop, in order to break through the enemy, and to join her comrades on the other side. The Feringhi horsemen of the Hussars, who knew not so far where she was, fired shot after shot on her and pursued her like hounds. But the Queen, with unexampled courage, cleared her way with her sword and marched on. Suddenly was heard a cry, 'I am dead, Bai Sahib, I am dead!' Alas, whose is this cry? Lakshmi turned round and found that it was her maid Mandar whom a white soldier had shot and killed! Angered, she attacked the Feringhi and her blow felled him on the spot. She had avenged the death of fair Mandar! She then marched on. She came to a small rill. Now one jump and Jhansi would have been out of the Feringhi's clutches. But her horse would not take that jump! If only she had had old horse! As if the fiery line of a magician was round him the horse moved in circles, round and round, but would not: cross. Before you could say 'one' the English horsemen closed on her! Still not a word of surrender or fear! One sword against their several swords,– yet she closed on them. She crossed sword with sword with them all, but one of them hit her on the head from behind. With that blow, the right part of her head, and even her right eye came out-just then, another blow hit her on the chest. Oh Lakshmi, Lakshmi ! the last drop of thy sacred blood is dripping and, therefore, now, Mother, take this last sacrifice for thee! Even at the point of death, she killed the British foe who had attacked her, and now the young Queen was breathing her last breath! A faithful servant, Ramchandra Rao Deshmukh, was near. He took her to a cottage near by. Ganga Das Bawa gave her cold water to drink to quench her thirst and a bed to lie down upon. Bathed in blood, this goddess of war reclined on the bed, and then her soul quietly fleeted from her body to heaven! As soon as she was dead, Ramchandra Rao, in accordance with her dying instructions prepared a pile of grass unseen by the enemy; he put her on that pyre and, before the touch of slavery could defile even her dead body, she was cremated.

On the pyre, if not on the throne! But Lakshmi is still with her sweetheart Liberty! She has forced open the gates or death by falling in battle and has now entered the other world. Pursuit can no longer harm her. Wicked Pursuit must pass through those roaring flames before it can do so.

Thus fought Lakshmi. She had achieved her purpose, fulfilled her ambition, carried out her resolve! One such life vindicates the whole existence of a nation! She was the concentrated essence of all virtues. A mere woman, hardly twenty-three yet, beautiful as rose, charming in her manners, pure of conduct, she had a power of organisation of her subjects, exhibited by very few, even among men. The flame of patriotism was always burning in her heart. And she was proud of her country's honour and pre-eminent in war! It is very rarely that a nation is so fortunate as to be able to claim such an angelic person, as a daughter and a queen. That honour has not yet fallen to the lot of England. In the Revolution of Italy, high ideals and heroism of the very highest type are to be found; yet, in all this period of glory, Italy could not give birth to a Lakshmi !

But, even our land could hardly have given birth to such a Queen but for this glorious War of Independence! The precious pearls in the ocean are not to be found on its surface. The *Suryakanta* jewel does not give out flames in the quiet of the night; nor does the flint give up its spark on soft cushions. They want resistance. Injustice must make the mind restless; really, not apparently, every drop of blood must actually boil; intense national feeling is thus set aflame in such a furnace, the particles of virtue begin to glow, the test goes on, the dross is eliminated, then, the concentrated essence of virtues begins to appear. In 1857, the heart of this our Motherland took fire; then, a terrible explosion which would deafen the world took place;—A spark at Meerut, and the whole country, which, under the roller or Dalhousie, had been reduced to the monotony of a dead level and seemed to be a heap of dust, proved to be a powder magazine filled with the most inflammable material. Just as when a mighty rocket in a fireplay, fired in the air, explodes, arrows and trees and various other picturesque objefis rise and burn and rush and die away, such was the case of this gigantic Revolutionary Rocket! Its length is from Meerut to the Vindhyas; its width from Peshawar to Dumdum ;and it was fired! Fire and flames raged in all directions. Blood coming down like rain,—sieges of Delhi, revenges of Plassey, massacres of Cawnpore, and the Sikandar Bagh of Lucknow! Thousands of heroes are fighting—and dying; cities are burning, Kumar Singh comes, struggles, falls, the Moulvie comes, struggles, and falls; the throne of Cawnpore, the throne of Lucknow, the throne of Delhi, the throne of Bareilly, the throne of Jagdishpur, the throne of Jhansi, the throne of Furrukabad, five thousand, ten thousand, fifty thousand, a lakh of swords, flags, banners, generals, horses, elephants-all are coming out one after another, move about in the turmoil of the raging fire! Some are ascending one flame, some another; they poise themselves a while, reel, fight, fall down unseen! Everywhere battle and thunder-storms! A veritable volcanic conflagration this! And the pyre, flaming near the cottage of Gangadas Bawa, is the last and the most lustrous flame of this raging volcanic conflagration of the War of Independence of 1857 !

END OF THE THIRD PART

PART IV

Temporary Pacification

CHAPTER I

A Bird's-Eye View

THE chief scenes in the War of 1857 being in Northern India, we had so long to dilate upon the warlike events in that region alone. But, in order to grasp even the general tenor of the War, it is necessary to see its manifestations in other provinces also. Therefore, while the tongues of fire of that tremendus conflagration are dancing up to the skies there, we must also cast a passing glance at the sparks in other regions.

We have already given a short description of the events in the Punjab, during the course of the siege of Delhi. After that, the Punjab was quiet on the whole, except for one or two spasmodic efforts at rising. The Hindu as well as the Mahomedan communities thoroughly sympathised at heart with the Revolutionaries and were full of hatred towards the British. But they did not care to help either party actively. The Sikh princes and people on the contrary, did not wish well to the Revolutionaries even at heart; nor did they remain neutral; nay, more, they did not hesitate to side openly with the English and shed the blood of their own countrymen on the field of battle.

It can be proved from many events that happened that the sympathies of the masses of Rajputana were on the side of the Revolutionaries. In towns like Jaipur, Jodhpur, and Udaipur, the curses that were heaped upon Indian soldiers fighting on the English side, the shouts of joy that went up in the bazaars, when Revolutionary victory was announced, and the grief with which they were filled when the news of their defeat came—all these showed from day to day that the Rajput masses were praying for victory to the Revolutionaries in the great national war. As regards the princes of Rajputana, most of them remained neutral and would not openly help either side, until a decisive conflict had taken place. But whenever they were forced to send some troops to help the English, these troops openly disobeyed the orders of their rulers and refused to fight against their brethren on behalf of the Feringhis!

The United Provinces, Oudh, Rohilkhand, Behar, Bundelkhand and Central India were the field of Kurukshetra of the. War of Independence of 1857. There was a slight rising at Rangoon, and in Burma, in general, but alas! it was a day after the fair, and was in vain!

After this bird's-eye view of the region north of the Vindhya mountains, let us now turn our eyes to the south. There, we first of all see the Empire of the Mahrattas founded by Shivaji. Their compatriots, who had migrated to the north, were fighting fierce battles at Cawnpore, Kalpi, and Jhansi. Thus, the Mahratta throne, ousted out of Raigarh, reappeared again in an ocean of blood at Cawnpore. And Tatia Tope was again flying aloft on high the banner once supported by heroes like Santaji and Dhanaji. If the magnificent unanimity, dash, and determination that characterised the rising in the north had also shown itself in the south, then even if the whole of England had gone to India to fight, the *Jaripatka* would never have been lowered! Where indeed, is a man of pure Mahtatta blood whose heart is not agitated by love and pride when the *Jaripatka* flies on the field, whether he shows it in his face or not? In 1857, also, the heroic inspiration, naturally took hold of the heart of all Mahrattas, but the diseases of indecision and indetermination stifled it in embryo. While the plan of the Revolution was being outlined in the north its messengers were also travelling in the south, visiting state after state, and town after town. Rango Bapuji of Satara was in correspondence with Nana Sahib of Cawnpore. In the various Sepoy regiments stationed at Poona, Satara, Dharwar, Belgaum, Hyderabad and other places, Brahmins, Moulvies, and the deputies of the northern Sepoys were travelling about secretly with the torch of Revolution in their hand. And, from Mysore right up to the Vindhya mountains, oaths were taken that a rising was to be made as soon as the north arose. But, though the south did not forget to rise, it forgot that it ought to arise as soon as the north, rose! The Rising in the north took place with an inconceivable, lightning-like rapidity, and with the determination to kill or die.

Instead of starting up immediately, the south waited for some time to watch the fortune of war in the north. In times of crisis like a Revolution, one moment decides the question of life or death. There are disadvantages in both alternatives, in haste as well as in delay. In such a dilemma, an able man fixes upon such a moment when boldness and spirit will reap the greatest possible fruits. Revolutions do not follow the rules of arithmetic. They succeed through the enormous strength of the spirit in the heart of man. They cool down by the sluggishness in action. They are kept up only by the heat of action. Calmness, mathematics, and the fixing of the day are all for the period of preparation. But when once the bugle has sounded and the drum been beaten, then there must be started at once determined fighting without any regard of life. One who hesitates then is certain to lose in the end. One who only just then begins to think out whether it is better to rise or not, is doomed for ever. Calmness in preparation but boldness in execution, this should be the watchword. During preparation, one may and even ought to proceed cautiously, step by step, even as on a carpet; but when the Revolution has once broken out, one must dart forth like an arrow without faltering a moment, even through living fire! Then let there be success or defeat, let there be life or death—there should be stubborn war, men should be ready to 'die while killing.' For when once the drum of war is beaten, the best road to success in a Revolution lies in advancing and never in waiting.

The south forgot this cardinal principle. It did nol rise as soon as the north rose. It proceeded slowly, staggering every now and then. Over-anxiety about success, and only spasmodic, isolated rising that followed as its consequence, necessarily led to nothing but certain failure. How this came to pass we shall review in brief.

There were three important regiments in the south, the 27th at Kolhapur, the 29th at Belgaum, and the 28th at Dharwar. When the plans of the Rising were made by means of correspondence, the 10th of August was fixed upon as the day on which they were to rise. But an English army was in the meanwhile being sent to Kolhapur to keep the population and the Sepoys there in check. This news was divulged to the Sepoys by an official of the Telegraph Department. Thus the Sepoys who were already infuritated, rose prematurely on the 31st of July, 1857. They killed some of their English officers, took the treasury in their charge, had a skirmish with the English troops that had just arrived, and went away towards the Ghats. The various Revolutionary bands united together under the leadership of Ramji Shirsal of Sawantwadi and began to harass the English force in the direction of the Kadi forest. They were defeated and dispersed after some months by the English with the help of the Portuguese of Goa. The new English officer, Jacob, who had come to Kolhapur, disarmed the remaining Sepoys there and had. their leaders shot.

But on the day on which the Sepoys at Kolhapur had risen, the town itself had not done so. In the meanwhile, emissaries from Nana Sahib of Cawnpore had an audience with the young king of Kolhapur and persuaded him to join the National Rising—He had also been presented with a sword by the Durbar of Lucknow. In the same manner, he was carrying on secret correspondence with the Rajas of Sangli, Jamkhandi and other southern states. But, more than the Maharaja, his younger brother, Chimna Sahib had in his veins the blood of Shivaji. He secretly began machinations to put right again the plans of the Revolution foiled by the recent turn of events. He prepared the irregular army of Kolhapur and many volunteers for a Rising, and in the early morning of the 15th of December Kolhapur rose again. The city gates were closed, guns were made ready, and the drum of Revolution was beaten in the streets. As soon as Jacob heard the news, he got the men under him ready and led an attack on a Kachcha gate. From that moment onward till the time that the English army took possession of the palace, a fierce battle raged. After defeat, the Raja, following the usual custom, declared that the Rising was organised by the army and the populace in spite of his orders to the contrary. When the names of the Revolutionary leaders were demanded, he replied that he knew nothing about it! Jacob tried his utmost to get hold of the leaders. He put many people, now and then, in prison, simply on suspicion; but he could get no scent of the vast and dangerous conspiracy. One of the leaders, even as he was being arrested, tore up an incriminating letter in his possession and swallowed it in the presence of his captors! Of the many who were blown from the mouths of cannon, one was only wounded at the first firing and was not killed. Still he proudly stood forth erect waiting for the second round. Just then, Jacob went up to him and said, , 'I pity you—you must have been betrayed into joining the Rebellion. So, if you help the Sirkar by divulging, the names of some mutineers, your life will be spared!' But the grand hero bore, without a murmur, the excruciating pain of his mangled body manfully, and, 'he looked at me (Jacob) with a scowl and scorn mingled and answered unhesitatingly — What I have done, I have done.' Without giving out a single name, he turned his face and stood forth boldly in front of the death-spitting cannon! Another Revolutionary, just before being blown up, muttered the name of a leader; at this, one of the Government servants present there quietly slunk away and warned that leader and others who were implicated in the town. When the English authorities, inquiring the whereabouts of the person named, came up to arrest him, he was already, out of Kolhapur and safe! With such fidelity to each other did the conspirators work, and the organisation of the various circles and batches was effected without much hitch or confusion.[1]

While affairs were in this state at Kolhapur, there were also signs of rising in Belgaum, about the 10th of August. But the Sepoy leader, Thakur Singh, and a bold Munshi, the leader of the citizens, were arrested just at the last moment. A new English army was soon on the scene and Belgaum and Dharwar soon became silent and submissive. The above-named Munshi was a Government servant and incriminating letters from him were found on the Sepoys at Poona and Kolhapur. So, on the evidence of these, he was blown from the mouth of a cannon.

At Satara, Rango Bapuji was from the first, in the bad books of the Government. Now, his son was hanged for preaching the doctrine of the Rising at Kolhapur. At the same time, two princes of the Satara royal family were banished. Seeing the throne, in the devoted service of which he had spent so many years, in such a plight, the faithful Rango Bapuji disappeared from Satara. Rewards were offered but nobody helped to hand him over to the English. And the fate

1. 'But it is difficult to describe the wonderful secrecy with which the whole conspiracy was conducted and the forethought supplying the schemes, and the caution with which each group of conspirators worked apart, concealing the connecting links, and instructing them with just sufficient information for the purpose in view. And all this was equal-led only by the fidelity with which they adhered to each other.'— *Western India* by Sir George Le Grand Jacob, K.C.S.I., C.B.

of that patriot is not known even to this day.

At this time, an able Englishman, called Lord Elphinstone, was appointed Governor of Bombay. He had not only borne the strain—small though it was—in his own presidency, but also sent troops to Rajputana. But, if it was anyone man whose cleverness prevented a rising in the city of Bombay itself, it was Forrest, the chief police officer. Bombay was a city full of easy-going, happy-go-lucky, and traitorous cowards. Thus, the only hearts susceptible to the flame of the national Revolution there were amongst the ranks of the Sepoys stationed there. And therefore it was that Forrest had kept a very close watch upon them. The *Dipavali* holidays were fixed upon as the opportune moment for rising and the Sepoys began to hold secret meetings. Forrest tried his utmost to send detectives into these meetings but did not succeed on account of the extraordinary caution displayed by the Sepoys. Therefore, he himself began to go about in various disguises, now as a Brahmin, now as some one else, and thus mixed with the people even in their exclusive dinner parties. At last he found out that the secret meetings were held in the house of a man called Ganga Prasad. Then he entered the house of Ganga Prasad after threatening to arrest him if he opposed, and saw what happened at one of those secret meetings through an aperture in the wall, unknown to the Revolutionaries who met there. Not only this, but also brought with him later on some English officers of the regiment and let them see the secret meetings for themselves. When the latter saw there coming into the meeting, one after another, Sepoys who were reckoned as the most loyal, they whispered in amazement, 'My God, my own men! is it possible?' The general plan of the Sepoys was to make a rising in Bombay at first, then to march towards Poona, capture that city, raise the banner of Mahratta Kingdom, and proclaim Nana Sahib as Peshwa.[2] But before the plans could be put into operation, Forrest broke up the

2. Forrest's *Real Danger in India.*

conspiracy, hanged two of the ringleaders as rebels and banished six of the prominent and leading military men; and thus the rising in Bombay was nipped in the bud.

At about the same time, the Revolutionary spark was about to strike Nagpur and Jubbulpur. The Sepoys near Nagpur had decided to rise on the 13th of June, 1857, and this plan was assented to by most of the prominent citizens. It was agreed that on the night of the 13th townspeople should send up in the air three burning balloons, and at this signal the military were to rise. The Revolutionaries there had another advantage; the English could spare no European troops for the province of Nagpur and Jubbulpore at that time. But soon the Indian regiments from Madras came and the sparks of Revolution were speedily extinguished. The Gond king of Jubbulpore, Shankar Singh, and his son were doing thier utmost for the Revolution. When they were arrested and their palace was searched, a small paper containing the king's morning-prayers was found folded in a silk cloth. Its English translation is as follows :-The king, Shankar Singh, meditating on the terrible image of the Goddess Chandi says, 'Shut the mouths of slanderers; trample the sinners! Shatru-Samharike! (Killer of enemies!) Listen to the cry of Religion; support your slave, Mathalike! Kill the British ; exterminate them; Mata Chandi!'[3] etc., etc.

King Shankar Singh and his son had tried to enlist the 52nd native regiment at Jubbulpore in the cause of the Revolution. Therefore, the two royal personages were blown from the mouth of cannon on the 18th of Septemper, 1857. At this news, the 52nd regiment, instead of being cowed down, was infuriated, rose immediately, killed an officer, called Mac Gregor, and marched away to the war.

There were risings in the Dhar state and at Mahidpur, Goria, and other places, organised by prince Feroze Shah of Delhi. We cannot describe the details of all these risings for

3. Charles Ball's *Indian Mutiny*, Vol, II, page 144.

want of space.

But, more than all the princes mentioned above, the fate of the English power in India lay in the hands of the Nizam of Hyderabad. The new Nizam, Afzul-ud-daulah, had just come to the throne in May 1857, and the Prime Ministership was in the hands of a man called Sir Salar Jung. The whole of the Deccan hung upon one word from the lips of Sir Salar Jung. If the Nizam of Hyderabad had joined the National Revolution, the whole of the Deccan would have risen like one man, and the cord of English rule, already strained to breaking point by the rising in the north, would have been snapped to pieces. Nor can we say that no one preached to Salar Jung the doctrine of a patriotic rising against the English. Though we take for granted that he was too 'loyal' to let love of religion, country, and independence even whisper such a thought into his mind, still the people of Hyderabad were precipitately urging him to join the Revolution. But, in spite of all these efforts, Salar Jung would not move. So, on the 12th of June 1857, Hyderabad assumed a more terrible form. On that day, proclamations signed by important Moulvies began to adorn the walls; Revolutionary handbills were seen everywhere in heaps; there were crowded meetings of Moslems in the Mosque and violent Revolutionary lecturers bound the people by oaths to drive the Kaffir Britishers out of the land! Still, Salar Jung would not move; nay, he even arrested some of the popular leaders and handed them over to the British authorities! Therefore, towards the evening of the 17th of July, the city of Hyderabad actually rose and ran with shouts of 'Din, Din!' to release their imprisoned leaders and, following the flag signifying independence, rushed at the British Residency. The Rohilla Sepoys of the Nizam's own army and about five hundred of townsmen actually began a battle. Under these circumstances, Hyderabad felt assured that, though Salar Jung would not openly join them, he would secretly sympathise with them, as other States had done, or at least that he would not join the side of the British. But Salar Jung disappointed them in every particular; he did not remain indifferent, but joined the Britisher and helped to slaughter the soldiers of his own state. In the skirmish, the Revolutionary leader, Torabaz Khan, was killed and Moulvie Alla-ud-din. fell into the hands of the enemy. Soon he was despactched to the Andaman islands, and the efforts of Hyderabad thus came to a disastrous end. The English historian frankly admits : 'For three months, the fate of India was in the hand or Afzul-ud-daulah and Salar Jung. Their wise policy proved that they preferred the certain position of a protected state to the doubtful chances of a resuscitation of the Delhi monarchy under the auspices of revolted Sepoys.'

Though the Nizam thus foiled the Revolution in the south, the young Hindu Raja of Zorapur, near the Nizam's territories, resolved to stake his everything in the War of Independence. Accordingly, he began by collecting an army of Arabs, Rohillas, and Pathans. Nana's Revolutionary messengers came to him and prepared him to fight under the Peshwas. The Brahmins and Moulvies of Raichur and Arcot also encouraged him in his plans. Not merely that, but, when he would not rise as soon as the people wanted him to, they—his own subjects—began to abuse him as cowardly and effeminate. Then he began the Revolution in the name of the Peshwas. The Nizam and the English together marched against him. From the moment he heard this, he knew his fate was sealed. Not being able to hold his own against the combined forces of the Nizam and the English, the young Raja went to Hyderabad itself about the month of February, 1858. While walking about there in the bazaars, he was arrested by Salar Jung's orders and handed over to the British! This Raja was from his childhood on very intimate terms with Meadows Taylor and used to call him by the familiar name of 'Appa'. Therefore the English authorities sent Meadows Taylor to the prison to find out from the Raja the secrets of the Revolutionary conspiracy and the names of the prominent leaders. There, as he was awaiting death, the Raja was very pleased to see Meadows Taylor and embraced him heartily. But when Taylor began to ask him some account of the Secret Society and as to how he got mixed up with it, to put in Taylor's own words—'He drew himself very proudly and replied haughtily,'No, Appa, I will never tell that! You ask me to go to see the Resident but I won't do that either. Perhaps he hopes that I will beg him for my life, but, Appa, I do not wish to live, like a coward, on charity, nor will I ever disclose the names of my countrymen!' Meadows Taylor went up to him once again and, showing him hopes of a pardon, suggested that he should disclose the story of the plot. Again, the Raja replied,'I shall tell everything else about my proceedings in this affair. But if they ask me the names of those who incited me to rise, I will not tell that. What? Should I, now ready to enter the jaws of death, should I betray the names of my own countrymen? No, no! Cannon, gallows, tbe region beyond the black waters none of them is as terrible as treachery!' Meadows Taylor then informed him that death awaited him with certainty. The Raja replied, 'But, I have one request, Appa; do not hang me, for I am not a thief. Blow me from a cannon. Just see how calmly I can stand before its mouth!'

However, through the intervention of Meadows Taylor the , 'Sentence of this patriotic young Raja was reduced from death to some years' transportation. A short time afterwards, when about to leave for the Andamans, the Raja took a pistol belonging to one of his English warders and, at a moment when no one was near, shot himself dead. He had previously said, 'I prefer death to transportation! Prison and transportation? The meanest mountaineer of my subjects will not remain in gaol—what then of me, their king?'[4]

4. Meadows Taylor's *Story of my Life.*

One of the men who had intimate and constant connection with the Raja of Zorapur was Bhaskar Rao Baba Sahib, the chief of Nargund. But, when Zorapur rose, Bhaskar Rao hesitated and was not sure if the proper time had arrived; he only rose when the former was completely crushed. On account of these lax, spasmodic, and inopportune risings in the south, no one was crowned with success. Baba Sahib was a cultured man and a great lover of learning. He had also collected together a large library of excellent books. His young wife was as spirited as she was beautiful and had resolved upon giving her whole life for the destruction of the Feringhis since the time she was refused the right of adoption. It was due to her inspiration that, at last, on the 25th of May, 1858, after long hesitation, Nargund openly rose and declared war with England. Baba Sahib threw off the yoke of slavery to the British ostentatiously. When the news came that the English officer, Monson, was marching against him, Baba Sahib took a few select men with him and surprised Monson at night in the woods near Nargund. In the skirmish, Monson was killed, his body was thrown in a fire near by, and his head was taken back triumphantly to Nargund. Next morning, it was hanging on the walls of Nargund. In the meanwhile, Baba Sahib's step-brother not only refused to join the Revolution but actually joined the English side. An English army then marched upon Nargund and defeated the army of Baba Sahib who himself escaped from the field. He was caught, a few days later, in disguise and hanged on the 12th of June. His young, beautiful, and daring Ranee did not surrender to the enemy, but in company with her mother-in-law committed suicide by throwing herself in the waters of the Malaprabha.

Besides these, Bhima Rao Komaldrug, the Bhils of Khandesh and their valiant spouses, armed with bow and arrow, and other small communities, organised risings in

4. Meadows Taylor's *Story of my Life.*

Maharashtra of greater or lesser magnitude. But, on account of the want of skill in choosing the proper time, on account of unripeness of preparation, and on account of the loose and spasmodic nature of the risings and their want of cooperation, the English had not to bear any severe strain in the south and could devote, practically, all their resources to the north.

After having thus taken a bird's-eye view of the affairs in the south, it is now high time that we should turn our eyes to take a last glance at the proud Ayodhya which is left groaning there at the end of the life story of the heroic Moulvie Ahmad Shah.

In the case of extraordinary brilliant heroes like Moulvie Ahmad Shah, their death is as noble and as extraordinary as their life. Others may die when they are killed in battle, but one whose very soul is on fire with a burning patriotism and who is dancing on the battle-field with shouts of 'Blood! Blood!' in order to quench that fire, knows no death; even if such a patriot falls in battle before his thirst for revenge is slaked, he does not die. Though the head was cut off, it has been seen, as a matter of fact, that the trunk of heroic men continued the fight in the field and there is a belief that when even this latter is cut to pieces their disembodied spirits harass the enemy at night.

There is, indeed, a philosophic truth underlying such superstitions. While Moulvie Ahmad Shah was still fighting, Lord Canning ha. published a proclamaltion to let the whole of Oudh know: 'Those who will voluntarily lay down their arms will not be considered as rebels and will be granted a free and complete pardon for their past actions, and those who help us now will receive back their lands and Vatans. Now that the British power has triumphed over the rebellion, if some still insist upon their cesistance to the British goverment, they shall all be most severely punished for this unwarrantable pertinacity.' After such a proclamation and after many of the leaders had died suddenly one after the other, the English naturally thought that the people of Oudh would soon calm down. And to add to the misfortunes of Oudh on the 5th of June, 1858, the news came that the villain, Powen, had assassinated the venerable Moulvie of Fyzabad. But instead of indulging in vain lamentations for the death of this sacred Moulvie, exhausted as she was by almost superhuman efforts, dispirited by defeat, and with surrender tempting her with hope of pardon, Oudh rose suddenly at his death-spell like one possessed, and jumped up in blood, with shouts of 'Revenge!' The base enemy hanged the Moulvie's body in the Chowdi-but his spirit, his ghost, began to fight with the English on the field! His ghost in order to satisfy its unquenched thirst, jumped at the neck of the English power, in its terrible unhuman form. Instead of being cowed down by his death, the whole of Oudh, the living ghost, ran up the battle-field again with fresh vigour brushing aside all thoughts of strength and weakness, success and defeat, hope and despair, life and death! To take revenge for the hanging of the Moulvie, Nizam Ali Khan marched up to Pilibhit; Khan Bahadur Khan with four thousand men ran to the field of action; the Farrukabad men rose taking five thousand followers; Vilayat Shah took three thousand men to the field and, with five thousand men, Nana Sahib, Bala Sahib, Ali Khan Mewati, and other leaders started a tremendous campaign in Rohilkhand and Oudh. Seeing these great masses of troops marching in haste, and thirsting for his blood, the cowardly traitor of Powen began to shudder with terror. The English immediately despatched troops for his protection. Around that part, the Revolutionaries were engaging in frequent and desperate encounters with the enemy. On the other side, at Chowk Ghat, on the banks of the Ghogra, the Begum and Sirdar Mamu Khan had established the headquarters of their army. Besides these, Raja Ram Baksh, Bahunath Singh, Canda Singh, Bhopal Singh, Hanumant Singh and other prominent and valiant Zemindars, with larger or smaller armies, were fighting to reconquer Oudh, which had been almost conquered by the English. Also, the celebrated Mogul prince Feroze Shah, who was lately fighting at Dhar, was now in Oudh. There was also there fighting in Oudh the famous Raja Narapat Singh, the valiant son of a valiant father. He it was who had so bravely defended the fortress of Ruiya. His father, Jussa Singh, was an intimate friend of Nana Sahib and had died at Brahmavarta while fighting on the side of Nana Sahib in the holy War of Independence. Narpat Singh, like a true Kshatriya, unsheathed the sword again for victory in the field in which his father lay dead; he gave shelter to Nana Sahib in his fortress at Ruiya; and he had been fighting ever since then against the Feringhi power. And even greater than all these, in power, in spirit, in determination, and in patriotism, the veteran Raja Veni Madhav also now left his fort and, with an extraordinary bold move, after marching along the Cawnpur road, was now ready to pounce upon Lucknow ! When those who have left all hopes of success fight only for honour and duty, even courting death, is there any limit to their magnificent courage? Simply for the honour of the Kshatriya race, this Veni Madhav, though without the slightest hope of success at this late hour, marched straight upon Lucknow ! And he caused placards to be posted in the town that all Indians residing there should leave it, for he was going to direct a tremendous attack upon the Feringhis. The Feringhis, though drunk with victory, and possessed of force, and good organisation, were astounded at his marvellous courage An attack on Lucknow? Forsooth, as if the war had begun only to-day, as if seas of blood had not at all flowed for the whole of the past year in Oudh !

So, on the 13th of June, Hope grant directed a surprise assault upon the Revolutionaries, gathering together at Nabobgaj near Lucknow. The surprise attack of the white and the black forces of Hope Grant would naturally have dispered the incautious Revolutionaries at once—but, Sepoys stop! It is not yet a week since the Moulvie was killed—so, stop! They stopped and they stood up ready to give battle even under such odds. And, lo! such an exhibition of bravery was seen on the side of the Revolutionaries as is rarely witnessed no matter anywhere. It was such as to make the usually spiteful enemy to be carried away by a natural admiration of heroic bravery. The English general, Hope Grant, writes :—'Still, their attacks were vigorous, if unsuccessful, and we had much ado to repel them. A large body of fine, daring Zemindari men brought two guns in the open and attacked us in the rear. I have seen many battles in India and many brave f llows fighting with a determination to conquer or die; but, I never witnessed anything more magnificent than the conduct of these Zemindars! In the first instance they attacked Hodson's horse, who would not face them and by their unsteadiness placed in great jeopardy two guns which had been attached to the regiment. I ordered up the 7th Hussars and the other four guns belonging to the battery to within a distance of five hundred yards from the enemy and opened a fire of grape which mowed them down with a terrible effect, like thistles before the scythe. Their chief, a big fellow with a goitre on his neck, nothing daunted, caused two green standards to be placed close to their guns and used them as a rallying point. But our grapefire was so destructive that whenever they attempted to save their pieces, they were struck. Two squadrons and more now came up to our side and forced the survivors to retire, waving the swords and spears at us and defiantly calling out to us to come on. Around the two guns alone there were one hundred and twentyfive corpses. After three hour's fighting, the day was ours.'[5]

Such desperate encounters took place in East Oudh, in

5. Hope Grant's *Incidents of the Sepoy War,* Page 292.

Middle Oudh, in North Oudh and, practically, all over Oudh. And that not with the enemy alone but with traitors like Man Singh and Powenkar who had been lured to join the enemy by , the proclamation of pardon. Oudh began to fight such a double battle. They directed attacks on Powen; they were fighting towards Lucknow; they fought at Sultanpur; they shut up the traitor Man Singh in his fort; they obstructed English routes; they sacked English station; and, by their noble sacrifice they made every space of the ground there worth worshipping as sacred soil! Cutting the cordon which the English drew round them, the patriots rushed about from place to place still persevering in their cry for war and revenge. Considerations of space alone for- bid us from minutely following all their movements.

Such was the terrible fight that Ayodhya fought! At last, in October, 1858, the English Commander-in-Chief again arranged a mass of white and brown troops in systematic order, made them march simultaneously from all sides against the Revolutionaries and, thus pressing them on all sides, gave orders to push them northwards towards Nepal. Still, Oudh would not be exhausted and would not retreat a step without fighting!

Veni Madhav's town, Shankarpur was surrounded on threo sides by three different armies. He was now weak in resources and the enemy was very strong; still, Veni Madhav would not lay down his arms. Then, the English Commander-in-Chief himself sent him a message telling him that a further coutinuance of the fight would mean only useless bloodshed, as he had no hope of victory. If he surrendered, he was promised full pardon and complete restoration of his property. Veni Madhav replied: 'It being henceforth impossible to defend the fort, I am going to leave It. But I will never surrender myself to you. For my person belongs not to me but to my king.' The fort will surrender, but not Veni Madhav![6]

In November, 1858, the famous proclamation of the Queen of England was published throughout India, and according to the prophecy, the company's rule did vanish after a hundred years! But, in its place came the rule of the Queen! Everyone who fought openly against the English in the war was to be given full pardon as soon as he laid down his arms; a promise was given that his property would not be confiscated'[7] not even an inquiry was to be held. The

---

6. How the people fought *pro rege* and *pro patria*, for the king and the Motherland, will be seen from the following. Charles Ball says;- 'After the proclamation, still the struggle in Oudh was wonderful, and all these bands of rebels were strengthened and encouraged to an in-conceivable degree by the sympathy of their countrymen. They could march without commissariat, for the people would always feed them. They could leave their baggage without guard, for the people would not attack it. They were always certain of their position and that of the British, for the people brought them hourly information. And no design could be possibly kept from them while secret sympathisers stood round every mess-table and waited in almost every tent in the British camp. No surprise could be effected but by a miracle, while rumour, communicated from mouth to mouth, outstripped even our cavalry.' Vol. II, page 572.

7. How this promise and similar promises were kept by the English is well-known to the people of India. The Government actually refused to return lakhs of Rupees lent to them on bonds and secuirties on the ground that the security-holders were rebels. Here is a sample of the general attitude of the English people at the time. In the biography of John Delane, the famous editor of the London *Times*, recently printed, we get some glimpses of the matter. At about the time of the mutiny, the *Times* had sent a special correspondent to India in the person of Sir W. H. Russel. It is recorded that at the end of January, 1859, Sir W. H. Russell was still with Lord Clyde, and, in one of his last letters from Lucknow, he tells a delightful story which he heard from the Commander-in-Chief. Alluding to his landlord at Allahabad (an Anglo-Indian general merchant), Lord Clyde said, 'You doubtless heard what he did?' 'No.' 'Well, he was much in debt to native merchants when the mutiny broke out. He was appointed special commissioner and the first thing he did was to hang all his creditors.' This 'delightful story,' is not, of course, contained in any 'History of the Indian mutiny.' It was not even contained in the Times' special corresdondentst letters to the *Times* intended for publication. It was meationed only in private letter of Sir W. H. Russell to John Delane.

right of Rajas to adopt an heir was recognised. A clause was also inserted that the religious beliefs of the people would never be interfered with; and an undertaking was given that promises would not thenceforth be broken.

The Queen proceeded to say: "And we do hereby confirm in their several offices, civil and military, all persons now employed in the service of the Honourable East India Company, subject to our future pleasure, and to such laws and regulations as may hereafter be enacted.

'We hereby announce to the native princes of India that all treaties and engagements made with them by or under the authority of the Honourable East India Company are by us accepted and will be scrupulously maintained; and we look for the like observance on their part.

'We desire no extension of our present territorial possession; and, while we will permit no aggressions upon our dominions or our rights to be attempted with impunity, we shall sanction no encroachment on those of others. We shall respect the rights, dignity, and honour of native princes as our own, and we desire that they, as well as our own subjects, should enjoy that prosperity and that social advancement which can only be secured by internal peace and good government.

'We hold ourselves bound to the natives of our Indian territories by the same obligations of duty which bind us to all our other subjects; and those obligations, by the blessing of Almighty God, we shall faithfully and conscientiously fullfil.

'And it is our further will that, so far as may be, our subjects, of whatever race or creed, be freely and impartially admitted to offices in our service, the duties of which they may be qualified by their education, ability, and integrity, duly to discharge.

'Our clemency will be extended to all offenders save

and except those who have been and shall be convicted of having, directly taken part in the murder of British subjects.

'To all others in arms against the Government, we hereby promise unconditional pardon, amnesty, and oblivion of all offences against ourselves, our crown, and dignity, on their return to their homes and peaceful pursuits."

In such a manner was this 'Magna Charta' (?) of Hindusthan published! The principal reason for its publication was, no doubt, the desire to extinguish the Revolution in Oudh. But Oudh did not care even to glance at it. The Begum of Oudh published the following counter-proclamation : 'In the proclamation, it is written that all the contracts and agreements entered into by the Company will be accepted by the Queen. Let the people carefully observe this artifice The Company has seized on the whole of Hindusthan , and if this arrangement be accepted, what is there new in it? The Company professes to treat the Chief of Bharatpur as a son and then took his territory. The chief of Lahore was carried off to London, never to return again. The Nabob Shams-ud-din Khan, on the one hand, they hanged, while, on the other hand, they salaamed to him. The Peshwa they expelled, from Poona and Satara and imprisoned for life in Bithoor. The Raja of Benares they imprisoned in Agra. They have left no names or traces of the chiefs of Behar, Orissa and Bengal. Our ancient possession they took from us on pretence of destributing pay and in the 7th article of the treaty, they wrote on oath that they would take no more from us. If, then, the arrangements made by the Company are to be accepted, what is the difference between the former and the present state of things? These are old affairs. But, even recently, in defiance of oath and treaties, and notwithstanding that they owed us millions of Rupess, without reason and on pretences of misconduct and the discontent of our people they took our country and property worth millions of Rupees. If our people were discontented with our royal predecessor,

Wajid Ali Shah, how comes it then, that they are content with us? And no ruler ever experienced such loyalty and devotion of life and goods as we have. What, then, is wanting that they do not restore to us our country? Further, it is written, in the proclamation, that they want no increase of territory, and yet they cannot refrain from annexation. If the Queen has assumed the government, why does she not restore our country to us when the people have unmistakably shown their wish to this effect?

'It is well known that no king or queen ever punished a whole army or a whole people for rebellion. All will be forgiven, for the wise cannot approve of punishing the whole army and people of Hindusthan and also they know that so long as the, word 'punishment' remains, the disturbance will not be suppressed. There is a well known proverb, '*Marta kya nahin karta.*'

'It is written in the proclamation, that they who harboured the rebels or who caused men to rebel shall have their lives, but that punishment shall be awarded after deliberation to them, that murderers and abettors of murders shall have no mercy shown to them, and that all the rest shall be forgiven. Now even a silly person will see that, under this proclamation, no one, be he guilty or innocent, can escape. Everything is written and yet nothing is, written. But one thing they have clearly said and that is that they shall let off no one who is implicated; and so, in whatever village or province our army has halted, the inhabitants of that place cannot escape. Deeply are we concerned for the condition of our beloved people on reading this proclamation which palpably teems with enmity. We now issue a distinct order, and trustworthy that all persons who may have foolishly presented themselves as heads of villages to the English shall, before the 1st of January, 1859, present themselves in our camp. No doubt their faults shall be forgiven. To believe in this Proclamation, it is only necessary to remember that Hindusthanee rulers are altogether kind and merciful. Thousands have seen this, millions have heard this. No one has ever seen the English have forgiven an offence.

'In this proclamation it is written that when peace is restored public works such as roads and canals, will be made in order to improve the condition of the people! It is worthy of a little reflection, that they have promised no better employment for Hindusthanees than the making of roads and the digging of canals!

'If people cannot see clearly what this means, then, there is no hope for them.

'Let no subject be deceived by the proclamation!"

And therefore Oudh would not take advantage of the un-conditional amnesty granted therein. She was still waving her sword, riding on horseback, fighting on, the field, bathing in blood and leaping into the fire of sacrifice! She wanted freedom or war to the end. She was more used to jump at the neck than fall at the feet of the enemy. She was still on the battle-fields of Shankarpur, Dhundiakhera, Rai Bareilly, Sitapur. She was killing, she was dying, but still she fought on!

So fought Oudh from June to November of 1858, from November to December, until April of 1859, when she was pushed from all sides towards Nepal. When the Revolutionaries entered Nepal, the English were still in hot pursuit; but still there was one hope—will the Hindu Raja of Nepal protect them?

At this time, the number of Revolutionaries who entered Nepal was about sixty thousand; they were led by Nana Sahib Bala Sahib, the Begum and her young son, and others. Jung Bahadur of Nepal wrote at this time a letter to them. The reply which Nana Sahib sent to him is so pointed and sarcastic that we cannot help quoting at least a part of it. It runs to this effect :— We have received your letter. We have been hearing the reputation of Nepal at distant places, all along the country. Indeed, In spite of my reading the history of many ancient kings of India and seeing the character of many present rulers, I believe that your Majesty's deeds stand matchless! For you did not hesitate to render help even to the British—the very people who have borne every sort of ill-will towards your people. And yet, as soon as they asked for help you have rushed to their assistance! There is no limit to this your generosity! Well then, shall it be unnatural, of me to expect that the descendant of the Peshwas who had all along been friendly towards your people will not be denied help from your Majesty, especially when you have given it so freely to the British who bore avowed enmity towards you? He who admitted the enemy inside will not at least turn his friend out!. It is utterly unnecessary to repeat here the well-known story of the wrongs under which Hindusthan is groaning, how the British people have broken treaties, trampled down their promises, snatched away the crowns of the Indian Rajas. It is equally unnecessary to describe how even the religion of the land is threatened as soon as the kingdoms of the land are destroyed. It is too well known. It is for this reason that this war is waged. We are sending Shrimant Bala Sahib, our brother, to you, and he will clear-up other things personally.'[8]

The letter was sealed with royal seal of the Peshwas and sent to lung Bahadur. After this letter, many consultations followed. Jung Bahadur sent one of his noblemen, Colonel Balbhadra Singh, to see personally the leaders of the Revolutionaries. The leaders told him unanimously, 'We have fought for the Dhrama of the Hindus. Maharaja Jung Bahadur too is a Hindu and therefore should help us. If he gives his help, even if he orders his officers to lead us, we shall again dash on Calcutta. We shall feed ourselves, and shall obey his orders. Whatever country we conquer in fight will become

8. Charles Ball's *Indian Mutiny,* Vol. II.

the possession of the Gurkha Government. If this is not possible, at least let him give us asylum in his country and we will live under his orders. Colonel Balbhadra Singh, the Gurkha representative, said: 'The English have opened wide the door of mercy. So, throw down your arms before the British and go to their asylum. They replied: 'We have heard of the proclamation. But we have no wish that some of our brothers should have their lives at the expense of others. Maharaja Jung is a Hindu and we do not want to fight against the Gurkhas. If he wants, we shall throw down our arms before him and even if we are to be murdered, we submit unresistingly. But how can we submit to the British by risking some of our own brethren to their vengeance?

Many such consultations took place, but at last Jung Bahadur finally told the Revolutionaries that if he had wanted to help them he would not have sent his men to massacre them at Lucknow ! Nay, he did not stop merely with sending this mean and cruel reply. He gave full permission to the English to enter Nepal and hunt the Revolutionaries within his territories!

Then Revolutionaries lost all hope, hid their arms, and quietly began to walk away to their homes. To encourage them in doing so, the English did not give them the slightest trouble for their past hostile attitude. Still, some grand-souled heroes, unable to bear the sight of the Britisher again treading the sacred soil of India, instead of returning to their homes, escaped to the jungles, knowing that it meant nothing short of dying by starvation! About that time, Nana Sahib wrote a letter to the British commander, Hope Grant. What does he say in that letter—any talk of surrender? Oh, no! After condemning at great length the unjust rule of the British in India, Nana asks : 'What right have you to occupy India and declare me an outlaw? Who gave you the right to rule over India? What! You, Feringhis, are the kings, and we, thieves, in this our own country? These are the last recorded words of Nana Sahib. No! This is the last challenge of the Peshwa throne of Balaji Viswanath! It is strong, proud, just, and self-respecting, worthy of the last descendant of Shivaji's Peshwas. The stain of effeminacy of the second Baji Rao was washed away in streams of the blood of the foreign foe, and the Gadi of the Peshwas passes away from the scene, like the Chitore Rajputanees of old, struggling, fighting, and burning amidst the leaping flames of the fire of sacrifice. This was her last shriek —'In India, foreigners are kings and the sons of Hindusthan thieves!'

History does not know for certain what happened to Nana Sahib after the episode of this letter. Bala Sahib died in the forest in circumstances of self-imposed misery. The Begum and her young son were, later on, given shelter by Jung Bahadur. The great martyr Gujaran Singh died in one of the numerous Skirmihes in the last stages of the war.

Thus ended the National Revolution of 1858, in Oudh. Nowhere in the world has a country fought for its independence with more stubborn bravery.

Malleson says: 'They (the people of Oudh) joined in the revolt inaugurated by their bretheren the Sepoys—the majority of them Oudh men—and fought for independence. How pertinaciously they waged the contest has been told in these pages. No other part of India gave an example of a resistance so determined, so prolonged, as did Oudh. Throughout the struggle, the sense of the injustice perpetrated in 1856 steeled the hearts of its people and strengthened their resolution. If on some occasion they too precipitately fled, it was in the hope of renewing the struggle with some chances of success another day. When, finally, the sweep made over Oudh by Lord Clyde forced the remnant of the fighting class to take refuge in the jungles of Nepal, the survivors often preferred starvation to surrender. The agricultural population, the talukdars, the landowners, the traders, accepted the defeat when, after that long struggle, they felt that it was final.[9]

* * *

9. Malleson's *Indian Mutiny,* Vol. V, page 207.

CHAPTER II

The Culminating Offering in the Sacrificial Fire

ON the 20th of June, 1858, in the fierce fight on the *Maidan* at Gwalior, Ranee Lakshmi Bai of Jhansi fell. But though one inveterate enemy of the English was thus taken away from the scene, the other, equally inveterate and, perhaps, more skilful in the tactics of war, had effected a clever retreat. He disappeared from Gwalior on the 20th, he disappeared, also, from the field of Jaura Alipur on the 22nd, and away he went out of the reach of the English—but where?

In a few days, allover central India, forests, cities, caves, villages, mountains, and rivers reverberated with a terrible war-cry, and jubilant shouts of 'Tatia Tope, Tatia Tope!'

For the Mahratta tiger, chased by the lances of the hunters, had now rushed into the forests of Central India. He had, as it were, lost his right hand by the death of Lakshmi Bai on the field of Gwalior. The Revolution was almost crushed by numerous defeats. He was now separated for ever from Nana Sahib. English power, through Indian strength, had now almost become invincible. He had now no army worth the name, no guns, no provision, and not even any hopes for getting these anywhere! Still the undaunted Tatia Tope, harassing the enemy, and maddening defeat itself, would not surrender the *Jaripatka* at the feet of the foreigner. Bend it before the foreigner, never! Such is the tree from which its staff is made that it might be broken by foreigners but it would never bend before them!

After the defeats of Gwalior and Jaura Alipur, Tatia Tope and Rao Sahib Peshwa took the remnants of the army and marched to a place called Sarmathura. They based all their future operations on three important principles. First, they were to try not to get entangled into any battle whatsoever with the English army. Secondly, they decided to make guerilla raids in the unguarded provinces. But these two stratagems would be impossible unless some means could be devised to ensure supply or provisions and good arms. So, to obtain these, the third rule of Tatia was to levy contributions of provisions, money, and arms, wherever an Indian state was to be found. In northern and central India, there are Indian states at almost every step. They had accumulated, in the course of years, huge stores of provisions and arms. And it was the duty of the kings there to use these stores for the protection of the country. But in 1857 these kings disregarded the earnest requests and entreaties of the country and their own subject. They would not openly join the Revolutionaries, because they were possessed by the sinful motive of looking to their own personal and individual gain. Was the Swadeshi army to starve while these selfish states had hoarded provisions lying uselessly in their store? To remedy such a tragic state of affairs, Tatia Tope and Rao Sahib hit upon the marvellous and just plan of snatching away from these unfaithful custodians, the means that were necessary for the defence of the country. This plan would give the Revolution sufficient money, provisions, and arms. Thus, the cost of maintaining the army of defence would not fall on the poor people of the country alone. These weak princes had generally only small armies, which were armies only in name, and even these more often than not sympathised with the Revolutionaries. To levy contributions on these kings was not at all a hard task. Since these states are at every step, the army need not be hindered with too much baggage on its marches. The army would have very little baggage to carry and, even if the enemy looted the provision sometimes, it would not give rise to great inconvenience, as the Revolutionary army could always find an Indian State on its way and make use of the provisions in its stores. For all these advantages, this plan was determined upon by Tatia Tope. If the kings gave provisions, on demand, willingly to the Swadeshi army—and many of them did give them then, well and good; if they did not, they were forced to give them, that was all.

On these three principles, therefore, the future operations of Tatia Tope depended; guerilla warfare, never to face the enemy in the open field, and to levy contributions on the Indian States and exact them if they refused. Tatia's ultimate object was to keep up such marches and cross the Narbada at the most favourable opportunity and thus to bring the Mahratta tiger to its native forests. The object of the English was not only to prevent him from crossing the Narbada, but not even to let him see it. And thus the race began.

First, Tatia had his eyes on Bharatpur. But, hearing that a strong English army had come there, he suddenly veered round to Jaypore. In the Jaypore Durbar, there were many people belonging to Tatia's party, and the army and the populace were also on his side. So, Tatia sent his messengers to that Durbar and intimated to his men to be ready. But the English got news of this quickly and an English army immediately marched to Jaypore from Nasirabad. When Jaypore plan thus fell through, Tatia descended towards the south. Here Colonel Holmes and an army pursued him. Suddenly, Tatia outwitted his pursuers and marched at once on the state of Tonk. The Nabob of the place shut himself up in the town and sent some select sepoys of his with four guns to engage with Tatia outside the walls. Now the battle would have begun, but suddenly the Tonk sepoys began to embrace Tatia's men in brotherly affection. They also handed over the four guns to Tatia, and in this manner Tatia got new troops, new guns, and fresh provisions, and continued his determined march to the south!

Tatia came right up to Indragarh and made a halt there. Behind him was Holmes, and on his flank was Roberts coming from Rajputana. At that time, it was raining tremendously and the Chambal was in front. The enemy behind and the unfordable Chambal in front! So, Tatia turned north-east towards Bundi, and after brilliant and strategic marches came to the province of Neemuch-Nasirabad which had risen in favour of the Revolution. Tatia encamped for rest near a village called Bhilwada. Hearing of this, Roberts came there hurriedly from Sarwargaon and fell on Tatia on 7th of August, 1858. After keeping him back all day, as soon as night fell, Tatia took his guns safely to Kotra within the dominions of Udaipur. While the army was resting there at night, Tatia went for worship in the temple of Shri Krishna at the famous place of pilgrimage near by, called Nathadwara. He returned to the camp at midnight and heard that the English army had come up close to them in pursuit. He at once gave orders to the army to break the camp and march on. But the army was so tired that the infantry replied bluntly, 'We cannot march a step till tomorrow-morning. Let the cavalry go in front.' Under these circumstances Tatia was obliged to give battle. As soon as it was dawn, Tatia arranged his troops as well as he could under the circumstances. In that battle, on the 14th of August, after some sharp fighting, Tatia's troops were routed and retreated about fifteen miles, leaving their guns behind. Now again Tatia was without guns, without provisions, and with an elated enemy in hot pursuit! So, avoiding the enemy at his back, he suddenly darted off again towards the river Chambal. The English armies followed him not only in his rear and flank but one English commander stood in front at the very banks of the Chambal. But Tatia put some on the wrong scent, eluded some, pushed back some, and thus, by clever marches, he came up to the Chambal and, almost under the nose of the English army waiting there, crossed that river!

Now it is true that the Chambal was between Tatia and the English pursuing forces. But then, he had no guns, no provisions, no money—and Narbada, he could not yet even think of it! He was thus beset with tremendous difficulties, and therefore he marched straight on Jhalrapattan. On seeing this, the loyal chief of the State took his faithful troops and his big guns and fell upon Tatia. But, as soon as Tatia was in sight the force of the State began to salaam him as their *Malik*! Immediately, Tatia took these troops under his command. In Jhalrapattan, he got cavalry horses, wagons, and plenty of provisions. He went there without a single gun and he had now got thirty-two guns! The Rao Sahib Peshwa ordered the Raja to pay twenty-five lakhs of Rupees as fine. The Raja pleaded for mercy and at last, it was agreed that he should pay fifteen lakhs. Tatia was in this place for five days. He distributed pay to the army at the rate of thirty Rupees a month to every cavalry-soldier and twelve to every infantry-man. Afterwards Rao Sahib, Tatia, and the Nabob of Bhanda began to deliberate upon their future plan of action in the south. The chief aim of the Peshwa army was to cross the Narbada and enter the Deccan. To oppose this, the English had woven nets of different armies and were guarding well nigh every outlet. But Tatia had now acquired thirty-two guns, a new army, new provisions and money, and was better prepared to continue the struggle. So, he silently whispered to his companions, 'Now, the next moves must be on Indore!'

This brilliant idea was quite in accordance with Tatia's daring. With not so much as one regular regiment in his hand, he had created new armies, new crowns, and new kingdoms. To a man of such magical talent, the plan of marching to Indore was not impossible to execute. It is the duty of the chief, Holkar, to help his master, the Peshwa. If he were not to do it willingly, service should be exacted from him by the Peshwa. The Indore army had secretly pledged itself to support Tatia. Even the Indore Durbar was secretly sending invitations to him! Therefore, Tatia decided. to play his game. He marched hastily from Pattan to- wards the south, rushed into Malwa, and appeared suddenly at Raigarh!.

Now, in pursuit of Tatia, there were marching from

different directions, the English commanders, Roberts, Holmes, Parke, Mitchell, Hope and Lockhart. All of them were thrown into consternation when they heard that Tatia was marching upon Indore. One moved from Mhow; one ran towards Nalkhera; one hesitated whether he should go to Raigarh or not. General Mitchell had just, with infinite difficulty, ascended a hill with his. army, when he saw Tatia just descending on the other side. But the English army was so tired that it could hardly go forth a step further. So it rested for a while; Tatia took advantage of it and continued his march. He was not tired! The next day, Mitchell recommenced the pursuit and at last came upon Tatia. The Revolutionaries were in their turn tired of the marches and prepared to give battle. They numbered at the time about five thousand and had about thirty guns. But the most wonderful thing is that, as soon as about one thousand of the English fell upon them, before even much blood was shed, they began to retreat, leaving their guns behind! It is on such occasions that we notice the difference between the guerilla tactics of Kumar Singh and of Tatia Tope. The latter's army did not take advantage of the opportunities that came in their way to deviate from the rule of not fighting an open battle with the English.

Leaving the *maidan* at Raigarh behind. Tatia's army entered into the forest on the banks of the river Betwa. and came out on the other side, at a place called Siranj. At Siranj, Tatia got four guns again. The English army could not move for some time on account of an excessive fall of rain. And so Tatia got some time to rest his troops. He, therefore, let his army rest for a week. At the end of the week, he marched again to the North. The town of Isagarh, in the Scindia's dominions, would not give him any provisions; so, it was taken by assault and Tatia again got eight guns. This was all right, but the Narbada was thus being left further behind. It appeared that the Mahratta lion could not get into his mountain cave on account of the numerous English lances blocking his way. While the many English armies are after one. man, why talk of the Narbada![1]

Now the Revolutionaries divided themselves into two parts one under Tatia and the other under Rao Sahib Peshwa. The two armies marched separately. But they did not give up their old tactics. They often eluded the enemy cleverly. got guns and lost them, fought when it was necessary as at Mangroli and Sindhwada, retreated in good order after skirmishes, were pursued for miles and escaped successfully; and again the two armies came together at Lalitpur. But, the Narbada was now no nearer. Nay, Tatia and Rao were now finally, almost in the grip of the enemy, Mitchell from the

1. An English writer says: 'Then commenced that marvellous series of retreats which, continued for ten months, seemed to mock at defeat, and made Tatia's name more familiar to Europe than that of most of our Anglo-Indian generals. The problem before him was not an easy one. He had to keep together an army of beaten Asiatics bound by no tie to his person and bound to each other only by one common hate and one common fear—hate of the Britisher's name and fear of the British gallows. He had to keep this ill-assorted army in constant motion at a pace which should baffle not only the english who pursued him but the enemies who streamed down at right angles to his line of march. He had, while thus urging his half-disciplined host to mad fight, to take some dozen cities, obtain fresh stores, collect new cannon and, above all, induce recruits to join voluntarily a service which promised only incessant flight at sixty miles a day. That he accomplished these ends with the means at his disposel indicates ability of no mean kind. Slightly as we may hold the marauding leader, he was of the class to which Haidar Ali belonged and had he carried out the plan attributed to him and penetrated through Nagpur to Madras, he might have been as formidable as his prototype. As it was the Narbada proved to him what the Channel was to Napoleon. He could accomplish anything except cross the stream. These columns, which moved at first as slowly as British columns are accustomed to move learnt to march, at last; and some of the later marches of Brigadier Parks and Colonel Napier were equal to half of Tatia's average rate. Still, he escaped; and through the hot weather and the rains, and the cold weather and the hot weather again, he was still flying, sometimes with two thousand 'dispirited' followers and sometimes with fifteen thousand men !'-From the *Friend of India.*

south, Colonel Liddell and Colonel Meade from the east and the north,Colonel Parke from the west Roberts from the Chambal—on all sides of Tatia, the enemy was closing round and narrowing the circle. Then, Rao and Tatja had a consulation and came suddenly to Kajuri; but there, too was an English army. They entered the jungle again and marched north-wards up to Talbahat. So, the English thought that at last Tatia had given up the idea of marching to the south. But, from there, Tatia and Rao Sahib suddenly dashed forth, crossed the Betwa, fought a skirmish with the English at Kajuri, and again at Raigarh and then marched straight to the south, now seen, now unseen. The English were in utter confusion at the audacity of the attempt; they ran in all directions to stop him, but, brushing aside and eluding these armies by extraordinary marches, this Mahratta with the speed of lightning, crossed *ghats*, forded rivers, rushed right through forests and pushed straight towards the south! Parke rushed from the flank, Mitchell in the rear and Becher from the front, but still Tatia persisted in his wonderful southward march! There, he has come to the Narbada, he is on the river—and the astonished and dumbfounded world clapped its hand in applause! —Tatia has, at last, crossed the Narbada! Malleson says: 'It is impossible to withhold admiration from the pertinacity with which this scheme was carried out.'[2]

2. 'Our very remarkable friend, Tatia Tope is too troublesome and clever an enemy to be admired. Since last June he has kept Central India in a fervour. He had sacked stations, plundered treasuries, emptied arsenals; collected armies, lost them; fought battles, lost them; taken guns from native princes, lost them; taken more, lost them; then, his motions were like forked lightning; and for weeks, he has marched thirty and forty miles a day. He has crossed the Narbada to and fro; he has marched between our columns, behind them, and before them. Ariel was not more subtle, aided by the best stage mechanism. Up mountains, over rivers, through ravines and valleys, amid swamps, on he goes, backwards and forwards, and sideways and zigzag ways, now falling upon a post-cart and carrying off the Bombay mails, now looting a village, headed and burned, yet evasive as Proteus.'—The *Times*, 17th January 1859.

At last, a Maharatta prince had entered the Deccan with an army! When it became known tbat Tatia had crossed the Narbada near Hoshangabad and had arrived near Nagpur, not only in the three presidencies, not only all over India, not only in England, but all over Europe even, all men, including even his enemies, shouted out in applause, Bravo! The whole Revolution had changed its colour at once![3] In front of him lay the Nizam's dominions where he had powerful party in Durbar supporting him, on the other side were Poona, Bombay and the whole of Maharashtra. The *Jaripatka* in the land of the Mahratta—who knew what hidden powers might not rise from that Raigarh, from that Pawankhindi, from that Wargaon! The Nizam of Hyderabad, Lord Harris at Madras, Lord Elphinstone at Bombay, and Lord Canning at Calcutta — all were bewildered with astonishment ! Such an astonishing feat did Tatia effect in this descent in to Maharashtra! But it was only astonishing; for the time had now gone by when it would also have been useful! A year before this crossing of the Narbada would have had a wounderful effect. Now, in the October of 1858, this wonderful strategy would excite admiration but would not lead to success! The Revolution had by now been crushed in almost all places. And the terrible bloodshed caused in the fierce struggle which was still fresh before its mind, had made the nation weak and stupid. In spite of this if the people of Nagpur had shown some perseverance, the aspect of the

3. It was accomplised. The nephew of the man recognised by the Mahrattas as heir of the last reigning Peshwa was on the Mahratta soil with an army... The Nizam was loyal. But the times were peculiar-...Instances had occured before, as in the case of the Scindia, of a people revolting against their sovereign when that sovereign acted in the teeth of the national feeling. It was impossible not to fear lest the army of Tatia should rouse to arms the entire Maharatta population and that the spectacle of a people in arms against the foreigner might act with irresistible force on the people of the Deccan-Malleson's Indian Mutiny "; Vol, IV, pages, 239, 240.

Revolution might have been changed. In the north of India, in village after village, the peasants would voluntarily and gladly give provisions to Tatia's men and look upon him with the reverence due to a patriotic hero—but such was the adverse fate that, in the country of the Mahratta themselves, the people were afraid to assist him. in his noble mission! What other fruits would the loyalty of the infamous Queen Banka bear? Undaunted however, by this adverse reception of his marvellous efforts, Tatia stayed there for some time and began to think out the future campaign.

Immediately, the English armies began to march thither from all directions. The English were at Melghat, Asirgarh was closed to him, and so were Gujarat, Khandesh, and Nagpur. The whole south was closed from be low, while, from above, from the north, the pursuing armies had now crossed the Narbada and come after him. Still the invincible hero did not lose heart; not only this, but the unbeaten warrior effected more marvellous feats in strategic marching. Keeping in check as far as possible the armies that were now encircling him, looting mails, breaking telegraphs, surprising outposts, Tatia marched straight to the source of the Narbada. Why? He had, now, actually set his heart upon Baroda. All the fords of the Narbada were watched by English armies on both sides of the river. Still, Tatia came to a village, called Kargun, to cross the river there. There he came across the English commandant Major Sunderland. The armies approached and a battle began. In the beat of the battle, Tatia ordered all his guns to be left behind, jumped into the Narbada, and was soon on the other side with his men. On this occasion, Tatia and his men, indeed, performed one of the most wonderful feats ever recorded in the history of warfare, in the rapid marches which they effected. Malleson clearly says, 'Now that the guns were lost, his men were able to display that capacity for rapid marching in which the natives of India are unsurpassed, I might almost say unequalled by any troops in the world'. Even in the midst of all this hurry and danger, Tatia continued his march straight towards Baroda. At Baroda, in the Durbar and in the army, the party which completely sided with Nana Sahib's policy was powerful and the Gaekwar's troops were only waiting for Tatia's arrival to join him openly. Tatia came up to Rajpura, exacted a ransom of money and horses from the chief there and, on the next day camped in the state of Chhota Udaipur. Baroda now Jay only fifty miles off!

But there were numerous English armies in hot pursuit trying to capture him. The enemies' troops used to proceed exactly on the line of his march, and it is most wonderful how he used to escape from their nets. At Chhota Udaipur, Parke came in with Tatia, and so Tatia had to give up the Baroda plan. Leaving the west aside, Tatia with his army marched again to the north and entered the jungles of Vasvara. But now, the Nabob of Banda had taken advantage of the Proclamation of the Queen of England and had laid down his arms. Tatia and Rao Sahib, the two leaders, were caught in a net which could not possibly be broken through. On the south there was the Narbada, on the west was Roberts and his army, on the north and east lay the steep and impassable Ghats! If, in such a state, Tatia and Rao had surrendered, who could have blamed them? But glory be to them that even in such a state they did not surrender! An English author, in surprise and admiration, writes: But, these two men were, in this hour of supreme danger, as cool, as bold, as fertile in resource as at any period of their careers'[4] On the 11th of December, Tatia came out of the jungle, obtained some provisions, from a Killadar and began to march straight on the city of Udaipur! But, immediately several English armies fell upon him. So he had to give up the design and re-enter the jungle. It seemed now evident that Tatia could not hold out for more than a week at the most and must eventually surrender. So the Revolutionary leaders began to discuss whether it was now necessary to give up

4. Malleson's *Indian Mutiny*, Vol. V, page 247.

the struggle. The place was not a jungle but a veritable cage into which the Mahratta tiger had been driven from all sides. Not only were English armies ready on every side, but they were narrowing the cordon every moment. Still Tatia would not think of giving up the fight. He and Rao Sahib one day marched out in the direction of Partapgarh It was now about four in the afternoon. Tatia's army had scarcely come out of the jungle when Major Rocke came up and blocked his way. Not that Tatia did not know that this part of the cage was also barred. But he took his choice and thought that this bar was the least strong of all, and so the tiger at once made an attempt to rush out there. Tatia's men marched straight on Major Rocke's troops and silenced them after a sudden onslaught. And thus the cage was broken through once again. The English commandants had to hang down their heads in shame!

On the 25th of December, 1858, Tatia left the Vasvara Jungle. About the same time, Feroze Shah, the illustrious hero whose work in Oudh has been described in a previous chapter, was coming with his army to meet Tatia.[5] This Prince Mirza Feroze Shah was a worthy son of the Delhi

---

5. 'One of the great results that have flowed from the rebellion of 1857-1858 has been to make inhabitants of every part of India acquainted with each other. We have seen the tide of war rolling from Nepal to the borders of Gujarat, from the deserts of Rajputana to the frontiers of the Nizam's territories, the same men overrunning the whole land of India and giving to their resistance, as it were, a national character. The paltry interests of isolated states, the ignorance which men of one petty principality have laboured under in considering the habits and customs of other principalities—all this has disappeared to make way for a more uniform appreciation of public events throughout India. We may assume that, in the rebellion of 1857, no national spirit was aroused, but we cannot deny that our efforts to put it down have sown the seeds of a new plant and thus laid the foundation for more energetic attempts on the part of the people if, in the course of future years, England has not done something towards reconciling the numerous inconsistencies and suppressing some of the dangerous tendencies of its rule in India.'-The *Times*, 25th of May, 1859.

dynasty. His marvellous exploit of crossing the Ganges and the Jumna, and the subsequent march up to where Tatia was, cannot be described in detail for want of space. Advancing to meet Feroze Shah and a Revolutionary Sirdar of the court of the Scindia called Man Singh, Rao Sahib and Tatia after many marches and skirmishes arrived at last at Indragarh on the 13th of January, 1859. And there the four leaders stopped for some time, discussing plans for future action. Tatia had always minute and correct information about the movements of the English. Seeing that they were closing round him again on all sides, Tatia arrived by forced marches at Dewasa. Now at last Tatia had not the smallest loophole through which to escape from the hands of the English. He had not even any hope of future success in his heart to encourage him to make another adventurous dash. Napier hemmed him from the north, Showers from the north-west, Somerset from the east, Smith from the south-east, Michel and Benson on the south, Bonner on the south-west and west:— thus, on all sides, he was surrounded by the enemy. Where and how could he with his fatigued men find a means of escape from these and other English forces? The English commandants swore that escape was absolutely impossible. How was it possible for Tatia to break through the net closing around him? It did in very deed seem impossible. The English cords were now tightly round the necks of the four leaders, Feroze Shah, Man Singh, Tatia and Rao Sahib. It was now impossible to escape!

At Dewasa, on the morning of the 16th of January, 1859, Tatia, Rao Sahib and Feroze Shah were discussing plans in a special council of war, when suddenly the last shout of despair was heard! Tatia felt an Englishman's hand at his back and the English had flooded into the camp. There was a joyous shout on the English side: 'Tatia is caught! Tatia is caught!' But soon the cry had to be varied. 'Oh ! he was here only just now! Run, soldiers, run!' They carried an exhaustive search in each and every corner but Tatia had disappeared!

That magician Tatia was to be seen again, together with Rao Sahib and Feroze at the town of Sikhar, near Alwar, on the 21st of January, and English forces were again running madly in pursuit. One of them, Holmes, actually fought a skirmish with. the Revolutionaries, who were defeated and pushed back.

The defeat at Sikhar destroyed not the hope of success or the Revolutionaries—that was gone even long before—but it made any further resistance absolutely impossible. Since the failure of the Baroda plan, after the crossing of the Narbada, Tatia and Rao Sahib had been discussing as to whether the guerilla tactics should be modified at last. Now, Tatia took leave of Rao Sahib and the army. He took with him two horses, a pony, two Brahmin cooks, and a man-servant. With these followers, Tatia came up to Sirdar Man Singh of Gwalior who was, at the time, hiding in the Paron jungles. Man Singh said to him,. 'You did not do well in leaving the army.' Tatia replied, 'Let that be for better or for worse I am now going to stay with you. I am tired of continual marching.'[6] Hearing that Tatia was now hiding with Man Singh in the jungle, the English now resorted to the plan of capturing through the base, and for them handy instrument of treachery and deceit, the enemy whom they would not capture in open war. First, they approached Man Singh. They told him that if he would surrender himself and help them in capturing Tatia, they would use their influence with the Scindia and not only have him pardoned but give him the kingdom of Narwar. This Man Singh was of such a base nature that he had before this tried to hand over even his own uncle to the English. The wretched Man, at once, consented and closed with the offer. He saw Tatia and informed him that he was going to surrender to the English. But, even after this, Tatia would not even think of surrender.

6. From Tatia's *Diary*.

Feroze Shah had just written to him to return to the camp. Tatia showed the letter to Man Singh and asked him 'Shall I then go or remain in this jungle? I will do as you tell me.' The treacherous Man replied, 'Wait for some time; I will soon let you know.' Though Tatia knew that Man Singh had surrendered to the English, he reposed full confidence in him. Man added, 'Until I return, you can remain in safety where my guide will take you to.' In the place showed by the guide, believing it to be the safest place, Tatia remained for three days. But on the third day, at midnight, the Mahratta tiger, who had hitherto evaded the enemy after fighting innumerable battles and skirmishes, marching thousands of miles, and effecting hair-breadth escapes was, by the treachery of a countryman, made a prisoner.

For, giving Tatia in charge of the guide, the basest-born of men returned to the English; hands were shaken to complete the agreement, and some Sepoys of the Bombay native regiment were sent to accompany Man. Such was the sympathy with Tatia in all Indian hearts that the English could not trust any Indian with him, as a rule. So, they did not even mention Tatia's name to the Sepoys. The order was simply 'to obey Man Singh's orders and to arrest the suspected person whom he would point out.' With this detachment, Man went his way to the Paron jungle. He had promised Tatia to return in three days to tell nim definitely whether he should go to Feroze Shah or not. And, he came at the appointed time, too! At midnight, on the- third day, Tatia was asleep in the place pointed out by the guide as the safest. Man came near the place and muttered an order to the Sepoys to rush forth. The Mahratta tiger was sound asleep in the jungle—the 'Beman Man' let loose on him his hands; Tatia just opened his eyes a little, and at once found himself a prisoner of the English!

On the 7th of April, 1859, at midnight, Tatia fell into this prison of treachery, and on the next day in the early morning, he was taken to the camp of General Meade at Sipri. Immediately, a court-martial sat and Tatia was charged with waging war against the British Power. On Wednesday, Tatia wrote down his statement in reply. 'Whatever I did, I did according to the orders of my master. Until Kalpi, I was under the orders of Nana Sahib, after Kalpi I was under Rao Sahib. Except in just battle, in warfare, neither I nor Nana have ever killed in cold blood or hanged any European, man, woman or child. I do not want to take part in this trial any more.' At the special request of the English, Tatia dictated his reliable, short, and important diary from the beginning to the end of the Revolution. The Munshi wrote it down and it was read out to him. Afterwards, he signed the diary as well as the statement given above in good English letters, 'Tatia Tope.' To all questions asked to him, he replied in Hindusthani, in the sense of the diary and the statement. His replies were straight, short, and spirited. If anyone asked him question in English, he would reply coolly in Hindusthani, 'Malum nahin,' (I don't understand). When minor English officers were walking about insolently near him, there was a look of indifference and disdain on his face. The inquiry lasted through Wednesday, Thursday and Friday. Crowds of Indians used to come up to see him, but permission was often refused them. Those who were admitted bowed to him with reverence and affection. When the English informed him that his trial was to take place and asked him to collect evidence for his defence, Tatia replied to the officer, 'I know full well that, having fought against the British as I have done, I shall have to prepare myself for death. I do not want any court nor do I wish to take any part in the trial;' and raising up his hands loaded with shackles, he continued, 'the only hope that I have is to get myself released from these chains either from the mouth of the cannon or from the loop of the gallows! Only one thing I have to ask, and that is, that, my family at Gwalior having had no connection with my actions, you should not take my old father to any task for my deeds.

On the 18th of April, the farce, called his trial, ended. Tatia was sentenced to death and taken to the gallows at about four o'clock in the afternoon. He was taken out of his tent under the guard of the 3rd Bengal Europeans. When Tatia approached the place where the gallows stood, the troops formed an extended square round it. There was a great crowd of Indian infantry, European cavalry, and the spectators. In the country surrounding, Indian villagers were standing up on eminences here and there. Tatia once again made a request that his father should not be persecuted. The charge and the sentence were read, and the *Mistri* broke the chains round Tatia's feet. Tatia walked boldly and with a firm step to the gallows and coolly ascended up the ladder. When, as is the custom, the executioners came up to bind Tatia's hands and feet on the platform, Tatia smiled pleasantly, and said, 'These formalities are not necessary.' With these words he himself put forth his head in the noose. The noose tightened, the block rose, and with a jerk... ...

Tatia Tope, the loyal servant of the Peshwas, the hero of 1857, the country's martyr, the defender of religion, the proud, the loving, the generous Tatia Tope, was hanging lifeless on the gallows of the English! The gallows became wet with blood and the country became wet with tears! His fault was that he suffered innumerable hardships for the sake of his country's independence; the baseness of a traitor's double-dealing was his 'reward; and the end ?—he was hanged on the gallows of the English like a criminal! Tatia ! Oh! Tatia! Why were you ever born in our unfortunate country! Why did you fight for these wretched, stupid and treacherous people! Tatia, can you see 'now the tears we shed for you? For the tears of weaklings, your blood!—What a bargain, indeed!

Seeing Tatia's body hanging mutilated there, the English heroes of the day turned back in satisfaction at their valour. His bleeding body was left hanging there till sunset. When the surrounding guard was withdrawn, the European spectators rushed forth in a crowd and there was a regular stampede to get hold of a lock of his hair as a souvenir.

In the sacrificial fire of the War of Independence of 1857, this was the last and culminating sacrifice!

The terrible volcano, which had opened wide its jaws and had vomited forth in rage a regular torrent of flesh, of blood, of corpses, of lightnings, of thunders, of burning red lava-that ,volcano then began to close its mouth again; its heated lava began to cool; its sword-tongues re-entered their scabbards; its fiery lightnings its deafening thunders, its whirl-winds, its terrible movings, and its dread awakenings— all entered again the magicians' bag and melted away into the invisible air. And the crater closed and green grass began again to grow on the top; cultivation recommenced; furrows were active; peace, safety, and softness reigned. And the surface of the volcano has now become so soft and smiling that nobody does believe that there slumbers a volcano under that surface!

* * *

CHAPTER III

Conclusion

Now that the volcano has temporarily subsided, readers might, however, ask what became of Feroze Shah and Rao Sahib?

After leaving Tatia, Rao Sahib fought desperately for a month and at last retired to the forests in disguise. At the end of about three years, he was also caught and was hanged at Cawnpore on the 20th of August, 1862. Feroze Shah was also roaming about in disguise, but, fortunately, in the end, he got out of India and stayed at Kerbela in Persia.

The Revolution of 1857, as such has been discussed, from time to time. Did the Revolution burst out too early, before the preparations were ripe? We think not. The prepartions that were made in 1857 are not usually found even in successful revolutions. When regiment upon regiment of soldiers, Princes, higher officers of the existing government, the police, and large towns, all one after another, gave promises to rise, who would not start at once? Besides, it is often the case that the real difficulty is at the start and the whole country rises only later on. This consideration also proves that the leaders of the Revolution did not at all precipitate matters. Those who dare not rise even with so many facilities are not the men who can ever rise at all!

Then, why was there the defeat? Several minor reasons have already been mentioned in their proper places. But the chief reason appears to be this. Though the plan of the destructive part of the Revolution was complete, its creative part was not attractive enough. Nobody was against destroying the English power; but what about the future? If it was only to re-establish the former internecine strife, if it was to bring again the same state of affairs as before, the same Mahrattas, and the same old quarrels-a condition, being tired of which, the nation, in a moment of mad folly, allowed foreigeners to come in—if it were only for this, the more ignorant of the populace did not think it worth while to shed their blood for it. Therefore, the Revolution worked out successfully as far as the destructive part was concerned; but, as soon as the time for construction came, indifference, mutual fear, and want of confidence sprang up. If there had been set clearly before the people at large a new ideal attractive enough to captivate their hearts, the growth and completion of the Revolution would have been as successful and as grand as its beginning.

Even had these people thoroughly understood at least so much that Creation comes only after the Deluge, the Revolution would have succeeded. But, let alone creation, the country could not accomplish even the deluge thoroughly! And, why? Because, the vice of treachery and baseness had not yet gone away from the land. The defeat was chiefly due to the treachery of those men who had not sense enough to understand that the English power was more harmful than even the former kind of Swaraj ever could be, and of those who had not the honesty and patriotism to refuse to give help to the foreigner against their own countrymen.[1]

---

1. 'Yet it must be admitted that, with all their courage, they (the British) would have been quite exterminated if the natives had been all and altogether, hostile to them. The desperate defences made by the garrisons were no doubt heroic; but the natives shared their glory, and they by their aid and presence rendered the defence possible. Our siege of Delhi would have been quite impossible, if the Rajas of Patiala and Jhind had not been our friends and if the Sikhs had not recruited in our battalions and remained quiet in the Punjab. The Sikhs at Lucknow did good service, and in all cases our garrisons were helped, fed, and served by the natives, as our armies were -attended and strengthened by them in the field. Look at us all, here in camp, at this moment! Our outposts are native troops, natives are cutting grass for our horses and grooming them, feeding the elephants, managing the transports, supplying the commissariat which feeds us, cooking our soldiers' food, clearing their camp, pitching and carrying their tents, waiting on our officers, and even lending us their money. The soldier who acts as my amanuensis declares that his regiment could not have lived a week but for the regimental servants, Doli bearers, hospital men, and other dependants. Gurkha guides did good service at Delhi and the Bengal artillerymen were as much exposed as the Europeans.'—Russell's *My Diary in India.*

And the whole sin of this defect lies on the head of these traitors! Had there been a clear and attractive ideal, even the traitors would have become patriots. When patriotism is profitable and paying, there is no advantage in playing the risky and shameful part of the betrayer. There is no special merit in that. The real glory belongs to those heroes who thoroughly understood that foreign domination is worse than Swaraj—Swaraj, democratic or monarchical, or even anarchical—and thus came out to fight for independence. Freedom is coveted not that the country might become wealthy but because in it alone consists the peace of the soul; honour is greater than loss or gain; the forest of independence is better than the cage though made of gold. Those who understood this principle, those who fulfilled their duty to their religion and to their country, those who lifted their swords for Swadharma and Swaraj and courted death if not for victory at least for duty, let their names be remembered, pronounced with reverence! Those who did not join them in the holy war, through indifference or hesitation, may their names never be remembered by their country. And, as for those who actually joined the enemy and fought against their own countrymen, may their names be for ever crushed! The Revolution of 1857 was a test to see how far India had come towards unity, independence, and popular power.[2] The fault of failure lies with the idle, effeminate, selfish and treacherous men who ruined it. But those who, wielding the sword dripping with their own hot

2. 'Among the many lessons the Indian mutiny conveys to the historians, none is of greater importance than the warning that it is possible to have a Revolution in which Brahmins and Sudras, Hindus and Mahomedans, could be united against us, and that it is not safe to suppose that the peace and stability of our dominions, in any great measure, depends on the continent being inhabited by different religious systems; for they mutually understand and respect and take a part in each other's modes and ways and doings. The mutiny reminds us that our dominions rest on a thin crust ever likely to be rent by titanic fires of social changes and religious revolutions. '-Forrest's *Introduction.*

blood, in that great rehearsal, walked boldly on the stage of fire and danced in joy even on the very breast of Death—let no tongue dare to blame those heroes! They were not mad; they were not hasty; they were not the sharers of defeat; they were not inconsiderate; and, therefore, they cannot be blamed. It was at their call that Mother India woke up from her deep sleep and ran forth to smite slavery down. But while one of her sons gave a terrific blow on the head of Tyranny, alas! her other son thrust a dagger in her own heart! And the wounded Mother was thrown down on the ground again! Now, which of these two sons was wicked, cruel treacherous, and accursed?

Emperor Bahadur Shah was a poet. During the heat of the Revolution be composed a Gazal. Some one asked him:

Dumdumay men dam nahin khair mango jan ki
Ai Zafar thandi hui shamsher Hindusthan ki.

'Now that, every moment, you are becoming weaker, pray for your life (to the English) : for, Oh! Emperor, the sword of India is now broken for ever!'

There is a tradition that the Emperor replied :

Ghazion men bu rahegi jabtalak iman ki
Tabto London tak chalegi teg Hindusthan ki.

'As long as there remains the least trace of love of faith in the hearts of our heroes, so long, the sword of Hindusthan shall be sharp, and one day shall flash even at the gates of London.'

VANDE MATARAM

GLOSSARY

Amir—a lord.
Ankush—a goading hook.
Arabisthan—Arabia.
Asura—an enemy of the gods.
Attar—perfumed extract.
Ayah—a waiting-woman.
Ayodhya—Oudh.

Babalog—Children.
Baberchi—Cook.
Badmash—a ruffian.
Bahadur—brave (man).
Bai—a lady's title.
Bania—merchant.
Bargeer—a Mahratta horseman.
Batti—a light turban.
Bazaar—shopping quarter in a city.
Begum—princess or lady of high rank.
Betichoot—incestuous.
Bhagavat Gita—a Hindu Scripture.
Bhagirathi—the Ganges.
Bhaldar—herald.
Bhaleghate—the chosen troops of the Scinda.
Bharata—a Hindu; also India.
Bharata-Bhumi—India.
Bharata-Mata—Mother India.
Bharata-Varsha—the imperial dominions of the Hindus.
Bhaubij—a Hindu feast.
Bheda—division : the principle of *divide et impera.*
Bheema—an ancient Hindu heir.
Bhishti—a water-carrier.
Bolo—say.
Brahmadesh—Burma.
Brahmin—a member of the Hindu sacerdotal caste.
Buggy—a gig.

Chalo—come along.
Chanderi—a kind of cloth (from the name of the place where it used to be manufactured).
Chandni—Goddess Kali (q.v.).
Chapatee—bread prepared in a particular fashion used by Indians.

Chauvis Perganna—a district in Bengal.
Chhabeli—darling.
Chato—cut down.
Chhatra—umbrella : the emblem of empire.
Chhatrapati—emperor.
Chintz—a kind of printed cloth.
Chobdar—herald.
Choughada—drum.
Chowdhury—chief.
Chowdi—a rest—house outside a village; government officers sometimes hold their court there.
Chowkidar—keeper.
Dak—post.
Dana—gift.
Dar—a suffix denoting possessor or owner.
Daroga—jail superintendent.
Desh—country.
Dewan-i-Khas—special audience hall.
Dewanji—minister.
Dharma—sacred duty or religion.
Dharamashala—place where charity is dispensed.
Dhoti—a long cloth.
Din—Faith : the war-cry of the Mahomedans during the Revolution of 1857.
Dipavali—the festival of lamps.
Doab—land between two rivers.
Doli—ambulance.
Dorakdar—an officer.
Dupeta—a long piece of cloth, used by soldiers round their waist and sometimes tied into a turban.
Durbar—levee or court.
Dushashasana—a wicked character in the Mahabharata.

Fakir—a Mohaomedan Sanyasi (q.v.) also common beggar.
Feringhi—a contemptuous term for an Englishman ; (it originally meant, a European).

Gadi—throne.
Ganga—the Ganges.
Gauri—a goddess.
Gazal—an Urdu couplet.
Ghanagarj—Sounding like thunder.
Gharry—a cab or carriage.
Ghat—the bank of a river, generally a bathing place ; also a chain of mountains.
Ghazi—a Mahomedan who fights fiercely for his faith and obtains victory.
Ghee—clarified butter.
Gully—small lane.
Guru—spiritual teacher.

Har Dev—God Shiva, who destroys evil.
Har Har Mahadev—the war-cry of Hindus (lit. Great God Shiva).
Hakim—physician.
Haridvar—the place where the Ganges leaves the mountains and enters the plains-metaphorically, origin or source.
Hatho—retire

Hawaldar—an army officer.
Hind—India.
Hindi—the language of India; also, Indian.
Hindusthan—India.
Hindusthanee—inhabitant of India.
Hindusthani—Indian ; also, a language of India.
Hiranyakashipu—a most powerful but wicked king of the Asuras (q.v.).
Homa—a sacrifice.
Hookah—smoking pipe.
Howdah—a covered seat on the back of an elephant.
Hujre—attendant.

Id—a Mahomedan feast.
Inam—land given as gift, free of taxes.
Islam—the Mahomedan world; Mahomedanism.

Jahgir—land given as recompense for service, generally military.
Jahgirdar—a man who owns a jahgir.
Jai Jumnaji!—victory to Jumna! —an invocation to the presiding Goddess of the river Jumna.
Jamadar—poniard.
Jaripatka—the banner of the Mahrattas.
Jat—Punjabee peasant.
Jatra—pilgrimage.
Jawan—a heroic young man.
Jehad—a religious war.
Juma Musjid—the principal mosque of a city.

Kaccha—useless, weak.
Kaffir—an abusive term for a non-Mahomedan.
Kalgitura—an ornament on the turban.
Kali—a Goddess who delights in destroying the foes of India.
Kali-Nadi—the river Kali.
Kalindi—the Jumna.
Kalpa—a mythological tree which bestows everything that is asked of it.
Kamadhenu—a mythical cow which bestows everything that is asked of it.
Karbhari—superintendent.
Kashi—Benares.
Kaustubha—gem worn by God Vishnu and Goddess Lakshmi.
Khalasa—the body of the fighting Sikhs.
Khalifa—the spiritual head of Islam.
Khan—a military title.
Khavind—Lord.
Killa—fort.
Killadar—fort-keeper.
Kinkhab—a rich velvet cloth worked in silver.
Koh-i-noor—the most ancient and most famous diamond of the world, robbed by the English from India.
Koran—the Scripture of the Mahomedans.
Kotwal—city commissioner of

police.
Kotwali—central police station.
Kripan—sword.
Kshatriya—the warrior caste among the Hindus.
Kshetra—a sacred place.
Kukri—a small hand-sword.
Kulkerni—a village tax-gatherer.
Kummerbund—a loin cloth worn by warriors.
Kunda—a sacrificial pit.
Kya Tamasha Hai—what fun!

Lakh—one hundred thousand.
Lashkar—army.
Lavani—a popular reed or lay.
Lota—tumbler, peculiarly shaped, used for drinking water from.

Mahabharta—the great Indian Epic.
Mahal—palace.
Mahalakshmi—the goddess of wealth and prosperity.
Mahalkuree—district officer.
Mahar—a low caste.
Maharaja—king (lit. great king).
Maharanee—queen (lit.great queen).
Maharashtra—the land of the Maharattas.
Mahut—the driver of an elephant.
Maidan—plain, battle-field.
Malik—master, governor.
Mangalya-Sutra—a sacramental string worn in the neck by the bride : it is removed only when she becomes a widow.
Mankaree—a courtier.
Mantap—hall generally of a religious character.
Mantra—Vedic hymn.
Maro Feringhi ko!—kill the Feringhis!
Marwari—a Marwar man, generally used in the sense of banker.
Mata—mother.
Mathalike—an epithet of Kali (q.v.).
Mat Maro—don't kill.
Maung—executioner.
Mawalas—Mahratta peasants led by Shivaji, and who fought with a courage rarely equalled.
Mem-Sahib—a term by which English women delight to be called by low-caste Indians.
Mera Jhansi Dongi Nahin—I will not give up my Jhansi.
Misal—a division of the Sikh Khalasa.
Mistri—executioner.
Moslem—Mahomedan.
Moulvie—a Mahoedan scholar.
Mourcha—an ornamental fan made of dear-hair.
Mullah—a Mahomedan priest.
Munsif—a civil judge.
Musjid—a Mahomedan place of worship.
Musnud—throne.
Mussulman—a Mahomedan.

Nabob—a Mahomedan lord (many of these Nabobs established independent thrones).
Nadar—bankrupt; used in the text in its literal sense of 'a man who is not a dar' (q.v.).
Nadi—a river.
Naga—a cobra snake.
Nagara—a kind of drum.
Nagarkhana—place where drums are kept and sounded.
Nagpurwalla—Nagpur-man
Narasimha—an incarnation of Vishnu in which he killed Hiranyakshipu (q.v.).
Nataka—a theatrical performance.
Nath—an ornament worn on the nose.
Nimakharam—traitorous
Nujeib—of noble birth; also a title.

Omra—a noble man.

Padre—a missionary (a term of contempt).
Padshah—emperor.
Padshahi—emperor.
Paga—stable.
Palkee—a palanquin.
Panday—a Revolutionary of 1857.
Pariah—a low caste Hindu.
Parthiva Puja—a worship.
Patel—head of a village.
Peshwa—literally, a minister; the Peshwa of the Mahratta empire soon became the head of the Mahratta confederacy.
Peshwai—the office and possessions of the Peshwa.
Powada—a popular song.
Prasad—anything blessed by being first dedicated to God.
Prayaga—Allahabad.
Prayagwal—Hindu priest of Prayaga (lit. any Prayaga man).
Prayaschitta—a purificatory ceremony.
Pudder—the end of ladies' cloth.
Puja—worship.
Pundit—a Hindu scholar.
Puran—a part of Hindu Scriptures.
Puranik—a Brahmin who reads and explains the Puran in public.
Purbhayya—a cast among the people of Oudh.
Pyjama—loose trousers.

Rabbi—a harvest season.
Raj—kingdom.
Raja—king.
Ramayana—a great Hindu Epic.
Ramchandra—the greatest Hindu hero and king—the hero of the Ramayana.
Rana—king; title assumed by Rajputs.
Ranalakshmi—the presiding Goddess of war.
Ranee—queen.
Rao—a title among the Mahrattas.
Rasaldar—an army officer.
Rishi—prophet or seer.

Roti—Bread.
Rupee—an Indian coin, originally worth two shillings, now depreciate to one shilling and four pence.
Rustom—a mighty Persian warrior —metaphorically, a great warrior.
Ryasat—State property.
Ryot—cultivator.

Sahib—Sir.
Sahukar—banker.
Salaam—respect or salute.
Sama—conciliation.
Samadhi—the state of perfect beatification.
Sanad—title-deed.
Sankalpa—preliminary of a religious ceremony.
Sanyasi—one who has renounced the world.
Saree—cloth worn over the shoulder by ladies.
Sarvahara—destroyer of everything
Sepoy—Indian soldier.
Shabash—well done!
Shahid—martyr who falls fighting.
Shankar—God Shiva (the same as Har Dev).
Shastra—science, generally theological.
Shatrusamharike—destroyer of foes.
Shazada—a prince of blood.
Shiledar—a Mahratta horseman.
Shirpana—an ornament worn on the turban.
Shiva—one of the Hindu Trinity.
Shri—blessed (used as part of the titles of persons or books).
Shrimant—a title of respect and honour (lit. prosperous).
Sirdar—an army officer of the higher grade.
Sirkar—Government.
Sowar—cavalryman.
Subahdar—an army officer.
Sudder Amin—sheriff.
Sudder Dewani—High Court.
Sudra—One of the four castes: among the Hindus.
Sultan—king.
Suryakanta—a gem, very cold to the touch, but which, when exposed to the sun, absorbs enormous heat and gives out sparks.
Suttee—the act of self-immolation by a Hindu wife on the pyre of her husband (lit. a pure spouse).
Swadesh—one's own country.
Swadeshi—belonging to one's own country.
Swadharma—one's own duty or religion.
Swaraj—independent self-government.
Swarajya—another form of Swaraj.
Swatantrya—independence.

Tahsil—revenue-jurisdiction.
Tahsildar—revenue-collector.
Taluk—a revenue-district.
Talukdar—baron of the court of Oudh having almost sovereign

authority.

Talukdari—the principality of a Talukdar.

Tamasha—fun, a show.

Tamashgar—a show man.

Tasmat Yuddhaya Yujyasva—Therefore, get ready for battle! (the trumpet-like words of Shri Krishna in a Gita).

Thakur—lord.

Thana—police station.

Tilaka—a mark on the forehead used by Hindus—a sign of purity and prosperity.

Tirtha—Sacred water.

Top-Khana—stand for mounting guns.

Tulsi—-a plant sacred to God Vishnu.

Vaisya—the merchant casts among the Hindus.

Vakil—attorney.

Varanasi—Benares.

Vatan—land almost tax-free, bestowed for service rendered.

Vatandar—holder of a vatan.

Veda—the Scripture of the Hindus.

Vizier—minister.

Waghnakh—a weapon made of or like tiger's claws.

Yajna—a Vedic sacrifice.

Yamadvitiya—a Hindu feast.

Yogi—a saint who has realised God.

Zemindar—land-owner

Zenana—ladies apartments.

List of Important Books Consulted

Arnold, Sir Edwin, K. C. I. E—*The Marquis of Dalhousie's Administration of British India.*

Ball, Charles—*The History of the Indian Mutiny.*

Coopland, Mrs.—*A Lady's Escape from Gwalior.*

Duff, Dr. Alexander—*The Indian Rebellion : Its Causes and Results in a series of Letters.*

Eyre, Sir Vincent—*Letters and Despatches.*

Forbes-Mitchell, William—*Reminiscences of the Great Mutiny, 1857-59.*

Forgett—*Real Danger in India.*

Forrest, George William—*State Papers (Several Series).*

Grant, Sir James Hope—*Incidents in the Sepoy War, 1857-58* (Compiled from the private journals of Sir Hope Grant ...... together with explanatory chapters by H. Knollys).

Gubbins, Martin Richard—*An Account of the Mutinies in Oudh and of the Siege of the Lucknow Residency.*

Holloway—*Essays on the Indian Mutiny.*

Holmes—*History of Indian Mutiny.*

Jacob, Sir George Le Grand—*Western India before and during the Mutinies* : pictures drawn from life.

Kaye, Sir John William—*A History of the Sepoy War in India*, 3 Vols.

Kaye and Malleson—*History of the Indian Mutiny*, 6 Vols.

Khan, Mu'in Al-Din Hasan—*Two Native Narratives.*

Leckey, Edward—*Fictions Connected with the Indian Outbreak of 1857 Exposed.*

Lowe, Thomas, M.R.C.S.—*Central India during the Rebellion of 1857.*

Malleson, G.B.—*Red Pamphlet.*

Martin, William—*Why is the English Rule Odious to the Natives of India?*

Mead, Henry—*The Sepoy Revolt : Its Causes and Consequences.*

Medley, Julius George—*A Year's Campaigning in India*

from March 1857 to March 1858.
Metcalfe—*Native Narratives.*
Roberts, Lord— *Forty-one Years in India.*
Russell, Sir Wm. Howard—*My Diary in India in the Year 1858-59. 2 vols.*
Shepherd—*Personal Narrative of Cawnpore.*
Sylvester—*Recollections.*
Tayler, William—*The Patna Crisis.*
Taylor, Meadows—*The Story of My Life.*
Thomson, Mowbray—*The Story of Cawnpore.*
Trevelyan, Sir George Otto—*Cawnpore.*
White—*Complete History of the Great Sepoy War*
Wilson—*The Defence of Lucknow,*
State Papers and several other books.
Anon—*History of the Siege of Delhi,* by an Officer who served there.
Anon—*Military Narrative.*
Anon—*Narrative of the Indian Revolt,* etc. Reprinted from the 'Illustrated Times'
शिपायांचें वंड—विनायक कोंडदेव ओक (मराठी)
शिपाई युद्धेर इतिहास—(बंगाली)
झांशीच्या राणीचें चरित्र—पारसनीस
गोडसे यांचा 'माझा प्रवास'—वैद्यांनी प्रकाशिलेलें